THE ADVANCED READING-WRITING CONNECTION

JOHN LANGAN

ATLANTIC CAPE COMMUNITY COLLEGE

Books in the Townsend Press Reading Series

Groundwork for College Reading with Phonics
Groundwork for College Reading
Ten Steps to Building College Reading Skills
Ten Steps to Improving College Reading Skills
Ten Steps to Advancing College Reading Skills
Ten Steps to Advanced Reading

Books in the Townsend Press Vocabulary Series

Vocabulary Basics
Groundwork for a Better Vocabulary
Building Vocabulary Skills
Building Vocabulary Skills, Short Version
Improving Vocabulary Skills
Improving Vocabulary Skills, Short Version
Advancing Vocabulary Skills
Advancing Vocabulary Skills, Short Version
Advanced Word Power

Supplements Available for Most Books

Instructor's Edition
Instructor's Manual and Test Bank
Online Exercises
PowerPoint Slides

Copyright © 2014 by Townsend Press, Inc.
Printed in the United States of America
9 8 7 6 5 4 3 2 1

Cover design: Akisia Grigsby

ISBN (Student Edition): 978-1-59194-425-6
ISBN (Instructor's Edition): 978-1-59194-426-3

Send book orders and requests for desk copies or supplements to:

Townsend Press Book Center
439 Kelley Drive
West Berlin, New Jersey 08091

For even faster service, contact us in any of the following ways:

By telephone: 1-800-772-6410
By fax: 1-800-225-8894
By e-mail: cs@townsendpress.com
Through our website: www.townsendpress.com

Contents

Part Two

Fifteen Selections for Readers and Writers   273

Part Three

Writing a Research Paper with Sources   449

Preface: To the Instructor

Have you, as a reading and/or writing instructor, asked yourself these questions:

- Is there a book that will help me teach both essential reading and essential writing skills?

- Is there a book that will clearly explain the connection between effective reading and effective writing?

- Is there a book that will provide selections that students will *want* to read and topics that students will *want* to write about?

If you've asked any of the above questions, *The Advanced Reading-Writing Connection* may be the book for you. Suitable for combined reading and writing classes, the book teaches students, in a step-by-step way, the skills needed to think, read, and write with clarity.

Part One of the book begins with chapters on main ideas and supporting details in reading. These are followed by a chapter on main ideas and supporting details in writing and a chapter on the steps in the writing process. Then chapters on relationships in reading are followed by chapters on relationships in writing. The final two chapters deal with inferences in reading and writing and argument in reading and writing.

Part Two of the book provides fifteen high-appeal reading selections for extended systematic practice in thinking, reading, and writing both paragraphs and essays.

Finally, **Part Three** of the book presents information on writing a research paper with sources, as well as a sample research paper in MLA format.

Other Features of the Book

Emphasis on clear thinking. A basic truth at the heart of both the reading process and the writing process is that any thoughtful communication of ideas has two basic parts: (1) a point is made and (2) that point is supported. As students work their way through this book, they will learn to apply the principle of point and support. They are encouraged when *reading* an essay to look for a central idea as well as for the reasons, examples, and other details that support that idea. They are reminded when *writing* to follow the same basic principle—to make a point and then provide support for that point. And they discover that clear *thinking* involves both recognizing ideas and deciding whether there is solid support for those ideas.

Frequent practice. Abundant practice is essential to learning, so this book includes numerous reading and writing activities. Each of the fifteen readings that make up Part Two is accompanied by this sequence of activities:

- **First Impressions.** A freewriting activity titled "First Impressions" helps students think about what they have read. The first question in this activity is always "Did you enjoy reading this selection? Why or why not?" The second and third questions focus on particular issues raised by the essay—issues about which each student should have something to say. Students can respond to one, two, or all three of these questions at the beginning of a class session; or, alternatively, students can record their responses in a "reading journal."

   The "First Impressions" activity provides two added benefits. First, it lays the groundwork for oral participation; many more students can contribute intelligently to classroom discussion after they have collected their thoughts on paper in advance. Second, as an integral step in the writing process, freewriting can supply students with raw material for one or more of the paragraph and essay assignments that follow the selections.

- **Words to Watch and Vocabulary Check.** Challenging words and phrases in each selection are defined in the "Words to Watch" section that precedes each reading. Then a "Vocabulary Check" activity helps students sharpen their skill at deriving meanings from context.

- **Reading Check.** The "Reading Check" is a series of ten comprehension questions that involve five key reading skills: finding the central point and main ideas, recognizing supporting details, making inferences, evaluating arguments, and understanding the writer's craft. The craft questions include such elements as introduction and conclusion strategies, types of support, patterns of organization, tone, purpose, intended audience, and appropriate titles. As students sharpen these crucial reading skills, they will become better, more insightful readers—and they will be ready to use the same techniques in their own writing.

- **Discussion Questions.** Four discussion questions follow the Reading Check. These questions provide a final chance for students to deepen their understanding of an essay and the issues and values that it presents. They also serve as a helpful intermediate step between reading a selection and writing about it. As noted below, these discussion questions can be used as additional writing topics.

- **Paragraph Assignments and Essay Assignments.** Four writing topics—two paragraph assignments and two essay assignments—conclude the activities for each selection. Half of the assignments involve personal experience topics and an "I" point of view; the other half are "objective" topics that call for a third-person point of view. All the assignments emphasize the basic principle of clear communication: that a student make a clear point and effectively support that point.

    Note that many of the model paragraphs and essays provided are deliberately first-person models. When students have third-person models, they tend to rely too heavily on them rather than attempting their own writing. Note also that in the interest of space, more paragraph than essay models are used in Part One; instructors should, however, feel free to ask students to write an essay rather than a paragraph for any given assignment.

High interest level. Dull and unvaried exercises, assignments, and readings work against learning. Students need to experience genuine interest in materials that they read and assignments that they write. Everything in the book, including the fifteen readings in Part Two, has been chosen not only for the appropriateness of its reading and writing levels but also for its compelling content.

Ease of use. The logical sequence in the chapters—from explanation to example to practice to mastery test—helps make the skills easier to teach.

Integration of skills. After learning the connections between reading and writing skills in Part One, students go on to apply the skills to the reading selections and writing assignments in Part Two. Through a great deal of practice in using reading and writing skills, they become effective readers and writers.

Instructor's edition. An *Instructor's Edition*—chances are that you are holding it in your hand—is identical to the student book except that it also provides answers to all the practices and tests, as well as comments on most answers.

Online supplements. PowerPoint presentations and online exercises are available in the Online Exercise Center at the Townsend Press website: **www.townsendpress.net**.

Acknowledgments

When my *Reading-Writing Connection* was published last year, many educators asked that I develop a sequel to the book that would emphasize more advanced reading and writing skills instruction. I thank them for helping to steer me in this direction. And I am grateful as always to my colleagues at Townsend Press who have made the book a team effort: Kathryn Bernstein, Bill Blauvelt, Denton Cairnes, Beth Johnson, Ruth A. Rouff, Tanya Savory, and Barbara Solot have all provided help along the way. I owe particular thanks to Janet M. Goldstein, who, from the time I started Townsend Press many years ago, has brought her extraordinary skills to almost every book the company has published. I have been fortunate to have by my side a colleague inspired by the same goals that have driven me: to help students learn by creating materials that are as clear and as human as possible. Janet, who is a great sports fan, would appreciate this line from Football Hall of Fame coach Vince Lombardi: "Perfection is not attainable, but if we chase perfection, we can catch excellence." Together, Janet and I have spent many years chasing perfection. I am grateful beyond words for her talents.

John Langan

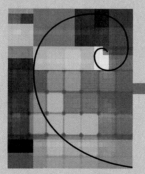

Introduction

Introduction:
The Reading-Writing Connection

The Core Reading and Writing Skills: Point and Support

You may already be aware that reading and writing are vital skills—in school, on the job, and in life. I completely agree! And I have written this book to help you become a better reader and a stronger writer.

To read and write well, you need to understand the difference between **point** and **support**. A **point** is an idea or an opinion. It is also called the **main idea**, and it is usually stated in one sentence. **Support** is the evidence that backs up the idea or opinion—the specific examples, reasons, facts, or other details that help prove the point. Here is a diagram that shows at a glance the two essential skills practiced by good readers and writers:

Following are two practice exercises that involve cartoons. Working through each exercise will give you a good sense of the difference between point and support.

PRACTICE 1

Look at the following cartoon:

"You are just not a dateworthy guy. You need to wear different clothes, put some meat on those bones, and get rid of that scythe."

See if you can answer the following questions:

● What is the **point** of the cartoon?

Your answer: The point is that _____

_____

● What is the **support** for the point?

Your answer: _____

_____

Explanation

The woman's point, of course, is that Death isn't good date material. There are two jokes here. The first is that no one would want to get romantically involved with Death in the first place! The second is that the woman seems to be rejecting just his hooded costume, his skeletal appearance, and the "tool of his trade"—the scythe he uses to cut off people's lives.

PRACTICE 2

Here are three more cartoons. What is the point of each cartoon, and what is the support?

Point: _____

Support: _____

_____

_____

Point: _____

Support: 1. _____

2. _____

3. _____

4. _____

"Things were good at work today. The boss was out sick. The computer network was working for a change. And the vending machine was giving everyone free cups of coffee."

Point: _____

Support: **1.** _____

2. _____

3. _____

More about Point and Support

Look at these two sentences:

_____ The apartment has two bedrooms.

_____ The apartment could use a good cleaning.

One of these sentences could be the point, or main idea, of a paragraph, with reasons and details to support the point. The other sentence does not express an idea or opinion. It is just a fact that does not call for any support. Put a check (✓) next to the sentence that is a point. Then read the explanation below.

"The apartment has two bedrooms" is just a fact. It does not need any support. On the other hand, "The apartment could use a good cleaning" expresses a point or opinion that needs support. As a reader, you should expect to see specific reasons or examples or details explaining exactly why a cleaning is needed. As a writer, you would be expected to provide evidence to support your point about the apartment.

Here in a nutshell is what effective reading and writing are about: a point (main idea) followed by solid support for that point.

PRACTICE 3

Put a check (✓) in front of the point (it can also be called the *main idea* or *opinion* or *topic sentence*) in each pair of sentences below.

1. _____ A. Lots of people text while they are driving.

   _____ B. Texting while driving should be illegal.

2. _____ A. Mr. McHenry was the nastiest boss I ever worked for.

   _____ B. Mr. McHenry's nickname for me was "Moron."

3. _____ A. Babies require a lot of attention.

   _____ B. Babies need to be fed every two to three hours.

4. _____ A. My brother has a new laptop computer.

   _____ B. My brother spends far too much time online.

5. _____ A. Our neighbors are painting their house and fixing up their yard.

   _____ B. Our neighbors must be getting ready to sell their house.

6. _____ A. There are many reasons why the divorce rate is so high.

   _____ B. Many people spend more time planning their wedding than thinking what their marriage will be like.

7. ___ A. My uncle should take better care of his health.

___ B. My uncle has diabetes and he smokes.

8. ___ A. Parents can be unwilling to admit their children's bad points.

___ B. A bully's parents might say "He's just all boy" instead of admitting he is mean.

9. ___ A. Gonzo is a die-hard sports fan.

___ B. Gonzo always tunes in to sports talk radio when he drives.

10. ___ A. We can do a lot to reduce our impact on the earth's environment.

___ B. Taking reusable bags to the grocery store is one way to save resources.

Supporting a Point

Look at the following point:

Point: The Beef and Burger Shop is a poor fast-food restaurant.

This statement hardly discourages us from visiting the Beef and Burger Shop. "Why do you say that?" we might legitimately say. "Give your reasons." Support is needed so we can decide for ourselves whether a valid point has been made. Suppose the point is followed by these three reasons:

1 The burgers are full of gristle.

2 The roast beef sandwiches have a chemical taste.

3 The fries are lukewarm and soggy.

Clearly, the details provide solid support for the point. They give us a basis for understanding and agreeing with the point. In light of these details, our mouths are not watering for lunch at the Beef and Burger Shop.

 **PRACTICE 4**

Following are groups of four sentences. In each case, one sentence is the point or main idea, and the other three sentences are details that support and develop this idea. Put a check (✓) in front of the point or idea in each group.

1. ___ A. You can keep your home as messy or neat as you like.

___ B. You can feel free to surf online dating sites for casual relationships.

___ C. There are certain advantages to being single.

___ D. You can have the bathroom all to yourself.

2. ____ A. The convenience store on Westlake Avenue is a good place to stop for lunch.

____ B. They have two people making sandwiches, so you never have to wait long for your order.

____ C. They have a wide selection of beverages, from coffee to fruit juice to smoothies.

____ D. They have healthier alternatives, like turkey burgers and garden salads with fresh local ingredients in season.

3. ____ A. My dad thinks any flavorings but salt and pepper are "weird."

____ B. My family is very difficult to cook for.

____ C. My mother is a vegan—she won't eat any animal products.

____ D. My sister is allergic to wheat, soy, egg, and milk.

4. ____ A. When Barry and Susan decided to get married, they were both drunk.

____ B. I do not think Barry and Susan's marriage is going to last long.

____ C. At their wedding reception, Susan was flirting and dancing with a former boyfriend.

____ D. Susan and Barry had a huge fight on their honeymoon and came home early.

5. ____ A. You are 1,000 times more likely to drown than to be bitten by a shark.

____ B. More people are killed by farm pigs every year than by sharks.

____ C. Sharks typically fear humans and go out of their way to avoid them.

____ D. It is incorrect to think of sharks as dangerous creatures that hunt humans.

6. ____ A. Finishing a marathon is a huge personal achievement.

____ B. People run marathons for many different reasons.

____ C. Training for a marathon is a good way to lose weight and get in shape.

____ D. Many people raise funds for charities by running a marathon.

7. ____ A. Professor Graham makes a point of calling on students she catches daydreaming or gazing out the window.

____ B. If a student is seen checking her cell phone in class, Professor Graham will mark the student as being absent for the entire class.

____ C. A student who falls asleep in Professor Graham's class is awakened by Graham blowing a whistle in his ear.

____ D. Professor Graham demands students' attention at all times and uses certain tactics to ensure attentiveness.

8. ____ A. Taking a year or so off between high school and college gives a young person time to work and save money for college expenses.

____ B. Gaining a year or more of life experience prior to college is invaluable to incoming college freshmen.

____ C. It is a good idea for high-school graduates to wait for a year or two before starting college.

____ D. A period of time after high school allows a young person more time to consider and evaluate his or her intended major.

9. ____ A. Young people, in general, no longer associate smoking cigarettes with being cool.

____ B. Cigarette smoking is not nearly as popular and accepted as it used to be.

____ C. More and more longtime smokers are making concerted efforts to quit.

____ D. Forty-five percent fewer people started smoking in 2011 than in 1960.

10. ____ A. Recent studies have shown that many people prefer texting to speaking on the phone or in person.

____ B. It is becoming more common for young people to interact through social media sites than in real life.

____ C. Many people report feeling lonely or anxious if they are separated for too long from phones or computers.

____ D. Increasingly, our society is becoming less comfortable with real human interaction and more dependent on electronic socializing.

Other Important Reading and Writing Skills

This book will help you practice and master the two essential reading and writing skills: identifying and providing main ideas and supporting details. The book will also cover other skills that are central to effective reading and writing: developing a good vocabulary, understanding relationships, making inferences, evaluating arguments, and appreciating the writer's craft.

Here is the sequence of chapters:

Part One

Reading and Writing Skills

What Is the Main Idea?

"I've got problems. I lost my job. My wife left me. My friends don't return phone calls. Even my dog won't go for a walk with me."

"What's the point?" You've probably heard these words before. It's a question people ask when they want to know the main idea that someone is trying to express. The same question can guide you as you read. Recognizing the **main idea**, or point, is the most important key to good comprehension. Sometimes a main idea is immediately clear, as in the above cartoon. The point—that the man on the couch has problems—is well supported by the statements about his job, wife, friends, and dog.

To find the main idea of a reading selection, ask yourself, "What's the point the author is trying to make?" For instance, read the paragraph on the following page, asking yourself as you do, "What is the author's point?"

¹Many people feel that violence on television is harmless entertainment. ²However, we now know that TV violence does affect people in negative ways. ³One study showed that frequent TV watchers are more fearful and suspicious of others. ⁴They try to protect themselves from the outside world with extra locks on the doors, alarm systems, guard dogs, and guns. ⁵In addition, that same study showed that heavy TV watchers are less upset about real-life violence than non-TV watchers. ⁶It seems that the constant violence they see on TV makes them less sensitive to the real thing. ⁷Another study, of a group of children, found that TV violence increases aggressive behavior. ⁸Children who watched violent shows were more willing to hurt another child in games where they were given a choice between helping and hurting. ⁹They were also more likely to select toy weapons over other kinds of playthings.

A good way to find an author's point, or main idea, is to look for a general statement. Then decide if that statement is supported by most of the other material in the paragraph. If it is, you have found the main idea.

Below are four statements from the passage. Pick out the general statement that is supported by the other material in the passage. Write the letter of that statement in the space provided. Then read the explanation that follows.

Four statements from the passage:

A. Many people feel that violence on television is harmless entertainment.

B. However, we now know that TV violence does affect people in negative ways.

C. One study showed that frequent TV watchers are more fearful and suspicious of others.

D. They try to protect themselves from the outside world with extra locks on the doors, alarm systems, guard dogs, and guns.

The general statement that expresses the main idea of the passage is _____.

Explanation

Sentence A: The paragraph does not support the idea that TV violence is harmless, so sentence A cannot be the main idea. However, it does introduce the topic of the paragraph: TV violence.

Sentence B: The statement "TV violence does affect people in negative ways" is a general one. And the rest of the passage goes on to describe three negative ways that TV violence affects people. Sentence B, then, is the sentence that expresses the main idea of the passage.

Sentence C: This sentence is about only one study. It is not general enough to include the other studies that are also cited in the paragraph. It is the first supporting idea for the main idea.

Sentence D: This sentence provides detailed evidence for the first supporting idea, which is that frequent TV watchers are more fearful and suspicious of others. It does not cover the other material in the paragraph.

The Main Idea as an "Umbrella" Idea

Think of the main idea as an "umbrella" idea. The main idea is the author's general point; all the other material of the paragraph fits under it. That other material is made up of **supporting details**—specific evidence such as examples, causes, reasons, or facts. The diagram below shows the relationship.

**TV VIOLENCE
DOES AFFECT PEOPLE
IN NEGATIVE WAYS**

Frequent TV watchers are more fearful
and suspicious of others.
Heavy TV watchers are less upset about real-life
violence than non-TV watchers.
TV violence increases aggressive behavior in children.

The explanations and activities on the following pages will deepen your understanding of the main idea.

Recognizing a Main Idea

As you read through a passage, you must **think as you read**. If you merely take in words, you will come to the end of the passage without understanding much of what you have read. Reading is an active process, as opposed to watching television, which is passive. You must actively engage your mind, and, as you read, keep asking yourself, "What's the point?" Here are three strategies that will help you find the main idea.

1 Look for general versus specific ideas.
2 Use the topic to lead you to the main idea.
3 Use key words to lead you to the main idea.

Each strategy is explained on the following pages.

1   Look for General versus Specific Ideas

You saw in the paragraph on TV violence that the main idea is a *general* idea supported by *specific* ideas. The following practices will improve your skill at separating general from specific ideas. Learning how to tell the difference between general and specific ideas will help you locate the main idea.

PRACTICE 1

Each group of words below has one general idea and three specific ideas. The general idea includes all the specific ideas. Identify each general idea with a **G** and the specific ideas with an **S**. Look first at the example.

Example

_S_ dishonesty

_S_ greed

_G_ bad qualities

_S_ selfishness

(*Bad qualities* is the general idea which includes three specific types of bad qualities: dishonesty, greed, and selfishness.)

1. _S_ handsome
   _G_ appearance
   _S_ well-dressed
   _S_ shabby

2. _G_ seafood
   _S_ oysters
   _S_ clams
   _S_ lobster

3. _S_ heavy traffic
   _S_ bus not on time
   _S_ alarm didn't go off
   _G_ excuses for being late

4. _S_ poor pay
   _S_ mean boss
   _S_ very dull work
   _G_ undesirable job

5. _S_ giggling
   _G_ childish behavior
   _S_ tantrums
   _S_ playing peek-a-boo

6. _S_ paper cuts
   _G_ minor problems
   _S_ broken nails
   _S_ wrong numbers

7. _S_ try to be kinder
   _S_ eat healthier foods
   _S_ go to bed earlier
   _G_ resolutions

8. _S_ take stairs instead of elevator
   _S_ ride bike instead of driving
   _G_ exercise opportunities
   _S_ walk instead of riding bus

9. _S_ skip breakfast
    _S_ grab a donut mid-morning
    _G_ poor eating habits
    _S_ order supersize portions

10. _S_ different goals
    _S_ no common interests
    _S_ dislike each other's friends
    _G_ reasons for breaking up

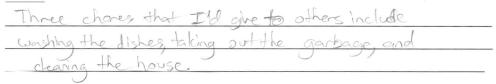

PRACTICE 2

Write out the answers to each question in the spaces provided. For each question, the answers are specific details that illustrate the general idea, which is underlined.

1. There are many material things in everyday life (appliances, electronic equipment, and the like) that we come to depend upon. What are three things that you would hate to be without?

    I would hate to live without a phone, a refrigerator, and a television.

2. If you were suddenly wealthy, you could hire other people to do tasks that you dislike. What are three specific chores that you'd hand over to somebody else?

    Three chores that I'd give to others include washing the dishes, taking out the garbage, and cleaning the house.

3. Most of us enjoy a good movie, but we have different ideas of what makes a film "good." What are three specific qualities that a movie needs in order for you to really like it?

    Three qualities that a good movie needs is thrilling action, good characters, and a compelling story.

4. We all know people whom we find difficult. Think of a person that you find hard to get along with. Name three specific reasons you find this person difficult.

    I find this person difficult because I'm not listened to and my ideas get turned down.

PRACTICE 3

In the following groups, one statement is the general point, and the other statements are specific support for the point. Identify each point with a **P** and each statement of support with an **S**.

1. ___ The vegetables were soggy and tasteless.

   ___ The chicken was hard to chew.

   ___ The meal was very unpleasant.

   ___ The rolls were rock-hard.

2. ___ The team's best player is averaging over 30 points a game.

   ___ The basketball team is in first place in its division.

   ___ The team has won eight of its first ten games.

   ___ The basketball team is off to a great start.

3. ___ The man doesn't use his turn signals.

   ___ The man drives too fast down narrow residential streets.

   ___ The man is an unsafe driver.

   ___ The man doesn't come to a complete stop at stop signs.

4. ___ Students stay in touch with friends through Facebook and e-mail.

   ___ Students write papers and share class notes online.

   ___ Students do much of their research on the Internet.

   ___ Students have practical uses for computers.

PRACTICE 4

In each of the following groups, one statement is the general point, and the other statements are specific support for the point. Identify each point with a **P** and each statement of support with an **S**.

1. ___ A. Among teenage girls, gossip contributes to bonding.

   ___ B. Political gossip often is leaked to the media as a way of learning how the public is likely to react to a particular policy.

   ___ C. Gossip takes many forms and serves various purposes.

   ___ D. In the business world, gossip can provide insights unavailable through official facts and figures.

2. ___ A. When answering the phone, some people's first words are "Who's this?"

   ___ B. Some people have terrible telephone manners.

   ___ C. Some people never bother to identify themselves when calling someone.

   ___ D. Some people hang up without even saying goodbye.

3. ___ A. Federal law should prohibit banks from giving credit cards to college students.

   ___ B. Credit-card debt is the leading cause of bankruptcy for young Americans.

   ___ C. Taking advantage of the fact that many parents will pay their children's credit-card debts, banks extend excessive credit to students.

   ___ D. When they receive their monthly credit-card bills, many students can pay only the minimum required and so have hefty interest charges on large unpaid amounts.

4. ___ A. Bats are so rarely rabid that a person has a better chance of catching rabies from a cow than from a bat.

   ___ B. Bats, in spite of their bad reputation, are not a danger to human beings.

   ___ C. Bats are afraid of humans and do their best to stay away from them.

   ___ D. Unlike movie vampires, bats do not bite people unless frightened or under attack.

PRACTICE 5

In each of the following groups—all based on textbook selections—one statement is the general point, and the other statements are specific support for the point. Identify each point with a **P** and each statement of support with an **S**.

1. ___ A. Companies that lose lawsuits usually pass the cost along to consumers.

   ___ B. To protect themselves from malpractice suits, doctors now give more patients unneeded tests, which cost hundreds of millions of dollars a year.

   ___ C. The cost of fighting a lawsuit forces some small businesses to close, even when they have successfully defended themselves.

   ___ D. The ever-growing number of lawsuits has had a number of negative consequences.

2. ___ A. Our social roles—whether we're students, employees, visitors, etc.— limit what emotions are acceptable for us to express.

   ___ B. Given the widespread habit of suppressing our emotions, many of us have trouble recognizing what we're really feeling.

   ___ C. Most of us rarely express our deepest emotions because of a number of factors.

   ___ D. We often hide our emotions rather than display them so as not to seem weak or needy to others.

3. ___ A. Disagreeing parties can accept the status quo, agreeing to just live with the situation as it stands.

   ___ B. When faced with a disagreement, the parties involved have several ways to proceed.

   ___ C. One party may use physical, social, or economic force to impose a solution on the others.

   ___ D. Negotiation, or reaching a mutually acceptable solution, is one means of dealing with conflict.

4. ___ A. With bribes, Prohibition-era bootleggers persuaded politicians, police, and other public officials to ignore the illegal sale of alcoholic beverages.

   ___ B. Prohibition glamorized drinking and made it fashionable for people to drink in illegal bars and break the law.

   ___ C. Prohibition encouraged the formation of organized-crime empires that illegally manufactured, transported, and sold liquor.

   ___ D. Prohibition, which banned alcoholic beverages in the United States from 1920 to 1933, resulted in much illegal activity.

2   Use the Topic to Lead You to the Main Idea

You already know that to find the main idea of a selection, you look first for a general statement. You then check to see if that statement is supported by most of the other material in the paragraph. If it is, you've found the main idea. Another approach that can help you find the main idea is to decide on the topic of a given selection.

The **topic** is the general subject of a selection. It can often be expressed in one or more words. Knowing the topic can help you find a writer's main point about that topic. Paying close attention to the topic of a selection can lead you to the main idea.

Textbook authors use the title of each chapter to state the overall topic of that chapter. They also provide many topics and subtopics in boldface headings within the chapter. For example, here is the title of a chapter in a psychology textbook:

Theories of Human Development (26 pages)

And here are the subtopics:

Psychoanalytic Theories (an 8-page section)

Learning Theories (a 9-page section)

Cognitive Theories (a 9-page section)

If you were studying the above chapter, you could use the topics to help find the main ideas.

But there are many times when you are not given topics—with standardized reading tests, for example, or with individual paragraphs in articles or textbooks. To find the topic of a selection when the topic is not given, ask this simple question:

Who or what is the selection about?

For example, look again at the beginning of the paragraph that started this chapter:

Many people feel that violence on television is harmless entertainment. However, we now know that TV violence does affect people in negative ways.

What, in just a few words, is the above paragraph about? On the line below, write what you think is the topic.

Topic: _____

You probably answered that the topic is "TV violence." As you reread the paragraph, you saw that, in fact, every sentence in it is about TV violence.

The next step after finding the topic is to decide what main point the author is making about the topic. Authors often present their main idea in a single sentence. (This sentence is also known as the **main idea sentence** or the **topic sentence**.) As we have already seen, the main point about TV violence is "we now know that TV violence does affect people in negative ways."

✔ Check Your Understanding

Let's look now at another paragraph. Read it and then see if you can answer the questions that follow.

[1]Recently a family of four was found dead in a suburban home in New Jersey—victims of carbon monoxide. [2]Such cases are tragically common. [3]Carbon monoxide is deadly for many reasons. [4]To begin with, it is created in the most ordinary of ways—by the burning of wood, coal, or petroleum products. [5]Once created, this gas is impossible to detect without instruments: it is colorless, odorless, and tasteless. [6]Also, carbon monoxide mingles with and remains in the air rather than rising and being carried away by the wind. [7]Then, when people unsuspectingly breathe it in, it chokes them, taking the place of the oxygen in their blood. [8]Furthermore, it can do its lethal work in very small quantities: anyone exposed to air that is just 1 percent carbon monoxide for even a few minutes will almost certainly die.

1. What is the *topic* of the paragraph? In other words, what is the paragraph about? (It often helps as you read to look for and even circle a word, term, or idea that is repeated in the paragraph.)

   _____

2. What is the *main idea* of the paragraph? In other words, what point is the author making about the topic? (Remember that the main idea will be supported by the other material in the paragraph.)

   _____

Explanation

As the first sentence of the paragraph suggests, the topic is "carbon monoxide." Continuing to read the paragraph, you see that, in fact, everything in it is about carbon monoxide. And the main idea is clearly that "Carbon monoxide is deadly for many reasons." This idea is a general one that sums up what the entire paragraph is about. It is an "umbrella" statement under which all the other material in the paragraph fits. The parts of the paragraph could be shown as follows:

Topic: Carbon monoxide

Main idea: Carbon monoxide is deadly for many reasons.

Supporting details:
1. Is easily created.
2. Is difficult to detect.
3. Remains in the air.
4. Chokes by taking the place of oxygen in the blood.
5. Deadly even in small quantities.

The following practices will sharpen your sense of the difference between a topic, the point about the topic (the main idea), and supporting details.

PRACTICE 6

Below are groups of four items. In each case, one item is the topic, one is the main idea, and two are details that support and develop the main idea. Label each item with one of the following:

T — for the **topic** of the paragraph
MI — for the **main idea**
SD — for the **supporting details**

Note that an explanation is provided for the first group; reading it will help you do this practice.

Group 1

_SD_ A. One bite from a piranha's triangular-shaped teeth can sever a person's finger or toe.

_T_ B. The piranha.

_MI_ C. The piranha—only eight to twelve inches long—is an extremely dangerous fish.

_SD_ D. A school of piranha can strip a four-hundred-pound hog down to a skeleton in just a few minutes.

Explanation

All of the statements in Group 1 are about piranhas, so item B must be the topic. (Topics are easy to identify because they are expressed in short phrases, not complete sentences.) Statements A and D are specific examples of the damage that piranhas can do. Statement C, on the other hand, presents the general idea that piranhas can be extremely dangerous. It is the main idea about the topic of "the piranha," and statements A and D are supporting details that illustrate that main idea.

Group 2

_SD_ A. Joint custody of a divorced couple's children has become more common.

_SD_ B. The number of men with sole custody of children has also grown.

_MI_ C. Alternatives to giving the mother sole child custody have increased in recent years.

_T_ D. Alternative child-custody arrangements.

Group 3

_SD_   A. In later adulthood, we begin to come to terms with our own mortality.

_T_   B. Stages of human development.

_SD_   C. Adolescence is typically a time of identity crisis.

_MI_   D. According to psychologists, we pass through various stages of human development throughout our lives.

Group 4

_T_   A. Kinds of power.

_SD_   B. Force, which the Italian statesman Machiavelli called "the method of beasts," is the use of physical coercion.

_SD_   C. Influence, the ability to control or affect the behavior of others, is also a form of power.

_MI_   D. Power, the ability to control or change the behavior of others, takes different forms.

PRACTICE 7

Following are four paragraphs. Read each paragraph and do the following:

1 Ask yourself, "What seems to be the topic of the paragraph?" (It often helps to look for and even circle a word or idea that is repeated in the paragraph.)

2 Next, ask yourself, "What point is the writer making about this topic?" This will be the main idea. It is stated in one of the sentences in the paragraph.

3 Then test what you think is the main idea by asking, "Is this statement supported by most of the other material in the paragraph?"

> *Hint:* When looking for the topic, make sure you do not pick one that is either **too broad** (covering a great deal more than is in the selection) or **too narrow** (covering only part of the selection). The topic and the main idea of a selection must include everything in that selection—no more and no less.
>
> For instance, in the example given in Practice 1, page 18, the topic is "bad qualities." "Character traits" would be too broad, because these would include good qualities as well as bad qualities. "Greed" would be too narrow, since this is only one type of bad quality mentioned.

Paragraph 1

¹ Shocking as it seems, cannibalism is common in the animal world. ²In species such as the red-back spider, the black widow spider, the praying mantis, and the scorpion, the female commonly eats the male after mating. ³Another widespread form of cannibalism is size-structured cannibalism, in which large individuals consume smaller ones. ⁴Octopus, bats, toads, fish, monitor lizards, salamanders, crocodiles, spiders, crustaceans, birds, mammals, and a vast number of insects have all been observed to engage in size-structured cannibalism. ⁵Yet another common form of cannibalism is infanticide. ⁶Classic examples include the chimpanzees, where groups of adult males have been observed to attack their infants; and lions, where adult males commonly kill infants when they take over a new harem after replacing the previous dominant males. ⁷Also, gerbils and hamsters eat their young if they are stillborn, or if the mothers are especially stressed.

1. What is the *topic* of the paragraph? In other words, what (in one or more words) is the paragraph about? _____ Cannibalism _____

_1_ 2. What point is the writer making about the topic? In other words, which sentence states the *main idea* of the paragraph? In the space provided, write the number of the sentence containing the main idea.

Paragraph 2

¹The Great Wall of China is a truly remarkable creation. ²At 4,500 miles long, taller than five men, and wide enough to allow at least six horses to gallop side by side atop it, the Great Wall is so huge it can be seen from space. ³The Wall is constructed of four-inch blocks made of compressed earth, stone, willow twigs, and the remains of laborers who died among the millions who worked on its construction. ⁴The Great Wall follows mountain slopes and has inclines as great as seventy degrees. ⁵The paths on the Wall are even more difficult to travel because the steps are of uneven depth, width, and height. ⁶Through much of its 2,500-year history, armies marched and camped on the Wall, keeping lookout for invaders and repelling trespassers who dared to pitch ladders to try to mount it. ⁷Today the Great Wall is a tourist attraction that brings many visitors to China. ⁸Tourists are eager to make the strenuous hike over precarious paths to take in the greatness of its size and history.

1. What is the *topic* of the paragraph? In other words, what (in one or more words) is the paragraph about? _The Great Wall of China_

_1_ 2. What point is the writer making about the topic? In other words, which sentence states the *main idea* of the paragraph? In the space provided, write the number of the sentence containing the main idea.

Paragraph 3

¹At the beginning of the twentieth century, families often hired older women known as chaperones to keep watch over their daughters. ²These women played an important role in courtship. ³When a young man asked a girl on a date, he automatically invited her chaperone as well. ⁴If a young lady entertained her boyfriend in the parlor, the chaperone did not budge from the room. ⁵Because of her responsibilities, the chaperone had the power to make courtship pleasurable or miserable. ⁶Some chaperones had soft hearts and gave young lovers some privacy. ⁷Others were such sticklers for appearances that they prevented the young couple even from exchanging personal remarks. ⁸In addition to being guardians, chaperones sometimes functioned as private eyes. ⁹They investigated the backgrounds of gentlemen who called on their charges to see which one would make the best match.

1. What is the *topic* of the paragraph? In other words, what (in one or more words) is the paragraph about? _____ Chaperones _____

_1_ 2. What point is the writer making about the topic? In other words, which sentence states the *main idea* of the paragraph? In the space provided, write the number of the sentence containing the main idea.

Paragraph 4

¹Cardiovascular disease—disease of the heart or blood vessels—is the leading cause of death in the United States, killing about 1 million people a year. ²Cardiovascular disease is actually a group of disorders. ³This group includes high blood pressure, or hypertension, which significantly increases the risk of other diseases in the group. ⁴Atherosclerosis, or coronary artery disease, is another member of the group. ⁵In this cardiovascular disorder, a fatty deposit, plaque, builds up on the walls of the arteries, restricting the flow of blood and causing strain to the heart, which must work harder to pump blood through the narrowed arteries. ⁶Sometimes an aneurysm occurs: the artery ruptures. ⁷Heart attack—technically, myocardial infarction—is also in this group. ⁸It happens when plaque builds up so much that blood flow to the heart is cut off and some heart muscle dies. ⁹Congestive heart failure, a chronic disease, is part of the group as well. ¹⁰In this disorder the heart has been weakened and can no longer pump enough blood. ¹¹Stroke, too, is a cardio-vascular disease: it occurs when blood flow to the brain is restricted or cut off.

1. What is the *topic* of the paragraph? In other words, what (in one or more words) is the paragraph about? ___ Cardiovascular disease ___

_2_ 2. What point is the writer making about the topic? In other words, which sentence states the *main idea* of the paragraph? In the space provided, write the number of the sentence containing the main idea.

3 Find and Use Key Words to Lead You to the Main Idea

Sometimes authors make it fairly easy to find their main idea. They announce it using **key words**—verbal clues that are easy to recognize. One group of these is **list words**, which tell you a list of items will follow. For example, the main idea in the paragraph about TV violence was stated like this: "However, we now know that TV violence does affect people in negative ways." The expression *negative ways* helps you zero in on your target: the main idea. You realize that the paragraph will most likely be about specific ways that TV violence affects people. As you read on and see the series of negative effects, you know your assumption about the main idea was correct.

Here are some common word groups that often announce a main idea. Note that each of them contains a word that ends in **s**—a plural that suggests the supporting details will be a list of items.

List Words

several kinds (or ways) of	several causes of	some factors in
three advantages of	five steps	among the results
various reasons for	a number of effects	a series of

When expressions like these appear in a sentence, look carefully to see if that sentence might be the main idea. Chances are a sentence containing list words will be followed by a list of major supporting details.

✓ Check Your Understanding

Underline the list words in the following sentences.

> *Hint:* Remember that list words usually end in *s*.

Example Emotional decisions can be divided into two main types.

1. At least five job trends deserve watching in today's world.

2. Pathologists identify four different stages of cancer in the body.

3. Several steps can be effective in helping people deal with prejudice.

4. Winners of presidential elections share various traits in common.

5. Giving birth to and raising a child will require a number of adjustments in the parents' lives.

Explanation

You should have underlined the following groups of words: *five job trends, four different stages, several steps, various traits,* and *a number of adjustments.* Each of these phrases tells you that a list of details may follow.

In addition to list words, addition words can alert you to the main idea. **Addition words** are generally used right before supporting details. When you see this type of clue, you can assume that the detail it introduces fits under the umbrella of a main idea.

Here are some of the addition words that often introduce supporting details and help you discover the main idea.

Addition Words

one	to begin with	also	further
first (of all)	for one thing	in addition	furthermore
second(ly)	other	next	last (of all)
third(ly)	another	moreover	final(ly)

✔ Check Your Understanding

Reread the paragraph about TV violence, underlining the addition words that alert you to supporting details.

¹Many people feel that violence on television is harmless entertainment. ²However, we now know that TV violence does affect people in negative ways. ³One study showed that frequent TV watchers are more fearful and suspicious of others. ⁴They try to protect themselves from the outside world with extra locks on the doors, alarm systems, guard dogs, and guns. ⁵In addition, that same study showed that heavy TV watchers are less upset about real-life violence than non-TV watchers. ⁶It seems that the constant violence they see on TV makes them less sensitive to the real thing. ⁷Another study, of a group of children, found that TV violence increases aggressive behavior. ⁸Children who watched violent shows were more willing to hurt another child in games where they were given a choice between helping and hurting. ⁹They were also more likely to select toy weapons over other kinds of playthings.

Explanation

The words that introduce each new supporting detail for the main idea are *One*, *In addition*, and *Another*. When you see these addition words, you realize the studies are all being cited in support of an idea—in this case, that TV violence affects people in negative ways.

That main idea includes the list words *negative ways*, which suggest that the supporting details will be a list of negative ways TV violence affects people. In this and many paragraphs, list words and addition words often work hand in hand.

The following chapter, "Supporting Details in Reading," includes further practice in the words and phrases that alert you to the main idea and the details that support it. But what you have already learned here will help you find main ideas.

Locations of the Main Idea

Now you know how to recognize a main idea by (1) distinguishing between the general and the specific, (2) identifying the topic of a passage, and (3) using key words. You are ready to find the main idea no matter where it is located in a paragraph.

A main idea may appear at any point within a paragraph. Very commonly, it shows up at the beginning, as either the first or the second sentence. However, main ideas may also appear further within a paragraph or even at the very end.

Main Idea at the Beginning

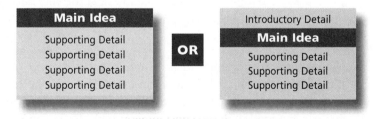

In textbooks, it is very common for the main idea to be either the first or the second sentence of a paragraph.

See if you can underline the main idea in the paragraph on the following page.

¹People tend to cling to their first impressions, even if they are wrong. ²Suppose you mention the name of your new neighbor to a friend. ³"Oh, I know him," your friend replies. ⁴"He seems nice at first, but it's all an act." ⁵Perhaps this appraisal is off-base. ⁶The neighbor may have changed since your friend knew him, or perhaps your friend's judgment is simply unfair. ⁷Whether the judgment is accurate or not, once you accept your friend's evaluation, it will probably influence the way you respond to the neighbor. ⁸You'll look for examples of the insincerity you've heard about, and you'll probably find them. ⁹Even if this neighbor were a saint, you would be likely to interpret his behavior in ways that fit your expectations.

In this paragraph, the main idea is in the *first* sentence. All the following sentences in the paragraph provide a detailed example of how we cling to first impressions.

✔ Check Your Understanding

Now read the following paragraph and see if you can underline its main idea:

¹For shy people, simply attending class can be stressful. ²Several strategies, though, can lessen the trauma of attending class for shy people. ³Shy students should time their arrival to coincide with that of most other class members— about two minutes before the class is scheduled to begin. ⁴If they arrive too early, they may be seen sitting alone or, even worse, may actually be forced to talk with another early arrival. ⁵If they arrive late, all eyes will be upon them. ⁶Before heading to class, shy students should dress in the least conspicuous manner possible—say, in the blue jeans, sweatshirt, and sneakers that 99.9 percent of their classmates wear. ⁷That way they won't stand out from everyone else. ⁸They should take a seat near the back of the room. ⁹But they shouldn't sit at the very back, since instructors sometimes make a point of calling on students there.

Explanation

In the above paragraph, the main idea is stated in the *second* sentence. The first sentence introduces the topic, shy people in class, but it is the idea in the second sentence—several strategies can lessen the trauma of attending class for shy people—that is supported in the rest of the paragraph. So keep in mind that the first sentence may simply introduce or lead into the main idea of a paragraph.

> **Hint:** Very often, a contrast word like *however, but, yet,* or *though* signals the main idea, as in the paragraph you have just read.

Main Idea in the Middle

The main idea at times appears in the middle of a paragraph. Here is an example of a paragraph in which the main idea is somewhere in the middle. Try to find it and underline it. Then read the explanation that follows.

> [1]A television ad for a new sports car showed scenes of beautiful open country that suggested freedom and adventure. [2]The car never appeared in the ad at all. [3]An ad for a hotel chain showed a romantic couple in bed together. [4]They were obviously on vacation and having a leisurely, romantic, sexy morning. [5]<u>As these ads suggest, advertisers often try to sell products and services by associating them with positive images rather than by providing relevant details about the product or service.</u> [6]An ad giving the car's gas mileage, safety rating, or repair frequency would be more important to a buyer, but it might not draw the viewer's interest as much as beautiful scenery. [7]Similarly, details on the hotel's prices and service would be more informative than images of a glamorous vacation. [8]But the romantic couple gets people's attention and associates the hotel in viewers' minds with a good time.

If you thought the fifth sentence states the main idea, you were correct. The first four sentences introduce the topic of advertisers and provide specific examples of the main idea. The fifth sentence then presents the writer's main idea, which is that advertisers often try to sell their products by associating them with appealing images rather than with relevant details. The rest of the paragraph continues to develop that idea.

Main Idea at the End

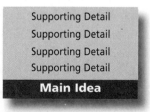

Sometimes all the sentences in a paragraph will lead up to the main idea, which is presented at the end. Here is an example of such a paragraph.

¹Only about 1 percent of insect species are destructive to crops and property. ²Nevertheless, this small group causes several billion dollars of damage each year in the United States alone. ³Harmful insects include household pests, such as termites; crop and livestock pests, such as boll weevils; and hosts of disease-causing organisms, such as mosquitoes infected with parasitic protozoa. ⁴Many insects, on the other hand, are beneficial to human society. ⁵Some insects pollinate fruit trees, flowers, and many field crops. ⁶Bees produce honey and beeswax, silkworms form cocoons from which silk is spun, and lac insects provide the raw material for commercial shellac. ⁷Some kinds of insects are natural enemies of destructive insects. ⁸For example, the larvae of certain wasps feed on caterpillars that destroy plants. ⁹**Clearly, insects are both harmful and beneficial to human society.**

Main Idea at the Beginning and the End

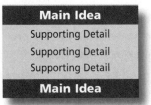

At times an author may choose to state the main idea near the beginning of the paragraph and then emphasize it (as a conclusion) by restating it in other words later in the paragraph. In such cases, the main idea is at both the beginning and the end. Such is the case in the following paragraph.

¹**An important result of medical advances is an increase in the number of conditions thought to be of medical concern.** ²In the not-too-distant past, birth and death usually occurred at home. ³Family members and friends were there or close by. ⁴Now most people are born and die in a hospital, surrounded by bright lights and expensive machines. ⁵People who were addicted to alcohol or drugs were once considered sinful or lacking in willpower. ⁶Now they are considered "sick." ⁷Problems that used to be accepted as part of life—baldness, wrinkles, small breasts, sleeplessness—are now deemed proper matters for medical attention. ⁸Some criminologists have even defined antisocial behavior as a medical problem. ⁹Lawbreakers of all kinds, from the shoplifter to the mass murderer, may potentially be labeled "sick." ¹⁰**Because of current medical knowledge, what were once thought to be problems of life or of character are now considered medical issues.**

Note that the main idea—because of medical advances, more problems are considered medical issues—is expressed in different words in the first and last sentences.

PRACTICE 8

The main ideas of the following paragraphs appear at different locations—in the beginning, somewhere in the middle, or at the end. Identify each main idea by filling in its sentence number in the space provided.

_2_   1. [1]Many people think of thieves as clever. [2]In reality, thieves can be remarkably foolish. [3]One evening, a Los Angeles woman was walking her miniature poodle when a man came up behind her, pushed her to the ground, grabbed the plastic bag she was holding, and drove away. [4]Afterward, when asked about the mugging, the woman cheerfully commented, "I only wish there had been more in the bag." [5]The woman had used the bag when she cleaned up her dog's messes. [6]In Baltimore, an even dumber burglar broke into a house while the woman who lived there was home, ransacked the place, and, having found only $11.50 in cash, demanded that the victim write him a check for $30. [7]When the woman asked to whom she should make the check payable, the thief gave his own name, in full. [8]He was arrested a few hours later. [9]But an Oklahoma thief may have been dumbest of all. [10]Charged with purse-snatching, he decided to act as his own attorney. [11]At his trial, he cross-examined the victim: "Did you get a good look at my face when I took your purse?" [12]Not surprisingly, he was convicted.

_3_   2. [1]For 250 million years, reptiles—which appeared on Earth long before the first mammals—have been fighting over territory. [2]Today, human beings do battle over property as well. [3]But the reptiles' way of fighting is generally more civilized and humane than the humans'. [4]Lizards will take a few rushes at one another to test which one is stronger. [5]After a few passes, the loser rolls over on his back to signal defeat. [6]The winner allows him to leave unharmed. [7]Rattlesnakes, similarly, will duel over territory. [8]But they do it with their necks twined together so that they cannot injure each other with their fangs. [9]Humans, of course, generally fight with the intent of injuring one another. [10]The victor often seems to feel he hasn't really won until he's wounded and humiliated his opponent, if not killed him.

_1_   3. [1]If asked to describe ourselves, most of us would not answer that we are mostly water, but that's exactly what we are. [2]A 150-pound person is actually 100 pounds of water and only 50 pounds of everything else. [3]Our blood plasma is 92% water, and our brains are 75% water. [4]We use the expression "dry as a bone," but in fact our bones are not dry at all—they are about 20% water.

⁵Our "inner sea" is constantly in motion, flowing through us every moment, bringing food and oxygen to our cells, carrying away wastes, lubricating our joints, cushioning our brains and regulating our temperatures. ⁶If the percentage of water in our bodies drops even 1 or 2 percent, we feel thirsty. ⁷A drop of 10% is usually fatal. ⁸Every day, we lose about two and a half quarts of water. ⁹Surprisingly, we replace less than half this lost water through drinking. ¹⁰The rest we replenish with food which, just like us, is mostly water. ¹¹A tomato, for example, is over 87% water, which is released into the body when we eat it.

_4_   4. ¹Today, as many as one and a half million children are believed to be homeschooled; twenty years ago, only 12,500 students were educated at home. ²This dramatic increase in the number of homeschooled children can be explained in part by the growth of membership in fundamentalist Christianity, whose members often choose to educate their children at home. ³While religious motivation is the reason that most families choose homeschooling, it is not the only reason. ⁴A number of reasons draw parents to homeschooling. ⁵Some parents prefer to educate their children in the security of their own homes away from the dangers of guns and violence in many urban schools today. ⁶Other parents believe that homeschooling provides their children a more intimate and nurturing learning environment. ⁷Economics can also play a role. ⁸One parent can stay home and be a home teacher, saving the high cost of childcare. ⁹Finally, motivations can even be negative: sometimes racism, anti-Semitism, or some other hateful reason can cause parents to reject public schooling for homeschooling.

The Central Point

Just as a paragraph may have a main idea, a longer selection may have a **central point**, also known as a **central idea** or **thesis**. The longer selection might be an essay, a reading, or a section of a textbook chapter. You can find a central point in the same way that you find a main idea—by identifying the topic (which is often suggested by the title of the selection) and then looking at the supporting material. The paragraphs within the longer reading will provide supporting details for the central point.

✓ *Check Your Understanding*

In the following essay, the central point is stated in one sentence. See if you can find and underline this sentence. Then write its number in the space provided.

Peer Pressure

[1]We often hear about the dangers of peer pressure to teenagers. [2]Teens take drugs, skip school, get drunk, or have sex to impress their friends. [3]However, there is another, perhaps equally bad, effect of peer pressure. [4]Desperate to conform to their friends' values, teens may give up their interests in school, in hobbies, and even in certain people.

[5]Teens may lose or hide their interest in school in order to be like their friends. [6]They adopt a negative attitude in which school is seen as a battlefield, with teachers and other officials regarded as the enemy. [7]In private, they may enjoy certain teachers, but in front of their friends, they put on a sarcastic or hostile act. [8]In addition, teenagers may stop participating in class. [9]They may refuse to join in class discussions, even when the topic interests them. [10]They may decide it is cool to show up without the assigned homework. [11]If their peers demand it, they may interfere with others' learning by disrupting class. [12]Conforming also means not joining in after-school activities.

[13]Teenagers also give up private pleasures and hobbies to be one of the crowd. [14]Certain pastimes, such as writing poems, practicing piano, reading books, or joining an after-school club may be off-limits because the crowd laughs at them.

[15]Most sadly, teenagers sometimes give up the people they love in order to be accepted. [16]If necessary, they sacrifice the old friend who no longer dresses well enough, listens to the wrong kind of music, or refuses to drink or take drugs. [17]Potential boyfriends or girlfriends may be rejected, too, if the crowd doesn't like their looks or values. [18]Teens can even cut their families out of their lives if they are too poor, too conventional, or too different from their friends' parents.

_____ is the number of the sentence that states the central point.

Explanation

The central point is a general statement that covers all or most of the details in a reading. To find the central point of the essay above, look first at its topic. Since the title is "Peer Pressure," and every paragraph is about that subject, we can say "peer pressure" is the topic. Then decide on what point is being made about the topic by looking at the major details of the essay. The first major detail, presented in the second paragraph, is about giving up interest in school as a result of peer pressure. The next major detail, in the third paragraph, is about giving up interest in hobbies; and the third major detail, in the fourth paragraph, is about giving up interest in certain people.

The central point, then, will be a general statement that covers all of the major details presented. As is often the case, the central point is stated in the first paragraph. Sentence 4 in that paragraph expresses the idea that peer pressure may cause students to give up interest in school, in hobbies, and in certain people.

PRACTICE 9

A. The author has stated the central point of the following textbook selection in one sentence. Find that sentence, and write its number in the space provided.

Prewriting Strategies

[1]Prewriting refers to strategies you can use to generate ideas before starting the first draft of a paper. [2]Prewriting techniques have various advantages. [3]They encourage imaginative exploration and therefore also help you discover what interests you most about your subject. [4]Having such a focus early in the writing process keeps you from plunging into your initial draft without first giving some thought to what you want to say. [5]Prewriting thus saves you time in the long run by keeping you on course.

[6]Prewriting can help in other ways, too. [7]When we write, we often interfere with our ability to generate material because we continually critique what we put down on paper. [8]"This makes no sense," "This is stupid," "I can't say that," and other critical thoughts pop into our minds. [9]Such negative, self-critical comments stop the flow of our thoughts and reinforce the fear that we have nothing to say and aren't very good at writing. [10]During prewriting, you deliberately ignore your internal critic. [11]Your purpose is simply to get ideas down on paper without evaluating their effectiveness. [12]Writing without immediately judging what you produce can be liberating. [13]Once you feel less pressure, you'll probably find that you can generate a good deal of material. [14]And that can make your confidence soar.

[15]One final advantage of prewriting: The random associations typical of prewriting tap the mind's ability to make unusual connections. [16]When you prewrite, you're like an archaeologist going on a dig. [17]On the one hand, you may not unearth anything; on the other hand, you may stumble upon one interesting find after another. [18]Prewriting helps you appreciate—right from the start—this element of surprise in the writing process.

_2_   is the number of the sentence that states the central point.

B. Sometimes an author does not state a main idea directly. In these cases, the main idea is **implied**—only suggested by the supporting details and not clearly stated in one sentence.

The central idea of the following textbook passage is unstated, and the passage is followed by four sentences. In the space provided, write the letter of the sentence that best expresses the unstated central idea. Ask yourself first, "What is the implied central idea?" Then test your answer by asking, "Does all or most of the material in the passage support this idea?"

[1]Between one-third and one-half of all adolescents and adults regularly fail to get enough sleep. [2]According to the National Sleep Foundation, adolescents need at least 9 hours of sleep a night, but 80% of them get less sleep than that. [3]As a result, at least once a week 28% of high school students fall asleep in class. [4]Another 22% fall asleep while doing homework, and 14% arrive late or miss school entirely because they oversleep. [5]Thus it is not surprising that chronic sleep deprivation among adolescents results in diminished attention, reduced arousal, and lower test scores.

[6]Sleep deprivation negatively affects reaction time, memory, judgment, and the ability to pay attention. [7]Experts estimate that sleep loss is a contributing factor in more than 200,000 automobile accidents each year in the United States, resulting in more than a thousand deaths and tens of thousands of injuries. [8]Research suggests that driving while sleepy is as dangerous as driving while drunk.

[9]Sleep deprivation may also affect the performance of people in high-risk positions such as nuclear power plant operators, who often have to make critical decisions on short notice. [10]For example, there was an accident at the nuclear power plant at Three Mile Island, Pennsylvania, in which human error transformed a minor mishap into a major nuclear disaster. [11]And certain hospital residents, who work long hours without rest, experience twice as many failures of attention while working at night compared to residents who work shorter shifts. [12]They make over one-third of serious medical errors regarding patients, including five times as many serious diagnostic mistakes that could be life-threatening. [13]To put the state of exhaustion into further perspective, residents working heavy schedules perform similarly on cognitive tasks to people with blood alcohol levels between 0.04% and 0.05%—the level reached when an average-sized man consumes three beers in a single hour.

[14]The lack of sleep also contributes to such diseases as heart attacks, asthma, strokes, high blood pressure, and diabetes. [15]In children, insufficient sleep is associated with increased risk of being overweight. [16]Sleep deprivation is also clearly related to depression in high school and college students. [17]According to Mary Alice Carskadon, a leading researcher in the area of sleep among college

students, "Every study we have done over the past decade on high school and college students shows that the less sleep they get, the more depressed moods they report." [18]Even for college students who are not depressed, research shows that a lack of sleep results in lower academic performance.

_C_ Which sentence best expresses the implied central idea of the entire selection?
  A. Businesses must require their employees to get enough sleep.
  B. Chronic sleep loss is widespread in America today.
  C. Not getting enough sleep has significant drawbacks.
  D. Sleep deprivation is a challenge faced by adolescents and adults alike.

A Final Thought

Whether we are readers, writers, listeners, or speakers, the "heart" of clear communication is the main idea, or point, and the support for the main idea. Look at the following diagram:

The diagram underscores the importance of the most important of all reading skills: the ability to identify main ideas. The diagram also shows that the ability to identify supporting details for the main idea is an almost equally important skill.

MAIN IDEAS IN READING: Mastery Test 2

A. In each of the following groups—all based on textbook selections—one statement is the general point, and the other statements are specific support for the point. Identify each point with a **P** and each statement of support with an **S**.

1. ____ A. In the summer, tenement apartments were so hot the Boston Board of Health recommended that mothers take their babies to the rooftops at night.

   ____ B. For many immigrants in the late 19th century, their first American home was less appealing than the place they had left behind.

   ____ C. In the winter, the tenements were so cold that people went to work even when they were sick just so they could get warm.

   ____ D. One tenement had 170 children but only a 14-foot-square yard for them to play in.

2. ____ A. There were ten women in the House of Representatives in 1970 and only one woman in the Senate.

   ____ B. In North Carolina, only a virgin could charge a man with rape.

   ____ C. Divorced women were regarded as high risks by insurance companies, and they had trouble getting credit cards.

   ____ D. In the early 1970s, women still had a long way to go in terms of gaining equal rights.

3. ____ A. The introduction of handguns in Europe in the early 1300s had a great impact on road travel.

   ____ B. The handgun allowed fourteenth-century travelers to protect themselves from highwaymen who robbed and assaulted travelers.

   ____ C. In the 1300s, most road travelers (being right-handed) kept their handguns under their left arms, leading to the common practice of keeping to the right side of the road.

   ____ D. Later in the fourteenth century, villages and towns began to hire men who could use handguns to protect travelers on sections of roadway; this practice was the forerunner of modern highway patrols.

(Continues on next page)

B. Each group of statements below includes one topic, one main idea, and two supporting details. In the space provided, label each item with one of the following:

T — for the **topic** of the paragraph
MI — for the **main idea**
SD — for the **supporting details**

Group 1

_____ A. Certain behaviors are considered especially serious signs that a child may later engage in violent criminal acts.

_____ B. "Red flags" in childhood for future criminal behavior.

_____ C. Cruelty to animals, such as beating or torturing pets, is often a sign of serious psychological problems in children.

_____ D. Children who show a fascination with setting fires have a strong tendency to later engage in violent criminal behavior.

Group 2

_____ A. Adults seek out spicy or bitter foods to stimulate their smaller supply of taste buds.

_____ B. Sensitivity to flavors.

_____ C. The difference in the sensitivity to flavors between children and adults lies in the taste buds, the tiny taste receptors that line the tongue.

_____ D. Young children's tongues are loaded with taste buds and are especially sensitive; therefore, sour or spicy flavors seem too intense to them.

MAIN IDEAS IN READING: Mastery Test 4

The main idea may appear at any place within each of the five paragraphs that follow. Write the number of each main idea sentence in the space provided.

_____ 1. [1]One writer spent nine hundred hours over the course of eight years watching the action in singles bars and learning about male-female relationships. [2]Although men may think of themselves as the aggressors, says this writer, it is really women who make the decisions when a courtship is beginning. [3]He has observed that women are the ones who pick a potential mate out of the crowd. [4]They position themselves near the man they've selected and, with a glance or a smile, invite him to make contact. [5]Similarly, as conversation begins, the woman initiates each increasingly intimate stage. [6]Her continuing eye contact, moving closer, and touching the man all signal her permission for him to make further advances. [7]In most cases, the woman's signals are so subtle that the man is only subconsciously aware of them.

_____ 2. [1]In everyday advertising, one observes many obvious attempts to package and sell products and ideas (toothpaste, aspirin, presidential candidates) through clever influence tactics. [2]Many people claim that such blatant attempts at persuasion are so pitifully obvious that they are not much affected by them. [3]Nevertheless, the sales of one cigarette brand increased seven times during a four-year period of heavy advertising. [4]A toy company increased its sales twenty-four times after it began to advertise extensively on television. [5]And one venerable but nearly forgotten cereal brand experienced a sudden 30 percent increase in sales when a well-known natural-foods enthusiast began plugging this rather bland cereal. [6]There are many other advertising success stories as well. [7]It appears that tremendous numbers of consumers are influenced by advertising, despite their claims to the contrary.

_____ 3. [1]Pedal error occurs when the driver of an automobile mistakenly presses down on the accelerator instead of the brake pedal. [2]This leads to unintended acceleration, which, in turn, can frequently result in an accident. [3]It seems as though stepping on the wrong pedal would be an unlikely occurrence. [4]However, an analysis of pedal error shows that this mistake is easier to make than you might think. [5]A driver sometimes turns his upper body a little to the left at the same moment that he moves his right foot toward the brake pedal. [6]The driver might turn his upper body to the right to look in the left side mirror or to reach for his seatbelt. [7]Or, if he is in reverse, he might look

(Continues on next page)

over his left shoulder to make sure that it is safe to back up. [8]This turning of the upper body could cause his right foot to move slightly to the right. [9]As he unconsciously moves his foot to the right, he may end up hitting the accelerator rather than the brake. [10]Instead of stopping and remaining stationary, the car in fact begins to accelerate. [11]Believing that his foot is on the brake, the driver presses his foot down harder in an effort to stop the car. [12]Obviously, this action only makes the problem worse.

_____ 4. [1]It appears that some pioneer women had more to fear from insects than from Indian attacks. [2]One of the most terrifying assaults of nature involved grasshoppers. [3]Swarms would appear suddenly, in huge clouds, and devour everything in sight. [4]If a housewife tried covering her garden with gunnysacks, the bugs simply went under them, or ate their way through them. [5]After they ate the crops, the grasshoppers moved into the barns and houses. [6]They ate all the food and devoured clothing, window curtains, furniture, fence boards, and cabin sidings. [7]In the summer, flies or gnats swarmed over everything. [8]In a desperate attempt to drive away mosquitoes, plainswomen burned buffalo chips—they could stand the smell better than the bugs could. [9]In the Southwest, women were instructed to place their beds at least two feet away from the walls, lest they wake up covered with scorpions. [10]Fleas were also a terrible problem, and some settlers burned their houses down when the fleas became too burdensome. [11]But American settlers had a yen for permanence, and a sturdy house that lasted forever was also a permanent abode for vermin.

_____ 5. [1]The American author Mark Twain is famous for the humor in his writing. [2]His novels, stories, and essays have brought laughter to millions. [3]However, Twain's own life in the sixteen years leading up to his death in 1910 was marked more by sorrow than humor, as he faced several personal tragedies. [4]He had invested a significant amount of money in the development of a mechanical typesetting machine. [5]In 1894 the project failed, and his investment was lost. [6]In addition, a publishing company that he had begun ten years earlier went bankrupt. [7]So at the age of 59, this once-rich man went on a two-year worldwide lecture tour in order to earn money. [8]He took his wife with him on this tour but left his three daughters at home in Hartford, Connecticut. [9]While he was gone, his favorite daughter, Susy, died of meningitis, an inflammation of the brain and spinal cord. [10]Although his wife, Olivia, was ten years younger than he, she had a long history of health problems and died in 1904. [11]In December 1909, just five months before Twain's own death, his daughter Jean died. [12]Only one of his three daughters outlived him.

MAIN IDEAS IN READING: Mastery Test 5

A. The main idea may appear at any place within each of the three paragraphs that follow. Write the number of each main idea sentence in the space provided.

_____ 1. ¹Just as there are rules of the road for drivers of cars, trucks, and buses, there are "rules of the sidewalk" for pedestrians. ²The sociologist Erving Goffman points out that, for one thing, pedestrians on a sidewalk keep to their right, relative to an imaginary dividing line in the middle of the sidewalk. ³Thus people sort themselves into lanes going in opposite directions, as on a vehicular roadway. ⁴And people who are walking slowly often tend to stay closer to the buildings, while to their left, in a "passing lane," are the people who are moving more quickly. ⁵Also, like drivers, pedestrians scan the route ahead so that they can swerve around obstacles—say, a puddle or a hole in the walkway—and so that they will not collide with anyone else. ⁶If a head-on collision seems possible, pedestrians will make eye contact and maneuver to keep out of each other's way. ⁷Goffman notes one obvious difference, though: rules of the road are often codified in laws and regulations, whereas rules of the sidewalk are informal social customs.

_____ 2. ¹When labor-management disputes are reported on news broadcasts, listeners sometimes think that mediation and arbitration are simply two interchangeable words for the same thing. ²But mediation and arbitration are very different processes, with different outcomes, though both involve the use of a neutral third party. ³In mediation, the third party (called a mediator) is brought in to assist in the negotiations so that the opponents will keep talking to each other. ⁴Mediators can only make suggestions about how to resolve a dispute; neither side is obliged to accept them. ⁵In arbitration, on the other hand, the third party—the arbitrator—is called in to settle the issue, and the arbitrator's decision is final and binding on both sides.

_____ 3. ¹A biological virus can attach itself to a human host cell and take charge, using the cell's functions to make the substances needed to form new virus particles, which then leave that cell and spread, repeating the process in other cells. ²Biological viruses cause many diseases—some minor, like the common cold; but some life-threatening, like polio or AIDS. ³Biological viruses may kill the host cell or make the cell itself malignant, or the virus may set off a dangerously violent response in the immune system. ⁴Biological viruses reproduce and spread in various ways, and they may be very hard to

(Continues on next page)

treat because they can take forms that the immune system cannot detect. ⁵Computer viruses are programs designed to attach themselves to ordinary software, take it over, and then reproduce and spread. ⁶A computer virus can do its damage by attacking the startup program, at which point antivirus devices cannot yet detect it; or by attacking the operating system; or by attacking applications such as databases. ⁷In any case, the virus can distort or kill computer memory. ⁸A computer virus, as the name implies, is very much like a biological virus.

B. (4.) The author has stated the central point of the following textbook selection in one sentence. Find that sentence, and write its number in the space provided.

Bug Protection

¹Almost all insects will flee if threatened. ²Many insects, however, have more specialized means of defense. ³Roaches and stinkbugs, for example, secrete foul-smelling chemicals that deter aggressors. ⁴Bees, wasps, and some ants have poisonous stings that can kill smaller predators and cause pain for larger ones. ⁵The larvae of some insects have hairs filled with poison. ⁶If a predator eats one of these larvae, it may suffer a toxic reaction. ⁷Insects that defend themselves by unpleasant or dangerous chemicals gain two advantages. ⁸On one hand, they often deter a predator from eating them. ⁹On the other hand, predators learn not to bother them in the first place.

¹⁰Other insects gain protection by mimicry, or similarity of appearance. ¹¹In one kind of mimicry, insects with similar defense mechanisms look alike, and predators learn to avoid them all. ¹²Bees and wasps mimic each other in this way. ¹³In another kind of mimicry, insects with no defenses of their own mimic the appearance of stinging or bad-tasting insects. ¹⁴Predators avoid the mimic as well as the insect with the unpleasant taste or sting. ¹⁵For example, syrphid flies look like bees but do not sting.

¹⁶Another kind of defense based on appearance is camouflage, or the ability to blend into surroundings. ¹⁷Many kinds of insects and animals have distinctive color markings that make them difficult to see. ¹⁸Predators have trouble locating prey that looks like its background. ¹⁹An insect is more likely to survive and produce offspring if it is camouflaged than if it is not.

_____ is the number of the sentence that states the central point.

MAIN IDEAS IN READING: Mastery Test 6

A. The main idea may appear at any place within each of the three paragraphs that follow. Write the number of each main idea sentence in the space provided.

_____ 1. [1]An old saying has it that "Many hands make light the work." [2]Thus we might expect that three individuals can pull three times as much as one person and that eight can pull eight times as much. [3]Research reveals that persons individually average 130 pounds of pressure when tugging on a rope. [4]However, in groups of three, they average 351 pounds (only 2.5 times the solo rate); and in groups of eight, only 546 pounds (less than 4 times the solo rate). [5]One explanation is that faulty coordination produces group inefficiency. [6]However, when subjects are blindfolded and believe they are pulling with others, they also slacken their effort. [7]Apparently when we work in groups, we cut down on our efforts, a process termed social loafing.

_____ 2. [1]Criminal and civil cases, the two types of court cases, differ in significant ways. [2]Criminal cases involve the enforcement of criminal laws, that is, laws against acts such as murder and robbery. [3]The case is brought by a government—a state or the federal government—against someone who is charged with committing a crime. [4]The government, then, is the prosecutor, and the accused is the defendant. [5]The defendant will be found "guilty" or "not guilty," usually by a jury. [6]A civil case involves a legal dispute between individuals and organizations, such as businesses. [7]One party to the case, the plaintiff, has filed a complaint against the other party, the defendant. [8]Civil lawsuits arise, for example, over personal injuries (as in automobile accidents), disagreements about contracts, and—more and more often these days—medical malpractice. [9]There is no verdict of "guilty" or "not guilty" in a civil case; instead, a jury, a judge, or a panel of judges will decide in favor of the plaintiff or the defendant.

_____ 3. [1]In one tribe in New Guinea, aggression is encouraged in boys from early infancy. [2]The child cannot obtain nourishment from his mother without carrying on a continuous battle with her. [3]Unless he grasps the nipple firmly and sucks vigorously, his mother will withdraw it and stop the feeding. [4]In his frantic effort to get food, the child frequently chokes—an annoyance to both himself and his mother. [5]Thus the feeding situation itself is "characterized by anger and struggle rather than by affection and reassurance" (Mead, 1939). [6]The people of another New Guinea tribe are extremely peaceful and do

(Continues on next page)

everything possible to discourage aggression. ⁷They regard all instances of aggression as abnormal. ⁸A similar tribe—the Tasaday of the Philippines—has been discovered. ⁹These people are extremely friendly and gentle. ¹⁰They possess no weapons for fighting or food-gathering; in fact, they are strict vegetarians who live off the land. ¹¹Evidence of this sort suggests that, rather than being basically aggressive animals, human beings are peaceful or aggressive depending upon their early childhood training.

B. (4.) The author has stated the central point of the following textbook selection in one sentence. Find that sentence, and write its number in the space provided.

¹Those who are fortunate enough not to live in poverty may equate "being poor" with "not having enough money to buy the things I'd like." ²Certainly, being poor does mean doing without many of life's material pleasures. ³But the impact of poverty goes far beyond the inability to buy goods.

⁴One fundamental effect of poverty is that the poor often live in substandard housing. ⁵They rent from landlords who may neglect the property, even to a criminal extent. ⁶The houses are often unsafe, with dangerous electrical wiring, non-functioning plumbing, and inadequate heat.

⁷Poverty also profoundly affects people's ability to receive an education. ⁸Public schools in poor areas are under-funded, poorly staffed, and supplied with outdated textbooks and sparse supplies. ⁹Classrooms are crowded and often chaotic; the schools function more as warehouses than as places of education. ¹⁰Children coming out of these schools are inadequately prepared for college, so they rarely advance beyond high school.

¹¹A third way in which poverty profoundly affects people's lives is in the area of employment. ¹²Without the career preparation that quality education provides, poor people are often qualified only for jobs with no future, no benefits, and a high chance of being laid off. ¹³When the poor do lose their jobs, they must deal with the tangled mess of unemployment insurance and welfare, adding stress and the increasing sense of failure to their lives.

_____ is the number of the sentence that states the central point.

In Chapter 1 you worked on the most important reading skill—finding the main idea. A closely related reading skill is locating *supporting details*—the added information that is needed for you to make sense of a main idea.

This chapter describes supporting details and presents three techniques that will help you take study notes on main ideas and their supporting details: outlining, mapping, and summarizing.

What Are Supporting Details?

"I know why I don't lose weight. Eating big meals and lots of snacks makes me happy. Drinking beer makes me happy. Not exercising makes me happy."

Supporting details are reasons, examples, facts, steps, or other kinds of evidence that explain a main idea. In the cartoon shown above, the main idea is that "I know why I don't lose weight." The joke in the cartoon is that the man's supporting details—big meals, snacks, beer, and not exercising—may make him *happy*, but they don't make him *healthy*.

On the next page is a paragraph with strong support for its point.

A Paragraph with Strong Support

In the paragraph below, three major details support the main idea that the penny should be phased out of our economy. As you read the paragraph, try to identify and check (✓) the three major details.

[1]"A penny saved is a penny earned," the old saying goes. [2]But there are now good reasons for our government to phase the penny out of the economy, allowing the nickel to stand as the lowest-valued coin. [3]For one thing, pennies take up more space than they are worth. [4]We can all recall a time when we needed a nickel, dime, or quarter to make an important phone call, buy a vending machine snack, or make a photocopy, and all we could come up with was a fistful of useless pennies. [5]Pennies are also a nuisance to the business community. [6]According to the National Association of Convenience Stores, 5.5 million hours and 22 million dollars are wasted by businesses on the extra time and effort it takes to handle pennies. [7]Finally, keeping pennies in circulation costs the nation as a whole. [8]The manufacturing, storage, and handling expenses involved in a penny's production and distribution add up to considerably more than the one cent it is worth.

✓ Check Your Understanding

See if you can complete the basic outline below that shows the three major details supporting the main idea.

Main idea: Our government should phase the penny out of the economy.

Supporting detail 1. _Pennies take up more space than they are worth._

Supporting detail 2. _Pennies are a nuisance to the business community._

Supporting detail 3. _Pennies cost the nation as a whole._

Explanation

You should have added (1) pennies take up more space than they are worth; (2) pennies are a nuisance to the business community, and (3) pennies cost the nation as a whole. These major supporting details help you fully understand the main idea. To read effectively, then, you must learn to recognize main ideas and the details that support these ideas.

Outlining

Preparing an outline of a passage often helps you understand and see clearly the relationship between a main idea and its supporting details. Outlines start with a main idea (or a heading that summarizes the main idea), followed by supporting details. There are often two levels of supporting details—major and minor. The **major details** explain and develop the main idea. In turn, the **minor details** help fill out and make clear the major details.

Below is the paragraph on TV violence that appeared in Chapter 1. Its supporting details are *factual evidence* found in two studies. Reread the paragraph, and put a check (✓) next to the each of three major supporting details.

> ¹Many people feel that violence on television is harmless entertainment. ²However, we now know that TV violence does affect people in negative ways. ³One study showed that frequent TV watchers are more fearful and suspicious of others. ⁴They try to protect themselves from the outside world with extra locks on the doors, alarm systems, guard dogs, and guns. ⁵In addition, that same study showed that heavy TV watchers are less upset about real-life violence than non-TV watchers. ⁶It seems that the constant violence they see on TV makes them less sensitive to the real thing. ⁷Another study, of a group of children, found that TV violence increases aggressive behavior. ⁸Children who watched violent shows were more willing to hurt another child in games where they were given a choice between helping and hurting. ⁹They were also more likely to select toy weapons over other kinds of playthings.

✓ Check Your Understanding

Now see if you can fill in the missing items in the following outline of the paragraph, which shows both major and minor details.

Main idea: We now know that TV violence does affect people in negative ways.

Major detail 1. Frequent TV watchers are more fearful and suspicious of others.

Minor detail: Protect themselves with extra locks, alarms, dogs, and guns.

Major detail 2. Heavy TV watchers are less upset about real-life violence than non TV watchers.

Minor detail: Constant violence on TV makes them less sensitive to the real thing.

Major detail: 3. _TV violence increases aggressive behavior_

Minor detail: _Children watching violent shows were more willing to hurt other children in games when given a choice._

Explanation

You should have added two major supporting details: (2) Heavy TV watchers are less upset about real-life violence than non-TV watchers; (3) TV violence increases aggressive behavior in children. And to the third major supporting detail you should have added the minor detail that children watching violent shows are more likely to choose toy weapons instead of other playthings.

Notice that just as the main idea is more general than its supporting details, major details are more general than minor ones. For instance, the major detail "Frequent TV watchers are more fearful and suspicious of others" is more general than the minor details about people protecting themselves with "extra locks on the doors, alarm systems, guard dogs, and guns," which illustrate the major detail.

Outlining Tips

The following tips will help you prepare outlines:

TIP 1 Look for words that tell you a list of details is coming. Here are some common list words:

List Words

several kinds of	various causes	a few reasons
a number of	a series of	three factors
four steps	among the results	several advantages

For example, look again at the main ideas in the two paragraphs already discussed and underline the list words:

- But there are now <u>good reasons</u> for our government to phase the penny out of the economy.

- <u>In fact</u>, we now know that TV violence does affect people in negative ways.

Here the words *good reasons* and *negative ways* each tell us that a list of major details is coming. But you will not always be given such helpful signals that a list of details will follow. For example, there are no list words in the paragraph on page 27 with this main idea: "Shocking as it seems, cannibalism is common in the animal world." However, you will want to note such list words when they are present, because they help you to understand quickly the basic organization of a passage.

 TIP 2   **Look for words that signal major details.** Such words are called **addition words**, and they will be explained further on pages 122–123. Here are some common addition words:

Addition Words

one	to begin with	also	further
first (of all)	for one thing	in addition	furthermore
second(ly)	other	next	last (of all)
third(ly)	another	moreover	final(ly)

✓ Check Your Understanding

Now look again at the selection on TV violence on page 55:

1. The word *one* (in *One study*) signals the first major supporting detail.

2. What addition words introduce the second major supporting detail?
    _____In addition_____

3. What addition word introduces the third major supporting detail?
    _____Another_____

And look again at the selection on phasing out the penny on page 54:

1. What words introduce the first major detail?___For one thing___

2. What word introduces the second major detail? ____also____

3. What word introduces the third major detail? ____Finally____

Explanation

In the selection on TV violence, the second major detail is introduced by the words *In addition*, and the third major detail by the word *Another*. In the selection on phasing out the penny, the first major detail is introduced by the words *For one thing*; the second major detail by the word *also*; and the third major detail by the word *Finally*.

TIP 3 When making an outline, put all supporting details of equal importance at the same distance from the margin. In the outline on TV violence on pages 55–56, the three major supporting details all begin at the same distance from the left margin. Likewise, the minor supporting details are all indented at a slightly greater distance from the margin. You can therefore see at a glance the main idea, the major details, and the minor details.

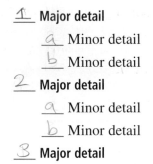

✓ *Check Your Understanding*

Put appropriate numbers *(1, 2, 3)* and letters *(a, b)* in front of the items in the following outline.

Main idea

<u>1</u> **Major detail**

   <u>a</u> Minor detail

   <u>b</u> Minor detail

<u>2</u> **Major detail**

   <u>a</u> Minor detail

   <u>b</u> Minor detail

<u>3</u> **Major detail**

Explanation

You should have put a *1, 2,* and *3* in front of the major details and an *a* and *b* in front of the minor details. Note that an outline proceeds from the most general to the most specific, from main idea to major details to minor details.

    The practice that follows will give you experience in finding major details, in separating major details from minor details, and in preparing outlines.

PRACTICE 1

Read and then outline each passage. Begin by writing in the main idea, and then fill in the supporting details. The first outline requires only major details; the second calls for you to add minor details as well.

A. [1]*Merriam-Webster's Collegiate Dictionary* defines *intimacy* as a state of "very close association, contact, or familiarity." [2]Researchers have identified four kinds of intimacy. [3]The first kind is physical. [4]Fortunate children are continually nourished by physical intimacy: being rocked, fed, hugged, and held. [5]As we grow older, we hug, shake hands, and continue to seek physical intimacy of all kinds. [6]Intimacy can also come from intellectual sharing. [7]When you engage another person in an exchange of important ideas, a kind of closeness develops that can be powerful and exciting. [8]Another kind of intimacy is emotional: exchanging important feelings. [9]Sharing personal information can both reflect and create feelings of closeness. [10]Last, shared activities can be seen as a dimension that achieves intimacy. [11]Shared activities can include everything from working side by side at a job or in a study group or meeting regularly for exercise workouts.

Main idea: _Researchers have Identified 4 kinds of_
intimacy.

    Major detail 1. _The first kind is physical._

    Major detail 2. _Intimacy can also come from intellectual_
sharing.

    Major detail 3. _Another kind of intimacy is emotional;_
exchanging important feelings.

    Major detail 4. _Last, shared activities can be seen as a_
dimension that achieves intimacy.

B. [1]A crowd is a temporary, relatively unorganized gathering of people. [2]Since a wide range of behavior is covered by the concept, sociologist Herbert Blumer distinguishes among four basic types of crowds. [3]The first, a casual crowd, is a collection of people with little in common except for participating in a common event, such as looking through a department-store window. [4]The second, a conventional crowd, is a number of people who have assembled for some specific purpose, such as attending a baseball game or concert. [5]Members of a conventional crowd typically act in accordance with established norms. [6]The third, an expressive crowd, is a group of people who have gotten together for self-stimulation and personal satisfaction, such as a religious revival or a rock festival. [7]And fourth, an acting crowd is an excited, explosive collection of people, including those who engage in rioting, looting, or other forms of aggressive behavior in which established norms carry little weight.

Main idea: According to sociologist Herbert Blumer, there are _____
_____four distinguished types of crowds._____

   Major detail: 1. _A casual crowd_
   _____

   Minor detail: _A collection of people with little in common._
   Major detail: 2. _A conventional crowd_
   _____

   Minor detail: _A number of people assembled together for a_
                    specific purpose.
   Major detail: 3. _An expressive crowd_
   _____

   Minor detail: _A group of people together for self-stimulation._
   Major detail: 4. _An acting crowd_
   _____

   Minor detail: _An excited, explosive collection of people._
   _____

Study Hint: At times you will want to include minor details in your study notes; at other times, it may not be necessary to do so. If you are taking notes on one or more textbook chapters, use your judgment. It is often best to be aware of minor details but to concentrate on writing down the main ideas and major details.

Mapping

Students sometimes find it helpful to use maps rather than outlines. **Maps**, or diagrams, are highly visual outlines in which circles, boxes, or other shapes show the relationships between main ideas and supporting details. Each major detail is connected to the main idea, often presented in the form of a title. If minor details are included, each is connected to the major detail it explains.

✓ *Check Your Understanding*

Read the following passage, and then see if you can complete the map and the questions that follow.

¹Weber says that there are three types of authority from which governments gain their right to command. ²One type of authority is based on tradition. ³Kings, queens, feudal lords, and tribal chiefs do not need written rules in order to govern. ⁴Their authority is based on long-standing customs and is handed down through generations from parent to child. ⁵People may also submit to authority because of charisma, the exceptional personal quality of an individual. ⁶Such leaders as Napoleon and Gandhi illustrate authority that derives its legitimacy from charismatic personalities. ⁷The political systems of industrial states are based largely on a third type of authority: legal authority. ⁸These systems derive legitimacy from a set of explicit rules and procedures that spell out the ruler's rights and duties. ⁹Typically, the rules and procedures are put in writing. ¹⁰The people pledge their obedience to "the law." ¹¹It specifies procedures by which certain individuals hold offices of power, such as governor or president or prime minister. ¹²But the authority is vested in those offices, not in the individuals who temporarily hold the offices.

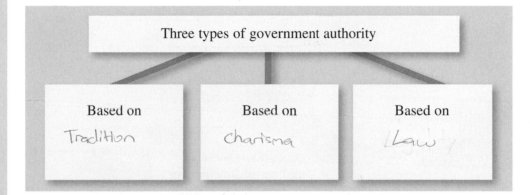

Three types of government authority

Based on	Based on	Based on
Tradition	Charisma	Law

Which word or words introduce:

1. The first major detail? _____ One _____
2. The second major detail? _____ Also; b _____
3. The third major detail? _____ Third _____

Explanation

The map sets off the major details in a very visual way. You see at a glance what Weber's three types of governmental authority are based on: tradition, charisma, and law. The words that introduce the major details are *One*, *also*, and *third*.

PRACTICE 2

Read each passage, and then complete the maps that follow. The main ideas are given so that you can focus on finding the supporting details. The first passage requires only major details. The second passage calls for you to add both major and minor details.

A. [1]Schools serve a number of functions in American society. [2]Because most students are unmarried, high schools and colleges act as matchmaking institutions. [3]It is at school that many young people find their future spouses. [4]Schools also establish social networks. [5]Some adults maintain friendships from high school and college; others develop networks that benefit their careers. [6]Another function of schools is to provide employment. [7]With 53 million students in grade and high schools, and another 15 million enrolled in colleges, U.S. education is big business. [8]Primary and secondary schools provide jobs for 2.9 million teachers, while another million work in colleges and universities. [9]Moreoever, schools help stabilize employment. [10]To keep millions of young people in school is to keep them out of the labor market, protecting the positions of older workers.

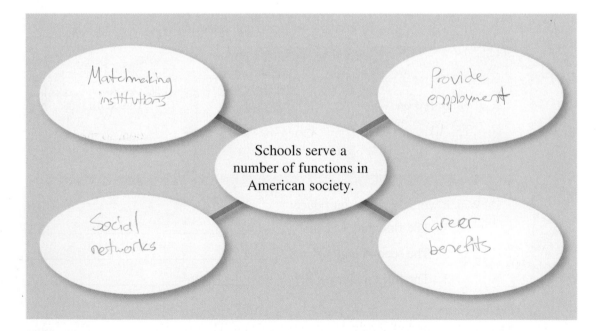

Matchmaking institutions

Provide employment

Schools serve a number of functions in American society.

Social networks

Career benefits

B. ¹In India, which has the largest number of cattle in the world, why is the slaughter of cows forbidden when there are many poor and starving people? ²Some social scientists have pointed out that the sacred cows serve several important, practical functions. ³First, they produce oxen, which Indians farmers desperately need to plow their fields and pull their carts. ⁴In addition, cows are of benefit when they die naturally. ⁵Their beef is eaten by the poor lower castes, and their hides are used by non-Hindu Indians to maintain one of the world's largest leather industries. ⁶Third, the cows produce an enormous amount of manure, which is used as fertilizer and cooking fuel. ⁷Fourth, the cows are easy to raise. ⁸They are tireless scavengers, eating garbage, stubble, and grass between railroad tracks, in ditches, and on roadsides. ⁹Thus, it costs nothing to raise the cows, and they provide many things of value.

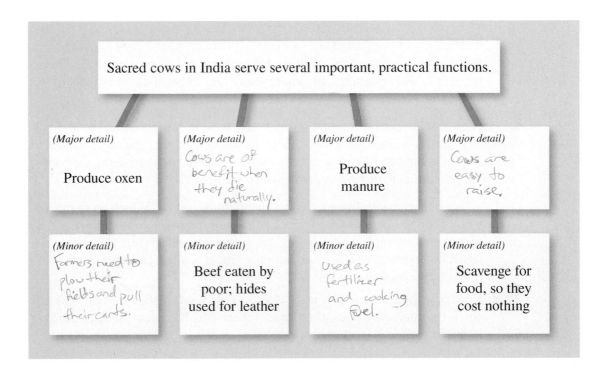

Sacred cows in India serve several important, practical functions.

(Major detail)	(Major detail)	(Major detail)	(Major detail)
Produce oxen	Cows are of benefit when they die naturally.	Produce manure	Cows are easy to raise.

(Minor detail)	(Minor detail)	(Minor detail)	(Minor detail)
Farmers need to plow their fields and pull their carts.	Beef eaten by poor; hides used for leather	Used as fertilizer and cooking fuel.	Scavenge for food, so they cost nothing

Summarizing

A **summary** is the reduction of a large amount of information to its most important points. The length and kind of summary will depend upon one's purpose as well as the material in question. Often, a summary will consist of a main idea and its major supporting details. As a general guideline, a paragraph might be reduced to a sentence or two, an article might be reduced to a paragraph, and a textbook chapter might be reduced to about three pages of notes.

One of the most common types of summarizing occurs when you are taking study notes on textbook material. Very often you will find it helpful to summarize examples of key terms. For instance, look at the following textbook passage and the summary that follows.

[1]People under severe stress may react to their problems with **regression**, a return to childlike behavior and defenses. [2]Adults who cry when their arguments fail may expect those around them to react sympathetically, as their parents did when they were children. [3]Other adults may use temper tantrums in a similar way. [4]In both examples, people are drawing on childish behaviors to solve current problems, in the hope that someone will respond to them the way adults did when they were children. [5]Inappropriate as it may seem, such immature and manipulative behavior often works—at least for a while.

Summary

Regression—a return to childlike behavior and defenses to solve current problems. For example, an adult whose argument fails may cry to get sympathy.

Note that a textbook definition of a key term (such as *regression*) should generally not be summarized, but should be worded in the language chosen by the author. On the other hand, it usually makes sense to summarize the supporting information. Summarizing often involves two steps:

1 *Select* one example from several that might be given. Which example you select is up to you, as long as it makes the term clear for you. In the summary above, the example about losing an argument and crying was chosen to illustrate regression. The other example, about temper tantrums, could have been chosen as well.

2 *Condense* the example if it's not already very brief. Notice that the example about the adult who cries when an argument fails has been condensed from a long sentence to a short one.

A definition of a key term followed by one condensed example is a very useful way to take notes—especially in introductory college courses, where many terms are defined and illustrated.

> *Study Hint:* If you have a textbook chapter to learn, very often you can get the information you need by doing two things: 1) writing down the definitions in the chapter and summarized examples of the definitions, and 2) writing down lists of major supporting details and any minor details that you think are important.

✓ *Check Your Understanding*

Read the selection below, taken from an introductory textbook for a college social science course. As is often the case in such introductory texts, a new term is presented and then followed by an extended example. Complete the study notes by circling the answer choice that best summarizes that example.

> [1]The tendency for members to be so intent on maintaining group agreement that they overlook or put aside the flaws in their decision is called **groupthink**. [2]Once a tentative decision has been made, members withhold information or opinions that might cast doubt on that course of action. [3]They do not want to be seen as criticizing their colleagues or as "rocking the boat." [4]If outside experts raise questions about the wisdom of their decision, members unite in opposing and discrediting the new information. [5]The classic example of "groupthink" occurred during President Kennedy's administration. [6]Kennedy sought the advice of a small group of trusted advisers in deciding whether to support the Bay of Pigs invasion of Cuba in 1961—an attempt by a force of Cuban exiles to overthrow the government of Fidel Castro. [7]Although several advisers had strong objections to the plan, not one expressed doubts. [8]As far as Kennedy knew, his advisers were unanimously in favor. [9]The invasion was a military and public relations disaster.

Study notes

Groupthink—the tendency for members to be so intent on maintaining group agreement that they overlook or put aside the flaws in the group's decision.

Example—

A. During Kennedy's administration, the Bay of Pigs invasion of Cuba in 1961 was a military and public relations disaster.
B. The classic example occurred during President Kennedy's administration.
C. Kennedy went ahead with the disastrous Bay of Pigs invasion because advisers withheld their objections.

Explanation

Useful study notes should clearly show how an example illustrates a new term. In the case of the paragraph above, the notes should include the key point that Kennedy's advisers overlooked the flaws in a decision. Only answer C includes the idea that advisers withheld their objections in order to seem unanimously in favor of the Bay of Pigs invasion, which turned out to be a disaster. Answer A tells about the results of the Bay of Pigs invasion, but says nothing about how the advisers withheld their true opinions. Answer B also makes no mention of what the advisers did. It refers to the example so generally that the event isn't even mentioned.

PRACTICE 3

Read each textbook selection below. Then complete the study notes by circling the letter of the answer that best summarizes an example of the term being defined.

A. ¹People are often motivated by the direct object of a desire, such as food or water. ²A **secondary reinforcer** is something one learns to desire through association with other, direct rewards. ³It is referred to as secondary not because it is less important, but because it is learned. ⁴A rat learns to get food by pressing a bar; then a buzzer is sounded every time the rat presses the bar and gets food. ⁵Even if the rat stops getting the food, it will continue to press the bar just to hear the buzzer. ⁶Although the buzzer by itself has no value to the rat, it has become a secondary reinforcer. ⁷For humans, money is a secondary reinforcer. ⁸Money is just paper or metal, but through its association with food, clothing, and other objects of desire, it becomes a powerful reward. ⁹Children come to value money only after they learn that it will buy such things as candy, something that has direct value to them. ¹⁰Then the money becomes a secondary reinforcer, something they have learned to want.

Study notes

Secondary reinforcer—something one learns to desire through association with other, direct rewards.

Example—

A. People are motivated by the direct objects of their desires, such as food, water, clothing, and candy.
B. Money is desired not for its own sake but because of its association with direct rewards of desire.
C. After a rat learns to get food by pressing a bar, a buzzer is sounded every time the rat presses the bar to get food.

B. ¹According to one sociologist, virtually every organization includes "higher participants" (such as the administrators) and "lower participants" (the rank and file). ²**Coercive organizations** are among the most common types of organizations. ³Prisons, concentration camps, and custodial mental hospitals are examples of coercive organizations. ⁴In each, force or the threat of force is used to achieve the organization's main goal: keeping the inmates in. ⁵The inmates obviously do not enjoy being imprisoned; they will run away if they have the chance. ⁶They are alienated from the organization and do not support its goals at all. ⁷Understandably, the higher participants—such as prison administrators—have to act tough toward the inmates, seeking compliance by threatening solitary confinement if they try to escape. ⁸In brief, in this kind of organization, coercion, or force, is the main form of power used, and the involvement by lower participants is alienating.

Study notes

Coercive organizations—organizations in which force or the threat of force is used to achieve the main goal: keeping in inmates, who are alienated from the organization.

Example—

A. Every organization includes "higher participants" (such as administrators) and "lower participants" (rank and file).
B. In coercive organizations, force is the main form of power used, and the involvement by lower participants is alienating.
C. In a prison, inmates will run away if they can, and the administrators seek obedience by threatening solitary confinement.

PRACTICE 4

Read each textbook selection below. Then take study notes by 1) writing down the key term and its definition, 2) selecting an example that makes the definition clear, and 3) writing that example in your notes, condensing it if possible.

A. [1]A **Pyrrhic victory** is a victory won at enormous cost. [2]A good example of such a victory is provided by the person whose name the term comes from: Pyrrhus, a Greek mercenary general who invaded Italy and attacked the Romans in 281 B.C. [3]Pyrrhus defeated the Roman army sent against him, but his own army suffered terrible losses. [4]"One more such victory and I am ruined," he exclaimed. [5]The Battle of Borodino in 1812 was another classic instance of a Pyrrhic victory. [6]Napoleon's invading French army defeated a defending Russian army near Moscow and occupied the city. [7]But the French suffered so greatly from the battle and the winter that followed that the invasion turned into a disaster that cost Napoleon his throne.

Study notes

A Pyrrhic victory— *A victory won at enormous cost.*

Example— *The French suffered so greatly from the battle with Russia and the winter that followed that the invasion turned into a disaster that cost Napoleon his throne.*

B. [1]To protect their self-esteem, some people will practice **suppression**, which is a deliberate attempt to avoid stressful thoughts. [2]For instance, Jeff wants to avoid thinking about an argument he had with his girlfriend. [3]To keep it out of his mind, he spends as much of his time as possible hanging out with his buddies, talking about and playing sports. [4]An elderly woman whose husband has died keeps herself busy with chores and volunteer work. [5]Scarlett O'Hara in the novel and movie *Gone with the Wind* is among the more famous practitioners of suppression. [6]Remember her line "I shall think about it tomorrow"? [7]Scarlett was suppressing her unpleasant thoughts.

Study notes

Suppression ———— A deliberate
attempt to avoid stressful thoughts.

Example— Jeff spent as much time as possible with his friends
to avoid an arguement with his girlfriend.

A Final Note

This chapter has centered on supporting details as they appear in well-organized paragraphs. But keep in mind that supporting details are part of readings of any length, including selections that may not have an easy-to-follow list of one major detail after another. In the readings that appear in Part Two (pages 281–441), you will be given practice in answering all kinds of questions about key supporting details. These questions will develop your ability to pay close, careful attention to what you are reading.

SUPPORTING DETAILS IN READING: Mastery Test 1

A. Answer the supporting-detail questions that follow the textbook passage.

[1]People who have no or low self-control share common traits. [2]First, they seem to have an unwillingness or inability to defer gratification. [3]Given a choice between getting five dollars today or fifteen dollars if they wait sixty days, they'll take the five dollars today. [4]People with weak self-control often pursue immediate gratification through such risky behaviors as too much smoking, drinking, or gambling, as well as by engaging in unprotected sex with strangers. [5]Second, they lack persistence in a course of action. [6]They prefer actions that are simple and easy, such as getting money without working or obtaining sex without establishing a relationship. [7]They tend to have poor work records, high rates of absenteeism when employed, unstable marital and family relationships, and other problems caused by an unwillingness to "work" at life. [8]At school, they usually learn little and quit early. [9]They lack all skills that require practice and training—they won't know how to fix a car or play a trumpet. [10]Finally, people with a lack of self-control are selfish. [11]Self-centered, indifferent, and insensitive to the suffering and needs of others, they impose loss and suffering on others. [12]They wreak havoc on all in their path without a qualm.

_____ 1. The first sentence provides
  A. the main idea.
  B. a major detail.
  C. a minor detail.

_____ 2. Sentences 3 and 4 provide
  A. the main idea.
  B. major details.
  C. minor details.

_____ 3. Sentence 5 provides
  A. the main idea.
  B. a major detail.
  C. a minor detail.

_____ 4. How many major supporting details does the paragraph include?
  A. Two
  B. Three
  C. Four
  D. Five

(Continues on next page)

B. (5–10.) Complete the outline of the following textbook passage by filling in the main idea and the major supporting details.

[1]According to social researcher Herbert Gans, there are five basic types of urban dwellers. [2]First are the cosmopolites—the intellectuals, professionals, and artists who have been attracted to the city. [3]They value the city's conveniences and cultural benefits. [4]The second type is the singles. [5]Roughly between the ages of 20 and their early 30s, the singles have not decided to settle in the city permanently. [6]For them, urban life is a stage in their life course. [7]Businesses and services, such as singles bars and apartment complexes, cater to their needs and desires. [8]After they marry, many singles move to the suburbs. [9]The next type of urban dweller is the ethnic villagers. [10]Feeling a sense of identity, working-class members of the same ethnic group band together. [11]They form tightly knit neighborhoods that resemble villages and small towns. [12]Family- and peer-oriented, they try to isolate themselves from the dangers and problems of urban life. [13]A fourth type of urban dweller is the deprived. [14]Destitute, emotionally disturbed, and having little income, education, or work skills, the deprived live in neighborhoods that are more like urban jungles than urban villages. [15]Some of them stalk those jungles in search of prey. [16]Neither predator nor prey has much hope for anything better in life—for themselves or for their children. [17]Finally, there are the trapped. [18]Some were trapped when an ethnic group "invaded" their neighborhood and they could not afford to move. [19]Others are "downwardly mobile"; they started in a higher social class but because of mental or physical illness, alcohol or other drug addiction, or other problems, they drifted downward. [20]Many are elderly and are not wanted elsewhere. [21]Like the deprived, the trapped suffer from high rates of assault, mugging, and rape.

Main idea: _____

_____

Major detail 1: _____

Major detail 2: _____

Major detail 3: _____

Major detail 4: _____

Major detail 5: _____

SUPPORTING DETAILS IN READING: Mastery Test 2

A. Answer the supporting-detail questions that follow the textbook passage.

¹All speakers have several vocal characteristics. ²Pitch refers to the highness or lowness of your voice. ³Fortunately, most people speak at a pitch that is about right for them, although a few persons talk using notes that are too high or too low for their voice. ⁴The volume or loudness of your voice is another vocal characteristic. ⁵Each person, regardless of size, can make his or her voice louder. ⁶If you have trouble talking loudly enough to be heard in a large classroom, work on increasing pressure from the abdominal area on exhalation. ⁷The rate of speech of our voice is the speed at which we talk. ⁸Although most of us utter between 140 and 180 words per minute, the optimal rate is a highly individual matter. ⁹The test of rate is whether listeners can understand what you are saying. ¹⁰The tone, the timbre, or the sound of your voice is known as its quality. ¹¹The best vocal quality is a clear, pleasant-to-listen-to voice. ¹²Problems of quality include nasality (too much resonance in the nose on vowel sounds), breathiness (too much air escaping during phonation), harshness (too much tension in the throat and chest), and hoarseness (a raspy sound to the voice).

_____ 1. In general, the major details of this paragraph are
    A. sounds.
    B. types of voices.
    C. pitches of voices.
    D. vocal characteristics.

_____ 2. Specifically, the major details of the paragraph are
    A. sound and voices.
    B. pitches that are about right, too high, and too low.
    C. pitch, volume, rate of speech, quality.
    D. tone, timbre, sound, and quality of the voice.

_____ 3. Sentence 1 provides
    A. the main idea.
    B. a major detail.
    C. a minor detail.

_____ 4. Sentence 4 provides
    A. the main idea.
    B. a major detail.
    C. a minor detail.

(Continues on next page)

_____ 5. Sentence 8 provides
   A. the main idea.
   B. a major detail.
   C. a minor detail.

6. *Fill in the blank:* One problem of voice _____ is harshness.

B. (7–10.) Complete the outline of the following textbook passage by filling in the missing supporting details.

[1]There are two main forms of survey, and each has its own advantages. [2]One type of survey is the interview. [3]An interview can obtain a high response rate because people find it more difficult to turn down a personal request for an interview than to throw away a written questionnaire. [4]In addition, a skillful interviewer can go beyond written questions and probe for a subject's underlying feelings and reasons. [5]Questionnaires, the second main form of survey, also have two advantages. [6]They are cheaper than interviews, especially when large samples are used. [7]Moreover, since the questions are written, the researcher knows that there is a guarantee of consistency, whereas five interviewers can ask the same question in five different ways.

Main idea: There are two main forms of survey, and each has its own advantages.

1. _____

   a. _____

   _____

   b. Can go beyond written questions

2. _____

   a. _____

   _____

   b. Guarantee of consistency (since questions are written)

SUPPORTING DETAILS IN READING: Mastery Test 3

A. Answer the supporting-detail questions that follow the textbook passage.

[1]More has been written on the fall of Rome than on the death of any other civilization. [2]While scholars are still debating this issue today, most agree that a number of factors led to Rome's demise at the hands of Germanic attackers in 476 A.D. [3]First, Rome was vulnerable to outside attackers because of internal political instability. [4]The Roman constitution did not have a clear law of succession. [5]As a result, each time a ruler died, civil war would break out—killing thousands and causing great political struggle. [6]Another factor that made Rome ripe for conquest was severe economic turmoil. [7]Rome's economy relied heavily upon slave labor. [8]However, years of harsh work and poor living conditions reduced the population of Rome's slaves. [9]Fewer slaves working on farms meant that the empire had fewer goods for trade and less food for its citizens. [10]Rome was also weakened by a lack of manpower. [11]The empire's long borders required more soldiers than were available to protect it from attack. [12]In addition, the need for soldiers abroad meant that there were fewer people to keep peace and order within the empire.

_____ 1. The main idea is expressed in sentence
     A. 1.
     B. 2.
     C. 4.
     D. 12.

_____ 2. The major supporting details of this paragraph are
     A. events.
     B. effects.
     C. theories.
     D. factors.

_____ 3. The second major detail of the paragraph is introduced in sentence
     A. 2.
     B. 4.
     C. 6.
     D. 8.

_____ 4. The third major detail of the paragraph is introduced in sentence
     A. 7.
     B. 8.
     C. 9.
     D. 10.

(Continues on next page)

_____ 5. Sentence 12 provides
   A. the main idea.
   B. a major detail.
   C. a minor detail.

B. (6–10.) Complete the map of the following textbook passage by filling in the missing major supporting details.

¹A good many factors influence whether a situation is seen as too crowded. ²Duration is one factor. ³For instance, people typically find it easier to tolerate a brief exposure to high-density conditions such as a ride on a crowded elevator than prolonged exposure on a cross-country bus. ⁴A second factor is predictability. ⁵People typically find crowded settings even more stressful when they are unable to predict them. ⁶A third factor has to do with frame of mind. ⁷There are times when individuals welcome solitude and other times when they prefer the presence of others. ⁸A fourth factor involves the environmental setting. ⁹People generally report that they can tolerate crowding better in impersonal settings such as a shopping center or an airline terminal than in a home or apartment. ¹⁰Finally, people's attitude toward a situation determines how they feel about crowding. ¹¹If people are fearful and antagonistic—or excited and friendly—crowding tends to intensify the feelings. ¹²Crowding makes a doctor's waiting room and a subway car all the more unpleasant, whereas it makes a football game and a party all the more enjoyable. ¹³And even though a crowded New York subway car turns people off, a crowded San Francisco cable car, crammed with people hanging over the sides, is defined as a "tourist attraction."

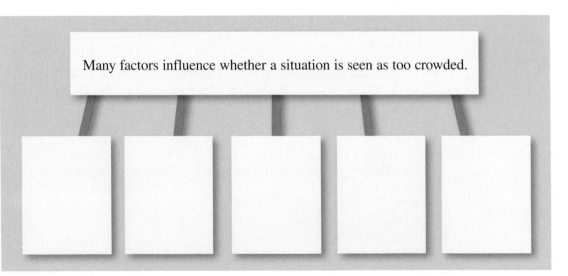

Many factors influence whether a situation is seen as too crowded.

SUPPORTING DETAILS IN READING: Mastery Test 4

A. (1–6.) Complete the outline of the following textbook passage by filling in the main idea and the major supporting details.

¹Psychologists believe that people progress through a sequence of stages as they make changes in their lives. ²The first stage of change is precontemplation. ³Whether or not they're aware of a problem behavior, people in this stage have no intention of making a change in the next six months. ⁴Busy college students in good health, for instance, might never think about getting more exercise. ⁵The second stage of change is contemplation. ⁶Individuals in this stage are aware they have a problem behavior, but are torn between the positives of the new behavior and the amount of time and energy required to change. ⁷For instance, students in a health class may start thinking about exercising but struggle to balance potential benefits with the effort of getting up early to jog or go to the gym. ⁸In the next stage—preparation—people intend to change a problem behavior in the next month. ⁹Some focus on a master plan. ¹⁰For instance, they might look into fitness classes, gyms, or other options for working out. ¹¹Others might start by making small changes, such as walking to classes rather than taking a campus shuttle bus. ¹²Next comes the action stage—people are modifying their behavior according to their plan. ¹³For instance, they might be jogging or working out at the gym three times a week. ¹⁴In the maintenance stage, individuals have continued to work at changing their behavior and have avoided relapse for at least six months. ¹⁵Lastly comes the termination stage. ¹⁶While it may take two to five years, a behavior becomes so deeply ingrained that a person can't imagine abandoning it. ¹⁷More than eight in ten college seniors who exercise regularly remain as active, or even more active, after graduation.

Main idea: _____

_____

Major detail 1. _____

Major detail 2. _____

Major detail 3. _____

Major detail 4. _____

Major detail 5. _____

Major detail 6. Termination

(Continues on next page)

B. (7–10.) Complete the map of the following textbook passage.

¹There have always been homeless people in the United States. ²But the homeless of today are more visible to the general public because they are much more likely to sleep on the streets or in other public places. ³Today's homelessness has arisen from at least three social forces. ⁴One is the increased shortage of inexpensive housing for the poor because of diminishing government subsidy of such housing. ⁵Another social force is the decreasing demand for unskilled labor. ⁶This decrease, which has occurred since the 1980s, has resulted in extremely high unemployment among young men in general and African Americans in particular. ⁷A third social force is the decrease in public welfare benefits that has taken place over the last two decades. ⁸These three social forces have enlarged the ranks of the extremely poor, thereby increasing the chances of these people becoming homeless.

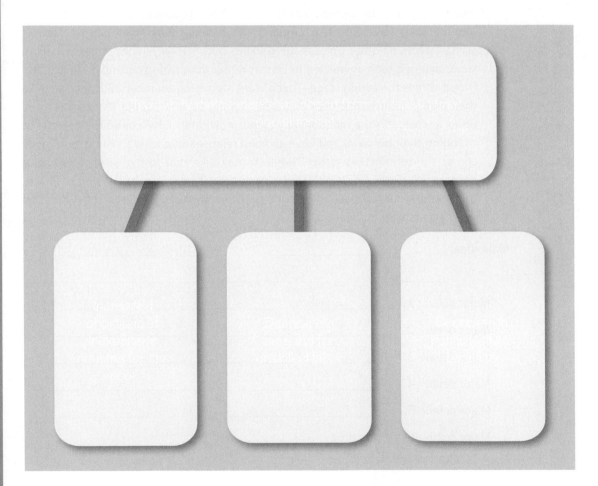

SUPPORTING DETAILS IN READING: Mastery Test 5

A. Answer the supporting-detail questions that follow the textbook passage.

¹*Heuristics* (pronounced *hyoo-ris'tiks*) are rules of thumb that help us to simplify problems. ²They do not guarantee a solution, but they may bring it within reach. ³A very simple heuristic method is hill-climbing. ⁴In this process, we try to move continually closer to our final goal without ever digressing or going backward. ⁵On a multiple-choice test, for example, one useful strategy in answering each question is to eliminate the alternatives that are obviously incorrect. ⁶Even if this does not leave you with the one correct answer, you are closer to a solution. ⁷Or in trying to balance a budget, each reduction in expenses brings you closer to the goal and leaves you with a smaller deficit to deal with. ⁸Another heuristic method is the creation of subgoals. ⁹By setting subgoals, we can often break a problem into smaller, more manageable pieces, each of which is easier to solve than the problem as a whole. ¹⁰A student whose goal is to write a history paper might set subgoals by breaking down the work into a series of separate tasks: choosing a topic, doing the research, preparing an outline, writing the first draft, editing, rewriting, and so on.

_____ 1. The main idea is expressed in sentence
   A. 1.
   B. 3.
   C. 4.
   D. 8.

_____ 2. The major supporting details of this paragraph are
   A. events.
   B. reasons.
   C. methods.
   D. questions.

_____ 3. The first major detail of the paragraph is introduced in sentence
   A. 2.
   B. 3.
   C. 4.
   D. 5.

_____ 4. The second major detail of the paragraph is introduced in sentence
   A. 5.
   B. 7.
   C. 8.
   D. 10.

(Continues on next page)

5–6. Complete the following study notes that summarize the paragraph.

Heuristics—rules of thumb that help us to simplify problems

1. Hill-climbing—try to move continually closer to final goal without digressing.

   Example— _____

   _____

2. Creation of subgoals—break a problem into smaller, more manageable pieces.

   Example— _____

   _____

B. (7–10.) Complete the map of the following textbook passage by filling in the main idea and the missing major details.

> [1]Public speaking is very different from everyday conversation. [2]First of all, speeches are much more structured than a typical informal discussion. [3]A speech usually imposes strict time limitations on the speaker. [4]In addition, for most situations, speeches do not allow listeners to interrupt with questions or commentary. [5]Another difference to keep in mind when speaking to groups is that public speaking generally requires more formal language. [6]Slang, jargon, and bad grammar have little place in public speeches. [7]Audiences usually react negatively to speakers who do not elevate and polish their language when giving a public talk. [8]A third significant difference between public and private discussion is that public speaking requires a different method of delivery. [9]Unlike casual conversation, which is usually quiet, effective public speakers adjust their voices to be heard clearly throughout the audience. [10]Speaking to a group also requires the speaker to assume a more erect posture and avoid distracting mannerisms and verbal habits.

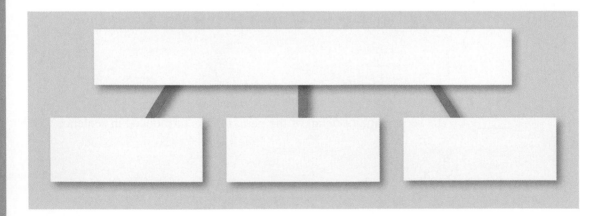

SUPPORTING DETAILS IN READING: Mastery Test 6

A. (1–3.) The main idea of the following textbook passage is **boldfaced**. Complete the map below by filling in the three major details, including brief explanations of each detail.

¹In Latin, *plagiarism* means "kidnapper." ²To plagiarize means to use another person's words or ideas as if they were one's own original creations. ³Quite simply, it is theft. ⁴Common thieves steal material goods that legally belong to others and then use this property as it if were rightfully theirs. ⁵Plagiarists do the same with words and ideas. ⁶**This theft can occur in three forms: global, patchwork, and incremental.** ⁷Global plagiarism is stealing all the words and ideas from another source and passing them off as one's own. ⁸This is the most blatant kind of plagiarism and is considered to be grossly unethical. ⁹Patchwork plagiarism occurs when words and ideas are pilfered from several sources and then patched together. ¹⁰In other words, instead of copying everything from one single source, the thief copies word for word from several sources. ¹¹In global and patchwork plagiarism, entire sections are copied verbatim. ¹²A third kind of plagiarism, incremental plagiarism, occurs when small portions (choice words or phrases) are borrowed from different parts of one source without proper credit being given.

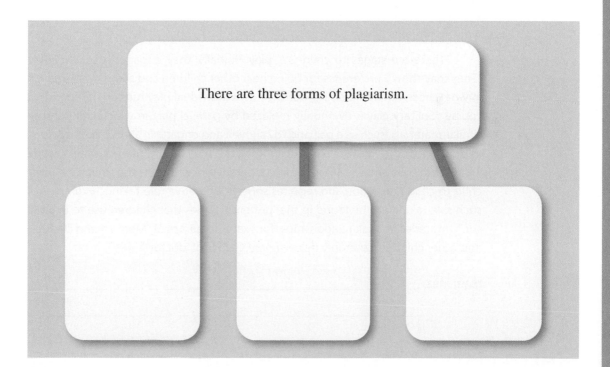

There are three forms of plagiarism.

(Continues on next page)

B. (4–6.) Outline the following textbook passage by filling in the main idea and the two major supporting details.

> ¹What causes forgetting? ²Research has established that most forgetting occurs because of interference from other information, which can take place in two ways. ³In proactive interference, prior information inhibits our ability to remember new information. ⁴For instance, if you have a new locker combination each year, you may have difficulty remembering it because you keep recalling the old one. ⁵In retroactive interference, new information inhibits our ability to remember old information. ⁶Now that you finally know your new locker combination, you may find that you have forgotten the old one. ⁷In both cases, we forget because competing information displaces the information we are trying to retrieve.

Main idea: _____

_____

1. _____

2. _____

C. (7–10.) Outline the following textbook passage by filling in the main idea and the major supporting details, including brief explanations of each detail.

   Note: The number of answer lines given does not indicate the number of major details in the passage.

> ¹There are stages to children's play. ²Initially, they engage in solitary play. ³They may show a preference for being near other children and show some interest in what those others are doing, but their own individual play runs an independent course. ⁴Solitary play is eventually replaced by parallel play, in which children use similar materials (such as a pail and toy shovel) and engage in similar activity (such as digging sand), typically near one another; but they hardly interact at all. ⁵By age 3, most children show at least some cooperative play, a form that involves direct child-to-child interaction and requires some cooperative role-taking. ⁶Examples of such role-taking can be found in the "pretend" games that children use to explore such mysteries as adult relationships (for example, games of "Mommy and Daddy") and other children's anatomy (for example, games of "doctor").

Main idea: _____

_____

_____

_____

_____

Main Ideas and Supporting Details in Writing

A Review of Paragraphs and Essays

You will probably be writing both paragraphs and essays for the course in which you are using this book. Following is a review of both types of writing.

Paragraphs

A **paragraph** is a series of sentences about one main idea, or **point**. A paragraph typically starts with a point (often called the **topic sentence**), and the rest of the paragraph provides specific details to support and develop that point.

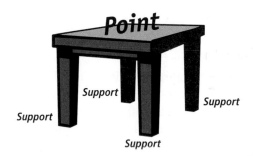

Look at the following paragraph, written by a student named Ben.

Some people struggle with "hard" addictions like alcohol or nicotine. But many others have to deal with everyday bad habits that have also become known as "soft" addictions. One soft addiction is drinking coffee. For some people, getting a cup of coffee is the first thing they think about when they wake up in the morning. Until they've had their coffee, they may be grumpy and not want to talk to anyone. Chances are that during their day, they will feel compelled to get and drink more coffee, even taking time away from work or school or people in their lives. Another soft addiction is television. Most people now watch, on average, over four hours of television a day! Their attention will stay half tuned in to a TV show even when they're eating or on the phone or listening to music or

> talking with other family members. But the most widespread and growing soft addiction today is the Internet. Even more now than with television, people spend hours staring at the screen of their laptop or smartphone. They're on Facebook; they're playing video games; they're reading and sending email; they're browsing almost nonstop on different sites. People carry their laptops or smartphones with them all during the day, take them along on their vacations, and keep them by their bed at night. If not watched carefully, even a "soft" addiction can interfere with having a happy and normal life.

- What is the point of Ben's paragraph? *People have everyday bad habits known as "soft" addictions.*

- What are the three supporting details that Ben has provided to back up his point?

  1. *Drinking coffee*
  2. *Watching television*
  3. *Using the Internet*

Ben begins his paragraph with an introductory comment. He then states his main idea, or point, in the second sentence. His point is that many people have everyday bad habits known as soft addictions. An effective paragraph must not only make a point but also support it with **specific evidence**—reasons, examples, and other details. Such specifics help prove to readers that the point is a reasonable one. Even if readers do not agree with the writer, at least they have the writer's evidence in front of them. Readers are like juries: they want to see the evidence for themselves so that they can make their own judgments.

As you have seen, the author of the paragraph above names and describes three soft addictions. To write an effective paragraph, always aim to do what the author has done: begin by making a point, and then go on to back up that point with strong specific evidence.

Essays

Like a paragraph, an **essay** starts with a point and then goes on to provide specific details to support and develop that point. However, a paragraph is a series of *sentences* about one main idea or point. An essay, on the other hand, is a series of *paragraphs* about one main idea or point, called the **central point** or **thesis**. Since an essay is much longer than a paragraph, the writer can develop a topic in more detail.

Look at the following essay, written by Ben after he was asked to develop more fully his paragraph on soft addictions.

Soft Addictions

Introductory Paragraph

Everyone has heard of people whose lives have been damaged and even ruined by addictions to alcohol, nicotine, or drugs. Such addictions are known as "hard addictions," because the substances cause actual physical dependence. But there is another kind of addiction—"soft addiction." That term describes everyday habits that have gotten so strong that they interfere with normal life. Three very common "soft addictions" include drinking coffee, watching TV, and using the Internet.

First Supporting Paragraph

Drinking coffee is a common part of many people's lives. But for many, coffee has become a soft addiction. To them, coffee is not just a pleasant beverage, but a necessity. When coffee addicts wake up in the morning, the first thing they think of is getting that first cup. Until they have had it, they tend to be grouchy and unwilling to interact with people. If coffee isn't available—for example, if they are staying with friends who don't keep coffee on hand—they become almost frantic. They have to go out to find a restaurant or coffee shop where they can get their "fix." This cycle often repeats itself in mid-afternoon, when the need for more coffee hits. They have to take a break, even if it means neglecting their work or stopping an important conversation, in order to get more coffee. Even though they know it will interfere with their sleep, many coffee addicts keep drinking it into the evening. Then they sleep poorly, wake up in a bad mood, and need even more coffee.

Second Supporting Paragraph

Like drinking coffee, watching television is another extremely common soft addiction. The average person now watches four hours of TV every day. This means spending four hours staring at a box, paying attention to the people on the screen while not paying attention to the real people in the same house. The sight of a family watching TV "together" is not a pretty one. Everyone sits looking passively at the flickering images, bathed in a sickly blue light. Their faces often look hypnotized, even drugged. In many homes, the television is on full-time and is almost like a member of the family, constantly talking and sending out its stream of pictures. When they are in the same room as the TV (and many homes have multiple sets), TV addicts are always half-watching it, even as they speak to family members, eat, listen to music, or talk on the phone.

Third Supporting Paragraph

A newer addiction than drinking coffee or watching television is the ever-increasing dependence on the Internet. Addicts are "plugged in" just about every waking minute of the day. If they aren't surfing the Web on their laptop computer, they're texting friends on their smartphone, playing a video game, or watching a

*Concluding
Paragraph*

YouTube video or Skyping on their tablet. Checking for messages or visiting their Facebook page is a near-constant activity. Scientists tell us that every new bit of data gives us a small burst of excitement—a dopamine squirt—and that it can be addictive. For Internet junkies, there is no such thing as taking a break from their addiction. They like to keep their smartphone with them all day, and it's on their bedside table at night. Being unplugged from the Internet for more than a few minutes results in a feeling of frantic anxiety.

While "hard addictions" to drugs or alcohol are clearly very serious, "soft addictions" can be far from harmless. Whenever any activity—even drinking coffee, watching TV, or using the Internet—gets out of control, it can upset the balance that people should aim to have in everyday life. For this reason, we should think seriously about any activity that is taking up significant time in our lives. We might all benefit from asking whether any of our everyday habits have become soft addictions.

- Which sentence in the introductory paragraph expresses the central point of the essay? ___4___

- How many supporting paragraphs are provided to back up the central point? ___3___

An Overview of the Essay

Here is the traditional structure of an essay:

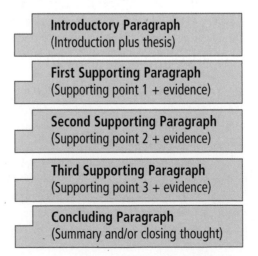

Title

Introductory Paragraph
(Introduction plus thesis)

First Supporting Paragraph
(Supporting point 1 + evidence)

Second Supporting Paragraph
(Supporting point 2 + evidence)

Third Supporting Paragraph
(Supporting point 3 + evidence)

Concluding Paragraph
(Summary and/or closing thought)

Note: While this book focuses on the traditional five-paragraph essay, there is no set number of paragraphs that an essay should contain. There might, for example, be only two supporting paragraphs; there might also be four or more supporting paragraphs.

The Parts of an Essay

Each of the parts of an essay is explained below.

Title

The title may summarize the topic of the essay in several words. It may also serve to create interest in the topic.

Introductory Paragraph

A well-written introductory paragraph will normally do the following:

- Gain the reader's interest by using one of several common methods of introduction.

- Present the thesis statement. The **thesis statement** expresses the central point of an essay, just as a topic sentence states the main idea of a paragraph. The central idea in Ben's essay is expressed in the last sentence of the introductory paragraph.

Four Common Methods of Introduction

Four common methods of introduction are (1) telling a brief story, (2) asking one or more questions, (3) shifting to the opposite, or (4) going from the broad to the narrow. Following are examples of all four.

1 Telling a brief story. An interesting story is hard for a reader to resist. In an introduction, the story should be no more than a few sentences, and it should relate meaningfully to the central idea. The story can be an experience of your own, of someone you know, or of someone you have read about. If Ben had used this approach, this is how his introductory paragraph might have looked:

> Jasmine was invited to spend a weekend at a friend's beach house. The weather was glorious. The house was beautiful. Jasmine and her friends were only a few moments' walk from the warm ocean waters. But when she got home, Jasmine told her family she would never go again. "There wasn't any Internet!" she complained. "It was horrible. I couldn't check my e-mail for three days. I could hardly sleep, wondering what I was missing." Her dependence on the Internet suggests that Jasmine is a victim of a "soft addiction."

2 Asking one or more questions. These questions may be ones that you intend to answer in your essay. They may also indicate that your topic is relevant to readers—it is something they care about. If Ben had used this approach, here is how his introductory paragraph might have looked:

> What is addiction? You probably instantly think of addiction to substances like heroin, nicotine, and alcohol. But can you become addicted to other, less harmful substances, and even activities? If **addiction** is defined as "the state of being enslaved to a habit or practice," the answer is definitely yes. Such less widely recognized addictions are known as "soft addictions."

3 Shifting to the opposite. Another way to gain the reader's interest is to first present an idea that is the opposite of what will be written about. Using this approach, Ben could have begun his essay like this:

> When you think of an addict, your mind probably goes to an extreme case—a junkie nodding off in a dark hallway, a needle dangling from his arm. But many people who have a problem with addiction look nothing like that guy. They're all around us, and at first glance they look totally normal and healthy. Spend a little time with them, though, and you'll realize that they are addicts, too. They're victims of "soft addictions."

4 Going from the broad to the narrow. Broad, general observations can capture your reader's interest; they can also introduce your general topic and provide helpful background information. Ben used this method of introduction for his essay:

> Everyone has heard of people whose lives have been damaged and even ruined by addictions to alcohol, nicotine, or drugs. Such addictions are known as "hard addictions," because the substances cause actual physical dependence. But there is another kind of addiction—"soft addiction." That term describes everyday habits that have gotten so strong that they interfere with normal life. Three very common "soft addictions" include drinking coffee, watching TV, and using the Internet.

Supporting Paragraphs

The traditional school essay has three supporting paragraphs. But some essays will have two supporting paragraphs, and others will have four or more. Each supporting paragraph should have its own main idea (also called a **topic sentence**) stating the point to be developed in that paragraph.

Notice that the essay on soft addictions has clear main ideas for each of the three supporting paragraphs:

- But for many, coffee has become a soft addiction.
- Like drinking coffee, watching television is another extremely common soft addiction.
- A newer addiction than drinking coffee or watching television is the ever-increasing dependence on the Internet.

Transitional Words and Sentences

In a paragraph, **transitional words** like *First, Another, Also, In addition,* and *Finally* are used to help connect supporting ideas. And in an essay, **transitional sentences** are sometimes used to help tie the supporting paragraphs together. Such transitional sentences often occur at the beginning of a supporting paragraph.

- Look at the main ideas (topic sentences) for the second and third supporting paragraphs in the essay on soft addictions. Explain how those sentences are also transitional sentences.

  The opening sentences for both paragraphs detail
  how both watching TV and drinking coffee are common addictions.

Concluding Paragraph

The concluding paragraph often summarizes the essay by briefly restating the thesis and, at times, the main supporting points. It may even provide a closing thought or two as a way of bringing the paper to a natural and graceful end.

- Look at the four sentences in the concluding paragraph of the essay on soft addictions. Which two sentences summarize the essay? _1, 2_
  Which two sentences provide a closing thought? _3, 4_

A Review of Outlining

Just as outlining helps in reading and understanding a passage, it also helps in planning and writing a paragraph or an essay. An outline shows at a glance the point of a paper and the numbered list of items that support the point. When Ben was writing his paragraph on three kinds of addiction, his starting point was an outline that showed his point and his support for the point:

Point: Everyday bad habits can become soft addictions.

    1. Drinking coffee

    2. Watching TV

    3. Using the Internet

The same outline helped guide Ben as he expanded his paragraph into an essay, with each kind of addiction serving as the topic of one of the three supporting paragraphs.

PRACTICE 1

Read the following two paragraphs and two essays, and then complete the outline of each. Notice that words such as *first, also, another,* and *finally* often signal each new item of support.

Outlining a Paragraph

A. ¹People are often confused about whether they have a bad cold or the flu. ²But the flu has some very specific symptoms that make it different than a cold. ³First, the flu comes on suddenly. ⁴You can be feeling fine at lunchtime and terrible by the end of the day. ⁵A second sign of the flu is a cluster of symptoms that include fever, headache, and muscle aches. ⁶Such a cluster is less likely to appear as part of a cold. ⁷And finally, the flu makes people feel more weak and exhausted than a cold does. ⁸A person with the flu often doesn't have enough energy to even get out of bed, while a person with a cold is more likely to get up and struggle through the day.

Point: _The Flu has some very specific symptoms that make it different than a cold._

Supporting detail 1. _First, the flu comes suddenly._

Supporting detail 2. _A cluster of symptoms that include fever, headache, and muscle aches._

Supporting detail 3. _The Flu makes people feel more weak and exhausted._

B. ¹There are certain times when you should definitely not text. ²First of all, texting in class is a bad idea. ³Since most schools forbid texting in class, you may be disciplined if you are caught. ⁴You may also miss valuable information or instructions. ⁵At the very least, you risk annoying your teacher, and who wants to needlessly aggravate a teacher? ⁶Secondly, it's only common sense to never text when you are behind the wheel of a car, SUV, or truck. ⁷You can't possibly text and keep your eyes on the road. ⁸Those who have tried have wound up getting into serious accidents—injuring or killing themselves and others. ⁹In addition, it's rude to text while having a conversation with someone. ¹⁰Texting while talking with someone gives the person you are with the impression that he or she is not worthy of your full attention. [11]Yet another place to avoid texting is at important ceremonies such as weddings and funerals. [12]These are deeply meaningful events that deserve your undivided attention.

Point: _There are certain times when you should definitely not text._

Supporting detail 1. _Texting in school is a bad idea._

Supporting detail 2. _Never text whenever you're behind the wheel._

Supporting detail 3. _It's rude to text while having a conversation._

Supporting detail 4. _Avoid texting at important ceremonies and events._

Outlining an Essay

C. [1]When you're not feeling well, if you're like most people, all you really want to do is crawl into bed and have some kind, motherly person who knows exactly what you need show up and take care of you while you just lie there and feel sorry for yourself. [2]Unfortunately, that's not likely to happen. [3]It's much more probable you'll have to go visit a doctor. [4]And you will get a lot more out of your doctor visit if you make a few simple preparations for it.

[5]First of all, you should make a list of all the medications you are currently taking. [6]Include not only prescription meds (such as antibiotics, birth-control pills, and blood pressure medication), but also over-the-counter pain killers, vitamins, herbal supplements, herbal teas, cold medicine, and sleeping aids. [7]Many medications, even the most innocent-sounding ones, can have dangerous side effects when combined with other meds. [8]They can even interact in a way that makes them ineffective. [9]Therefore, your doctor must know exactly what you're already taking before she prescribes anything new.

[10]Secondly, take along a list of all your symptoms. [11]That might seem obvious, but especially when people aren't feeling well, they sometimes mention only the major source of discomfort and forget minor symptoms that might be important. [12]So, of course, mention the immediate reasons you're at the doctor—nausea, joint pain, headache, dizziness—but take some time to think about and write down anything that's been bothering you since your last doctor visit. [13]Maybe it doesn't seem important that, for example, you've been thirsty a lot, or that you've suddenly lost some weight, but you should mention any such observation. [14]Such a list will help the doctor make an accurate diagnosis, and will also insure that you don't forget anything that you should mention.

[15]Finally, be sure to write down any questions you want to ask the doctor. [16]You might want to ask, for instance, "Should I take this medication with food? [17]Am I contagious? [18]How soon can I expect to feel better? [19]What caused this problem? [20]Should I restrict my activities?" [21]Many doctors see as many as twenty patients in the course of the day. [22]They can't spend a lot of time explaining diagnoses and treatments to each of those patients. [23]So in order to make the best use of your

appointment, have your questions prepared ahead of time. [24]Otherwise you're likely to be on your way home when you think, "Why didn't I ask that?"

[25]It may seem tiresome to have to prepare for a doctor's visit, especially when you're not feeling well. [26]But taking some time to be a pro-active patient will help you get the most out of your appointment and, hopefully, be on the road to recovery that much more quickly.

Point: _You'll get more out of a doctor's visit if you make simple preparations for it._

Supporting detail 1. _Make a list of medications you're taking._

Supporting detail 2. _Take a long list of all your symptoms._

Supporting detail 3. _Write down any questions for your doctor._

D. [1]Getting into college can be a very stressful experience. [2]You've got to choose colleges you think you can get into, then get your test scores together, fill out endless applications, write essays, fill out financial aid forms, and then sit and bite your nails nervously until the happy day when you find out that you've been accepted. [3]Finally you can relax! [4]For many students, however, the anxiety is just beginning. [5]In fact, attending college can be more stressful than many incoming students realize.

[6]One common cause of college stress is choosing a major. [7]When it's time to declare a major, it's tempting to choose the subject you enjoy the most. [8]But what if that subject is creative writing, or religion, or anthropology? [9]Are there going to be any jobs available in your field once you graduate? [10]Especially in today's economy, with unemployment numbers scarily high, a lot of college graduates are working as coffee shop baristas and bartenders. [11]As students get closer to graduation and see their friends with more practical degrees, such as engineering, nursing, and medical technologies, lining up promising job interviews, they often begin to panic. [12]Many wish they'd minored in their beloved subject and majored in something else that had better employment prospects. [13]Nothing stresses a college senior out more than the thought, "I'll never get a job in my field!"

[14]A second major source of stress among college students is the need to hold a part-time or even full-time job while in school. [15]Unless they were lucky enough to be born to a rich family, most college students have to work while they're in school. [16]Even if they are attending an affordable school, there is a constant demand for money for textbooks, food, and rent, as well as tuition. [17]It's not unusual for students to work up to forty hours a week just to keep afloat, leaving little time for their studies, not to mention housework, a personal life, and often even childcare. [18]The pressure to get good grades in order to make all this stress worthwhile is overwhelming.

[19]Thirdly, there's the problem of balancing your studies with your social life. [20]The majority of college students are young single people who are very naturally looking for friends, fun, and even a significant other. [21]The college years are the best opportunity most of us will ever have to get together with a large number of people whose company we will enjoy. [22]That's great, but it also creates a big potential problem. [23]It's difficult to concentrate on cranking out that difficult research paper

or studying for that midterm when people you like are encouraging you to ditch the studies and come to a great party! [24]Even the most serious students are likely to find themselves stressed and scrambling to make up for an overly social weekend when Monday rolls around.

[25]Finally, and most stressful of all, most students are increasingly aware, as the years go on, of the debt they are accumulating. [26]Even if they have dodged the bullet of choosing an impractical major, almost all students graduate owing a substantial amount of money to the government or private lenders. [27]Will they land a job that will allow them to repay that debt? [28]What if they don't? [29]Will they be dragging that debt around for decades to come, interfering with their ability to marry, to buy a house, to have children? [30]Talk about stress!

[31]While the college years are often thought as a fun and carefree time, in reality they can be anything but that. [32]Many college students struggle with stress that they never anticipated when they looked ahead to "the best years of their lives."

Point: _Attending college is very stressful for many incoming students._

Supporting detail 1. _One common cause of college stress is choosing a major._

Supporting detail 2. _The need to hold a part-time or full-time job while in school._

Supporting detail 3. _Balancing your studies with your social life._

Supporting detail 4. _As the years go on more student debt is being accumulated._

A Review of Topics and Topic Sentences

As you learned in Chapter 1, the **topic** is a general subject. A good reader looks for the topic of a selection and then the idea that is expressed about that topic. A good writer starts with a topic and then decides what idea to advance about that topic. In the outlines you have just considered, it is easy to identify the topics and the ideas about the topics:

Topic	Topic sentence (main idea)
Cold versus flu	The flu has some very specific symptoms that make it different from a cold.
Texting	There are certain times when you should definitely not text.
Doctor visit	You will get a lot more out of your doctor visit if you make a few simple preparations for it.
College stress	Attending college can be more stressful than many incoming students realize.

PRACTICE 2

Here are fifteen topics. See if you can write main ideas about any five of them. Put your topic sentences in the spaces provided.

Examples

Soda	Soda drinking can be dangerous to one's health.
Basic fears	Everyone has certain basic fears in their lives.
Football	Given a choice, I much prefer watching football to either baseball or basketball.

Watching sports on television	Cosmetic surgery	Giving a party
Student uniforms	Disciplining children	First job
Obesity	Body art	Marijuana
Violent video games	Gun control	Horror movies
Elderly drivers	Credit cards	Having a pet

1. Playing violent video games is often claimed to cause rises in gun violence.

2. The debates on gun control have been both controversial and complicated throughout history.

3. Having a pet in your home brings about many other daily responsibilities.

4. Horror movies are some of the most popular and attention-grabbing genres in film history.

5. There are many ways you can properly discipline your children.

Staying on Point

One common mistake in writing a paper is to go off point. Think of your point as the bull's-eye in a target. Every sentence and detail in a paper should be **relevant**, meaning that it hits the bull's-eye—it supports your point. Otherwise, your paper will not be convincing. Instead of hitting the target and proving your point, your "support" will be **irrelevant**. In other words, it will miss the point completely.

Let's say you decide your point is going to be that your family car is a lemon. If you then provide details about the car's good features, you are going off point. Or perhaps your point is that your aunt is a generous person. If you provide details about her sense of humor or odd habits, you are going off point. Or your point could be that your apartment is not a good place to live. If you provide details about the convenient location of the apartment, you're missing the target.

Look at the following list of items for a possible paragraph. The point is followed by six facts, only three of which are on target in supporting the point. The other facts are irrelevant to the point. See if you can check (✓) the three **relevant** statements of support—the ones that hit the bull's-eye.

Point: My sister should break up with her boyfriend.

_____ 1. They have been dating more than two years.

✓ 2. He speaks rudely to her in front of his friends.

✓ 3. He says nasty things to her, like "If you ever get fat, I'm out of here."

_____ 4. He is studying to be a certified public accountant.

✓ 5. He often disappears for long periods and won't tell her where he's been.

_____ 6. His parents are good friends with our parents.

Now read the following comments on the six items to see which ones you should have checked and why.

Explanation

1. The fact that they have been dating for more than two years does not indicate a problem. You should not have checked this item.

2. Speaking rudely to her in front of his friends indicates a lack of respect and concern for her. Such behavior is definitely a problem. You should have checked this item.

3. Threatening to leave her if she does not conform to his expectations is controlling and hostile behavior, and you should have checked this item.

4. Studying to be a CPA indicates a plan for the future and good prospects for a job. You should not have checked this item.

5. For someone to disappear and refuse to say why indicates at least a domineering, controlling personality and maybe involvement in shady activities. Both are red flags in a relationship. You should have checked this item.

6. Many dating couples have parents who are friends with each other. This doesn't indicate a problem with the relationship. In fact, it could be an asset!

PRACTICE 3

Each point is followed by three statements that provide relevant, on-target support and three that do not. In the spaces, write the letters of the three **relevant** statements of support.

1. **Point: I'd rather rent a movie and watch it at home than go to the theater.**

   A. Some really spectacular movies are worth seeing on the big theater screen.
   B. At home I can wear my pajamas and cuddle up with a blanket.
   C. People in theaters are often noisy and distracting.
   D. The sound system in a theater is certainly better than mine at home.
   E. I like to be able to pause the movie if I want a bathroom or snack break.
   F. Video stores are rare these days, as most people can get movies directly on their TVs.

   Items that logically support the point: __B__   __E__   __F__

2. **Point: Homeschooling has definite benefits.**

    A. Homeschooled children can learn at their own pace, rather than on a set schedule.

    B. Parents who homeschool may do so because of their religious or political beliefs.

    C. Homeschooled children get one-on-one attention from their parent-teachers, rather than having to compete for attention in a classroom.

    D. Homeschooled children don't have to deal with the peer pressures and bullying that often exist in schools.

    E. Homeschooled children may miss the opportunity to develop social relationships outside their families.

    F. About 3 percent of American children are homeschooled.

    Items that logically support the point: ___A___   ___C___   ___D___

3. **Point: There are advantages to taking online college courses rather than attending classes on campus.**

    A. Parents with small children don't need to hire a babysitter if they access an online course at home.

    B. Students who take online courses aren't able to interact socially with other students.

    C. People who work odd hours can take online courses at whatever time of day or night is convenient for them.

    D. Because there is no commuting to online courses, students can save time and gas money by learning at home.

    E. Students who take online courses need to be extra careful not to fall behind on assignment deadlines.

    F. In general, degrees from traditional colleges and universities are still more respected than degrees from online schools.

    Items that logically support the point: ___C___   ___D___   ___E___

4. **Point: Alcohol and tobacco are among the most dangerous drugs that Americans use today.**

    A. Cancer from cigarette smoking kills numerous Americans every year.

    B. During Prohibition (1920–1933), liquor bootleggers fought one another in the same way drug dealers do today.

    C. About half of all fatal traffic accidents are due to drunk driving.

    D. Nothing is more annoying than trying to enjoy a restaurant meal when the people at nearby tables are smoking and drinking heavily.

   E. We often don't think of alcohol and tobacco as "drugs" because they are legal.

   F. Alcohol abuse causes many people to become more aggressive and violent.

   Items that logically support the point: ___A___   ___C___   ___F___

Providing Enough Support

STRONG, SPECIFIC SUPPORT   THIN, VAGUE SUPPORT

Another common mistake in writing a paper is not providing enough *specific* details. Truly specific details excite the reader's interest; they *show* what the writer means. They are the opposite of dull, wordy writing that provides thin support for a point.

Specific details, as shown in the illustration above, provide solid support for a point. Thin and vague details do not. Lazy writers are content to produce undersupported paragraphs, but good writers are willing to take the time needed to think carefully about and to build a solid paper.

PRACTICE 4

Each of the four points below is followed by two items of support. Put a check (✓) next to the item that is specific and clearly shows us the writer's point. By contrast, the other item will be vague, dull, or wordy and lack sharp details.

1. **Sitting in the emergency waiting room was stressful.**

   ✓ A. ¹We had no idea how Dad was doing after his heart attack, and that made us really scared. ²Plus, it didn't help that some of the other people in the room looked and acted even more upset than we did. ³No one appeared to be relaxing, to say the least. ⁴Unpleasant sounds and smells kept drifting into the room, too, and that sure didn't make things any easier.

_____ B. [1]Mom and I stared at each other with tears in our eyes, waiting to hear about Dad after his heart attack. [2]Mom whispered, "I just wish I knew how your father is doing." [3]Across the room, an elderly man held his head in his hands. [4]A young woman slammed her hands on the nurse's desk and shouted. [5]And every time the heavy hospital doors opened, sharp antiseptic odors blasted the room along with the eerie beeps and alarms of heart monitors.

2. **My great-grandmother had a hard childhood.**

   _____ A. [1]Instead of going to school, she was forced to do hard work when she was only ten years old. [2]She didn't have the everyday comforts most of us take for granted today. [3]Because her family was unusually poor, there was often not enough to eat. [4]What there was to eat was often not very healthy.

   ___✓___ B. [1]She worked in a textile mill for ten hours a day at an age when most girls were playing with dolls and going to grade school. [2]She slept on a mattress made of pine straw and used an outhouse for a bathroom. [3]Sometimes, the family ate greasy roasted squirrel when there was no other food available.

3. **It can be costly to maintain a house.**

   ___✓___ A. [1]This past spring my dryer broke. [2]Since it was over 20 years old, I had to buy a new one. [3]After that, the water heater broke and had to be replaced, which put me out about $600. [4]As if that weren't enough, this past fall a squirrel crawled down through the chimney into my basement and began chewing the insulation. [5]I had to pay for someone to trap the squirrel, replace the insulation, and put up a metal grate over the chimney so no more squirrels could get in. [6]And in winter, I wind up paying at least $200 a month for gas. [7]Still, I enjoy owning a home and wouldn't want to go back to living in an apartment.

   _____ B. [1]It seems like there's never a month that goes by that something major doesn't break down and have to be replaced. [2]And the cost of appliances these days isn't cheap. [3]As if that weren't enough, I've had a problem with a squirrel finding its way into the basement and causing damage. [4]It caused me time and money to get the squirrel out of there and to see that it didn't happen again. [5]In winter, the heating bills are astronomical because the temperature outside is often below freezing. [6]With all the expense, I still prefer owning a house to living in an apartment.

4.   **Sharing an apartment with Kenny is not working out.**

✓ A. ¹It's getting to be a habit with Kenny to leave greasy plates and dirty glasses lying around the living room. ²Today I found a few soggy Cheerios in the couch cushions. ³This past Saturday it was his turn to clean the bathroom, but he got up early, went out, and didn't return until after midnight. ⁴So I wound up scrubbing the floor, tub, sink, and toilet. ⁵Because he never seems to wash his sheets and clothes, there's an odor coming from his room lately that smells like moldy cheese. ⁶Yesterday he and his friend Victor were playing Nerf football inside and shattered a lamp my mom gave me. ⁷"Sorry, dude," Kenny said. ⁸All I could do was shake my head.

B. ¹He's probably the sloppiest person I've ever met, and doesn't seem to care one bit if the apartment looks like a mess. ²If that's not bad enough, he's unreliable when it comes to doing his share of the weekly chores. ³Because he can't be counted on, I often wind up doing the chores myself. ⁴And lately, there's been a strange smell coming from his bedroom. ⁵It's not just Kenny's sloppiness that I find irritating; the friends he hangs out with are annoying too. ⁶They like to play around a lot, and sometimes their rowdiness gets out of hand and things get broken. ⁷I don't even know how to respond when he manages to damage one thing or another.

MAIN IDEAS AND SUPPORTING DETAILS IN WRITING: Mastery Test 1

Read the following two paragraphs and one essay, and then complete the outline of each. (Some of the answers have been filled in for you.) Notice that words such as *first, also, another,* and *finally* often signal each new item of support.

A. [1]Are you always late? [2]Do you know someone who is? [3]Researchers have discovered some of the main characteristics of people who are always late. [4]Risk-takers are addicted to the thrill of leaving for their appointed destination only when they absolutely must. [5]They don't mind the risk of being late, because they don't want to risk being early and waiting for others. [6]Freedom-makers are those who felt powerless as children. [7]Their strong desire not to be controlled by others may be at the root of their lateness. [8]Organization-slackers are those who have difficulty figuring how long each of their tasks will take and how long it will take them to get to their appointments on time. [9]These people generally have poor organizational skills, though they may be very intelligent. [10]Finally, trouble-avoiders are people who, unconsciously or consciously, wish to avoid the people they are supposed to meet or the place where they are going. [11]Since they're angry that they must go to an appointment, they make others wait for them.

Point: _____

_____

Supporting detail 1. _____

Supporting detail 2. _Freedom-makers_____

Supporting detail 3. _Organization-slackers_____

Supporting detail 4. _____

B. [1]These days, it's very easy to shop online. [2]But online shopping will never entirely replace shopping in stores. [3]For one thing, people like to use their senses when they shop. [4]They like to touch soft sweaters, see colorful displays, and perhaps hear music. [5]They even like to smell pleasant aromas, like candle scents and freshly baked goods. [6]In contrast, when you're shopping online, the only things you touch are the plastic keys and mouse on your computer. [7]And you don't smell anything. [8]Shopping at real "brick and mortar" stores is also enjoyable because you can do it with friends. [9]Shopping with a friend can be helpful when you're weighing whether or not to make a purchase. [10]In contrast, shopping online is basically a solitary activity. [11]Moreover, shopping in stores can be an opportunity to simply do some walking. [12]Sometimes it's nice to take a leisurely stroll around a large store or mall, especially if you have a job that puts you in front of a computer screen in a cubicle all day long.

(Continues on next page)

Point: _____

_____

Supporting detail 1. People like to use their senses when they shop.

Supporting detail 2. _____

Supporting detail 3. _____

C. ¹Owning a dog isn't always easy. ²Dogs require a commitment of time, energy, and money. ³They have to be fed, bathed, groomed, and taken to the vet. ⁴It's a pain to find someone to take care of them when you go away. ⁵They can eat your shoes, tear up your books, leave muddy paw prints on your furniture, shed all over the house, and occasionally leave presents you'd really rather not have to deal with on your floor. ⁶And they are totally worth it. ⁷For a number of reasons, owning a dog is a great experience.

⁸First of all, dogs are truly man's, and woman's, best friend. ⁹Dogs provide love that is unconditional. ¹⁰They don't care if you're rich or poor, fat or thin, black or white, straight or gay, if your ancestors came over on the Mayflower or arrived in this country last week. ¹¹If you show the dog kindness, it will reward you richly. ¹²After a rough day, there is nothing better than to come home to a furry friend who thinks you are wonderful. ¹³That joyous look and wagging tail can make you forget your troubles.

¹⁴Secondly, dogs can provide security and other forms of help. ¹⁵Even a gentle, friendly dog will alert its owners to a possible intruder. ¹⁶A dog's barking, especially if it is loud and threatening-sounding, can scare off a prowler, as well as give the owner time to call the police. ¹⁷Dogs have also been known to alert neighbors that something is wrong inside the house—perhaps that their owner is sick or injured and needs help. ¹⁸Dogs have also alerted their owners to house fires.

¹⁹Thirdly, owning a dog is a great way to teach children responsibility. ²⁰Kids learn that having a pet means being responsible for feeding it, exercising it, training it, and taking care of it when it's sick or injured. ²¹Helping to take care of another creature helps kids develop a sense of compassion.

²²And finally, owning a dog can help people make new friends. ²³Because most dogs need to be walked, their owners have to get outdoors. ²⁴They are likely to see other people walking *their* dogs. ²⁵It's not hard for two owners to strike up a conversation about their common interest in dogs. ²⁶Some towns and cities even have dog parks, where owners can sit and chat as their pets romp with one another.

²⁷The benefits of owning a dog far outweigh the problems. ²⁸Dogs are delightful pets that enrich their owners' lives.

Point: _____

_____

Supporting detail 1. _____

Supporting detail 2. _____

Supporting detail 3. _____

Supporting detail 4. _____

MAIN IDEAS AND SUPPORTING DETAILS IN WRITING: Mastery Test 2

Each point is followed by three statements that provide relevant, on-target support and three that do not. In the spaces, write the letters of the three **relevant** statements of support.

1. **Point: My father-in-law, Ken, should not be driving anymore.**

    A. Ken never learned to drive a stick-shift car.

    B. Twice in the last six months, Ken has passed out for brief periods.

    C. Ken's reflexes have noticeably become very slow.

    D. Ken does all the driving since his wife is now legally blind.

    E. Ken's vision is so bad he can no longer read.

    F. Ken is very concerned about losing his independence.

    Items that logically support the point: _____ _____ _____

2. **Point: Oakville is a dangerous part of the city.**

    A. There were more robberies in Oakville last year than in any other city neighborhood.

    B. Several popular bars and restaurants have opened in Oakville in recent years.

    C. Poor street lighting in Oakville makes it easy for criminals to hide in dark areas.

    D. Because Oakville is right on the subway line, muggers can rob someone, jump on the subway, and quickly disappear.

    E. An Oscar-winning movie was filmed on the streets of Oakville in the late 1980s.

    F. Oakville residents hosted a "Clean Up Our Community" day in April.

    Items that logically support the point: _____ _____ _____

3. **Point: Convenience stores live up to their name.**

    A. Convenience store are close to home.

    B. Small local businesses should be supported by the community.

    C. Some convenience store chains sell products under their own brand name.

    D. Convenience stores are open until late or all night.

    E. Parking is right outside the convenience store's door.

    F. The produce at most of our supermarkets is usually terrible.

    Items that logically support the point: _____ _____ _____

(Continues on next page)

4. **Point: The Internet has not replaced socializing in person—only made it easier.**

   A. Many online courses enable students to e-mail their assignments to their teachers.

   B. Internet "meet-up" groups allow people in the same geographic area who share common interests to easily get together in person.

   C. Families in China have turned to training camps that offer to "wean" their children from overuse of the Internet.

   D. The first online gambling website opened in 1995, paving the way for the hundreds that exist now on the Internet.

   E. Organizations can send out e-mail "blasts" to remind everyone on their mailing list of upcoming events, thus increasing attendance at the events.

   F. Roughly 20% of heterosexual couples and 50% of homosexual couples have met through online dating sites.

   Items that logically support the point: _____ _____ _____

5. **Point: It makes sense to give alternative sentences, not jail, to some nonviolent offenders.**

   A. Everyone, no matter how terrible a crime he or she has been accused of, is entitled to legal representation.

   B. Alternative sentences cost less than jail and can be handed down more quickly than sentences involving jail time.

   C. Despite the best efforts of law enforcement, the crime rate goes up every year.

   D. Prisons are already overcrowded; adding more prisoners could create dangerous security situations.

   E. The courts always have a backlog of cases, and some of them are thrown out because there isn't time for the DA's office to prepare a case.

   F. Evidence suggests that alternative sentences offer a better chance of rehabilitating the offender.

   Items that logically support the point: _____ _____ _____

MAIN IDEAS AND SUPPORTING DETAILS IN WRITING: Mastery Test 3

Each of the five points below is followed by two items of support. Put a check (✓) next to the item that is specific and clearly shows us the writer's point. By contrast, the other item will be vague, dull, or wordy and lack sharp details.

1. **Seeing the Grand Canyon was an unforgettable experience.**

   _____ A. [1]Until you actually see the Canyon, you really can't comprehend how huge and beautiful it is. [2]The colors of the rocks are really pretty. [3]There are strange stone formations everywhere you look. [4]The biggest birds I've ever seen were soaring overhead. [5]I really can't describe how awesome a sight it is.

   _____ B. [1]The Grand Canyon is about a mile deep and up to 18 miles across, and it is breathtaking. [2]Especially at sunset, the canyon walls blaze with orange, red, gold, and blue colors. [3]Massive birds called condors fly over the canyon. [4]Their nine-foot wings make a loud rushing sound. [5]The canyon is so amazing, I found tears rolling down my cheeks as I looked at it.

2. **The elementary school needs to be replaced.**

   _____ A. [1]The classrooms are shabby and ugly, and are far too crowded. [2]There aren't nearly enough seats in the cafeteria for all the students, so they have to eat lunch at ridiculous times. [3]The hallways are creepy-looking, the playground is inadequate, and the gymnasium is a joke.

   _____ B. [1]Many of the classrooms have broken windows and peeling paint on the walls. [2]The children have to sit so close to each other that they can barely move without hitting someone. [3]The cafeteria is so tiny the kids have to eat lunch in four shifts, beginning at 10:30. [4]Poor lighting in the hallways makes them dark and scary-looking. [5]The merry-go-round and jungle gym on the playground are both broken, and the gymnasium doesn't even have a basketball hoop.

3. **Fear of heights limits travel for my mom.**

   _____ A. [1]The one time Mom went up in a plane, she put her head down and cried and shook the entire time. [2]On that same trip, she made my dad stop the car before going over the Brooklyn Bridge, because her hands were sweating and she felt nauseated. [3]While the rest of us went to the top of Rockefeller Center, she sat alone in a coffee shop.

   _____ B. [1]It's hard for my mom to go on a trip, because she won't fly, and she's afraid of bridges. [2]And once she gets to where she's going, she can't go up in any elevators, because just the thought of how high she's going really freaks her out and almost makes her sick. [3]It's really a problem for her.

(Continues on next page)

4. **My two-year-old nephew Anthony loves to get into things.**

_____ A. ¹One day when I was babysitting him, I saw him dialing on the phone. ²A few minutes later, a police officer came to my door and explained that someone had dialed 911. ³I told him that my nephew Anthony must have done it. ⁴Then I had to prove to him that Anthony wasn't in any danger by calling him to the door. ⁵Anthony wasn't scared. ⁶"I can dial 911," he proudly told the policeman. ⁷"My parents taught me."

_____ B. ¹You can't take your eyes off of him for a second because he will be doing something he's not supposed to. ²It's really amazing the trouble he can get into the second you turn your back. ³One time he actually called 911 when I was baby-sitting him. ⁴That was embarrassing to me, but it didn't bother Anthony one bit when a policeman showed up to check out the "emergency."

5. **The pizza in this restaurant is the best.**

_____ A. ¹I've never tasted pizza anywhere this good, and I've eaten a _lot_ of pizza. ²You can tell by the smell when you walk in the front door that it's going to be good. ³The cheese is always good and they really pile it on. ⁴And the choice of toppings is unbelievable so one can really create their own individual pizza. ⁵I've created some of the most unusual pizzas imaginable!

_____ B. ¹The moment the door opens, the scent of baking crust, basil, and sausage makes my mouth water, and my stomach growls in anticipation. ²This pizzeria loads each pizza with a special imported mozzarella that is always bubbly and rich. ³I top my pizzas with pineapple, barbecued chicken, and bacon.

4 Understanding the Writing Process

Now that you know the two basic goals in effective writing—to make a point and support that point—it's time to write some simple paragraphs and to experience the writing process. (Note that all of the following advice applies to writing essays as well.)

Even professional writers do not sit down and write a paper in a single draft. Instead, they work on it a step at a time. Writing a paper is a process that can be divided into the following steps:

Step 1   Getting Started through Prewriting

Step 2   Preparing a Scratch Outline

Step 3   Writing the First Draft

Step 4   Revising and Editing

Step 5   Reading the Paper Aloud

With each of the three paragraph assignments that follow, you will learn a different prewriting strategy that will help you generate supporting details. The three strategies are freewriting, questioning, and list making.

PRACTICE 1: Using Freewriting to Develop a Paragraph

Write a paragraph that supports the following main idea:

Main idea: Attending college is a stressful experience for me.

How to Proceed

1. Freewrite. Your purpose in the paragraph is to provide specific support for your main idea or point. To help think about and develop your support, spend some time freewriting. **Freewriting** is just sitting down and writing whatever comes into your mind about your point. Do this for ten minutes or so. Write without stopping and without worrying in the slightest about spelling, grammar, and the like. None of that matters at this early draft stage while you are thinking on paper. Simply get down all the information that occurs to you about your point.

Look at some of the freewriting done by a student named Mason:

> Stress in college begins with what to major in. A person just can't just chose anything it needs to be something that will mean a job later on. This is a very stressful decision to have to make. A problem also is working while going to school. This just piles on the presure, trying to have enough time for classes and homework and also keeping the boss happy by being at work. And lots of luck having time for much social life and just having enough fun to make it all seems worthwhile. All work and no play is not a good thing to have to put up with.

Notice that there are mistakes with spelling, grammar, and punctuation in Mason's freewriting. He is not concerned about such matters—*nor should he be*—at this stage. He is just concentrating on getting thoughts and details down on paper, and he knows that writing things down at random can help him think about his topic.

You should take the same approach when freewriting: explore your topic without worrying at all about writing "correctly." In this early stage of the writing process, you are just trying to figure out what you want to say.

2. Prepare a Scratch Outline. Your freewriting will eventually help you figure out different ways that college is stressful. Your goal is to have three supporting items for your paragraph. Write down your supporting items and number them 1, 2, and 3.

Here are the supporting items that Mason decided to focus on in a scratch outline:

> Attending college can be stressful.
> 1. deciding on major
> 2. working while taking classes
> 3. having time for a social life

3. Writing the First Draft. The first draft is just that—a rough first draft as you put at least some of your details down and get an overall sense of the shape of your paper. You still do not have to worry about spelling or punctuation at this stage of the writing process. You want to create the foundation of your paper—its main point and its supporting details. In later drafts, you can build on what you have in the first draft.

Here is Mason's first draft:

> There is a lot of stress in going to college. First, figuring out a major. Everybody wants a major they will enjoy but also a major that is going to result in a job after they graduate. Finding the right major is easier said than done. It may be one of the most important decisions in one's life, and there's a lot of stress in making the right choice. Number 2 as far as stress is having to work at the same time one is taking classes. I have to work 40 hours a week to be able to help pay for college costs. But there is only so much time in a day for work and trying to keep up with studying and get decent grades. Then there is the stress in trying to have any kind of social life while doing everything else. Should I be expected to live like a monk?

4. Revise and Edit. Ideally, put your paper aside for a while before doing later drafts. When you revise, try to do all of the following:

- Omit any details that do not truly support the topic sentence.
- Add more details as needed, making sure you have enough specific details for each of your supporting items.
- Add addition words such as *first, another, second, also,* or *finally* to signal to the reader you are moving from one supporting item to another.
- Include a final "caboose" sentence that rounds off the paper, bringing it to a close.

Here is the paragraph that Mason eventually produced after revising and editing it. Underline the addition words in his paper that show he is moving from one cause of stress to the next.

> Attending college can be stressful. One common cause of college stress is selecting a major. In my case, the major I would really enjoy is history, and I'd love to be a history teacher. But what I've learned is that there is little demand for history teachers in the job market. So do I need to major in something I don't really like, such as accounting, when my goal in life is to find work I enjoy doing? Having to decide just what to do is a very stressful situation. Secondly, many students find it stressful to have to work either part-time or full-time while attending college. Some students—and I'm one of them—have to work almost forty hours a week to pay for college expenses.

> This demanding work schedule leaves me with barely enough time to keep up with my coursework, and it makes it all the more challenging to earn good grades. Furthermore, many college students find it stressful having to balance studying and socializing. I find it difficult to muster the willpower to study for a mid-term exam or complete a ten-page paper when friends invite me to a party. Finally, thinking about what will happen after you graduate can lead to stress. I am well aware that when I graduate from college I will have over $35,000 in college debt, and I will be expected to start paying that amount back in regular installments. But because of today's uncertain job market, what if I can't get a decent-paying job? This worry is never far from my mind.

Note: At a later point, Mason was asked to expand his paragraph into an essay. It appears on pages 90–91.

5. Read the Paper Aloud. Always proofread a paper by reading it out loud. Make sure you read exactly what is on the page. Hearing how your writing sounds is an excellent way to pick up grammar and punctuation problems in your writing. Chances are that you'll find sentence mistakes at every spot where your paper does not read smoothly and clearly. This point is so important that it bears repeating: *To help find mistakes in your paper, read it out loud!*

By consulting a grammar and punctuation handbook as needed, you'll learn to identify and correct mistakes that you may be making.

An Important Final Note: When writing *your* "college stress" paragraph, you should personalize it by making it specifically about your experience. Use a first person "I" point of view. *All the supporting details you provide should be unique to your situation.* You could also decide to develop alternative stressors—for example, transportation problems or family problems or relationship problems.

Your goal is to prove to your reader, through convincing details, that college is stressful for *you*. Imagine you're presenting your evidence to a jury. Do your best to provide such strong specific evidence that the jury—your readers—will all conclude that college is indeed very stressful for you.

PRACTICE 2: Using Questions to Develop a Paragraph

Write a paragraph that supports the following point:

Main idea: There have been some real high points in my life so far.

How to Proceed

1. Ask Questions. Your purpose in the paragraph is to provide specific support for your point. To help think about and develop your support, spend some time asking yourself questions. As you do, write down answers to those questions. Your questions can start with words like *what, when, where, why*, and *how*.

Here are some questions that a student named Jack asked while developing a paper about high points in his life:

> What was one high point?
> Why was it so special and memorable?
> How did other people react?
> What were other high points?
> What did I say and do, and what did other people say and do?

2. Prepare a Scratch Outline. Your questioning will eventually help you develop the specific details about why the event was such a high point in your life. Your goal is to have at least several supporting items for your paragraph. Write down those details and number them 1, 2, and 3. Here are the details that Jack decided to focus on.

> 1. basketball award
> 2. helping at home
> 3. falling in love

3–4. Write a First Draft, Revise, and Edit. On the next page is the paragraph that Jack eventually produced. Underline the addition words that show he is moving from one high point to the next.

> When I think about high points in my life, I think of three very special times. The first happened when I was a junior in high school and was named "Most Motivated Player" on my basketball team. I'd worked very hard on my game, and it made me feel terrific to be recognized by my coach and teammates. I told my father the news, and he smiled and said, "The family is very proud of you, Jack." I've never forgotten that. Another

> high point in my life occurred when my father got sick and I had to step in to keep things going. I watched my sisters while my mother was at the hospital, and I took care of dishes and trash and helped with homework and did a lot of other things without being asked. My father said to me one night when I saw him at the hospital, "We've really needed you in this trying time." I felt I had moved from being a child to an adult. A third high point was years later when I really fell in love for the first time. Even though that time ended, I'll never forget how Mary Ellen made the world glow for me. Every bit of loneliness I had ever had in life just disappeared, and we would hold hands and laugh together and the sun was shining all the time.

5. Read the Paper Aloud. Always proofread a paper by reading it out loud. Make sure you read exactly what is on the page. Hearing how your writing sounds is an excellent way to pick up grammar and punctuation problems in your writing. Chances are that you'll find sentence mistakes at every spot where your paper does not read smoothly and clearly. This point is so important that it bears repeating: *To help find mistakes in your paper, read it out loud!*

By consulting a grammar and punctuation handbook as needed, you'll learn to identify and correct mistakes that you may be making.

PRACTICE 3: Using a List to Develop a Paragraph

Write a paragraph that supports the following point:

Main idea: Getting eight hours of sleep a night would be a real challenge for me.

How to Proceed

1. Make a List. In **list making** (also known as **brainstorming**), you make a list of ideas and details that could go into your paper. Simply pile these items up, one after another, without worrying about putting them in any special order. Try to think of as many details as possible and to make them as specific as possible. Here are the initial items on the list of a student named Grace.

> Give up late night talks with boyfriend
> Cut down on my coffee drinking
> Stop late-night TV
> Stop late-night snacks
> Shut off my cell phone
> No more quiet time for myself
> . . .

Expand your list with one detail after another—as many things as you can think of. Don't worry about which items you will use or putting your items in order at this point—just get down a list of as many items as you can think of. You can easily delete or add more items and put them into the right sequence later. At this prewriting stage, you're just accumulating raw material and thinking about your topic by putting a long list of details on paper.

2. Prepare a Scratch Outline. Once you have your list, prepare a scratch outline of your paragraph. It will serve as a guide to just how to proceed in writing your paragraph. Here is Grace's scratch outline:

> 1. Giving up a lot of my coffee
> 2. Turning my phone off
> 3. Cut down on TV watching

3–4. Write a First Draft, Revise, and Edit. Here is the paragraph that Grace eventually produced. Underline the signal words that Grace uses to move from one item to the next.

> Getting eight hours of sleep a night would require changing some habits that I've been following for years. First of all, I'd need to cut out drinking about ten cups of coffee a day, which would be hard to do. Coffee is like lifeblood to me! I can't imagine making it through the day without it, but it also keeps me up at night. Next, I'd need to turn my phone off. Texts and beeps wake me up a lot. This seems like a simple enough fix, but I'm addicted to my phone. I'd be afraid of missing something! Finally, I'd just need to force myself to get in bed earlier. I watch a lot of TV at night, and one show leads to another. However, staying up every night to watch the late show is not a great idea when you have to be up at six a.m.

5. Read the Paper Aloud. Always proofread a paper by reading it out loud. Make sure you read exactly what is on the page. Hearing how your writing sounds is an excellent way to pick up grammar and punctuation problems in your writing. Chances are that you'll find sentence mistakes at every spot where your paper does not read smoothly and clearly. This point is so important that it bears repeating: *To help find mistakes in your paper, read it out loud!*

By consulting a grammar and punctuation handbook as needed, you'll learn to identify and correct mistakes that you may be making.

A Final Thought

To master the two basic goals in effective writing—making and supporting a point—and to learn to use the prewriting techniques of freewriting, asking questions, and list making, you need to practice. Do so by writing paragraphs or essays on each of the three assignments in Mastery Tests 2, 3, and 4.

UNDERSTANDING THE WRITING PROCESS: Mastery Test 1

Each item below is an example of one stage in the writing process for the following assignment:

Assignment: Write a paragraph or an essay in which you describe an irresponsible person you have known. In it, be sure to provide specific details that illustrate the person's lack of responsibility.

Identify each item by labeling it with one of the following:

A. Freewriting	**B.** List making	**C.** Questioning
D. Scratch outline	**E.** First draft	

_____ 1. irresponsible person
my cousin Jules
mother's car and flat tire
not watching sister's baby
talks about community college
never gets around to paperwork

_____ 2. ¹My cousin Jules is an irresponsible person. ²For example, once my aunt—his mother—let him borrow her car to go to a party. ³The next day when it was time to go to work, my aunt couldn't find her car. ⁴She woke Jules up, and he told her he'd had a flat tire. ⁵Instead of fixing the flat, he called a friend for a ride and just left her car miles from home. ⁶Another example of Jules's irresponsibility happened when he was spending the evening at my sister's house. ⁷Amy mentioned that she needed to pick up a prescription for her son from the drug store. ⁸Jules offered to stay at the house while she went out. ⁹When my sister got back to the house, Jules had left! ¹⁰He'd gotten a call from a friend and just gone, leaving my baby nephew sleeping alone in the house. ¹¹A final example of Jules's irresponsibility is his attitude toward school. ¹²He keeps saying he's going to take some courses at community college, but then he "forgets" to fill out the paperwork and misses the deadline to register. ¹³I don't have much hope that Jules is ever going to become a responsible person.

_____ 3. *Who was irresponsible?* My cousin Jules
When was he irresponsible? One time when he borrowed my aunt's car
How was he irresponsible? He didn't get a flat tire fixed
What is another example of irresponsibility? Didn't watch his baby nephew
What is yet another example? Talks about going to school but doesn't

(Continues on next page)

___ 4. ¹I definitely know people who are not responsible at times. ²Sometimes members of my own family drop the ball on things they should do. ³But now that I think of it my cousin Jules really takes the cake. ⁴There have been plenty of times when he did not do what he should have done. ⁵One thing I remember: he took his mom's car and got a flat tire when he was going to a party or something . . . then he never even got it fixed. ⁶Everybody in the family yelled at him for that. ⁷His reputation just got worse. ⁸Community college is something he talks about. ⁹But you never see him follow through. ¹⁰All talk and no action. ¹¹Not taking charge of his own life.

___ 5. My cousin Jules is irresponsible.
    1. Borrowed his mom's car and didn't get a flat tire repaired
    2. Left his babysitting post with his sister's son
    3. Talks about going to college but forgets to register

UNDERSTANDING THE WRITING PROCESS: Mastery Test 2 (Freewriting)

Use the prewriting technique of freewriting to help you write a paragraph or an essay on the following assignment.

Personal Quality. Think of someone you know—a sister, brother, father, mother, grandparent, friend, boss, teacher, neighbor—and think of a personal quality you associate with him or her. (The quality can be positive or negative: honest, reliable, generous, selfish, shy, materialistic, bossy, hardworking, lazy—or any other trait.) Then write a description of that person, showing that he or she possesses that quality. Your main idea can simply be a sentence like this:

- My brother Brett is hardworking.
- Our next-door neighbors are the most selfish people I know.

How to Proceed

1. **Freewrite.** Before you actually write the first draft, spend ten or fifteen minutes freewriting. Just sit down and write whatever comes into your mind about the person you have in mind. Write without stopping and without worrying at all about spelling, grammar, and the like. Write about things the person says and does that show what he or she is like. In general, think on paper and try to get down as much information as you can about the person. You are using the freewriting process to try to figure out what you want to say. When you are done, you'll probably have a sense of whether the person you've chosen and the quality you've identified will be a topic you can write about and support in a paper.

2. **Ask questions and/or make a list.** You may find it then helps to also use other prewriting techniques. Perhaps ask yourself questions about what are especially good examples of the personal quality you want to write about. Or see if you can make up a list of as many examples as you can think of about that personal quality. The goal of your prewriting techniques is to help you determine whether you have a good topic to develop and support in a paper. You'll then be ready to do a scratch outline.

3. **Prepare a scratch outline.** Write out your main idea and briefly list your supporting items.

   Main Idea
       Supporting example 1
       Supporting example 2
       Supporting example 3

(Continues on next page)

4. **Write and revise.** Write a first draft of your paper, and then go on to revise it in one or more additional drafts. Remember that your goal is to advance a point and then do a solid job of supporting that point. Use addition words such as *first, second,* and *finally* to signal to the reader that you are moving from one example to another.

Here, as a model, is one student's response to the assignment.

> The main thing in my life that's kept me strong and directed is my loving mother. There have been times when I've doubted my own self-worth, and she was able to restore my confidence in myself. One of these times occurred when I was flunking out of college my freshman year. Instead of giving up on me, my mom encouraged me and assured me I could do better. She believed in me, so I began believing in myself. A second example happened not long after that, when I made a pretty big mistake and got into a car accident (my mom's car!) after I'd been drinking. Mom had to come and pick me up at the jail, and was she ever mad. But when I saw the tears in her eyes and she said, "You could have gotten yourself killed!" I knew it wasn't the car she was upset about. If a friend had totaled my car, I might never speak to him again. But the unconditional love of a parent isn't like that. It stays steady and strong even when the child's life is rocky. And in the end, it makes the child steady and strong.

5. **Read your paper aloud.** After you have edited and proofread your paper, be sure to *read it out loud.* Hearing how your writing sounds is an excellent way to pick up grammar and punctuation problems in your writing. Chances are that you'll find sentence mistakes at spots where your paper does not read smoothly and clearly. Use a grammar handbook, if necessary, to see what corrections are needed. Make the required corrections to remove the trouble spots.

UNDERSTANDING THE WRITING PROCESS: Mastery Test 3 (Asking Questions)

Use the prewriting technique of asking questions to write a paragraph on the following assignment.

I've had to go through some hard times in my life.

Alternatively, write about someone you know who has had to go through hard times.

How to Proceed

1. **Ask questions.** Here are some questions you might ask in thinking about how to do this assignment.

   1. What is the worst hard time I've had to go through?
   2. When and where did this hard time take place?
   3. How did I respond to this challenging time?
   4. How were people I care about affected by this hard time?
   5. What is another hard time, or what are other hard times, that I've had to cope with in my life?

   As you ask questions and think of answers, write out your thoughts and responses as they occur to you. Remember not to worry about spelling, grammar, and the like. You just want to do some thinking on paper as you gradually figure out what you want to say about each hard time in your life and the people it affected.

2. **Freewrite and/or make a list.** You may then find it helps to also use other prewriting techniques. Perhaps freewrite about one of the hard times. Or see if you can make up a list of the details that made that time such a difficult one. You'll eventually be ready to do a scratch outline.

3. **Prepare a scratch outline.** Write out your main idea and a brief list of the challenging time or times you have had to deal with.

   Main Idea
   1. **Supporting example 1**
   2. **Supporting example 2**
   3. **Supporting example 3**

4. **Write and revise.** Write a first draft of your paper, and then go on to revise it in one or more additional drafts. Remember that your goal is to advance a point and then do a solid job of supporting that point. Use addition words such as *one, another*, and *last* to signal to the reader that you are moving from one example to another.

   Alternatively, you may want to develop in great detail just one hard time, and you may want to use time signals such as *then, next, while*, and *finally* as you move from one detail about that time to the next.

(Continues on next page)

5. **Read your paper aloud.** After you have edited and proofread your paper, be sure to *read it out loud*. Hearing how your writing sounds is an excellent way to pick up grammar and punctuation problems in your writing. Chances are that you'll find sentence mistakes at spots where your paper does not read smoothly and clearly. Use a grammar handbook, if necessary, to see what corrections are needed. Make the required corrections to remove the trouble spots.

UNDERSTANDING THE WRITING PROCESS: Mastery Test 4 (List Making)

Use the prewriting technique of list making to help you do a paragraph on the following assignment.

Based on their behavior, some students that I know probably should not be in college.

How to Proceed

1. **Make a list.** See if you can make up a list of behaviors of students who are acting as if they don't want to be in college. Write down as many of their words and actions as you can think of that help reveal their attitude toward being a student. Below are some details to get you started, but make sure that you add your own observations to this list:

   > Sit through classes without taking notes
   > Often stare out into space
   > Never seen in the library, bookstore, or lab
   > . . .

2. **Prepare and/or ask questions.** You may also find it helpful to freewrite about one or more of these students and why you suspect they do not want to be (and probably should not be) in school. Or you may want to ask a series of questions, such as "Are they late for class or do they miss classes? Do they do things other than take notes in class? Do they seem prepared for exams? How can you sense they don't want to be present?" You'll eventually be ready to do a scratch outline.

3. **Prepare a scratch outline.** Write out your main idea and the main details that you have to support it.

   Main Idea
   1. Supporting example 1
   2. Supporting example 2
   3. Supporting example 3

4. **Write and revise.** Write a first draft of your paper, and then go on to revise it in one or more additional drafts. Remember that your goal is to advance a point and then do a solid job of supporting that point. Use addition words such as *to begin with, next, then,* and *after* to signal to the reader that you are moving from one direction to the next.

(Continues on next page)

5. **Read your paper aloud.** After you have edited and proofread your paper, be sure to *read it out loud*. Hearing how your writing sounds is an excellent way to pick up grammar and punctuation problems in your writing. Chances are that you'll find sentence mistakes at spots where your paper does not read smoothly and clearly. Use a grammar handbook, if necessary, to see what corrections are needed. Make the required corrections to remove the trouble spots.

5 Relationships in Reading

Good readers and writers understand the relationships between ideas. This chapter explains the basic relationships you should recognize as a reader.

Ideas in a reading selection are almost always connected to each other. Learning to recognize these connections, or **relationships**, will help you become a better reader.

As you will see, authors use two common methods to show relationships and make their ideas clear. These two methods—**transitions** and **patterns of organization**—are explained in turn in this chapter.

Transitions

Look at the following items and put a check (✓) by the one that is easier to read and understand:

_____ One way to lose friends is to talk but not listen. A way to end friendships is to borrow money and not pay it back.

✓ One way to lose friends is to talk but not listen. Another way to end friendships is to borrow money and not pay it back.

You probably found the second item easier to understand. The word *another* makes it clear that the writer is adding a second way to lose friends. **Transitions** are words or phrases (like *another*) that show relationships between ideas. They are like signs on the road that guide travelers. Or they can be seen as "bridge" words, carrying the reader across from one idea to the next:

One way to lose friends is to talk but not listen. **ANOTHER** way to end friendships is to borrow money and not pay it back.

Two major types of transitions are words that show addition and words that show time.

Words That Show Addition

Once again, put a check (✓) beside the item that is easier to read and understand:

_____ Many people rent DVDs because rental is cheaper than tickets to a movie theater. DVDs are now available online as well as in stores.

✓ Many people rent DVDs because rental is cheaper than tickets to a movie theater. Also, DVDs are now available online as well as in stores.

The word *also* in the second item makes the relationship between the sentences clearer. The author is providing reasons why renting movies is popular. The first reason is that renting DVDs is cheaper than buying tickets to the movies. A *second* reason is that the movies are so readily available. The word *also* makes it clear that another reason is being given. *Also* is an addition word.

Addition words signal added ideas. These words tell you a writer is presenting one or more ideas that continue along the same line of thought as a previous idea. Like all transitions, addition words help writers organize their information and present it clearly to readers. In the cartoon on the next page, the words *For one thing* introduce a list, and the words *Also* and *Finally* add to the list of reasons why the man is a terrible pet owner (in the dog's opinion).

"You're a terrible pet owner. For one thing, you keep me on a chain. Also, you make me eat on the floor. Finally, you never let me go out in public alone."

Here are some common words that show addition:

Addition Words

one	to begin with	also	further
first (of all)	for one thing	in addition	furthermore
second(ly)	other	next	last (of all)
third(ly)	another	moreover	final(ly)

Examples

The following items contain addition words. Notice how these words introduce ideas that *add to* what has already been said.

- Garlic improves the flavor of many dishes. *In addition*, it lowers cholesterol, fights heart disease, and kills certain viruses.

- Rivers serve as highways for migrating birds. *Also*, the nearby wetlands provide the birds with places in which to rest and feed.

- My neighbors are so safety-conscious that they had the wooden front door of their apartment replaced with a steel one. *Moreover*, they had iron bars installed on all their apartment windows.

PRACTICE 1

Complete each sentence with a suitable addition word from the box on the previous page. Try to use a variety of transitions.

Hint: Make sure that each addition word or phrase that you choose fits smoothly into the flow of the sentence. Test each choice by reading the sentence aloud.

1. To avoid car thieves, lock valuables in the trunk or glove compartment. You should _____*also*_____ try to park in the middle of a block on a busy, well-lit street.

2. There are several ways to use old jeans. _____*First*_____, you can use them for patching other jeans.

3. One million stray dogs live in the New York City metropolitan area. _____*In addition*_____, there are more than 500,000 stray cats in the same area.

4. "_____*Last*_____, and most important," said my adviser, "you've got to complete that term paper or you won't graduate on time."

5. Part-time workers have second-class status. For one thing, they are easily laid off. Second, they get no fringe benefits. _____*Finally*_____, they are often paid less than half the hourly rate of a full-timer.

Words That Show Time

Put a check (✓) beside the item that is easier to read and understand:

_____ The two neighboring families used to get along well. They are not on speaking terms.

_✓_ Previously, the two neighboring families got along well. Now they are not on speaking terms.

The words *previously* and *now* in the second item clarify the relationship between the sentences: *Before*, the families got along well; and *now* they don't speak to each other. *Previously* and *now* and words like them are time words.

Time words indicate a time relationship. These transitions tell us *when* something happened in relation to when something else happened. They help writers organize and make clear the order of events, stages, and steps in a process. In the cartoon below, the words *First* and *Then* mark two steps in a process.

"First you eat the worm. Then you floss with the string."

GLASBERGEN

Copyright 2001 by Randy Glasbergen.

Here are some common time words:

Time Words

before	immediately	when	until
previously	next	whenever	often
first (of all)	then	while	frequently
second (ly)	following	during	eventually
third (ly)	later	as (soon as)	final(ly)
now	after	by	last (of all)

Note: Some additional ways of showing time are dates ("In 1890 . . . ," "Throughout the 20th century . . . ," "By 2018 . . .") and other time references ("Within a week . . . ," "by the end of the month . . . ," "in two years . . .").

Examples

The following examples contain time words. Notice how these words show us *when* something takes place.

- *While* the nurse prepared the needle, I rolled up my sleeve. *Then* I looked away.

- Many people get sleepy *after* eating a heavy meal.

- *During* my last semester in college, I spent more time job hunting than I did studying.

Helpful Tips about Transitions

Here are two points to keep in mind about transitions:

 TIP 1 Some transition words have the same meaning. For example, *also, moreover,* and *furthermore* all mean "in addition." Authors typically use a variety of transitions to avoid repetition.

 TIP 2 In some cases the same word can serve as two different types of transitions, depending on how it is used. For example, the word *first* may be used as an addition word to show that the author is presenting a series of points, as in the following sentences:

> For many athletes, life after a sports career is a letdown. *First,* they are often not prepared for nonathletic careers. In addition, they . . .

First may also may be used to signal a time sequence, as in these sentences:

> A trip to a giant supermarket can be quite frustrating. *First,* you have trouble finding a parking space close to the store. Then, . . .

PRACTICE 2

Complete each sentence with a suitable time word from the box on page 125. Try to use a variety of transitions.

> *Hint:* Make sure that each time word or phrase that you choose fits smoothly into the flow of the sentence. Test each choice by reading the sentence aloud.

1. _____*After*_____ my cousin took a long shower, there was no hot water left for anyone else in the house.

2. To make chicken stock, begin by putting a pot of water on the stove to boil. _____*Then*_____ drop in a chicken and some diced celery and onions.

3. Gerald waited impatiently all day for the Monday night football game to begin on TV, but _____*during*_____ the first half, he fell asleep.

4. Recent advances in medicine make it possible to treat babies even _____*when*_____ they are born.

5. Some students listen to their iPods, eat snacks, and talk on their cell phones _____*while*_____ doing their homework.

Patterns of Organization

You have learned that transitions show the relationships between ideas in sentences. In the same way, **patterns of organization** show the relationships between supporting details in paragraphs, essays, and chapters. It helps to recognize the patterns in which authors arrange information. You will then be better able to understand and remember what you read.

The rest of this chapter discusses two major patterns of organization:

- The **list of items pattern**
  (Addition words are often used in this pattern of organization.)

- The **time order pattern**
  (Time words are often used in this pattern of organization.)

Noticing the transitions in a passage often can help you become aware of its pattern of organization. Transitions can also help you find the major supporting details.

1   The List of Items Pattern

List of Items
Item 1
Item 2
Item 3

To get a sense of the list of items pattern, try to arrange the following sentences in a logical order. Put a *1* in front of the sentence that should come first, a *2* in front of the sentence that comes next, a *3* in front of the third sentence, and a *4* in front of the sentence that should come last. The result will be a short paragraph. Use the addition words as a guide.

__2__   One common strategy is to consume massive quantities of junk food, which is easily done thanks to all the ever-present convenience stores and fast-food restaurants.

__1__   There are some widely popular, inappropriate methods that people use to combat stress.

__4__   Finally, watching hours of nonstop TV can put people in a stupor that helps them forget the problems of everyday life.

__3__   Another way to deal with stress is to doze or sleep for hours and hours, even during the day.

This paragraph begins with the main idea: "There are some widely popular, inappropriate methods that people use to combat stress." The next three sentences go on to list three of those methods, resulting in the pattern of organization known as a list of items. The transitions *One, Another,* and *Finally* introduce the points being listed and indicate their order:

> [1]There are some widely popular, inappropriate methods that people use to combat stress. [2]One common strategy is to consume massive quantities of junk food, which is easily done thanks to all the ever-present convenience stores and fast-food restaurants. [3]Another way to deal with stress is to doze or sleep for hours and hours, even during the day. [4]Finally, watching hours of nonstop TV can put people in a stupor that helps them forget the problems of everyday life.

A **list of items** refers to a series of reasons, examples, or other points that support an idea. The items have no time order, but are listed in whatever order the author prefers. Addition words, such as those in the box on the following page, are often used in a list of items to tell us that other supporting points are being added to a point already mentioned. Textbook authors frequently organize material into lists of items, such as a list of types of economic systems, symptoms of heart disease, or reasons for teenage drinking.

✔ *Check Your Understanding*

Below is a paragraph that gives directions. Complete the outline of the paragraph by listing the missing steps in the correct sequence. To help yourself identify each step, do two things:

- Underline the time words that introduce each item in the sequence;
- Number (*1, 2, . . .*) each step in the sequence.

> ¹Here is a six-step technique that will help you relax quickly. ²First, lie down with your arms at your sides and your fingers open. ³When you are comfortable, close your eyes and put all distracting thoughts out of your mind. ⁴Next, tighten all the muscles of your body at once. ⁵Do this by pushing your toes together, tightening your buttocks and abdomen, clenching your fists, and squeezing your eyes shut. ⁶Then, let everything relax, and feel the tension flow out of your body. ⁷After that, take a deep breath through your mouth, hold it for twenty seconds, and then let it out slowly, breathing slowly and easily, as you do when you are sleeping. ⁸Finally, think of a pleasant scene as you feel your whole body becoming calm and relaxed.

Main idea: Here is a six-step technique that will help you relax quickly.

1. _____
2. _____
3. Tighten all muscles at once.
4. _____
5. _____
6. _____

Explanation

You should have added these steps to the outline:

1. Lie down, arms at your sides and fingers open. (The author signals this stage with the time word *First*.)
2. When you are comfortable, close your eyes and clear your mind. (The author signals this stage with the time word *When*.)
4. Let everything relax, and feel the tension flow out of your body. (The author signals this stage with the time word *Then*.)
5. Take a deep breath, hold it, let it out, and breathe slowly and easily. (The author's signal is the time word *After*.)
6. Think of a pleasant scene as you feel yourself relax. (The author signals this last step with the time word *Finally*.)

As indicated by the transitions used, the relationship between the steps is one of time: The second step happens *after* the first, and so on.

PRACTICE 5

The following passage gives directions involving several steps that must be done in order. Complete the map below by writing the main idea in the top box and filling in the three missing steps.

> *Hint:* Underline the time words that introduce each step in the sequence, and number each step.

¹There are several steps to remembering your dreams. ²To begin with, you must make up your mind to do so, for consciously deciding that you want to remember increases the likelihood that it will happen. ³Then put a pen and a notebook near your bed, so that you can write down what you remember as soon as you wake up. ⁴When possible, turn off your alarm before you go to sleep so that you can wake up gradually; this will increase the likelihood of remembering your dreams. ⁵Finally, when you wake up in the morning and remember a dream, write it down immediately, even before getting out of bed.

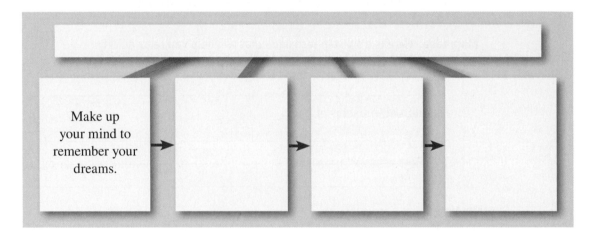

Make up your mind to remember your dreams.

A Note on Main Ideas and Patterns of Organization

A paragraph's main idea often indicates its pattern of organization. For example, here's the main idea of the paragraph you just read: "There are several steps to remembering your dreams." The words *several steps* suggest that this paragraph will be organized according to time order. Another good example is the main idea of the earlier paragraph on aging: "Various theories explain the aging process." The words *various theories* suggest that this paragraph will be a list of items.

Paying close attention to the main idea, then, can give you a quick sense of a paragraph's pattern of organization. Try, for instance, to guess the pattern of the paragraph with this main idea:

While there are thousands of self-help groups, they all fall into three basic categories.

The phrase "three basic categories" is a strong indication that the paragraph will list those categories. The main idea helps us guess that the paragraph will be a list of three items.

PRACTICE 6

Most of the main ideas below have been taken from college textbooks. In the space provided, write the letter of the pattern of organization that each main idea suggests.

_____ 1. The process of digestion can be divided into four stages.
   A. List of items   B. Time order

_____ 2. A federal form of government has advantages and disadvantages.
   A. List of items   B. Time order

_____ 3. The stock market crash resulted from a number of basic weaknesses in the economy.
   A. List of items   B. Time order

_____ 4. Serious relationships in our lives often evolve gradually, going several phases.
   A. List of items   B. Time order

_____ 5. Law enforcement officers are taught a series of steps to follow up arriving at the scene of a violent crime.
   A. List of items   B. Time order

_____ 6. There are several search aids that can be of great help when you are looking for information online.
   A. List of items   B. Time order

_____ 7. Educational opportunities vary greatly in different regions of the United States.
   A. List of items   B. Time order

_____ 8. Treating the allergic patient often involves a three-stage process.
   A. List of items   B. Time order

_____ 9. Convenience products can be subdivided into four groups on the basis of how people buy them.
   A. List of items   B. Time order

_____10. The worldwide fall of communism was marked by a series of dramatic events.
   A. List of items   B. Time order

Two Final Points

1 While many passages have just one pattern of organization, often the patterns are mixed. You may find that part of a passage uses a list of items pattern, and another part of the same passage uses a time order pattern. (For example, in the paragraph on page 135 about relaxing, the steps are given in time order, but the third step contains a list of four sets of muscles to tighten.)

2 Remember that not all relationships between ideas are signaled by transitions. An author may present a list of items, for example, without using addition words. So as you read, watch for the relationships themselves, not just the transitions.

RELATIONSHIPS IN READING: Mastery Test 1

A. Fill in each blank with an appropriate transition from the box. Use each transition once. Then, in the spaces provided, write the letter of the transition you have chosen.

A. after	**B.** also	**C.** another
D. moreover	**E.** then	

Hint: Make sure that each word or phrase that you choose fits smoothly into the flow of the sentence. Test your choices by reading each sentence to yourself.

_____ 1. [1]If you're used to e-mail, sending an actual letter can seem like a long, drawn-out process. [2]First you have to get a pen and paper, an envelope, and stamps. [3]_____ you write the letter, you have to fold it, place it in the envelope, and attach a stamp. [4]Finally you need to find a place to mail the letter. [5]No wonder people mail so few real letters these days!

_____ 2. [1]I have a limited interest in people whose main topic of conversation is themselves and who never show any interest in what is happening to me. [2]_____ group I avoid is people who never allow facts to interfere with their opinions.

_____ 3. [1]The world of business is one area in which technology has isolated us. [2]Many people now work alone at a display terminal that connects to a large central computer. [3]Personal banking has _____ become a detached process. [4]To deposit or withdraw money from their accounts, customers often interact with machines rather than people.

_____ 4. [1]By today's standards, early automobiles were difficult to operate and uncomfortable to drive. [2]A driver had to start the car's engine by cranking it by hand, and the crank sometimes sprang back and broke the driver's thumb. [3]_____, early cars were open on top, so driving on unpaved roads left riders choking on dust and dirt.

_____ 5. [1]Many television ads proceed in three stages: the problem, the advice, and the resolution. [2]For example, a mouthwash commercial will first establish the problem—that someone has bad breath. [3]_____ it will suggest that the person try the advertised mouthwash. [4]This is followed by an obvious resolution of the problem: the person's being chased by attractive members of the opposite sex.

(Continues on next page)

139

B. (6–9.) Fill in each blank with an appropriate transition word from the box. Use each transition once.

A. after	B. last	C. next
D. then		

¹Two Minnesota brothers, Ed and Norman, are engaged in a war. ²It all started (6)_____ Ed's wife gave him a pair of pants that didn't fit. ³Ed wrapped up the pants and put them under Norman's Christmas tree. ⁴As soon as Norman opened the box, he recognized the unwanted pants.

⁵The (7)_____ year, he gave them back to Ed, sealed in a heavy carton tied with knotted ropes. ⁶The War of the Pants was on. ⁷Each year, on one of the brothers' birthdays, or on Christmas, the dreaded pants reappear. ⁸Two years ago, Norman bought an old safe, put the pants in it, welded it shut, and delivered it to Ed's house. ⁹Somehow, Ed retrieved the pants. ¹⁰(One of the rules of the war is that the pants must not be damaged.)

¹¹(8)_____ year Ed took the pants to an auto junkyard. ¹²The pants were placed in an ancient Ford's backseat, and the car (9)_____ went through the auto crusher. ¹³On his birthday, Norman found a four-foot square of smashed metal on his doorstep. ¹⁴He knew it could only be Ed's doing, and the pants must be inside. ¹⁵Norman is still trying to get at the pants and prepare next year's "topper."

_____10. The pattern of organization of the above selection is
    A. list of items.
    B. time order.

RELATIONSHIPS IN READING: Mastery Test 2

A. Fill in each blank with an appropriate transition from the box. Use each transition once. Then, in the spaces provided, write the letter of the transition you have chosen.

A. also	**B. before**	**C. first**
D. then	**E. when**	

_____ 1. ¹Big snapping turtles don't get to weigh so much without eating a lot of food. ²Here's how they do it: ³Most snapping turtles float, or lie motionless on the bottom of a pond or river. ⁴_____ a fish, frog, or other prey swims close enough, the turtle snaps very fast with powerful jaws.

_____ 2. ¹Experts cite several reasons for Japan's low crime rate. ²_____, Japan has had strict gun control for four hundred years. ³In addition, the country relies on some fifteen thousand small neighborhood police stations known as *koban*. ⁴Police officers and their families actually live as part of the neighborhood, helping prevent the growth of conditions that might lead to crime.

_____ 3. ¹For much of my life, I have been haunted by dreams of falling. ²In a typical dream, I have fallen off a tall building or over the edge of a cliff or out of a plane, and I am plunging at a breathtaking speed toward the ground. ³_____, just as I am about to crash into the ground, I wake up in a cold sweat, my heart racing.

_____ 4. ¹According to legend, tea was discovered quite by accident. ²One day about 4,000 years ago, a Chinese emperor was boiling water outside when leaves from a bush fell into the open pot. ³_____ the emperor could remove the leaves, they began to brew. ⁴He smelled the sweet aroma of the mixture, and once he tasted it, tea was born.

_____ 5. ¹Whoever you are, whatever you look like, chances are you're not happy with your appearance. ²Our culture constantly sends out the message that you're not attractive enough. ³Television is one of the most powerful message-carriers, showing you an endless parade of impossibly thin, beautiful people. ⁴Magazines are _____ designed to make you feel ugly, with glossy airbrushed models on every page providing an impossible ideal of thin, ageless beauty.

(Continues on next page)

141

B. Read the passage and answer the question that follows.

¹Probably every child remembers digging a hole in his or her backyard and being told, "If you dig deep enough, you'll go to China." ²What would really happen if a man dug a hole through the center of the Earth and then jumped into it? ³The traveler entering the tunnel would first fall rapidly under the force of gravity. ⁴Eventually, as he approached the Earth's center, the jumper's weight would decrease. ⁵By the time he reached the center of the Earth, he would be weightless. ⁶An equal amount of the Earth's mass on all sides of him would cancel out the forces of gravity. ⁷Still, the traveler's original momentum would carry him past the center toward the opening on the far side of the world. ⁸After almost reaching that point, he would fall back up the hole toward his starting point. ⁹Back and forth he would then go, like a yo-yo, gradually slowing down until coming to a stop at the very center of the Earth.

_____ 6. The main pattern of organization of the passage is
    A. list of items.
    B. time order.

C. (7–9.) Fill in each blank with an appropriate transition word from the box. Use each transition once. Then answer the question that follows.

A. also	B. finally	C. first

¹The microbes that cause infection are transmitted to people in several ways. ²_____, there is direct transmission, which involves bodily contact with an infected person. ³Examples are passing along a cold through handshaking or herpes through sexual relations. ⁴There is _____ indirect transmission, which occurs when microbes are passed from an infected person to an individual via airborne particles, water, food, or anything else the infected person touches. ⁵For example, someone might catch the flu by drinking from a glass that has been used by a person with the flu. ⁶_____, animals and insects can transmit microbes. ⁷Flies, for instance, carry harmful microbes on their feet, and can transmit them to people by landing on their food.

_____ 10. The pattern of organization of the above selection is
    A. list of items.
    B. time order.

RELATIONSHIPS IN READING: Mastery Test 3

A. (1–4.) Arrange the scrambled sentences below into a logical paragraph by numbering them *1, 2, 3,* and *4* in an order that makes sense. Then, in the space provided, write the letter of the pattern of organization used.

Note that transitions will help you by clarifying the relationships between sentences.

____ In addition, check the puppy's personality by watching how it plays with other puppies.

____ There are some important points to keep in mind when choosing a puppy.

____ Last, since curiosity is a sign of intelligence, clap your hands to see if the puppy is curious and interested.

____ For one thing, look for signs of good health, including clear, bright eyes and firm, pink gums.

_____ 5. The pattern of organization of the above selection is
     A. list of items.
     B. time order.

B. Read the passage and answer the question that follows. You may find it helpful to underline transitions as you read.

[1]In January of 1954, Ernest and Mary Hemingway left Nairobi on a vacation trip on which they flew over grazing elephants, hippos bathing in the lakes, and huge flocks of feeding flamingos. [2]As they were circling a spectacular waterfall, a flock of ibises flew in front of the plane. [3]When the pilot dived to avoid the birds, he struck an abandoned telegraph wire that crossed the gorge. [4]In the crash that followed, Ernest sprained his shoulder; Mary was only slightly injured. [5]Luckily, a boat came down the river the next morning, and its crew rescued them. [6]By that evening, they were on board a small plane bound for Entebbe. [7]The plane lifted from the plowed field that served as a runway, then crashed and burst into flames. [8]Ernest escaped by breaking through a window with his head and injured shoulder, and Mary got out through another window. [9]Twice in two days they had crashed and come out alive, but Ernest had injured his head, his backbone, and a kidney. [10]After this, even writing a letter was difficult for him.

_____ 6. The pattern of organization of the above selection is
     A. list of items.
     B. time order.

(Continues on next page)

C. Read the textbook passage below, and then answer the question and complete the outline.

> ¹Prevention against injury involves a combination of two types of preventive measures. ²First is active prevention, which refers to methods that require people to do something to reduce the risk of being injured. ³Examples include the use of seat belts, the use of bicycle and motorcycle helmets, following drunk driving laws, and obeying traffic regulations. ⁴The second type of preventive measure is passive prevention. ⁵Passive prevention refers to methods requiring little or no action on the part of those being protected. ⁶These measures include anti-lock brakes that automatically engage when roads become slippery, automobile air bags, better street lighting, and built-in safety switches on power tools and electrical equipment.

_____ 7. The pattern of organization of the above selection is
   A. list of items.
   B. time order.

8–10. Complete the outline of the passage.

Main idea: _____

_____

Major supporting details:

1. _____

   _____

   Examples—use of seat belts; bike helmets

2. _____

   _____

   Examples—anti-lock brakes; air bags

RELATIONSHIPS IN READING: Mastery Test 4

A. (1–5.) Arrange the scrambled sentences below into a logical paragraph by numbering them *1, 2, 3,* and *4* in an order that makes sense. Then, in the space provided, write the letter of the pattern of organization used.

Note that transitions will help you by clarifying the relationships between sentences.

_____ When you have chosen your apartment, have a lawyer or another person knowledgeable about leases examine your lease before you sign it.

_____ If you're looking for an apartment, begin by making a list of promising openings. Check the classified ads and two or three real estate offices for apartments within your price range and desired locale.

_____ As you inspect each apartment, make sure that faucets, toilets, stoves, and electrical wiring and outlets are functioning efficiently and safely.

_____ After you have made a solid list, visit at least five of the most promising available apartments.

_____ 5. The pattern of organization of the above selection is
   A. list of items.
   B. time order.

B. Read the textbook passage below and answer the question that follows.

[1]Did you ever wonder how trainers get porpoises to do all those tricks, like leaping over a high bar or jumping through a hoop? [2]Wild porpoises are first taught to eat fish from their trainer's hand. [3]When the animal accepts a fish, the trainer blows a whistle. [4]The porpoise associates the whistle with "correct" behavior. [5]Once the porpoise touches a human hand to get a fish, it will touch other things, like a red target ball. [6]For example, the trainer will hold the ball high above the water while leaning over a kind of pulpit. [7]Seeing the ball, the porpoise leaps out of the water; it knows it will be rewarded with a fish. [8]A hoop can then be substituted for a ball, and the porpoise's behavior can be "shaped" so it will jump through the hoop. [9]If the porpoise misses by jumping too low, the fish reward is withheld. [10]The intelligent animal will associate "no fish" with "wrong" behavior; very quickly, the porpoise will be leaping gracefully through the center of the hoop.

_____ 6. The pattern of organization of the above selection is
   A. list of items.
   B. time order.

(Continues on next page)

C. (7–10.) Complete the map of the following textbook passage.

> ¹Work shapes human lives in fundamental ways. ²First, work consumes enormous amounts of people's time. ³Most people spend about one-third of their adult lives working. ⁴According to a recent survey, almost half of all employed people spend 40 hours or more per week at work; only 10 percent work less than 30 hours a week. ⁵Work also gives life a structure and rhythm. ⁶The traditional eight-hour "shift" allows people to balance their days with productive time and recreational time. ⁷This daily pattern promotes mental health. ⁸In fact, many studies show that when people are unable to work, they experience emotional distress and low self-esteem. ⁹A third way work shapes life is that it causes stress. ¹⁰For some this stress can be positive—resulting in increased performance and professional success. ¹¹For others, however, the stress can be extreme and lead to health problems and illness.

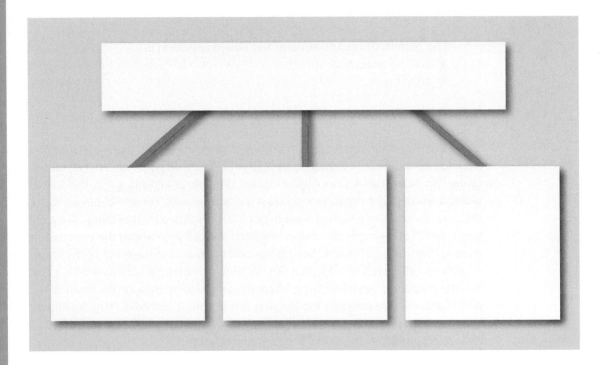

RELATIONSHIPS IN READING: Mastery Test 5

Read each textbook passage, and then answer the questions or follow the directions provided.

A. [1]Scoundrels have cheated their victims throughout history, but the term "confidence man" was apparently coined only in 1849, and it immediately achieved widespread currency. [2]It originated in the story of a swindler of gentlemanly appearance and remarkable boldness named Samuel Thompson. [3]He would approach a well-dressed stranger on the streets of a city and greet him as if he were an old acquaintance. [4]After a brief conversation, Thompson would ask, "Have you confidence in me to trust me with your watch until tomorrow?" [5]The victim, embarrassed to have forgotten this courteous and friendly gentleman and reluctant to deny such a direct request, would lend his watch. [6]Then the "confidence man" would walk off laughing, never to return. [7]He was finally caught by the police only after he was spotted by a previous victim.

_____ 1. The pattern of organization of the above selection is
    A. list of items.
    B. time order.

    2. One of the transitions that signals the pattern of organization is

_____.

B. [1]Many food products are stamped with dates that tell consumers when the product is still fresh. [2]Products are dated in one of three ways. [3]Some food products contain the words "sell by" followed by the date. [4]These foods remain fresh for about one week after the date on the label. [5]Other foods list the date after the words "best if used by." [6]Products with this label can still be used for a few weeks after the date on the label, but they might not have the same quality.

[7]_____, certain products, such as baby formulas, have an expiration date. [8]These products should not be used after the date on the label.

_____ 3. The paragraph
    A. lists ways in which food products are dated.
    B. describes stages in dating food products.

_____ 4. The transition that would best fit the blank space in sentence 7 is
    A. *After.*
    B. *Eventually.*
    C. *Third.*

(Continues on next page)

C.   ¹Dr. Elisabeth Kübler-Ross has identified five stages in the reactions of dying patients. ²The first stage, she says, is denial. ³Patients will at first deny the seriousness of their illness, claiming that some error has been made. ⁴Then patients become angry. ⁵They ask, "Why me?" ⁶Their anger may be directed against God, fate, or even their doctors. ⁷Next comes depression. ⁸During this stage, patients feel hopeless and lose interest in life. ⁹After depression comes bargaining—patients try to bargain for their lives. ¹⁰They may promise God or their doctors that they'll be good, stop smoking, give up alcohol, or do whatever is necessary if only they can survive. ¹¹The fifth stage is that of acceptance. ¹²Patients finally resign themselves to the inevitable. ¹³They are not joyful, but they gain a sense of inner peace. ¹⁴While there has been some criticism of Kübler-Ross's stages, her work has contributed much to making death a more comfortable and better-understood subject.

_____ 5. The pattern of organization of the above selection is
   A. list of items.
   B. time order.

6–10. Complete the map of the paragraph.

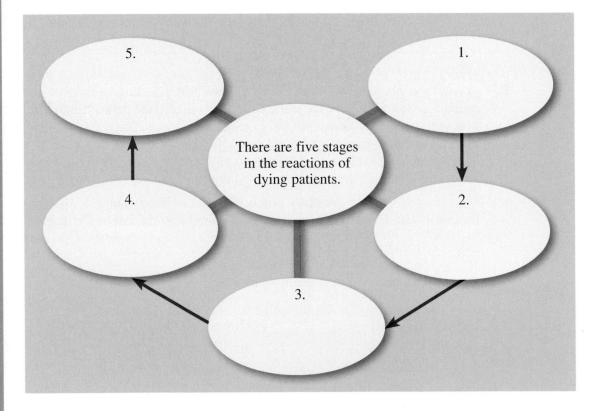

RELATIONSHIPS IN READING: Mastery Test 6

Read each textbook passage, and then answer the questions or follow the directions provided.

A. [1]According to the National Institute on Drug Abuse, thirty million Americans—one out of eight people—suffer from a drug or alcohol dependency. [2]The development of an addiction typically unfolds in four stages. [3]First, some stimulus—drugs, alcohol, sex, chocolate—holds out the promise of short-lived pleasure or excitement. [4]Next, a person discovers that indulging in one of these activities temporarily satisfies some psychological need, making him or her feel good, if only for a short time. [5]Third, certain recurring situations start to trigger the addictive behavior, and the pattern repeats itself. [6]Finally, the habit takes control, and the individual loses self-control. [7]Often, by this stage, a physical dependency will have been added to a psychological one, thereby making the addictive behavior pattern even more difficult to break.

_____ 1. The pattern of organization of the above selection is
    A. list of items.
    B. time order.

2–3. Two of the transitions that introduce the major details of the paragraph are

_____   _____

B. [1]After World War II began, women's roles changed. [2]The most visible change was the sudden appearance of large numbers of women in uniform. [3]The military organized them into auxiliary units with special uniforms, their own officers, and, amazingly, equal pay. [4]Most either filled traditional women's roles, such as nursing, or replaced men in noncombat situations.

[5]Women also substituted for men on the home front. [6]During the war, three million women entered the labor force, and for the first time in history, married working women outnumbered single working women. [7]The war challenged the public's image of proper female behavior, as "Rosie the Riveter" became the popular symbol of women who abandoned traditional jobs as domestic servants and store clerks to work in construction and heavy industry.

_____ 4. The pattern of organization of the above selection is
    A. list of items.
    B. time order.

5. The second major detail is signaled with the transition _____.

_____ 6. The total number of major details is
    A. two.
    B. three.
    C. four.

(Continues on next page)

C.   ¹There are three main ways that children learn their gender roles. ²One is conditioning through rewards and punishments. ³For example, boys who play with model airplanes and girls who play with dolls will usually be encouraged by their parents. ⁴On the other hand, boys who prefer dolls and girls who prefer airplanes will often be criticized or even punished. ⁵Another element is imitation. ⁶Young children will usually imitate adults who they think are like themselves. ⁷This means that boys will usually imitate their fathers and girls their mothers. ⁸The third and perhaps most important element is self-definition. ⁹Children quickly learn that all people are either male or female and define themselves as belonging to one sex rather than the other. ¹⁰They then use this self-definition to choose their future interests and to develop their personalities and social roles.

_____ 7. The pattern of organization of the above selection is
  A. list of items.
  B. time order.

8–10. Complete the outline of the paragraph.

  Main idea: _____

  Major supporting details:

  1. Conditioning through rewards and punishments

  2. _____

  3. _____

6 Relationships in Writing

You learned in Chapter Three that the first two goals in writing are to advance a main idea and to support that idea. A third goal in writing is to organize the support you provide for your main idea. This chapter explains the two most common ways to organize your support: listing order and time order. **Just as a knowledge of listing and time order can make you a better reader, it can make you a better writer.**

Listing Order

Often the supporting material in a paper is organized by using a listing order. A **listing order** uses addition words such as *first, also, another,* and *last of all.* The list might be a list of reasons or of actions or of qualities or of any series of items that are similar in some way. Most of the paragraphs you have looked at so far have had a listing order.

Here is yet another paragraph that uses a list:

> ¹If parents decide to use punishment to control their children, its effectiveness can be increased in several ways. ²The first involves consistency. ³Punishment that is unpredictable is related to especially high rates of disobedience in children. ⁴When parents permit children to act inappropriately on some occasions but scold them on others, children are confused about how to behave, and the unacceptable act persists. ⁵In addition, a warm relationship with children increases the effectiveness of an occasional punishment. ⁶Children of involved and caring parents find the interruption in parental affection that accompanies punishment to be especially unpleasant. ⁷As a result, they want to regain the warmth and approval of parents as quickly as possible. ⁸Last, punishment works best when it comes with an explanation. ⁹The explanation helps children understand the misbehavior and be on guard to not repeat it in the future.

The paragraph orders its supporting details by presenting three ways that parents can use punishment effectively. The addition words that introduce the items in the list are *first, In addition,* and *Last.*

In the previous chapter, you learned that addition words, like all transitions, help writers organize their information and present it clearly to readers. Addition words are as helpful to you as a writer as they are to you as a reader.

Here are words that show addition:

Addition Words

one	to begin with	in addition	last
first	another	next	last of all
first of all	second	moreover	final
for one thing	also	furthermore	finally

PRACTICE 1: Writing a Paragraph with a Listing Order

Write a paragraph that supports one of the following three main ideas:

- There are three ways I am different from my brother (or my sister, or my mother, or my father).

- Although there is a lot I would do if I won the lottery, there are three things in particular that I would do right away.

- There are several advantages (*or* disadvantages) to being an only child.

A Model Paragraph

Here is one student's response to the assignment.

My brother and I look quite a bit alike. But we are very different in three important ways. One way is that I am very social, while Greg is more private. I always want to be with people, the more the better, but he likes being alone or with just one close friend. A second way we are different is how we express ourselves. I am a big talker—it seems that every thought I have comes straight out of my mouth. Greg is much quieter. He thinks things through, and only then will he speak. Finally, I am a pessimist. When a problem comes up, I immediately think, "Oh, no; what a disaster!" Greg is much more optimistic. He calmly says, "Oh, it's not that bad—we can deal with this." Although we are sister and brother and also close friends, we are certainly different.

● What are the addition transitions used in the model paragraph on the previous page? Write them here:

_____   _____   _____

Writing Your Own Paragraph

1. As explained in Chapter 4, there are three prewriting techniques that can help you think about a paper: freewriting, questioning, and list making. Apply one or another of these techniques to each of the three topic sentences on the previous page. You might, for example:

 ● Make up a list of ways that you are different from your brother (or your sister, or your mother, or your father).

 ● Ask yourself what are five or ten things you might want to do right away if you won the lottery.

 ● Freewrite for a page or two about advantages or disadvantages to being an only child.

2. These prewriting techniques will help you determine the topic sentence for which you'll be able to provide the best support. Choose that topic sentence to develop in your paper.

3. Make a scratch outline in which you list the three supporting items in your paper and the order in which you'll present them.

4. Go on to write the first draft of your paper. If you find that you get "stuck" in a major way in providing enough supporting information, remember that you can always go back and choose one of the other topic sentences instead.

5. When writing your paper, perhaps in the second draft, remember to use addition transitions—words such as *first, a second, also, another, a third, last of all*—to signal to your readers each of your three supporting items.

6. After you have completed your next-to-final draft, read it out loud to yourself. If you come upon snags in your reading, chances are there may be grammar or punctuation problems at those points. Use a grammar handbook, if necessary, to see what corrections are needed. Make the required corrections so that every sentence in your paper reads smoothly and clearly.

Time Order

Time order is another very common way to present supporting details. In **time order**, supporting details are presented in the order in which they occurred.

Read the paragraph below, which is organized in a time order. In the spaces provided, write appropriate transitions to show the time relationships. Use each of the following transitions once: *after, as, first, later, then.*

¹In one of the most terrifying scenes in all of literature, George Orwell in his classic novel *1984* describes how a government known as Big Brother destroys a couple's love. ²The couple, Winston and Julia, fall in love and meet secretly, knowing the government would not approve. ³_____ informers turn them in, a government agent named O'Brien takes steps to end their love. ⁴_____ he straps Winston down and explains that he has discovered Winston's worst fear. ⁵_____ he sets a cage with two giant, starving sewer rats on the table next to Winston. ⁶He says that when he presses a lever, the door of the cage will slide up, and the rats will shoot out like bullets and bore straight into Winston's face. ⁷_____ Winston's eyes dart back and forth, revealing his terror, O'Brien places his hand on the lever. ⁸Winston realizes that the only way out is for Julia to take his place. ⁹Suddenly, he hears his own voice screaming, "Do it to Julia! Not me! Julia!" ¹⁰Orwell does not describe Julia's interrogation, but _____, when Julia and Winston see each other, they realize that each has betrayed the other. ¹¹Their love is gone. ¹²Big Brother has won.

The writer makes the main point of her paragraph in the first sentence: "In one of the most terrifying scenes in all of literature, George Orwell in his classic novel *1984* describes how a government known as Big Brother destroys a couple's love." She then supports her point with a detailed description of what the government does. Time words that are used to help connect Orwell's details include the following: "*After* informers turn them in," "*First* he straps," "*Then* he sets," "*As* Winston's eyes," and "but *later*, when."

In the previous chapter, you learned that time words, like all transitions, help writers organize their information and present it clearly to readers. Time words are as helpful to you as a writer as they are to you as a reader.

Here are words that show time:

Time Words

before	immediately	when	until
previously	next	whenever	often
first (of all)	then	while	frequently
second (ly)	following	during	eventually
third (ly)	later	as (soon as)	final(ly)
now	after	by	last (of all)

Note: Some additional ways of showing time are dates ("In 1890 . . . ," "Throughout the 20th century . . . ," "By 2020 . . .") and other time references ("Within a week . . . ," "by the end of the month . . . ," "in two years . . .").

PRACTICE 2: Writing a Paragraph with a Time Order

Write a paragraph about a specific experience you've had that was one of the following:

- nerve-racking
- humbling
- terrifying
- humorous
- depressing
- gratifying
- anger-inducing
- instructive

A Model Paragraph

Here is one student's response to the assignment.

> Flying back from visiting my family in Indiana recently, I had a humorous encounter with a little girl in the airport. Little Maya was a talkative four-year-old who was also headed for Philadelphia. I was flying standby, so I wasn't sure I'd actually get on the flight. We'd been having a great time discussing the plane (we agreed that silver was the prettiest color) and our dogs waiting at home. When Maya and her mom were called to board the plane, she grabbed my hand and said, "Come on! It's time to get on!" I then tried to explain to her that there might not be room for me on the flight. Maya said, "That's just silly!" She immediately dragged me over to the boarding clerk and told him, "This is my friend. She can sit on my lap!"

- What are the time transitions used in the model paragraph above? Write them here:

_____   _____   _____

Writing Your Own Paragraph

1. As explained in Chapter 4, there are three prewriting techniques that can help you think about a paper: freewriting, questioning, and list making. Apply one or another of these techniques to the possible topics on the previous page. You might, for example:

   - Ask yourself what was one of the most nerve-racking or gratifying experiences in your life, when and where this experience happened, why it happened, and what were the details that made it so nerve-racking or gratifying.

   - See if you can make a list of as many details as you can think of about an experience that was anger-inducing or very instructive.

   - Freewrite for a page or two about a humorous or humbling experience in your life.

2. These prewriting techniques will help you determine the experience for which you'll be able to provide the best support. Express that experience in your topic sentence. You might write, for example, "The most nerve-racking experience of my life took place when I was in sixth grade" or "In my senior year of high school, I had the most humbling experience of my life" or "I was never as angry as when a supposed friend of mine betrayed my confidence" or "One of the most instructive moments of my life happened when my dying father spoke to me."

3. Make a scratch outline in which you list the major supporting items in your paper and the time order in which you'll present them.

4. Go on to write the first draft of your story. If you find that you get "stuck" in a major way in providing enough supporting information, remember that you can always go back and choose another experience instead.

5. To help your experience come alive, include some dialog—words that you said or that someone else said. In the model paragraph, you'll notice, we hear the exact words that Maya said.

6. When writing your story, remember to occasionally use time transitions— words such as *first, a second, next, then,* and *eventually*—to help connect one part of your experience with the next as it goes from beginning to end.

7. After you have completed your next-to-final draft, read it out loud to yourself. If you come upon snags in your reading, chances are there may be grammar or punctuation problems at those points. Use a grammar handbook, if necessary, to see what corrections are needed. Make the required corrections so that every sentence in your paper reads smoothly and clearly.

RELATIONSHIPS IN WRITING: Mastery Test 1

A. Complete each sentence with a suitable addition word or words from the box below. Try to use each transition once. Then, in the space provided, write the letter of the transition you have chosen.

A. also	**B.** another	**C.** for one thing
D. in addition	**E.** second	

Hint: Make sure that each word or phrase that you choose fits smoothly into the flow of the sentence. Test your choices by reading each sentence to yourself.

_____ 1. ¹The weather at the North Pole is truly extreme. ²_____, the average winter temperature is more than 20 degrees below zero.

_____ 2. ¹We communicate to exchange information. ²We _____ communicate to develop relationships.

_____ 3. ¹An important dental warning sign is a tooth that shows sensitivity to hot or cold. _____ sign is bleeding gums.

_____ 4. ¹Paranoid people often believe that someone is plotting against them. ²_____, they may believe that everyone is staring at them and talking about them.

_____ 5. ¹Students should get a college degree because it opens more job doors. ²A _____ reason is that their average yearly salary will be much higher.

(Continues on next page)

B. (6–10.) Complete each sentence with a suitable time word from the box below. Use each transition once.

A. final	B. first	C. next
D. secondly	E. then	

¹Are you living with a person who verbally abuses you? ²If so, you owe it to yourself to change your situation. ³The way to succeed is to break the process into manageable steps. ⁴_____ and most important, you must believe that you are not to blame for the abuse. ⁵No doubt your abuser has convinced you that if only you would do A, B, or C differently, he or she would not "have" to become abusive. ⁶This is a lie. ⁷No one "has" to be abusive. ⁸_____, educate yourself about verbal abuse. ⁹Use books or the Internet to read about verbal abuse and how to deal with it. ¹⁰You'll find you are not alone, and that leads to the _____ step: Find a support group. ¹¹Identify people (friends, relatives, a teacher or minister or counselor) you can speak frankly to about your situation and who will give you help. ¹²With increased confidence, you are _____ ready to talk to your partner. ¹³As calmly and firmly as possible, state that you are a person who deserves respect and civil behavior, and that you will accept no less. ¹⁴Offer to go with your partner to a counselor who will help both of you learn new ways to communicate. ¹⁵If your partner does not respond, you must consider the _____ step: Leaving. ¹⁶You were not put here on earth to have your self-esteem destroyed by serving as someone else's verbal punching bag.

RELATIONSHIPS IN WRITING: Mastery Test 2

A. (1–4.) Fill in each blank with an appropriate transition from the box. Use each transition once.

A. also	**B.** final	**C.** first of all
D. second		

[1]A review of the ways the United States deals with its garbage reveals the ongoing problems that we face in getting rid of and limiting our waste. [2]_____, most of the 500,000 tons of waste generated each day in the United States is buried in landfills. [3]Landfills are expensive to construct, fill up rapidly, and can contaminate ground water. [4]A _____ method, incineration, is cheaper and theoretically can pay for itself by producing energy in the form of electricity or steam. [5]The initial construction expense, however, is enormous, and mechanical problems are common. [6]_____ disturbing is the potential threat incinerators pose to public health because of the dangerous toxic gases they emit during burning. [7]The _____ and most important way to deal with our garbage problem lies in recycling—a process that can reduce the amount of garbage produced in the first place. [8]It has been estimated that up to 80 percent of our garbage can be eliminated through separation and recycling. [9]To succeed, this method will have to be much more widely used than it is now.

_____ 5. The pattern of organization of the above selection is
    A. list of items.
    B. time order.

(Continues on next page)

B. (6–9.) Fill in each blank with an appropriate transition from the box. Use each transition once.

A. finally	B. first	C. then
D. while		

¹There has been an overwhelming interest in the story of King Kong from its first appearance in a 1933 movie to the popular remake of that film in 2005. ²The basic story is pretty simple. ³The _____ thing that happens is that filmmakers go to a mysterious island to make a movie about an enormous ape. ⁴The ape _____ snatches the leading lady, with whom he falls in love. ⁵After the ape is captured, he is taken back to the United States and put on display in New York. ⁶The next turn in the plot is that he escapes, grabs the girl again, rampages through the city, and climbs to the top of the Empire State Building. ⁷_____ all of this action is happening, he manages to tenderly protect the girl. ⁸_____, he is mortally wounded by fighter planes, and the massive creature falls to his death. ⁹The story will probably be around forever, having a grip, for whatever mysterious reasons, on our collective imagination.

_____10. The pattern of organization of the above selection is
    A. list of items.
    B. time order.

RELATIONSHIPS IN WRITING: Mastery Test 3

Write a paragraph or essay that you develop by using a list of three or four items. You may want to choose one of the following ideas that you have not yet written about:

- There are three ways I am different from my brother/sister/mother/father.

- Although there is a lot I would do if I won the lottery, there are three things in particular that I would do right away.

- There are several advantages (or disadvantages) to being an only child.

Or you may choose one of the following topics:

- I love visiting my grandparents for several different reasons.

- There are three reasons why students should take a year or more off between high school and college.

- If I could have a makeover, I can think of three things about myself I would definitely want to change.

A Model Paragraph

Here is one student's response to this assignment.

> I always love visiting my grandparents. There are many reasons I enjoy these visits, but three stand out for me. To begin with, they make me feel so welcome. Grandma always rushes out to give me a big hug, and Grandpa beams at me and says, "Well, well—how's my favorite girl?" Secondly, they always take the time to really listen to me. They remember things I've talked about before and will say things like, "And your friend Doug, who was sick—how is he doing?" and "Is your math course still giving you problems?" And last of all, I love visiting them because they are such a wonderful link to my past. They'll pull out photographs of my mother when she was a baby, or my parents as young newlyweds, and tell me stories that really bring the past alive for me. For these reasons and many more, I love visiting my grandparents.

- Underline the topic sentence—the sentence that expresses the main idea of the above paragraph. (You'll note it is not the first sentence.)

- What three addition words does the writer use to signal each of her three supporting reasons?

_____ _____ _____

(Continues on next page)

Writing Your Own Paragraph or Essay

Pick out the topic sentence you think you might be able to write about. Then explore that topic by freewriting about it, or asking questions such as *what, when, where, how,* and *why* about it, or making a list of all the details you can think of about it. Prewriting will help you determine the topic for which you can provide the best supporting details.

See if you can develop the topic with even more details, and prepare a scratch outline of the paragraph or essay. Then go on to write the first and later drafts of your paper.

RELATIONSHIPS IN WRITING: Mastery Test 4

You have probably already written at least one paragraph that uses a time order and time words: a story about a specific experience. Now write a paragraph or an essay on one of the processes described below. A **process** involves a series of steps carried out in a time order: first one does this, then this, next this, and so on.

- How to cook a favorite dish
- How to throw a successful party
- How to sell your car
- How to get over an everyday fear
- How to make a diet work
- How to achieve a healthier lifestyle
- How to win friends and influence people
- How to get a high grade in a class

A Model Paragraph

Here is a paragraph a student wrote on a similar topic—how to eat a healthier diet.

> You want to eat a healthier diet? Of course you do. But it's hard to know where to begin. That's why I'm here to help! In order to eat better, you need to follow these helpful steps. First, go through your kitchen and throw away every item of processed food you own. I'm looking at you, Double Stuff Oreos. Don't try to hide back there in the cupboard, Velveeta Shells and Cheese. Out with them! Processed foods are loaded with sugar, salt, and fat, and those are all the enemies of weight loss. If they aren't in your house, you won't be tempted to eat them. Next, go back to the grocery store. Push your cart (at a good quick pace—you're burning calories!) around the periphery of the store—the outer edge only. That is where you will find the fruits and vegetables and lean meat and fish that should be the bulk of your diet. Do not go into the other aisles! The other aisles are evil! It's there that you'll be tempted to stock up on the likes of Memphis BBQ Pringles, Dr. Pepper, and the Pasta Roni Fettuccine Alfredo. Lastly, take your wonderful, healthy bags of fruits, veggies, lean meat and fish home and hit the Internet. Type in "healthy recipes" and the names of the ingredients you've bought. Have fun experimenting with the recipes that come up. In no time, you'll be eating a healthier diet than you have ever eaten before.

(Continues on next page)

- Underline the topic sentence—the sentence that expresses the main idea of the above paragraph. (You'll note it is not the first sentence.)

- What three transitions (signal words) does the writer use to guide the reader from one part of the process to the next?

_____   _____   _____

Writing Your Own Paragraph or Essay

Pick out the process you think you might be able to write about. Then explore that topic by freewriting about it, or asking questions such as *what, when, where, how,* and *why* about it, or making a list of all the details you can think of about it. Prewriting will help you determine the topic for which you can provide the best supporting details.

See if you can develop the topic with even more details, and prepare a scratch outline of the paper. In the outline, first write out the point of your paragraph or essay. Here is the scratch outline prepared by the author of the model paragraph shown above:

> In order to eat better, follow these helpful steps.
> 1. Throw away all your processed food.
> 2. Visit the periphery of your grocery store to get real food.
> 3. Find healthy recipes on the Internet.

After you prepare your scratch outline, go on to write the first and later drafts of your paper. When you think you have the final draft of your paper, read it aloud to make sure that every sentence reads smoothly and clearly. If that is not the case, you still have a bit of work to do. Use a grammar handbook, if necessary, to help remove the trouble spots.

7 More Relationships in Reading

Good readers and writers understand the relationships between ideas. This chapter explains four additional basic relationships you should recognize as a reader.

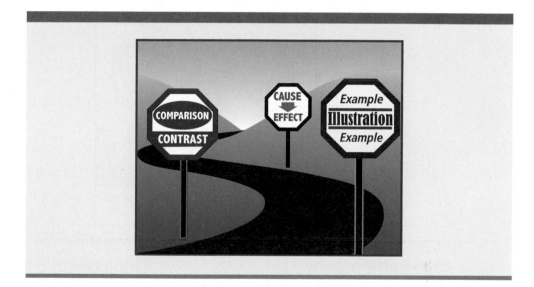

In Chapter 5, "Relationships in Reading" (pages 121–138), you learned about two common types of relationships: ones that involve **addition** and ones that involve **time**. In this chapter, you will learn about more relationships you should recognize as a reader: **illustration, comparison, contrast, and cause and effect**.

1 Illustration

Words That Show Illustration

Put a check (✓) beside the item that is easier to understand:

___ I've become very absent-minded. Last week I went to work on my day off.

___ I've become very absent-minded. Last week, for instance, I went to work on my day off.

The second item is easier to understand. The words *for instance* make it clear that what happened on that day off is just one example of the absent-mindedness. *For instance* and other words and phrases like it are illustration words.

Illustration **words** indicate that an author will provide one or more *examples* to develop and clarify a given idea. In the cartoon above, the speaker gives an example of a food that is high in protein.

Here are some common words that introduce examples:

Illustration Words

(for) example	including	(as an) illustration	one
(for) instance	specifically	to illustrate	once
such as	to be specific		

Examples

The following items contain illustration words. Notice how these words signal that one or more *examples* are coming.

● Certain colors are associated with particular emotions. *For instance*, green represents jealousy, red stands for anger, and blue means "gloomy."

● My grandmother doesn't hear well anymore. *For example,* whenever I say, "Hi, Granny," she answers, "Fine, just fine."

● A cat's curiosity can get it into ridiculous situations. *Once,* a neighbor's cat got its head stuck in the garbage disposal.

PRACTICE 1

Complete each item with a suitable illustration word or phrase from the box on the previous page. Try to use a variety of transitions.

> *Hint:* Make sure that each word or phrase that you choose fits smoothly into the flow of the sentence. Test each choice by reading the sentence aloud.

1. Animals were once tried for crimes. _____, in 1740 a cow convicted of witchcraft was hanged by the neck until dead.

2. Some soap opera fans take the shows too seriously. There are viewers, _____, who actually send threats to soap opera "villains."

3. My mother believes in various superstitions, _____ the idea that if you drop a fork, it means company's coming.

4. When a couple divorces, the partners often experience a wide range of emotions, _____ anger, regret, depression, and relief.

5. People have chosen to end their lives in a variety of unusual ways. As an _____, in ancient China, people committed suicide by eating a pound of salt.

Illustration words are common in all types of writing. One way they are used in textbooks is in the pattern of organization known as the definition and example pattern.

The Definition and Example Pattern

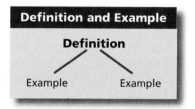

To get a sense of the definition and example pattern, try to arrange the following sentences in an order that makes sense. Put a *1* in front of the sentence that should come first, a *2* in front of the sentence that comes next, and a *3* in front of the sentence that should be last. The result will be a short paragraph.

____ Someone might, for instance, sit calmly through a friend's criticism and act as if it didn't bother him or her.

____ Apathy is an avoidance response in which a person acknowledges unpleasant information but pretends he or she does not care about it.

____ Another example is responding to the loss of a job by acting indifferent: "Who cares? It was a dumb job anyhow."

This paragraph begins with a definition: "Apathy is an avoidance response in which a person acknowledges unpleasant information but pretends he or she does not care about it." The second sentence makes clear this meaning of *apathy* with an example: "Someone might, for instance, sit calmly through a friend's criticism and act as if it didn't bother him or her." The third sentence then provides an added example: "Another example is responding to the loss of a job by acting indifferent: 'Who cares? It was a dumb job anyhow.'" The second and third sentences include the illustration words *for instance* and *example*. As you can see, the **definition and example** pattern of organization includes just what its name suggests: a definition and one or more examples.

An Important Study Hint: Good textbook authors want to help readers understand the important ideas and terms in a subject—whether it is psychology, sociology, business, biology, or any other field. Such authors often take time, then, to include key definitions. The ideas and terms being defined are usually set off in *italic* or **boldface** type, and the definitions are signaled by such words as *is, are, is called, termed,* and *refers to.* Here are some definitions from a variety of textbooks:

- An **instinct** is a form of behavior that occurs in all normal members of a species without having been learned.

- **Phobias** are fears that are out of proportion to the actual danger involved in a situation.

- **Divergent thinking** refers to the ability to generate unusual, yet nonetheless appropriate, responses to problems or questions.

- Once a tumor has been detected, cells can be removed from it in a procedure called a **biopsy**; the cells are then examined under the microscope by a pathologist.

- Party funding, along with the money a candidate receives from individual contributors and interest groups, is termed **hard money** since it goes directly to the candidate and can be spent as he or she chooses.

- Both rapidly growing countries and slowly growing countries can have a problem with their **dependency ratio**—the number of nonworking compared to working individuals in a population.

If an author defines a term, you can assume that it is important enough to learn. So when reading and taking notes on a textbook, always do two things:

1) Write down key definitions.

2) Put an "Ex" in the margin next to a helpful example for each definition. When a definition is general and abstract, examples are often essential to make its meaning clear.

✔ Check Your Understanding

The following paragraph defines a word, explains it a bit, and then gives an example of it. After reading the paragraph, see if you can answer the questions that follow.

> [1]Acrophobia is an intense, unreasonable fear of high places. [2]People with acrophobia exhibit emotional and physical symptoms in response to being at great heights. [3]For instance, one sufferer of extreme acrophobia, Sally Maxwell, is unable to go above the third floor of any building without feeling enormous anxiety. [4]Her acrophobia began one evening when she was working alone in her office on the eighth floor of a large building. [5]Suddenly she was struck with terror by the idea that she might jump or fall out the open window. [6]She crouched behind a steel filing cabinet, trembling, unable to move. [7]When she finally gathered her belongings and left the building, she was sweating, her breathing was rapid, and her heart was pounding. [8]Yet she had no rational explanation for her fears.

What word is being defined? _____

What is the definition?   _____

_____

Which sentence explains more about the word? _____

In which sentence does the example begin? _____

Explanation

The word *acrophobia* is defined in the first sentence—"an intense, unreasonable fear of high places." The second sentence explains a bit more about acrophobia. The story about Sally Maxwell, which begins in the third sentence, provides an example of how acrophobia affects one sufferer. The example helps make the new term clear to the reader. The author introduces that illustration with the transition *For instance.*

PRACTICE 2

A. The following passage includes a definition and two examples. Underline the term being defined. Then, in the spaces provided, write the number of the definition sentence and the number of the sentence where each example begins.

[1]Shaping is a way to teach a new behavior by encouraging a series of small bits of the whole behavior. [2]This approach, for instance, was used to teach a disturbed little boy named Dickey to wear eyeglasses after cataract surgery. [3]His physician feared that without glasses, his vision would deteriorate permanently. [4]At the mere mention of eyeglasses, however, Dickey threw terrible temper tantrums. [5]So researchers used shaping to ease him into the idea of wearing his glasses. [6]Dickey was deprived of his breakfast so that food could be used as a reward. [7]He received a bit of food each time he picked up some glasses frames. [8]Later in the procedure, he had to put glasses on in order to receive a reward. [9]Within eighteen days, Dickey had learned through gradual steps to wear his glasses for twelve hours a day.

[10]Another example is teaching a circus tiger to jump through a flaming hoop. [11]The tiger might first be rewarded for jumping up on a pedestal and then for leaping from that pedestal to another. [12]Eventually, the hoop would be set on fire, and the tiger would have to leap through the burning hoop to be rewarded.

Definition _____ *Example 1* _____ *Example 2* _____

B. The following passage includes a definition and one example. Underline the term being defined. Then take study notes on the selection by doing two things: (1) filling in the word being defined and its definition; (2) in a few words, summarizing the example.

[1]Jonathan Swift (1667–1745), author of *Gulliver's Travels,* often used irony—saying one thing but meaning another—in his writing. [2]For example, in his famous essay "A Modest Proposal," he makes this suggestion for ending the famine in Ireland: the Irish should raise babies to be eaten. [3]Swift did not mean his suggestion to be taken seriously. [4]His actual goal was to shock his British audience into facing the mass starvation and misery in Ireland that British policies had produced at that time.

_____ — _____

_____

Example— _____

_____

2 Comparison and Contrast

Words That Show Comparison

Put a check (✓) beside the item that is easier to understand:

____ Driving a car is a skill that we learn through practice. Writing a paper is a skill that we learn through hands-on experience.

____ Driving a car is a skill that we learn through practice. Similarly, writing a paper is a skill that we learn through hands-on experience.

The first item makes us wonder, "What has learning to drive a car got to do with writing a paper?" The word *similarly* makes it clear that the author intends to compare learning to write a paper with learning to drive a car. *Similarly* and words like it are comparison words.

© Randy Glasbergen
www.glasbergen.com

"You and I are more alike than most people think. We have similar habits—we demand to be fed several times a day, and we enjoy sleeping on the furniture. And we both shed a lot."

Comparison words signal similarities. Authors use a comparison transition to show that a second idea is *like* the first one in some way. In the above cartoon, the words *alike, similar,* and *both* show the dog is making a comparison between himself and the cat. The dog names three ways he and the cat are similar: both of them want to be fed several times a day, sleep on the furniture, and shed a lot.

Here are some common words that show comparison:

Comparison Words

(just) as	both	in like fashion	in a similar fashion
(just) like	equal(ly)	in like manner	in a similar manner
alike	resemble	similar(ly)	(in) the same way
same	likewise	similarity	(in) common

Examples

The sentences below contain comparison words. Notice how these words show that things are *alike* in some way.

- When buying milk, my mother always takes a bottle from the back of the shelf. *Similarly,* when my father buys a newspaper, he usually grabs one from the middle of the pile.

- Moviemakers with a big hit tend to repeat the winning idea in their next film, *just like* authors who use a successful plot over and over.

- The printing press greatly changed the way people learned news and ideas. *In a similar manner,* the Internet has revolutionized the way in which people obtain information.

PRACTICE 3

Complete each sentence with a suitable comparison word or phrase from the box on the previous page. Try to use a variety of transitions.

1. Checking messages on your cell phone in a darkened theater will not win you any friends. _____, talking out loud with your movie partner will soon make people scowl in your direction.

2. _____ an athlete in training, the mind of a reader grows stronger with practice.

3. Spicy foods make me very thirsty. Believe it or not, ice cream affects me _____.

4. The Amish people farm their land _____ their 18th-century relatives did, without benefit of gasoline-powered tractors or other modern equipment.

5. _____ rats become hostile when they live in a crowded cage, humans become aggressive in crowded conditions.

Words That Show Contrast

Put a check (✓) beside the item that is easier to understand:

___ A roller coaster scares many people. They love riding on it.

___ Even though a roller coaster scares many people, they love riding on it.

In the first item, the two sentences seem to contradict each other. We want to ask, "Do people like a roller coaster, or don't they?" In the second item, the phrase *even though* makes clear the relationship between the two ideas: In spite of the fact that a roller coaster is scary, people still love riding on it. *Even though* and other words and phrases like it are contrast words.

www.glasbergen.com

"The main difference between us is that I spend all my money on shoes."

Contrast words show that things *differ* in one or more ways. In the above cartoon, the speaker uses the contrast word *difference* to signal a major distinction between two insects.

Here are some common words that show contrast:

Contrast Words

but	instead (of)	even though	difference
yet	in contrast	as opposed to	different(ly)
however	on the other hand	in spite of	differ (from)
although	(on the) contrary	despite	unlike
nevertheless	converse(ly)	rather than	while
still	opposite		

Examples

The above cartoon and the sentences below contain contrast words. Notice how these words signal that one idea is *different from* another idea.

● People used to think that getting chilled would lead to catching a cold. *However,* getting chilled has nothing to do with getting sick.

- Skunks are unpopular creatures, *yet* they eat lots of mice and bugs and don't spray unless they feel threatened.

- Some people look upon eating as something to be done quickly so they can get on to better things. *In contrast,* others think eating *is* one of the better things.

PRACTICE 4

Complete each sentence with a suitable contrast word or phrase from the box on the previous page. Try to use a variety of transitions.

1. Most of us could live without food for a month; _____, we need two quarts of water a day to survive.

2. _____ going up a ladder is easy, looking down from the top can be difficult.

3. At first we were planning on spending our vacation at a campground,

   _____ now we've decided to save money by relaxing at home.

4. Paula was not satisfied with her paper _____ the fact that she had already written five drafts.

5. We use seventeen muscles to smile. _____, we have to use forty-three muscles to frown.

Comparison and contrast transitions are often used in paragraphs organized in the comparison and/or contrast pattern.

The Comparison and/or Contrast Pattern

To get a sense of the comparison and/or contrast pattern, try to arrange the following sentences in an order that makes sense. Put a *1* in front of the sentence that should come first, a *2* in front of the sentence that comes next, and a *3* in front of the sentence that should be last. The result will be a short paragraph.

____ Yet the large, hairy tarantula is relatively harmless, while the small brown recluse is dangerously poisonous.

____ The tarantula and the brown recluse are more different than they are similar.

____ It's true that both spiders are alike in inspiring a great deal of fear.

The first sentence of this paragraph is the general one, the one with the main idea: "The tarantula and the brown recluse are more different than they are similar." The words *similar* and *different* suggest a comparison and/or contrast pattern of organization. The comparison word *alike* and the contrast words *yet* and *while* in the other two sentences show that the spiders are indeed being compared *and* contrasted: "It's true that both spiders are alike in inspiring a great deal of fear. Yet the large, hairy tarantula is relatively harmless, while the small brown recluse is dangerously poisonous."

The **comparison-contrast** pattern shows how two things are alike or how they are different, or both. When things are compared, their similarities are pointed out; when they are contrasted, their differences are discussed. (The tarantula and the brown recluse spider are alike in the fear they inspire; they are different in the effects of their bites, as well as in their appearance.)

You will find authors using a **comparison** pattern to show how two things are alike and a **contrast** pattern to show how they are different. Sometimes an author will compare and contrast in the same paragraph, pointing out both similarities and differences between two things. Comparison or contrast transitions will signal what an author is doing.

✓ *Check Your Understanding*

In the following paragraph, the main idea is stated in the first sentence. As is often the case, the main idea suggests a paragraph's pattern of organization. Here the transition *differently* is a hint that the paragraph may be organized in a comparison and/or contrast pattern. Read the paragraph and answer the questions below. Then read the explanation that follows.

> [1]In middle age, men and women often view life very differently, especially if they are couples who have led traditional lives. [2]By middle age, the husband is often comfortable in his position at work and has given up any dreams of advancing further. [3]He may then become more family-oriented. [4]In contrast, once the children are grown, the wife may find herself free to explore interests and develop abilities she has had no time for in the previous fifteen or twenty years. [5]Unlike her husband, she may be more interested in non-family activities than she was before.

1. Is this paragraph comparing, contrasting, or both? _____

2. What two things are being compared and/or contrasted? _____

   _____

3. What three comparison or contrast transition words or phrases are used in

   the paragraph? _____

Explanation

This paragraph is only contrasting, not comparing—it discusses only differences, not similarities. The two things being contrasted are the views of traditional middle-aged men and women. The transition words or phrases that show contrast are *differently*, *In contrast*, and *Unlike*.

PRACTICE 5

A. The following passage uses the pattern of either comparison or contrast. Read the passage and answer the questions that follow.

> ¹Employment policies are quite different in Japan and the United States. ²In Japan, teamwork is an essential part of hiring and promotion. ³College graduates who join a corporation are all paid about the same starting salary. ⁴To learn about the company's various departments, they are rotated as a team through the organization. ⁵They are also promoted as a team. ⁶Only in later years are individuals singled out for recognition. ⁷When there is an opening in the firm, outsiders are not even considered.
>
> ⁸In the United States, on the other hand, an employee is hired on the basis of what the firm thinks that individual can contribute. ⁹Employees try to outperform others, and they strive for raises and promotions as signs of personal success. ¹⁰The individual's loyalty is to himself or herself, not to the company. ¹¹Outsiders are considered for openings in U.S. firms.

Check (✓) the pattern which is used in this passage:

_____ Comparison

_____ Contrast

What two things are being compared or contrasted?

1. _____   2. _____

B. The following paragraph uses the pattern of either comparison or contrast. Read the passage and then answer the questions and complete the map that follows.

> ¹Among the school experiences new to young children is the regimented environment. ²At home, children may have been able to do what they wanted when they wanted to do it. ³But in school, they are given a set time for talking, working, playing, eating, and even going to the toilet. ⁴Another source of anxiety may be the public method of discipline that some teachers use. ⁵Whereas at home children are scolded in private, in school they may be held up to embarrassment in front of their peers. ⁶"Mandy," the teacher may say, "why are you the only one in

the class who didn't do your homework?" ⁷Or, "Scott, why are you the only one who can't work quietly at your seat?" ⁸Last, a child may be scared by the competitive atmosphere of the school. ⁹At home, one hopes, such competition for attention is minimal. ¹⁰In school, however, children may vie for the teacher's approving glance or tone of voice, or for stars on a paper, or for favored seats in the front row.

Check (✓) the pattern which is used in this passage:

___ Comparison

___ Contrast

Complete the following map of the paragraph:

There are three differences between _____ and _____.	
1. Regimentation in school	Free movement at home
2.	
3.	

3 Cause and Effect

Words That Show Cause and Effect

Put a check (✓) beside the item that is easier to understand:

_____ The paint has worn off the wooden siding. Fungus has begun to grow on it.

_____ Because the paint has worn off the wooden siding, fungus has begun to grow on it.

In the first item, it seems the author is simply listing two things that have happened to the wooden siding. The word *because* in the second item makes clear the relationship between the two ideas—the protective paint wore off, and for this reason, the fungus was able to grow. *Because* and words like it are cause and effect words.

© 2007 by Randy Glasbergen.
www.glasbergen.com

GLASBERGEN

"It's an adjustable mortgage. If interest rates go up,
then your payment increases. If interest rates go down,
then your payment increases."

Cause and effect words signal that the author is explaining *the reason why* something happened or *the result* of something happening. In the cartoon above, the applicant is told that the result of interest rates going up or down will, unfortunately for him, be the same: Either way, his mortgage payment will go up!

Here are some common words that show cause and effect:

Cause and Effect Words

therefore	so	owing to	because (of)
thus	(as a) result	effect	reason
(as a) consequence	results in	cause	explanation
consequently	leads (led) to	if . . . then	accordingly
due to	since	affect	depend(s) on

Examples

The above cartoon and the sentences that follow contain cause and effect words. Notice how these words introduce a *reason* for something or the *result* of something.

● My sister became a vegetarian *because* she doesn't want to eat anything that had a mother.

● *If* the weather gets too humid, *then* the wooden doors in our house swell up and begin to stick.

● At one time in history, birth records were not kept for ordinary people. *As a result,* the only birthday parties given were for kings, queens, and other royalty.

PRACTICE 6

Complete each sentence with a suitable cause and effect word or phrase from the box on the previous page. Try to use a variety of transitions.

1. _____ property taxes in the city have gone sky-high, many corporations are moving to the suburbs.

2. Maria's resumé is impressive; _____, she has already had several job interviews.

3. My family is full of great Italian cooks, _____ canned ravioli tastes like cardboard to me.

4. _____ car dealers have a monthly quota of cars to sell, they are more likely to offer good deals near the end of a month.

5. Some zoo animals have not learned how to be good parents. _____, baby animals are sometimes brought up in zoo nurseries and even in private homes.

Cause and effect transitions often signal the cause and effect pattern of organization.

The Cause and Effect Pattern

To get a sense of the cause and effect pattern, try to arrange the following sentences in an order that makes sense. Put a *1* in front of the sentence that should come first, a *2* in front of the sentence that comes next, and a *3* in front of the sentence that should be last. The result will be a short paragraph.

____ Growing up without parents around resulted in the monkeys drinking enormous amounts of alcohol.

____ A study of monkeys suggests two factors may lead to alcoholism.

____ Low levels of serotonin in the brain also caused the monkeys to drink more.

As the words *resulted in, lead to,* and *caused* suggest, this paragraph is organized in a cause and effect pattern. The paragraph begins with the general idea: "A study of monkeys suggests two factors may lead to alcoholism." Next come two causes: "Growing up without parents around resulted in the monkeys drinking enormous amounts of alcohol. Low levels of serotonin in the brain also caused the monkeys to drink more."

Note that even in the cause and effect pattern—or any other pattern—addition words may be used to introduce points and show their order. The last sentence of the above paragraph, for example, includes the word *also,* showing that a second point is being added to the first: "Low levels of serotonin in the brain also caused the monkeys to drink more."

Information in a **cause and effect** pattern addresses the questions "Why does a behavior or event happen?" and/or "What are the results of a behavior or event?" An author may then discuss causes, or effects, or both causes and effects.

Authors usually don't just tell what happened; they try to explain both what happened and why. A textbook section on the sinking of the ship *Titanic*, for example, would be incomplete if it did not include the cause of the disaster—going at a high speed, the ship collided with an iceberg. Or if the number of homeless families in the country increases, journalists will not simply report the increase. They would also explore the reasons for and effects of that increase.

✔ *Check Your Understanding*

Read the paragraph below and see if you can answer the questions about cause and effect that follow. Then read the explanation to see how you did.

> [1]Even the best listeners are unable to listen carefully to everything they hear. [2]One reason is the overload of messages we encounter each day. [3]Besides the numerous hours we spend hearing others speak, we may spend several more hours listening to the radio or television. [4]It just isn't possible to avoid having our attention wander at least part of this time. [5]Another cause of poor listening is a preoccupation with personal concerns. [6]A romance gone sour or a good grade on a test may take prominence in our mind even as someone is speaking to us. [7]In addition, being surrounded by noise may result in poor listening. [8]For example, many voices at a noisy party or the sound of traffic may make it difficult for us to hear everything that is being said.

1. What are the three causes described in this paragraph?

   A. _____

   B. _____

   C. _____

2. The three causes lead to what result or effect? _____

_____

3. What three cause and effect signal words or phrases are used?

_____

Explanation

The paragraph begins with the main idea: "The best listeners are unable to listen carefully to everything they hear." That point is then supported by three reasons, or causes. The first is the overload of messages we hear each day. The second reason is our preoccupation with personal concerns. The third cause given is that we are at times surrounded by interfering noise. The effect is stated in the main idea—our inability to listen carefully to everything we hear. The cause and effect signals used are *reason, cause,* and *result in.*

PRACTICE 7

A. Read the paragraph below, looking for one cause and three main effects (the three major details). Then complete the map that follows.

> ¹Chronic stress can lead to many serious health problems. ²One effect of stress is painful muscle tension. ³Headaches, backaches and sore shoulders are direct consequences of this tension. ⁴Another result of long-term exposure to stress is a weakening of the body's immune system. ⁵The body is then more vulnerable to infection and diseases, and normal colds or minor infections are more likely to develop into serious illnesses. ⁶Third, stress can result in psychological disorders, including depression, anxiety, phobias, and addictions. ⁷In one way or another, our bodies will eventually protest a prolonged exposure to stressful situations.

(Cause)

(Effect)

(Effect)

(Effect)

B. Read the paragraph below, looking for the one effect and the four causes. Then complete the outline that follows.

> ¹There are a number of motivations for shoplifting. ²Poverty is one cause; research indicates that poor people are more likely than others to shoplift, in particular when unemployment is high. ³A second reason is to stretch a budget by stealing some things rather than buying them. ⁴Shoplifters also steal because of the sense of excitement that they experience in daring to break the law. ⁵Yet another explanation, especially among youngsters, is the desire for social acceptance; when asked why they shoplift, many young people say, "Because my friends are doing it."

Main idea *(the effect):* _____

Major supporting details *(the causes):*

1. _____

2. _____

3. _____

4. _____

A Note on Main Ideas and Patterns of Organization

Remember that a paragraph's main idea often indicates its pattern of organization. For example, here is the main idea of a paragraph you worked on earlier:

> In middle age, men and women often view life very differently, especially if they are couples who have led traditional lives.

This sentence may have made you expect that the paragraph would go on to contrast the views of middle-aged men and women. If so, the paragraph would be organized according to the comparison and/or contrast pattern.

✓ *Check Your Understanding*

Finding the main idea of a paragraph may help you decide on its pattern of organization. Try, for instance, to guess the pattern of paragraphs with these main ideas:

> The development of the automobile in the early twentieth century resulted in a number of changes in U.S. society.

Pattern: _____

> A franchise is a business arrangement in which an individual obtains rights from a larger company to sell a well-known product or service.

Pattern: _____

Explanation

In the first sentence, the words *resulted in* suggest that the paragraph will have a cause and effect pattern, discussing the social effects of the introduction of the automobile. In the second sentence, the word *franchise* is defined, suggesting that the paragraph will follow a definition and example pattern, with examples of various franchises to follow.

PRACTICE 8

Most of the main ideas below come from college textbooks. In the space provided, write the letter of the pattern of organization that each suggests.

_____ 1. A communicable disease is one in which an infectious organism is usually passed from person to person.
    A. Definition and example   B. Comparison and/or contrast   C. Cause and effect

_____ 2. Following are three reasons for the existence of stereotypes.
    A. Definition and example   B. Comparison and/or contrast   C. Cause and effect

_____ 3. College students in their thirties and forties face many of the same pressures as younger students, but they are often better equipped to withstand these pressures.
    A. Definition and example   B. Comparison and/or contrast   C. Cause and effect

_____ 4. A growing concern with health has affected the way that many Americans eat.
    A. Definition and example   B. Comparison and/or contrast   C. Cause and effect

_____ 5. A mission statement is an organization's declaration of how it will achieve its purpose.
    A. Definition and example   B. Comparison and/or contrast   C. Cause and effect

_____ 6. Americans typically think of men as naturally better suited to perform the most strenuous physical labor, but not all peoples of the world hold the same view.
    A. Definition and example   B. Comparison and/or contrast   C. Cause and effect

_____ 7. Because of economic pressures, increasing numbers of people are seeking housing assistance.
A. Definition and example   B. Comparison and/or contrast   C. Cause and effect

_____ 8. Nonverbal communication behaviors are those bodily actions and vocal qualities that accompany a verbal message and have agreed-upon interpretations within a culture.
A. Definition and example   B. Comparison and/or contrast   C. Cause and effect

_____ 9. There are several possible explanations for why retail prices often end on certain numbers.
A. Definition and example   B. Comparison and/or contrast   C. Cause and effect

_____10. First-year college students who expect to do well in school need to learn quickly the right and wrong ways of preparing for exams.
A. Definition and example   B. Comparison and/or contrast   C. Cause and effect

A Final Point

Keep in mind that a passage may often be made up of more than one pattern of organization. For instance, the paragraph in this chapter about acrophobia (the unreasonable fear of high places) uses the definition and example pattern. But the example itself—a series of events on one evening in Sally Maxwell's life—uses a time order pattern.

Or consider the following passage:

> [1]Have you ever had the experience of recognizing someone's face but not being able to recall his or her name? [2]The reason is that the information about that person is split up and stored in the two different sides of your brain, and each side has its own way of thinking and remembering. [3]Recalling someone's face is the task of the right side of your brain, which understands whole things at once and is responsible for visualizing, recognizing similarities, and supplying intuitions. [4]This side of your brain provides insights that are hard to put into words. [5]The left side of your brain deals with language and stores words themselves, including the person's name that you have temporarily forgotten. [6]This is the side responsible for speaking, reading, writing, and listening.

The paragraph uses, in part, a cause and effect pattern, explaining the reason why we may recognize a face but not recall a name. It also uses a contrast pattern, explaining the different functions of the two sides of the brain.

MORE RELATIONSHIPS IN READING: Mastery Test 1

A. Fill in each blank with an appropriate transition from the box. Use each transition once. Then, in the spaces provided, write the letter of the transition you have chosen.

A. because	**B.** for example	**C.** in contrast
D. just as	**E.** therefore	

Hint: Make sure that each word or phrase that you choose fits smoothly into the flow of the sentence. Test your choices by reading each sentence to yourself.

_____ 1. ¹Some thieves read the newspapers to find out good times to rob houses. ²_____, after reading the obituaries, such thieves may "clean out" a home while the family is at a loved one's funeral.

_____ 2. ¹Whenever something bad happens to me, my grandmother tries to help me through it. ²When I was depressed after breaking up with my boyfriend, she told me, "_____ we must go through the storm before seeing the rainbow, we often must experience sorrow before joy."

_____ 3. ¹Honeybees attack just to protect their hives. ²_____, if you run away from the hive when attacked, the bees will eventually lose interest in you.

_____ 4. ¹_____ there are no clocks in gambling casinos, gamblers can easily lose all sense of time. ²That is clearly what the casino management wants to happen. ³The longer people stay at the tables or in front of the slot machines, the better.

_____ 5. ¹Most birds are born in either of two very different states. ²Some are born weak, blind, and usually naked. ³About all they can do for themselves is open their mouths for food. ⁴_____, other newborn baby birds are bright-eyed and covered with down. ⁵As soon as their down is dry, they are able to peck at things and run after their parents.

(Continues on next page)

B. Label each item with the letter of its main pattern of organization.

    A Definition and example
    B Comparison and/or contrast
    C Cause and effect

_____ 6. ¹Phobias are intense, irrational fears that are out of proportion to the actual danger in a situation. ²For example, people with the fear of open places (agoraphobia) are often reluctant to leave their homes.

_____ 7. ¹Bread made with whole-wheat flour is brown, but not all brown bread is whole-wheat bread. ²Some manufacturers add molasses or honey to white-flour dough to give it a brown color, and they are allowed to label the product "wheat bread." ³For this reason, it is important to read the package label before buying.

_____ 8. ¹Prison overcrowding is dangerous because it increases unrest among inmates and produces a climate in which violence is more likely. ²Riots, escapes, and hostage taking become more of a problem. ³Prison overcrowding also makes it more difficult for correctional officers and prison administrators to manage the prison. ⁴The result is that prisons are more costly to run.

_____ 9. ¹In the 1890s, most Americans were struggling to reach a middle-class lifestyle. ²By the 1990s, in contrast, an overwhelming majority had achieved the middle class but were either losing it or struggling to hold on to it. ³In the 1890s, government responded to the prodding of reform-minded citizens and began to create a framework of rules to control the excesses of giant businesses and to protect the interests of the average citizen. ⁴But in the 1990s, that framework of controls on large corporations was steadily dismantled.

_____10. ¹What sociologist George Ritzer has termed the "McDonaldization of society"—the standardization of everyday life—does not refer just to the robotlike assembly of food. ²As Ritzer points out, this process is occurring throughout our society—and it is transforming our lives. ³For instance, shopping malls offer one-stop shopping in controlled environments. ⁴Travel agencies offer "package" tours. ⁵They will transport middle-class Americans to ten European capitals in fourteen days. ⁶All visitors experience the same hotels, restaurants, and other scheduled sites—and no one need fear meeting a "real" native. ⁷The newspaper *USA Today* spews out McNews—short, blank, unanalytical pieces that can be digested between gulps of the McShake or the McBurger.

MORE RELATIONSHIPS IN READING: Mastery Test 2

Read each textbook passage and answer the questions or follow the directions provided.

A. [1]The incomes of middle- and working-class Americans were dealt a severe blow during the 1980s. [2]A major reason was a decline in industrial jobs. [3]The economy became less devoted to manufacturing goods and more focused on providing services. [4]Many manufacturing jobs, especially in the steel and auto industries, were transferred from the United States to Third World countries. [5]As a result, millions of blue-collar workers in the Midwest and Northeast were stranded. [6]They were forced into much lower-paying jobs with fewer benefits and opportunities for advancement.

_____ 1. The main pattern of organization of the paragraph is
   A. definition and example.
   B. cause and effect.
   C. comparison and/or contrast.

2. One transition that signals the pattern of organization of this paragraph is _____.

B. [1]Boys who mature early physically have a decided advantage over their more slowly maturing peers. [2]Early maturers become heroes in sports and leaders in both formal and informal activities. [3]Other boys look up to them; girls have crushes on them. [4]Even adults tend to trust them. [5]They are more self-confident and independent than other boys. [6]In contrast, their less mature male peers, with their high-pitched voices and underdeveloped physiques, feel inadequate. [7]They are weaker at sports and more awkward with girls.

_____ 3. The main pattern of organization of the paragraph is
   A. definition and example.
   B. cause and effect.
   C. comparison and/or contrast.

4. The transition that signals the pattern of organization of this paragraph is _____.

C. [1]There are often more than two sides to a question, and offering only two choices when more actually exist is called an either-or fallacy. [2]For example, the statement "You are either with us or against us" assumes that there is no middle ground. [3]Or consider the following conclusion: People opposed to total freedom of speech are really in favor of censorship. [4]This argument ignores the fact that a person could believe in free speech as well as in laws that prohibit slander or that punish someone for falsely yelling "Fire!" in a crowded theater.

(Continues on next page)

_____ 5. The main pattern of organization of the paragraph is
      A. definition and example.
      B. cause and effect.
      C. comparison and/or contrast.

      6. The transition that signals the pattern of organization of this paragraph

       is _____.

D. [1]Why does lightning make such a loud sound? [2]The answer has to do with the electrical energy it gives off. [3]A single bolt may produce as much as 3,750 million kilowatts of electrical energy. [4]Most of this energy—75 percent—turns into heat, causing the temperature of the surrounding air to rise greatly. [5]Since heated air expands, the sudden increase in temperature leads to a rapid expansion of the air around the lightning. [6]And that air expansion causes sound waves—thunder—which can be heard up to eighteen miles away.

_____ 7. The main pattern of organization of the paragraph is
      A. definition and example.
      B. cause and effect.
      C. comparison and/or contrast.

      8. One transition that signals the pattern of organization of this paragraph

       is _____.

E. [1]People are different from other primates, but not as different as they might like to think. [2]It's true that that there are significant contrasts in size and proportion between humans and other primates. [3]And, of course, humans are by far the more intelligent. [4]Nevertheless, to use chimpanzees as an example, both they and humans have the same muscles and bones, located in almost the same places and working in nearly the same ways. [5]The internal organs of both animals are also very much alike, as are their blood and other body fluids. [6]Seen under a microscope, even their genes are strikingly similar.

_____ 9. The main pattern of organization of the paragraph is
      A. definition and example.
      B. cause and effect.
      C. comparison and/or contrast.

      10. One transition that signals the pattern of organization of this paragraph

       is _____.

MORE RELATIONSHIPS IN READING: Mastery Test 3

A. (1–4.) Arrange the scrambled sentences below into a logical paragraph by numbering them *1, 2, 3,* and *4* in an order that makes sense. Then, in the space provided, write the letter of the pattern of organization used.

Note that transitions will help you by clarifying the relationships between sentences.

____ Also, high tuitions affect the amount of time available for studying; because loans and scholarships are hard to get, many students have to put in numerous hours at work in order to afford school.

____ For one thing, it undoubtedly prevents some students from attending college in the first place.

____ Finally, those who do manage to get loans know that they must begin their careers with large debts.

____ The high cost of college today causes problems for many students in more ways than one.

_____ 5. The main pattern of organization is
    A. contrast.
    B. comparison.
    C. cause and effect.
    D. definition and example.

B. Read the passages and answer the questions that follow. You may find it helpful to underline transitions as you read.

    [1]Men and women may interpret women's actions on a date very differently. [2]One study found that acts such as speaking in a low voice or smiling were interpreted by men as indicating that the woman was interested in sex. [3]Women, in contrast, tended to see the same behaviors as simply friendly. [4]Drinking with a man, going to the man's apartment, or wearing sexy clothes were all seen by men as indicating a desire for sex, while women regarded these behaviors as appropriate or fashionable.

_____ 6. The main pattern of organization of the paragraph is
    A. definition and example.
    B. cause and effect.
    C. comparison and/or contrast.

    7. One transition that signals the main pattern of organization of this

    paragraph is _____.

(Continues on next page)

¹Mass hysteria is a type of group behavior that involves a widely held and contagious anxiety, usually as a result of a false belief. ²The reaction in part of the country to the 1938 radio broadcast of *The War of the Worlds* is one example. ³This dramatization of Martians landing on Earth was so realistic that people began to panic and flee before the realization set in that they were reacting to a radio play. ⁴The medieval witch-hunts are another good example of mass hysteria. ⁵They were based on the belief that witches were the cause of many problems in late medieval society, including natural disasters and illness. ⁶Those accused of being witches (mainly old women) were tortured until they confessed or they died. ⁷As many as 500,000 people were burned to death by the clergy between the fifteenth and seventeenth centuries.

_____ 8. The major supporting details of the selection are
    A. definitions.
    B. causes.
    C. comparisons.
    D. examples.

_____ 9. The main pattern of organization of the paragraph is
    A. definition and example.
    B. cause and effect.
    C. comparison and/or contrast.

10. The transition that signals the main pattern of organization of this paragraph is _____

MORE RELATIONSHIPS IN READING: Mastery Test 4

A. (1–4.) Arrange the scrambled sentences below into a logical paragraph by numbering them *1, 2, 3,* and *4* in an order that makes sense. Then, in the space provided, write the letter of the main pattern of organization used.

Note that transitions will help you by clarifying the relationships between sentences.

____ In contrast, the original Italian story is the gruesome tale of the Princess Talia, who falls into a deep magical sleep in the woods, where she is raped by a nobleman and, later on, gives birth to twins, whom the nobleman's wife tries to have killed and cooked for dinner.

____ It is often said that fairy tales, with their heavy doses of terror and violence, are too scary for young children.

____ Consider the story of Sleeping Beauty that today's children know, which involves a princess who is put to sleep by a wicked witch and then awakened by the kiss of her true love.

____ But today's versions of fairy tales are actually less frightening than the original stories.

_____ 5. The main pattern of organization is
    A. contrast.
    B. comparison.
    C. cause and effect.
    D. definition and example.

B. Read each paragraph and answer the questions that follow.

[1]A small sausage in a bun received the name "hot dog" in 1906 as the result of a cartoonist's poor spelling ability. [2]A sausage vendor, Harry Stevens, sold what he called "dachshund sausages" (named after the short-legged dog) at New York City baseball games. [3]During one of those games, newspaper cartoonist Tad Dorgan was in the audience. [4]He sketched a cartoon of a live dachshund, smeared with mustard and folded into a bun. [5]Not knowing how to spell "dachshund," however, he settled on "dog," giving the cartoon the caption "Get your hot dogs!" [6]Once the cartoon was published in newspapers, readers began demanding their own "hot dogs."

_____ 6. The main idea is expressed in the
    A. first sentence.
    B. second sentence.
    C. last sentence.

(Continues on next page)

_____ 7. The selection mainly
   A. defines and illustrates the term "hot dog."
   B. gives the reason small sausages are now called hot dogs.
   C. contrasts "dachshund sausage" with "hot dog."

8. The transition that signals the main pattern of organization of this

   paragraph is _____.

> ¹When a crowd is watching as someone threatens to jump from a building, its behavior seems affected by the time of day. ²In daylight, the crowd is usually quite quiet, but under the cover of darkness, many individual members will shout encouragement to the person to kill himself or herself. ³A similar reaction was seen when women college students took part in an experiment where they were asked to press a button to shock other volunteers. ⁴When the women pushing the buttons were visible to the victims, they administered only brief shocks. ⁵However, when they were allowed to wear gowns and masks that hid their identity, they shocked the volunteers twice as much. ⁶Clearly the feeling of being anonymous causes people to engage in antisocial behavior.

_____ 9. One pattern of organization of the selection is
   A. definition and example.
   B. cause and effect.
   C. comparison and/or contrast.

_____10. Another pattern of organization of the selection is
   A. definition and example.
   B. cause and effect.
   C. comparison and/or contrast.

MORE RELATIONSHIPS IN READING: Mastery Test 5

A. Read the textbook paragraph below. Then answer the question and complete the outline that follows.

> ¹There are several reasons why middle-aged adults are returning to school. ²Some want to learn to do their jobs better. ³College courses can help them improve their job skills and keep up in their fields. ⁴Others return to school because more credits may mean a raise or promotion. ⁵Teachers, for instance, get raises for reaching certain levels of education. ⁶Also, some adults return to the classroom because of interest in a new field, such as health care, telecommunications, or computer programming. ⁷Finally, others want to study subjects such as foreign languages, history, or literature for the sake of learning. ⁸Such classes help adults spend their time in more productive and interesting ways and deepen their understanding of themselves and their world.

_____ 1. The organizational patterns of the paragraph are list of items and
    A. definition and example.
    B. cause and effect.
    C. comparison and/or contrast.

2–5. Complete the outline of the paragraph by writing in the four major supporting details.

Main idea: There are several reasons why middle-aged adults are returning to school.

    Major supporting details:

    1. _____

    2. _____

    3. _____

    4. _____

(Continues on next page)

B. Read the textbook paragraph below. Then answer the question and complete the map that follows.

> ¹Why do people have differing needs for achievement? ²One researcher found that the need for achievement is related to parental attitudes. ³Parents who are high achievers themselves usually demand independence from their children. ⁴The children must become self-reliant at a relatively early age. ⁵As a result, the children develop a sense of confidence and find enjoyment in their own achievements. ⁶On the other hand, parents who have low needs for achievement are more protective of their children. ⁷They help their children perform everyday tasks, such as dressing and feeding, far more than necessary. ⁸The consequence is that children are less independent and often have low achievement needs.

_____   6. The paragraph
   A. defines and illustrates *achievement*.
   B. compares two types of parents and their effects.
   C. contrasts two types of parents and their effects.

7–10. Complete the map of the paragraph by writing in the missing supporting details.

One researcher found that the need for achievement
is related to parental attitudes.

_____-achiever parents

_____

_____

_____

Children thus develop sense of confidence and enjoy their own achievements.

_____-achiever parents

More protective of their children and do more for them.

_____

_____

_____

_____

MORE RELATIONSHIPS IN READING: Mastery Test 6

A. Read the textbook paragraph below. Then answer the question and complete the outline that follows.

> ¹One researcher has identified five basic causes of frustration above and beyond daily hassles. ²To begin with, delays are hard for us to accept because our culture stresses the value of time. ³Anyone who has been caught in a traffic jam is familiar with the frustration of delay. ⁴Lack of resources is another cause of frustration, especially to low-income Americans, who cannot afford the new cars or vacations that TV programs and magazine articles would have us believe everyone must have. ⁵Losses, such as the end of a love affair or a cherished friendship, are frustrating because they often make us feel helpless, unimportant, and worthless. ⁶Failure is a frequent source of frustration in our competitive society. ⁷The aspect of failure that is hardest to cope with is guilt. ⁸We imagine that if we had done certain things differently, we might have succeeded, and so we feel responsible for our own or someone else's pain and disappointment. ⁹Discrimination can also be a source of frustration. ¹⁰Being denied opportunities or recognition simply because of one's sex, age, religion, or skin color, regardless of one's personal qualifications or accomplishments, is immensely frustrating.

_____ 1. The organizational patterns of the paragraph are list of items and
  A. definition and example.
  B. comparison and/or contrast.
  C. cause and effect.

2–6. Complete the outline of the paragraph by writing in the five major supporting details.

Main idea: There are five causes of frustration above and beyond daily hassles.

Major supporting details:

1. _____

2. _____

3. _____

4. _____

5. _____

B. Read the textbook paragraph below. Then answer the question and complete the map that follows.

> [1]Role conflict is a situation in which the different roles an individual is expected to play make incompatible demands. [2]A working mother provides one example. [3]In meeting the requirements of a full-time job, she automatically violates the expectation that a mother will put her children's needs before everything else. [4]In meeting the cultural demands of motherhood (staying home if the child is sick, attending school plays), she automatically violates the requirements of a nine-to-five job. [5]A priest provides another example. [6]He is expected to treat confessions as strictly confidential. [7]But a priest, like any other citizen, has responsibilities toward the community. [8]What should he do if a parishioner confesses that he has committed several rapes and cannot control his behavior? [9]In living up to one role expectation (confidentiality), the priest violates another (community responsibility). [10]The key point here is that the difficulties the individuals in these positions experience—the feelings of conflict, inadequacy, and anguish—are not of their own making. [11]They are built into their roles.

_____ 7. The main pattern of organization of the passage is
   A. cause and effect.
   B. definition and example.
   C. comparison.
   D. contrast.

8–10. Complete the map of the passage. In doing so, you will need to summarize the main idea and the two supporting details.

8 More Relationships in Writing

This chapter will show you how to write papers that involve illustration, comparison, contrast, and cause and effect—the patterns of organization you learned about in the previous chapter. **Just as a knowledge of these patterns can make you a better reader, it can also make you a better writer.**

When you learn and practice these new writing patterns, the goals of effective writing will remain the same:

1 Start with a main idea or point.

2 Provide truly specific details that support your main idea or point.

3 Think about your paper by using one or more of the prewriting strategies already discussed: freewriting (writing nonstop about your topic for ten minutes or so without worrying about mistakes while you think on paper); asking questions (*who, when, what, how,* and *why* about your topic); and list making (jotting down a random list of as many details as you can think of about your topic). Keep in mind that effective writing begins with messy prewriting!

4 The eventual result of your prewriting should be a scratch outline that shows at a glance your main idea and the key supporting items that support that main idea.

5 You can then go on to a first draft and later drafts, with revision and editing.

The Illustration Pattern

Illustration paragraphs use one or more *examples* to clarify and support a main idea. Here are words that show illustration:

Illustration Words

(for) example	(for) instance	to illustrate
including	such as	once

PRACTICE 1: Writing a Paragraph That Uses Examples

Write a paragraph that uses examples to support one of the following three main ideas:

● A person I know always seems to act in wise/foolish/selfless/self-serving ways.

● The place where I live is in need of some repairs.

● Some people use their cell phones in inappropriate places.

A Model Paragraph

Here is one student's response to a similar assignment using the illustration pattern—providing examples that support the idea that the holiday season has become too commercialized.

Since I was a child, the holiday season has become more and more commercialized, and now it's totally ridiculous. To begin with, stores begin letting shoppers know that Christmas is coming even before Halloween hits. Decorations go up in late October along with glaring signs that bark "Lay Away Now!" as a not-so-subtle warning that the holiday is going to cost you a lot. Next is the horror of Black Friday, the crazy holiday shopping frenzy that happens on the day after Thanksgiving. Of course, now it's gotten so bad that many sales actually begin on Thanksgiving evening, ruining many salespeople's day. Nothing says being thankful like stampeding people pushing one another out of the way in a Wal-Mart at 3 in the morning. And every year there are more reports about fistfights over certain sales items. Finally, because there is so much emphasis placed on expensive gifts, big parties, and outdoing your neighbor with decorations, most people have forgotten the point of the holidays. They are not about wearing yourself to a frazzle and emptying your wallet. They are about family, faith, and friends. However, as the commercialization of the season continues to snowball, those things become harder and harder to remember.

● Underline the topic sentence—the sentence that expresses the main idea of the paragraph.

● Circle the number of examples that are provided in the paragraph to support the topic sentence: 1   2   3   4

Writing Your Own Paragraph

1. As explained in Chapter 4, there are three prewriting techniques that can help you think about a paper: freewriting, questioning, and list making. Apply one of these techniques to each of the three topic sentences on the previous page. You might, for example:

   ● Ask yourself what are specific examples of the person's wise (*or* foolish *or* selfish *or* self-serving) behavior.

   ● Make a list of specific repairs your home or apartment needs.

   ● Freewrite for a page or two about instances in which people use their cell phones in rude or otherwise inappropriate places.

2. These prewriting techniques will help you determine the topic sentence for which you'll be able to provide the best support. Choose that topic sentence to develop in your paper.

3. Make a scratch outline in which you list the three supporting items in your paper and the order in which you'll present them.

4. Go on to write the first draft of your paper. If you find that you get "stuck" in a major way in providing enough supporting information, remember that you can always go back and choose one of the other topic sentences instead.

5. When writing your paper, perhaps in the second draft, remember to use addition transitions—words such as *first, a second, also, another, a third, last of all*—to signal to your readers each of your three supporting items.

6. After you have completed your next-to-final draft, read it out loud to yourself. If you come upon snags in your reading, chances are there may be grammar or punctuation problems at those points. Consult a grammar handbook, if necessary, to see what corrections are needed. Make the required corrections so that every sentence in your paper reads smoothly and clearly.

The Comparison Pattern

Comparison paragraphs show how two things are *like* each other. Here are words that show comparison:

Comparison Words

(just) as	in like (similar) manner	same
(just) like	similar(ly)	in the same way
alike	similarity	resemble
likewise	both	equally

PRACTICE 2: Writing a Paragraph That Uses Comparison

Write a paragraph that supports one of the following three main ideas:

● In several ways, I'm like a _____ (my favorite animal).

● The best teachers I've had shared several things in common.

● My girlfriend/boyfriend/spouse is similar in some ways to my mother/father.

A Model Paragraph

Here is one student's response to the assignment.

> I've realized that my wife is quite similar, in some ways, to my mom. My wife is a very intelligent person who is earning her bachelor's degree in nursing. My mom wasn't able to go to college, but she's an equally smart woman who would have made a terrific nurse. Also, my wife is an unconventional woman who puts purple streaks in her hair, wears crazy clothing she finds in thrift stores, and plays the bongo drums. Although Mom isn't quite that bold, she is likewise a rebel in her own way. She got a tattoo when she was 40, loves rocking out to Pearl Jam, and enjoys wearing long shoulder-duster earrings. Finally, my wife has a mouth on her. She swears like a sailor when she's upset. Mom is a little more polite, but when she's not happy with me, she resembles my wife in using very colorful language!

- Underline the topic sentence—the sentence that expresses the main idea of the paragraph.

- Underline the comparison words that are used in the paragraph.

- Circle the addition words that move the reader from one point of comparison to the next.

Writing Your Own Paragraph

Pick out—or create from scratch—a topic sentence you think you might be able to write about. Then explore that topic by freewriting about it, or asking questions such as *what, when, where, how,* and *why* about it, or making a list of all the details you can think of about it. Prewriting will help you determine the topic for which you can provide the best supporting details.

See if you can develop the topic with even more details, and prepare a scratch outline of the paragraph. Then go on to write the first and later drafts of your paper. When you think you have the final draft of your paper, read it aloud to make sure that every sentence reads smoothly and clearly. If that is not the case, you still have a bit of work to do. Use a grammar handbook, if necessary, to see what corrections are needed. Make the required corrections to remove these trouble spots.

The Contrast Pattern

Contrast paragraphs show how two things are *different*. We might, for example, contrast two instructors, two jobs, or two friends. Contrast helps us understand the two things more clearly and why we feel the way we do about them. Here are common words that show contrast:

Contrast Words

but	instead	still	difference
yet	in contrast	as opposed to	different(ly)
however	on the other hand	in spite of	differs from
although	on the contrary	despite	unlike
nevertheless	even though	rather than	while

PRACTICE 3: Writing a Paragraph That Uses Contrast

Write a paragraph about two quite different people or events or things. You may use one of the following main ideas, or start with a topic sentence of your own:

- I act differently around my parents than I do around my friends.

- The technology I use in my everyday life is much different from what my parents or grandparents had.

- Watching a movie in a theater is really different from watching it on TV.

A Model Paragraph

Here is one student's response to a related assignment—two different ways of handling stress.

My friend Jen's way of dealing with stress is almost the total opposite of how I handle it. When we were college roommates last semester, I got to see that difference firsthand during final exams. As the pressure began building for our final exam in chemistry, I was bouncing all over the dorm room and chattering a mile a minute. Jen, on the other hand, kind of shut down and went into her own head. She ignored me, put on headphones, and listened to music as she continued to study. Around 3 a.m., when the stress was peaking, I was chugging coffee and complaining irritably. In contrast, Jen did some yoga and deep breathing, drank some green tea, and told me politely to calm down. She even helped me understand a chemical reaction, explaining it clearly and patiently. In the morning on the way to the exam, I was all gloom and doom and already deciding that I wasn't going to do well. But Jen just shrugged and said, "We studied really hard. We'll do the best we can. That's all we can do." I thought of that as the exams were passed out, and I credit Jen's cool handling of stress for helping me pass chemistry.

- Underline the topic sentence—the sentence that expresses the main idea of the paragraph.

- Underline the contrast words that are used in the paragraph.

- Circle the time words that move the reader from one part of the story to the next.

Writing Your Own Paragraph

Pick out—or create from scratch—a topic sentence you think you might be able to write about. Then explore that topic by freewriting about it, or asking questions such as *what, when, where, how,* and *why* about it, or making a list of all the details you can think of about it. Prewriting will help you determine the topic for which you can provide the best supporting details.

See if you can develop the topic with even more details, and prepare a scratch outline of the paragraph. Then go on to write the first and later drafts of your paper. When you think you have the final draft of your paper, read it aloud to make sure that every sentence reads smoothly and clearly. If that is not the case, you still have a bit of work to do. Use a grammar handbook, if necessary, to see what corrections are needed. Make the required corrections to remove these trouble spots.

The Cause-Effect Pattern

Cause and effect paragraphs show *reasons* or *results.* They seek to explain the *causes* of some behavior or event. Or they describe the *effects* or *consequences* of some behavior or event. Here are words that show cause and effect:

Cause and Effect Words

therefore	so	owing to	because (of)
thus	(as a) result	effect	reason
(as a) consequence	results in	cause	explanation
consequently	leads to	if . . . then	accordingly
due to	since	affect	

PRACTICE 4: Writing a Paragraph That Uses Cause and Effect

Write a paragraph that uses one of the following main ideas, or start with a topic sentence of your own:

● Losing a job can have painful consequences in a person's life.

● My parents' divorce (or the death of a loved one) had a real impact on my life.

● There are several reasons why I am a good/poor reader.

A Model Paragraph

Here is one student's response to a related assignment—giving reasons why regular exercise has been helpful in her life.

> Running regularly has not only kept me in shape; it's helped my life in a number of other ways. For one thing, it's kept me out of trouble. When I began jogging as a teenager, I just did it to lose a few pounds. But when it became a habit, I didn't want anything to interfere with my morning runs. As a result, several years later, when a lot of my friends stayed out drinking and partying until all hours, I usually came home earlier so that I'd feel good in the morning. Another effect of running is that it's helped me create a circle of like-minded friends. We share a love for a healthy hobby that's often the basis for getting together. And because we all talk about our frustrations while running together, our problems always seem smaller by the end of the run. Last, running helped me understand the work it takes to reach a goal. At one time, I never would have believed I could run ten miles without stopping. But day by day, then week by week, I added miles and got stronger. One day, I could run that far. As a consequence of that experience, I now know that steady planning and working are the keys to success in life.

- Underline the topic sentence—the sentence that states the main idea of the paragraph.
- Underline the cause and effect words that are used in the paragraph.
- Circle the addition words that move the reader from one cause or effect to the next.

Writing Your Own Paragraph

Pick out—or create from scratch—a topic sentence you think you might be able to write about. Then explore that topic by freewriting about it, or asking questions such as *what, when, where, how,* and *why* about it, or making a list of all the details you can think of about it. Prewriting will help you determine the topic for which you can provide the best supporting details.

See if you can develop the topic with even more details, and prepare a scratch outline of the paragraph. Then go on to write the first and later drafts of your paper. When you think you have the final draft of your paper, read it aloud to make sure that every sentence reads smoothly and clearly. If that is not the case, you still have a bit of work to do. Use a grammar handbook, if necessary, to see what corrections are needed. Make the required corrections to remove these trouble spots.

MORE RELATIONSHIPS IN WRITING: Mastery Test 1

A. Complete each sentence with a suitable illustration word from the box below. Use each transition once. Then, in the space provided, write the letter of the transition you have chosen.

A. example	**B.** for instance	**C.** including
D. specifically	**E.** such as	

Hint: Make sure that each word or phrase that you choose fits smoothly into the flow of the sentence. Test each choice by reading the sentence to yourself.

_____ 1. Throughout history, men have chosen to marry for different reasons. One _____ is that in ancient Sparta, men needed wives solely for childbearing.

_____ 2. Common courtesies, _____ saying *please* and *thank you,* are becoming less and less common.

_____ 3. Sometimes drivers don't seem to be paying full attention to their driving. _____, this morning I saw people driving while talking on cell phones, combing their hair, and glancing at newspapers.

_____ 4. Color in the workplace can serve a functional purpose. _____, different colors can be used to mark secure and unsecured areas, areas where visitors are and are not allowed, or various levels of safety and danger.

_____ 5. We have come to understand in recent years how the English language is riddled with sexism. Most blatant is the generic "he," which excludes women from whatever group is being discussed, _____ in the line "When a college student studies for an exam, he should be sure to review all his lecture notes."

(Continues on next page)

B. Complete each sentence with a suitable comparison word from the box below. Try to use each transition once. Then, in the space provided, write the letter of the transition you have chosen.

A. in the same way	**B. just as**	**C. like**
D. likewise	**E. similarly**	

Hint: Make sure that each word or phrase that you choose fits smoothly into the flow of the sentence. Test each choice by reading the sentence to yourself.

_____ 1. A swarm of locusts looks _____ a massive dark cloud moving across the sky.

_____ 2. As a young boy, Raymond was often beaten by his parents. Unfortunately, he now treats his own children _____.

_____ 3. _____ people put their best foot forward for romance, birds show off their skills or looks during courtship.

_____ 4. My cousin, who gets around in a wheelchair, had kitchen counters built at a convenient height for him. _____, he created a flower container garden at a height he can easily reach.

_____ 5. American films are enormously popular in almost every country. _____, American clothing styles influence fashions around the world.

MORE RELATIONSHIPS IN WRITING: Mastery Test 2

A. Complete each sentence with a suitable contrast word from the box below. Use each transition once. Then, in the space provided, write the letter of the transition you have chosen.

A. although	**B. however**	**C. in contrast**
D. nevertheless	**E. unlike**	

Hint: Make sure that each word or phrase that you choose fits smoothly into the flow of the sentence. Test each choice by reading the sentence to yourself.

_____ 1. People are capable of making some adjustment to a constant noise level. _____, if the noise exceeds eighty-five to ninety decibels, their productivity will decrease over the course of the workday.

_____ 2. _____ Americans claim to be concerned with fitness, the typical adult can't climb a flight of steps without getting short of breath.

_____ 3. _____ perennial plants, which return year after year, annuals survive for only one season.

_____ 4. Most American-born college students cannot converse in a foreign language. _____, it is a rare student in Europe who cannot speak at least one language besides his or her own.

_____ 5. The most effective bridge from low levels of reading ability to higher levels is pleasure reading. _____, this is exactly the kind of reading that is missing from the lives of many students.

(Continues on next page)

B. Complete each sentence with a suitable cause and effect word from the box below. Use each transition once. Then, in the space provided, write the letter of the transition you have chosen.

A. because	**B.** cause	**C.** consequence
D. reason	**E.** result	

Hint: Make sure that each word or phrase that you choose fits smoothly into the flow of the sentence. Test each choice by reading the sentence to yourself.

_____ 6. The _____ many people support organic farming is that it is less destructive to the environment than farming with chemicals and pesticides.

_____ 7. If you're taking an antibiotic, you must continue taking it until all the pills are gone. Failure to do so could _____ in a relapse or in the emergence of resistant bacteria strains.

_____ 8. Human behavior is so complicated that we are not always aware of the _____s of our own actions.

_____ 9. Although reduced-fat foods may sound healthy, the fat is often replaced by carbohydrates that may _____ weight gain.

_____ 10. Information overload is all around us, coming with terrifying speed via the Internet as well as fax, phone, text messaging, e-mail, and scores of cable channels. _____ so much information bombards us constantly, we fail to remember a great deal of it.

MORE RELATIONSHIPS IN WRITING: Mastery Test 3

Following are four paragraphs that use either illustration, comparison, contrast, or cause and effect. Fill in the blanks in each paragraph with an appropriate transition from the box. Use each transition once. Then answer the questions that follow each paragraph.

1.

A. alike	B. both	C. similar

[1]My grandmother and I have a few things in common. [2]For one thing, we are _____ physically. [3]We are both short—just over five feet—with curly black hair and brown eyes. [4]In addition, we are _____ in our emotional makeup. [5]She and I are both quick-tempered, but after we shout angrily for a few minutes, we calm down and apologize. [6]And finally, we are _____ crazy about cooking. [7]When we get together, we spend our time chopping garlic and vegetables and comparing recipes. [8]I love being my grandmother's Mini-Me!

● What is the main idea, or point, of the paragraph? _____
_____

● _____ Which pattern of organization is used in the paragraph?
    A. Illustration   C. Contrast
    B. Comparison   D. Cause and effect

2.

A. example	B. for instance

[1]Cults are movements that represent religious traditions different from established religions. [2]In fact, many of today's great world faiths began as cults and, at first, were treated with hostility and ridicule. [3]_____, first-century Romans laughed at the notion that a messiah and his tiny flock in faraway Palestine could threaten their mighty pagan temples. [4]But from an obscure cult movement, Christianity arose. [5]Islam and Buddhism are other _____s of major religions that began as cults.

● What is the main idea, or point, of the paragraph? _____
_____

● _____ Which pattern of organization is used in the paragraph?
    A. Illustration   C. Contrast
    B. Comparison   D. Cause and effect

(Continues on next page)

3.

A. on the other hand	B. unlike

¹My two dogs are completely _____ each other. ²Physically, Cosmo is a big, goofy dog, about 55 pounds, with long silver-reddish hair. ³Logan is a small terrier, 20 pounds of muscle, with a very short brown and white coat. ⁴Behaviorally, Cosmo has never met a stranger. ⁵Upon meeting new people, he leans against them as if they're his long-lost best friends and gazes adoringly into their eyes. ⁶Logan, _____, is suspicious. ⁷He barks frantically and lets them know that if they make one wrong move, he'll rip their throats out.

● What is the main idea, or point, of the paragraph? _____
_____

● _____ The pattern of organization of the above selection is
   A. illustration.   C. contrast.
   B. comparison.   D. cause and effect.

4.

A. cause	B. due to	C. explanation
D. leads to	E. reasons	

¹Almost everyone daydreams at times, and there are a number of _____ we do so. ²One _____ of daydreaming is boring jobs that are bearable only when workers imagine themselves doing something else. ³Deprivation also _____ daydreaming. ⁴People on a diet sometimes deal with their hunger by picturing all the favorite foods they would love to be eating. ⁵Another _____ for daydreaming is that it discharges hostile feelings. ⁶An angry student may picture getting his instructor fired as a way of dealing with the hostility he feels about the teacher. ⁷Finally, daydreaming can occur _____ our wish to plan for a future that will offer more happiness to us than might be the case in the present.

● What is the main idea, or point, of the paragraph? _____
_____

● _____ The pattern of organization of the above selection is
   A. illustration.   C. contrast.
   B. comparison.   D. cause and effect.

MORE RELATIONSHIPS IN WRITING: Mastery Test 4

Write a paragraph or an essay that uses examples to support its point. You may want to choose one of the following ideas from page 198 that you have not written about:

- A person I know always seems to act in wise/foolish/selfless/self-serving ways.

- The place where I live is in need of some repairs.

- Some people use their cell phones in inappropriate places.

Or choose one of the following:

- Organizational skills can come in handy in everyday life.

- There are some truly ridiculous current fashion trends.

- Most fad diets do more harm than good.

A Model Paragraph

You have already seen on page 198 a model paragraph that uses *illustration*. Here is another model paragraph:

> There is no doubt that my bad habits make my life more difficult than it needs to be. For instance, I am a terrible procrastinator. Whether it's doing a school assignment or cleaning the house before guests come over, I wait until the last minute. This habit makes me constantly stressed and incapable of doing my best work. Another example of my bad habits is that I am always running late. I don't build in enough time to get to work or to school or to social events on time. This causes me to be in constant trouble with my teachers, my employer, and my friends. A final bad habit that makes my life harder is my compulsive need to be funny. In the most inappropriate moments, I blurt out something intended to make people laugh. Depending on the situation, I come across as either really insensitive or just stupid. My bad habits definitely get in the way of my having a pleasant life.

- Underline the topic sentence—the sentence that expresses the main idea of the above paragraph.

- Circle the number of examples that are provided in the paragraph to support the topic sentence: 1   2   3   4

(Continues on next page)

Writing Your Own Paragraph or Essay

Pick out—or create from scratch—a topic sentence you think you might be able to write about. Then explore that topic by freewriting about it, or asking questions such as *what, when, where, how,* and *why* about it, or making a list of all the details you can think of about it. Prewriting will help you determine the topic for which you can provide the best supporting details.

See if you can develop the topic with even more details, and prepare a scratch outline. Then go on to write the first and later drafts of your paper. When you think you have the final draft of your paper, read it aloud to make sure that every sentence reads smoothly and clearly. Use a grammar handbook, if necessary, to see what corrections are needed. Make the required corrections to remove the trouble spots.

MORE RELATIONSHIPS IN WRITING: Mastery Test 5

Write a paragraph or an essay that uses *comparison* or *contrast* to support its point. You may want to choose one of the following ideas from pages 200 and 202 that you have not written about:

- In several ways, I'm like a _____ (my favorite animal).
- The best teachers I've had shared many things in common.
- My girlfriend/boyfriend/spouse is similar in some ways to my mother/father.
- I act differently around my parents than I do around my friends.
- The technology I use in my everyday life is much different from what my parents or grandparents had.
- Watching a movie in a theater is really different from watching it on TV.

A Model Paragraph

You have already seen on pages 200–202 model paragraphs that use comparison and contrast. Here is another model paragraph—one that uses contrast:

> My friend Evan and I handle stress in definitely different ways. When I am stressed out, the whole world knows about it. I complain, loudly, to everyone in the neighborhood. My brother, my parents, my friends, and the guy I buy vegetables from at the produce market all know that I'm upset about something, because I tell them about it. The next time I see any of them, they're all asking, "So, are you feeling better now?" Unlike me, Evan hunkers down when he is feeling stressed. He goes radio silent. No one sees him or hears from him for days. When he finally emerges, after he's gotten over whatever it was, he will tell his closest friends a little bit about what was going on, but not in any great detail. I deal with stress by broadcasting it to the world. In contrast, Evan deals with stress by going deep within.

- Underline the topic sentence that expresses the main idea of the above paragraph.
- Underline the contrast words used in the paragraph.

(Continues on next page)

Writing Your Own Paragraph or Essay

Pick out—or create from scratch—a topic sentence you think you might be able to write about. Then explore that topic by freewriting about it, or asking questions such as *what, when, where, how,* and *why* about it, or making a list of all the details you can think of about it. Prewriting will help you determine the topic for which you can provide the best supporting details.

See if you can develop the topic with even more details, and prepare a scratch outline. Then go on to write the first and later drafts of your paper. When you think you have the final draft of your paper, read it aloud to make sure that every sentence reads smoothly and clearly. Use a grammar handbook, if necessary, to see what corrections are needed. Make the required corrections to remove the trouble spots.

MORE RELATIONSHIPS IN WRITING: Mastery Test 6

Write a paragraph or an essay that uses *cause and effect* to support its point. You may want to choose one of the following ideas from page 203 that you have not written about:

- Losing a job can have painful consequences in a person's life.
- My parents' divorce (or the death of a loved one) had a real impact on my life.
- There are several reasons why I am a good/poor reader.

Or choose one of the following:

- Breaking my bad habit of _____ has had positive effects on my life.
- Peer pressure has made me do some pretty stupid things.
- Not carrying a cell phone would make a big difference in my day.

A Model Paragraph

You have already seen on page 204 a model paragraph that uses cause/effect. Here is another model paragraph.

> Being a big brother to my little brother Eli has made me a more responsible person. Because I know that he is always watching me, I want to set a good example for him. Therefore, I choose my words with a bit more care, I'm more thoughtful about what I eat, and I pay more attention to what I watch on TV and for how long I watch it. Also, since I need to watch Eli when my parents are working, I really think about how he's spending his time. If I were just babysitting some kid for a few hours, I'd probably let him veg in front of the TV, but I don't want Eli to become a couch potato. As a result, I read to him and encourage him to do art projects and other constructive activities.

- Underline the topic sentence—the sentence that expresses the main idea of the preceding paragraph.

- Circle the cause and effect words used in the paragraph.

(Continues on next page)

Writing Your Own Paragraph or Essay

Pick out—or create from scratch—a topic sentence you think you might be able to write about. Then explore that topic by freewriting about it, or asking questions such as *what, when, where, how,* and *why* about it, or making a list of all the details you can think of about it. Prewriting will help you determine the topic for which you can provide the best supporting details.

See if you can develop the topic with even more details, and prepare a scratch outline. Then go on to write the first and later drafts of your paper. When you think you have the final draft of your paper, read it aloud to make sure that every sentence reads smoothly and clearly. Use a grammar handbook, if necessary, to see what corrections are needed. Make the required corrections to remove the trouble spots.

9 Inferences in Reading and Writing

You have probably heard the expression "to read between the lines." When you "read between the lines," you pick up ideas that are not directly stated in what you are reading. These implied ideas are often important for a full understanding of what an author means. Discovering the ideas that are not stated directly in writing is called **making inferences**, or **drawing conclusions**.

Look at the cartoon below. What inferences can you make about it? Check (✓) the **two** inferences that are most logically based on the information suggested by the cartoon.

✓ A. The couple is not likely to have a good dining experience at the restaurant.

___ B. The couple will never eat at the restaurant.

___ C. The restaurant was recently closed for health violations.

✓ D. Whoever is running the restaurant is not doing a good job.

Explanation

A. *The couple is not likely to have a good dining experience at the restaurant.*

The "help wanted" sign indicates that the restaurant is seriously understaffed. It would be logical, then, to infer that the restaurant cannot provide patrons with a good dining experience. You should have checked this item.

B. *The couple will never eat at the restaurant.*

The man's comment that "this isn't the best time" suggests that he may be willing to try the restaurant once it has solved its staffing problems. Also, experience suggests that it is common for restaurants to change ownership and/or management. You should not have checked this item.

C. *The restaurant was recently closed for health violations.*

Nothing in the cartoon suggests that the restaurant was recently closed for health violations. Perhaps if it continues to operate without sufficient staff, it *may* be closed, but we have no way of knowing that. You should not have checked this item.

D. *Whoever is running the restaurant is not doing a good job.*

Experience tells us that good managers are able to hire and retain qualified employees. The "help wanted" sign suggests quite the opposite—that a number of employees have recently quit or been fired. The lack of staff, in turn, has caused the couple to decide against dining there. Clearly, this is no way to run a business! You should have checked this item.

Inferences in Reading

In reading, we make logical leaps from information stated directly to ideas that are not stated directly. As one scholar has said, inferences are "statements about the unknown made on the basis of the known." To draw inferences, we use all the clues provided by the writer, our own experience, and logic.

Chances are you already make inferences in your everyday reading. For example, let's say you read the following sentence:

Many of us have *ambivalent* feelings about our politicians, admiring them but also distrusting them.

That sentence does not tell us the meaning of *ambivalent*, but it does suggest that *ambivalent* involves both positive and negative feelings. Thus you can infer from this sentence that *ambivalent feelings* probably means "mixed feelings," and you'd be correct.

✓ *Check Your Understanding 1*

Read the following passage and check (✓) the **two** inferences that are most firmly based on the information given. Then read the explanation that follows.

> [1]A sociology professor wrote on the board, "A woman without her man is nothing" and, with a smile, asked students to punctuate the sentence correctly. [2]The men all wrote, "A woman, without her man, is nothing." [3]However, the women wrote, "A woman: Without her, man is nothing."

____ A. The professor was definitely a man.

____ B. The professor did not believe students could punctuate the words correctly.

____ C. The professor knew there was more than one way to punctuate the words correctly.

____ D. The professor is not a good teacher.

____ E. Gender differences caused students to read and punctuate the professor's words differently.

Explanation

A. There is no indication of the professor's gender in the passage. You should not have checked this item.

B. Nothing in the passage implies that the professor doubted students' ability to punctuate the words correctly. You should not have checked this item.

C. Since the professor chose the particular sentence and smiled while writing the words, we can conclude that the professor was aware of more than one punctuation possibility. Therefore, you should have checked this item.

D. There is no suggestion in the passage that the professor is a poor teacher. In fact, the professor has chosen a dramatic way to suggest that each sex sees the world from its own point of view. You should not have checked this item.

E. Male and female students had very different responses to the sentence. Gender was the only apparent difference among the students, so we can conclude that it caused the different responses. You should have checked this item.

✓ Check Your Understanding 2

Read the following passage, and then check (✓) the **three** inferences that can most logically be drawn from it. Then read the explanation that follows.

[1]A famous psychology experiment conducted by Dr. John B. Watson demonstrates that people, like animals, can be conditioned—trained to respond in a particular way to certain stimulations. [2]Watson gave an eleven-month-old baby named Albert a soft, furry white rat. [3]Each time Albert tried to stroke the rat, Dr. Watson hit a metal bar with a hammer. [4]Before long, Albert was afraid not only of white rats but also of white rabbits, white dogs, and white fur coats. [5]He even screamed at the sight of a Santa Claus mask.

____ A. Dr. Watson did not like small children.

✓ B. Before the experiment, Albert was not afraid of white rats.

____ C. Albert had been familiar with rats before the experiment.

____ D. If he had seen a black fur coat, Albert would have screamed.

✓ E. Albert connected the loud noise of the hammer striking the metal bar with the white rat.

✓ F. Albert was afraid of unexpected loud noises.

Explanation

A. This is not a logical inference. We might certainly question the way the baby was used, but the passage doesn't give enough information for us to infer logically that Watson did not like small children.

B. This is a logical inference. Because Albert tried to pet the rat, it is fair to assume that he wasn't frightened of the animal.

C. This is not a logical inference. The passage gives no clues about Albert's having previous experience with rats.

D. This is not a logical inference. The passage makes no mention of Albert's response to any color but white.

E. This is a logical inference. Because the noise appears to have changed Albert's attitude toward the rat, we can assume he associated the noise with the rat.

F. This is a logical inference. Since the noise is what made Albert afraid of the rat, we have to infer that he was afraid of the noise. In addition, experience tells us that babies are likely to be frightened of unexpected loud noises.

Guidelines for Making Inferences in Reading

The exercises in this chapter provide practice in making careful inferences when you read. Here are three guidelines for that process:

1 **Never lose sight of the available information.** As much as possible, base your inferences on the facts. For instance, in the paragraph about Watson's experiment, we are told, "Albert tried to stroke the rat." On the basis of that fact, we can readily conclude that the baby had no fear of rats.

   It's also important to note when a conclusion lacks support. For instance, the idea that Albert would have screamed at the sight of a black fur coat has no support in the paragraph. We are told only that Albert was frightened by white furry things.

2 **Use your background information and experience to help you in making inferences.** Our understanding and experience with babies, for example, help us realize that Albert was frightened of unexpected loud noises.

   The more you know about a subject, the better your inferences are likely to be. So keep in mind that if your background in an area is weak, your inferences may be shaky. For example, if you develop a rash and fever that will not go away, a doctor's inferences about the cause are likely to be more helpful than your inferences.

3 **Consider the alternatives.** Don't simply accept the first inference that comes to mind. Instead, consider all the facts of a case and all the possible explanations. For example, the doctor analyzing your rash and fever may first think of and then eliminate several possibilities before coming to the right conclusion.

PRACTICE 1

Read the following passage. Then, in the space provided, write the letter of the most logical answer to each question, based on the information given in the passage.

[1]A corporate president recently made a visit to a nearby Native American reservation as part of his firm's public-relations program. [2]"We realize that we have not hired any Indians in the five years our company has been located in this area," he told the assembled tribespeople, "but we are looking into the matter very carefully." [3]"*Hora, hora,*" said some of the audience. [4]"We would like to eventually hire 5 percent of our total work force from this reservation," he said. [5]"*Hora, hora,*" shouted more of the audience. [6]Encouraged by their enthusiasm, the president closed his short address by telling them that he hoped his firm would be able to take some hiring action within the next couple of years. [7]"*Hora, hora, hora,*" cried the total group. [8]With a feeling of satisfaction, the president left the hall and was

taken on a tour of the reservation. [9]Stopping in a field to admire some of the horses grazing there, the president asked if he could walk up closer to the animals. [10]"Certainly," said his guide, "but be careful not to step in the *hora*."

_____ 1. To get the main point of this passage, the reader must infer
      A. the location of the reservation.
      B. what kind of company the president headed.
      C. the meaning of the word *hora*.

_____ 2. From the passage, we can infer that the audience
      A. believed the president's speech.
      B. did not believe the president's speech.
      C. was confused by the president's speech.

_____ 3. From the passage, we can infer that the president
      A. thought the Native Americans deserved to be hired.
      B. thought his company should not hire the Native Americans.
      C. misinterpreted the Native Americans' reaction to his speech.

_____ 4. From the passage, we can infer that the main reason the president spoke to the Native Americans about jobs was that
      A. they needed the jobs.
      B. he thought promising jobs to Native Americans would make his company look good.
      C. he thought hiring Native Americans would be good for his company.

PRACTICE 2

Read the following passage. Then, in the space provided, write the letter of the most logical answer to each question, based on the information given in the passage.

[1]During World War II, the troop ship *SS Dorchester* steamed out of New York harbor with 904 men headed for Greenland. [2]Among those leaving anxious families behind were four chaplains: Methodist preacher George Fox, Rabbi Alexander Goode, Catholic priest John Washington, and Reformed Church minister Clark Poling. [3]Some 150 miles from their destination, a Nazi submarine sighted the *Dorchester* in its crosshairs. [4]Within moments of a torpedo's impact, reports a survivor, stunned men were pouring out from their bunks as the ship began tilting. [5]With power cut off, the escort vessels, unaware of the unfolding tragedy, pushed on in the darkness. [6]Onboard, chaos ruled as panicky men came up from the hold without life jackets and leaped into overcrowded lifeboats.

[7]When the four chaplains made it up to the steeply sloping deck, they began guiding the men to their boat stations. [8]They opened a storage locker, distributed life jackets, and coaxed the men over the side. [9]In the icy, oil-smeared water, Private William Bednar heard the chaplains preaching courage and found the strength to

swim until he reached a life raft. [10]Still onboard, Grady Clark watched in awe as the chaplains handed out the last life jackets, and then, with ultimate selflessness, gave away their own. [11]As Clark slipped into the water, he saw the chaplains standing—their arms linked—praying, in Latin, Hebrew, and English. [12]Other men, now calm, joined them in a huddle as the *Dorchester* slid beneath the sea.

_____ 1. We can infer from this passage that
   A. the Nazis had been hunting for the *Dorchester* for a long time.
   B. the *Dorchester*'s passengers and their families knew that because the ship carried soldiers, it might be attacked.
   C. the Nazi submarine was eventually found and destroyed.

_____ 2. We can infer that the chaplains and others remaining on the boat didn't jump off because
   A. there was no more room in the lifeboats, and they knew they could not survive in the icy sea without a life jacket.
   B. they couldn't swim.
   C. they assumed a friendly ship would soon pass by and save them.

_____ 3. We can infer from the passage that Grady Clark
   A. was one of the men who died in the *Dorchester* tragedy.
   B. survived the attack and reported what the chaplains had done.
   C. was the sole survivor of the attack on the *Dorchester*.

_____ 4. The passage suggests that
   A. the chaplains had known each other for many years.
   B. religious faith may strengthen courage.
   C. the chaplains had no fear of death.

PRACTICE 3

Read the following textbook passages. Then put a check (✓) by the **three** inferences that are most logically based on the given facts in each passage.

A. [1]George Washington's honesty is a trait that has been well publicized. [2]The famous story of how little George chopped down his father's favorite cherry tree, then bravely admitted to the deed, has an honored place in American presidential history. [3]The cherry tree story was first recorded in 1806 by Parson Mason Weems, a Maryland preacher and storyteller. [4]Unfortunately, Parson Weems was none too honest himself, and it appears that he invented the story of George and the cherry tree. [5]There is no record of the cherry tree incident anywhere until it appears in Weems's book. [6]The parson, it seems, thought it acceptable to teach the virtue of honesty through a made-up story. [7]We can judge Weems's own truthfulness by the fact that he describes himself in the book as "formerly rector of Mount Vernon Parish." [8]Such a parish never existed.

____ 1. The passage suggests that George Washington was not so honest after all.

____ 2. We can conclude that Parson Weems knew George Washington well.

____ 3. Widely accepted stories about history are not necessarily true.

____ 4. Parson Weems wrote about a virtue he didn't have himself.

____ 5. The author of this passage doubts that George Washington was a great leader and president.

____ 6. In his stories and sermons, Weems may well have told other false stories.

B. [1]The *Chicago Tribune* once wrote that Henry Ford, the founder of the Ford Motor Company, was an ignorant man. [2]Ford sued, challenging the paper to "prove it." [3]During the trial, Ford was asked dozens of simple, general information questions: "When was the Civil War?" "Name the presidents of the United States," and so on. [4]Ford, who had little formal education, could answer very few. [5]Finally, exasperated, he said, "I don't know the answers to those questions, but I could find a man in five minutes who does. [6]I use my brain to think, not store up a lot of useless facts."

____ 1. Henry Ford was probably angered by the article in the *Chicago Tribune*.

____ 2. Ford frequently sued people.

____ 3. The *Tribune* won the case in court.

____ 4. Ford believed that knowing where to find a fact is good enough.

____ 5. Ford would have been even more successful in his career had he had a formal education.

____ 6. Ford believed that knowing how to think is more important than knowing facts.

C. [1]Most people would like to think that they choose their friends solely on the basis of personal characteristics. [2]A classic study of a housing complex for married students at the Massachusetts Institute of Technology (MIT) suggests that proximity— nearness and availability—can be an important factor. [3]Researchers asked couples to list their friends in the complex. [4]They found that residents were far more likely to list the couple in the next apartment than one that lived two doors away, and more likely to visit with a couple two doors away than with one three or four doors away. [5]A distance of thirty feet or a short elevator ride made the difference between friends and strangers! [6]More recent studies have confirmed the importance of proximity. [7]One possible explanation is that whenever people encounter strangers, they feel tense. [8]The more they see a person, the more they come to think of that person as predictable and safe, and hence the more likely they are to strike up a conversation that leads to friendship. [9]This would explain why the most popular couples in the MIT housing complex were those who lived at the bottom of the stairs near the garbage cans that everyone used.

_____ 1. Most people probably think their personal preferences determine whom they choose for friends.

_____ 2. In fact, our personal preferences have no effect on who our friends are.

_____ 3. A person who lives in a big country is more likely to have more friends than someone who lives in a small country.

_____ 4. Someone living in an apartment house is likely to have more friends than someone who lives on a farm.

_____ 5. A garbage collector is likely to have more friends than a letter carrier.

_____ 6. Someone who works in a busy office is likely to have more friends than someone who works at home.

Inferences in Writing

An excellent way to enrich your writing is to practice creative writing techniques that encourage readers to make inferences. Three such techniques, described on the pages that follow, are:

1 Details that show rather than tell
2 Figures of speech
3 Dialog

The techniques add to a reader's experience by asking him or her to make inferences about what has been read.

Details That Show Rather Than Tell

While writers of factual material usually state directly much of what they mean, creative writers often provide verbal pictures that *show* what they mean. It is up to the reader to infer the point of what the creative writer has said. For instance, a nonfiction writer might write the following:

My brother is accident-prone.

But the creative writer might say:

> Once my brother tried to open a tube of Krazy Glue with his teeth. When the cap came loose, glue squirted out and sealed his lips shut. They had to be pried open in a hospital ER.

Rather than merely stating that his brother was accident-prone, the author *shows* this quality with specific details.

> Now look at the following statement that a nonfiction writer might produce:

> It would be really hard to feel the pain that others feel. It is better not to know.

Compare the above with the following lines about the pain in human life from George Eliot's *Middlemarch*, considered by many the greatest of English novels:

> If we had a keen vision and feeling of all ordinary human life, it would be like hearing the grass grow and the squirrel's heart beat, and we should die of that roar which lies on the other side of silence. As it is, we walk about well wadded with stupidity.

Eliot uses vivid images that help us infer a profound human truth—that behind the surface we often carry around a great deal of pain—a "roar . . . on the other side of silence." So as to not die from experiencing the pain of others, we protect and wad ourselves with ignorance and stupidity. To get the most out of creative writing and literature, you must often infer the meanings behind the words—just as you do in everyday life.

Figures of Speech

Creative writers often use comparisons known as **figures of speech** to imply their meanings and give us a fresh and more informed way of looking at something. The two most common figures of speech are similes and metaphors.

Simile—a comparison introduced with *like, as,* or *as if.*

In the cartoon, Snoopy writes about a pair of beautiful eyes that they are "like two supper dishes"! (The joke, of course, is that the comparison is hardly a flattering one.)

In the quotation from *Middlemarch*, George Eliot uses two similes. To see and feel all ordinary human life, Eliot says, would be "like hearing the grass grow and the squirrel's heart beat."

Here's another example. Instead of saying, "The morning after the party, my mouth felt awful," you could express the same idea vividly by saying, "The morning after the party, my mouth felt like a used ashtray." The simile shows just how nasty your mouth felt. It gives us more information than the line that simply tells us your mouth felt awful.

Here are some other similes:

- Abandoned houses lined the city street *like tombstones*.

- That too-thin teenage girl has arms *like matchsticks*.

- The look the hostess gave me was *as welcoming as a glass of ice water in my face*.

- The used car salesman attached himself to prospective customers *like Velcro*.

- My mind was becoming *as calm as the surface of a quiet mountain lake*.

Metaphor—an implied comparison, with *like, as,* or *as if* omitted.

The 23rd Psalm in the Bible is the source of some of the world's best-known metaphors, including "The Lord is my shepherd." The comparison suggests that God is like a shepherd who looks after his sheep.

Here are some other metaphors:

- The candidate waded into *a sea of people* to shake hands.

- The movie was *a bomb*.

- Her disapproval was *an ice pick to my heart*.

- The algebra problems were *a forest of tiny enemies*, jeering at me from the page.

- To people searching for information, the Internet is a vast *candy store* of facts.

PRACTICE 4

Use a check (✓) to identify each figure of speech as either a simile or a metaphor.
Then, in the space provided, answer each inference question that follows.

_____ 1. To Jennifer, the psychology course was a banquet of ideas.

   ___ simile   ___ metaphor

   You can infer that Jennifer
   A. finds her psychology course rather tedious.
   B. likes to eat during her psychology course.
   C. finds her psychology course quite interesting.

_____ 2. After I ate that meal, I felt as if I had swallowed a barbell.

   ___ simile   ___ metaphor

   You can infer that the meal was
   A. sweet.
   B. heavy.
   C. spicy.

_____ 3. When Don started to run track again after his knee operation, he felt like
   a bus on the racetrack at the Indy 500.

   ___ simile   ___ metaphor

   You can infer that Don
   A. felt slow and awkward.
   B. felt cheerful and optimistic.
   C. knew he would never regain his old form.

_____ 4. Tina says that her first boyfriend was an economy car, but her current
   one is a luxury sedan.

   ___ simile   ___ metaphor

   You can infer that Tina's current boyfriend
   A. is a big improvement over her first one.
   B. is an auto mechanic.
   C. is a family man.

_____ 5. The CEO of the company gave a talk to his employees that was one part
   sugar and one part sandpaper.

   ___ simile   ___ metaphor

   You can infer that the CEO
   A. was hard to understand.
   B. led a company that sold both groceries and home products.
   C. was both encouraging to and critical of his employees.

Dialog

Another way to write creatively is to use dialog that presents the exact words of the persons in your writing. Seeing and hearing speakers' exact words makes it seem as if we are present in a scene—or listening to the words in a film. Exact words can often help readers infer more about what a character is thinking and feeling than a great deal of description would.

PRACTICE 5

To appreciate the power of dialog, read the following story. Without stating the obvious, the dialog tells us a great deal about the attitudes of the two people involved. After reading the story, answer the inference questions about it.

[1]A girl who had been late every day so far came up to see me after class.

[2]"Hi," she said. "I'm probably going to be late a lot for this class. [3]I wanted to let you know so you won't be marking me late."

[4]"Why are you going to be late?" I asked.

[5]"The traffic is just so heavy between my house and school. [6]The drive takes longer than it should."

[7]"Doesn't that mean you need to leave your house earlier?" I asked.

[8]She looked exasperated and said, "No! I LEAVE at 7. [9]I only live 30 miles away. [10]It shouldn't take more than an hour to get here."

[11]There was a brief silence as I waited for her to say something that made sense. [12]Nothing was forthcoming. [13]I finally said, "But apparently it does take more than an hour, so . . . I think the only solution is for you to leave earlier."

[14]She wailed, "But that would mean leaving home at SIX-THIRTY. [15]Can't I do some extra credit work or something?"

[16]Again, we just looked at each other as I shook my head. [17]Did she expect me to say to her, "Oh, of course, YOU don't have to be on time. [18]Just the other students."

_____ 1. We can infer from the passage that the writer
   A. has had many students ask for favors.
   B. knows the student has a good reason for being late.
   C. is a teacher.
   D. is a parent whose children are college students.

_____ 2. We can conclude from the passage that the writer
   A. will no longer mark the student late for class.
   B. will continue to mark the student late for class.
   C. will probably give the student extra credit work.
   D. will tell the student that she is acting like a spoiled brat.

_____ 3. The passage suggests that
   A. teachers need to be more flexible about classroom rules.
   B. it is not a good idea to schedule classes in the morning.
   C. some students are unwilling to do what it takes to succeed in school.
   D. the student will probably drop out of school.

_____ 4. The passage suggests that the student
   A. knows she is not making sense.
   B. is used to getting her own way.
   C. is also late for her other classes.
   D. drives an old, beat-up car that can't go very fast.

_____ 5. We can infer that the writer
   A. lives closer to school than the student does.
   B. sometimes arrives late to class herself.
   C. is amazed at the student's request.
   D. will advise the student to drop her class.

INFERENCES IN READING AND WRITING: Mastery Test 1 (Reading)

A. (1–3.) Put a check (✓) by the **three** inferences that are most logically based on the information suggested by the cartoon.

____ 1. Lucy has just criticized the boy, Linus.

____ 2. Linus feels Lucy's criticism is valid.

____ 3. Lucy feels very guilty that Linus has taken her criticism badly.

____ 4. Lucy doesn't seem to realize that people may accept constructive criticism but not destructive criticism.

____ 5. The cartoonist believes we should never criticize others.

____ 6. The cartoonist believes it's best to criticize others in a constructive way.

B. (4–6.) Read the passage below. Then check (✓) the **three** inferences that are most logically supported by the information given.

> [1]Shortly after the young woman sat down in the bus, she lit a cigarette. [2]The man next to her waved some smoke away, nudged her, and pointed to the sign at the front of the bus.
>
> [3]The woman did not turn to look at the man and continued smoking calmly. [4]The man got up and spoke to the bus driver, who continued driving and shook his head. [5]At the next stop, the man, looking disgusted, got off the bus.

____ 1. The man had never smoked.

____ 2. The smoke was bothering the man.

____ 3. The man pointed to a no-smoking sign.

____ 4. The driver refused to get involved.

____ 5. The man got off the bus because it was his stop.

____ 6. The driver was related to the woman.

(Continues on next page)

C. Read the passage below, taken from the autobiographical book *Move On* by the television journalist Linda Ellerbee. Then, in the spaces provided, write the letter of the most logical answer to each question, based on the information given in the passage.

¹Television changed my family forever. ²We stopped eating dinner at the dining-room table after my mother found out about TV trays. ³We kept the TV trays behind the kitchen door and served ourselves from pots on the stove. ⁴Setting and clearing the dining-room table used to be my job; now, setting and clearing meant unfolding and wiping our TV trays, then, when we'd finished, wiping and folding our TV trays. ⁵Dinner was served in time for one program and finished in time for another. ⁶During dinner we used to talk to one another. ⁷Now television talked to us. ⁸If you had something you absolutely had to say, you waited until the commercial, which is, I suspect, where I learned to speak in thirty-second bursts. ⁹As a future writer, it was good practice in editing my thoughts. ¹⁰As a little girl, it was lonely as hell. ¹¹Once in a while, I'd pass our dining-room table and stop, thinking I heard our ghosts sitting around talking to one another, saying stuff.

_____ 7. We can infer that as a child, Ellerbee
   A. preferred eating at the dining-room table to eating in front of TV.
   B. was glad that she no longer had to set and clear the dining-room table.
   C. wished that her parents watched TV programs that she enjoyed.

_____ 8. Ellerbee suggests that
   A. TV can help people feel less lonely.
   B. it's possible to feel lonely even when others are around.
   C. talking with others does not help to reduce loneliness.

_____ 9. We can infer that in Ellerbee's home
   A. her mother was aware that Ellerbee was unhappy with TV.
   B. there were no other children for Ellerbee to talk to.
   C. watching TV became more important than talking and listening to family members.

_____ 10. We can infer that when Ellerbee imagined ghosts, she
   A. was remembering better times with her family.
   B. was scared of passing by the dining room.
   C. realized her childhood home was haunted.

INFERENCES IN READING AND WRITING: Mastery Test 2 (Reading)

A. (1–2.) Put a check (✓) by the **two** inferences that are most logically based on the details in the cartoon below.

_____ 1. The children are enjoying themselves.

_____ 2. The house was built on stilts so the children could play underneath it.

_____ 3. The children probably seldom watch real television.

_____ 4. The cartoonist wishes to emphasize how television keeps children from more active play.

_____ 5. The cartoonist means to emphasize the children's creativity in building a realistic sand sculpture.

B. (3–4.) Read the passage below. Then check the **two** inferences that are most logically supported by the information given.

> [1]"Does the chili have any meat in it?" the woman asked. [2]"No," answered the waiter. [3]"I'll have chili, then." [4]The waiter was disappointed, since chili was one of the restaurant's least expensive items. [5]"The lobster special is delicious," he suggested, "and healthy." [6]The woman shook her head and responded, "Not for the lobster."

_____ 1. The woman is a vegetarian.

_____ 2. The woman was brought up as a vegetarian.

_____ 3. The waiter was hoping to get a larger tip for a more expensive meal.

_____ 4. The woman is on a tight budget.

_____ 5. The woman was alone.

(Continues on next page)

C. (5–8.) Read the passage below. Then, in the spaces provided, write the letter of the most logical answer to each question, based on the information given in the passage.

[1]Mutual attraction may get us into a love relationship, but it is not the determining factor in making the relationship grow and last. [2]Two factors that make relationships endure have to do with expectations and equity. [3]When two people first fall in love, they often enjoy a mixture of romantic, sexual, and other intense feelings of love. [4]In healthy, lasting relationships this passionate love gradually shifts into compassionate love, which blends friendship, intimacy, commitment, and security. [5]If both people in the relationship anticipate and welcome this shift, the transition is managed comfortably. [6]Expectations are aligned with reality. [7]If not, the relationship can become troubled or even end because of this surprise about the nature of love or any number of other unrealistic expectations that can occur. [8]In addition, each person in the relationship needs to experience a balance between what he/she puts into the relationship and what he/she gets out of it. [9]Each needs to feel that neither too little nor too much is received when compared with what is given. [10]This equity helps make for a happy relationship.

_____ 5. We can infer that the author of this passage believes
   A. romantic love can be damaging to a relationship.
   B. the happiest couples are not physically attracted to one another.
   C. physical attraction is often strongest early in a relationship.

_____ 6. We can conclude that the author of this passage
   A. has learned through personal experience about the uncertainties in relationships.
   B. believes that realism about love increases the chance of happiness.
   C. believes that love inevitably fades after people have been together a long time.

_____ 7. We can infer from this passage that the author believes
   A. the changes that people in love go through are sad, but inevitable.
   B. compassionate love can be richly rewarding.
   C. people should change partners when feelings of romantic love fade.

_____ 8. We can conclude from the author's remarks that
   A. ideally, people in a relationship will enjoy both giving and receiving.
   B. a person who really wants a relationship to succeed will ignore his or her own needs.
   C. there is no such thing as receiving too much from a partner.

INFERENCES IN READING AND WRITING: Mastery Test 3 (Reading)

A. (1–2.) Put a check (✓) by the **two** inferences that are most logically based on the information suggested by the cartoon.

"But we can't break up. Without you I'd be like a burger without fries."

___ 1. This is the couple's first date.

___ 2. The woman in the cartoon wants to break up with the man.

___ 3. The woman likes the man more than he likes her.

___ 4. The man is a very independent person.

___ 5. The woman may not like the man comparing their relationship to a hamburger and frics.

B. (3–4.) Read the following passage. Then put a check (✓) by the **two** inferences that are most logically based on the information given.

> [1]The goal of our lives must be to reach out in kindness, love, and care. [2]We must change the world by our relationships with other people—that will be our immortality. [3]We will not be remembered for job or financial success. [4]There is no gravestone that says, "Effective CEO" or "A Multimillionaire." [5]Hopefully our grave will have words such as "Loving father" or "Devoted daughter" or "Caring husband" or "Beloved sister."

___ 1. Family members should help each other out financially.

___ 2. The writer of this passage is a minister.

___ 3. We will be remembered for how we treated people.

___ 4. Gravestones should describe people's careers.

___ 5. Matcrial success is not the same as human success.

(Continues on next page)

C. Read the following passage. Then, in the spaces provided, write the letter of the most logical answer to each question, based on the information given in the passage.

[1]My friends have no friends. [2]They are men. [3]They think they have friends, and if you ask them whether they have friends they will say yes, but they don't really. [4]They think, for instance, that I'm their friend, but I'm not. [5]It's OK. [6]They're not my friends either.

[7]The reason for that is that we are all men—and men, I have come to believe, cannot or will not have real friends. [8]They have something else—companions, buddies, pals, chums, someone to drink with and someone to lunch with, but no one when it comes to saying how they feel—especially how they hurt.

[9]Women know this. [10]They talk about it among themselves. [11]To women, this inability of men to say what they feel is a source of amazement and then anguish and then, finally, betrayal. [12]Women will tell you all the time that they don't know the men they live with. [13]They talk of long silences and of drifting off and of keeping feelings hidden and never letting on about troubles or bothers or whatever.

_____ 5. We can infer that the author of this passage
    A. has genuine friends himself.
    B. believes men have no need of genuine friends.
    C. feels something prevents men from having genuine friends.

_____ 6. We can infer that the author
    A. is proud he is able to share his feelings better than other men.
    B. believes women want the men in their lives to share their feelings.
    C. believes men have more hurt feelings than women do.

_____ 7. We can infer that the author believes women
    A. have genuine friends.
    B. prefer "strong, silent" men.
    C. understand why men do not talk about their feelings.

_____ 8. We can conclude that the author thinks
    A. men realize they don't have friends.
    B. women should try to be more like men when it comes to friendship.
    C. men's relationships aren't deep enough to be genuine friendships.

INFERENCES IN READING AND WRITING: Mastery Test 4 (Writing)

A. Use a check (✓) to identify the item in each pair that shows us sharp and vivid details rather than vague and general ones.

1. ____ A. Robert's frequent complaints about aches and pains and other health problems make me think he is a bit of a hypochondriac.

   ____ B. In one week, Robert announced that he thought he had a broken rib, a brain tumor, tuberculosis, and poison ivy, none of which turned out to be true.

2. ____ A. We knew immediately from his face and his attitude that our boss was angry about something when he arrived at work this morning.

   ____ B. The boss walked in with his face as tense and hard as granite. He didn't say a word to anyone, but his fists were clenched tight.

3. ____ A. I had my first broken heart when I was 15, and I was so upset that I lost ten pounds and about ten nights of sleep. My mom was afraid to turn on the radio, because any cheesy love song could make me burst into tears.

   ____ B. When I went through my first breakup, it was harder than anything I'd ever been through before. I couldn't eat or sleep, and the slightest thing could upset me and make me cry.

4. ____ A. The movie *Toy Story* was a huge hit with my little nephew. He laughed so much, it was clear he thought it was hilarious!

   ____ B. While watching *Toy Story*, my little nephew actually fell off the couch from laughing so hard. Once on the floor he just lay there, giggling helplessly.

5. ____ A. There are not enough parking spaces in our neighborhood, and it is becoming a real problem. More and more, people are leaving their cars illegally parked.

   ____ B. Because parking is limited, the people across the street park their cars in their front yard, and our neighbors practically block the road with their SUV parked on the narrow shoulder.

6. ____ A. Today Janna wore a faded army shirt with a pair of black velvet trousers that were two sizes too large. On her feet were men's work boots.

   ____ B. Janna doesn't have very good taste in clothes. She puts together odd-looking outfits out of mismatched garments that don't fit her well.

(Continues on next page)

7. ___ A. Dolphins are thought to be the most intelligent animals after humans, and their activities also indicate that they have a well-developed sense of humor.

    ___ B. Dolphins huddle together and use clicks and whistles to communicate and plan actions. When they're bored, they sneak up behind pelicans and nip at their tail feathers.

B. (8–10.) Use sharp and specific details—visual details and actions, sounds, smells, tastes, and textures—to turn any **three** of the following sentences into vivid ones. Use the spaces provided.

Example

Our daughter has an unusual interest in bugs.

Six-year-old Katie often spends hours with a huge magnifying glass inspecting ants and crickets in our backyard. And just yesterday, she carried a giant water beetle up to her room, hoping to keep it as a pet.

1. The coffee was bad.
2. The party sounded like fun.
3. My brother bought a new car.
4. Only one other passenger was on the bus.
5. The house looked deserted.
6. I heard a noise.
7. The cat slept.
8. The singer walked on stage.
9. The driver was angry.
10. Thanksgiving dinner was delicious.

INFERENCES IN READING AND WRITING: Mastery Test 5 (Writing)

Use a check (✓) to identify each figure of speech as a simile or a metaphor. Then, in the space provided, answer each inference question that follows.

_____ 1. The car was like a trash can on wheels.

    ___ simile   ___ metaphor

    You can infer that the car
    A. was neat and well-kept.
    B. was dirty and messy.
    C. did not run well.

_____ 2. When the rainstorm hit, it was as if a giant water balloon in the sky had suddenly burst.

    ___ simile   ___ metaphor

    You can infer that the rainfall was
    A. heavy.
    B. fun.
    C. dangerous.

_____ 3. After their fight, Jason sent Brianna a long letter full of apologies and cotton-candy words.

    ___ simile   ___ metaphor

    You can infer that Jason's letter was
    A. insincere.
    B. sweet.
    C. funny.

_____ 4. The vampire passed through the streets at midnight like a fleeting shadow.

    ___ simile   ___ metaphor

    You can infer that the vampire
    A. moved quickly and quietly.
    B. moved in stops and starts.
    C. was wearing black.

_____ 5. When she's in a good mood, our math teacher is Mother Teresa; at other times, she's the Terminator.

    ___ simile   ___ metaphor

    You can infer that the teacher
    A. is very skilled in teaching algebra.
    B. is sometimes very kind and sometimes cruel.
    C. has been teaching for a long time.

(Continues on next page)

_____ 6. Antonio's anger is a cancer that eats away at any joy that comes into his life.

___ simile   ___ metaphor

You can infer that Antonio's anger
A. is making him very sick.
B. keeps him from being happy.
C. makes him hungry.

_____ 7. People taking pictures with cell phones surrounded the celebrity like bees surrounding a flower.

___ simile   ___ metaphor

You can infer that the people with cell phones
A. thought the celebrity smelled nice.
B. avoided the celebrity.
C. gathered tightly around the celebrity.

_____ 8. Brendan is a big puppy dog of a guy.

___ simile   ___ metaphor

You can infer that Brandan
A. has a nasty temper.
B. is friendly and playful.
C. is fond of animals.

_____ 9. That doctor's bedside manner is as warm as a snowdrift in the Arctic.

___ simile   ___ metaphor

You can infer that the doctor
A. has cold hands.
B. is neither friendly nor encouraging.
C. has not been a doctor for very long.

_____10. When I drank those three cups of espresso, I suddenly felt as if someone had strapped two rocket engines to me.

___ simile   ___ metaphor

You can infer that the espresso was
A. hot.
B. bitter.
C. energizing.

INFERENCES IN READING AND WRITING: Mastery Test 6 (Writing)

Make up and write a *realistic and lively* dialog between two or more people. Don't have your characters talk like cardboard figures; have them talk the way people would in real life. Also, make sure their voices are consistent. (Don't have them suddenly talk out of character.)

The dialog might, for example, be a discussion or an argument between two friends, or a husband and wife, or a parent and child, or a brother and sister, or a clerk and customer, or a doctor and patient, or a police officer and suspect. The verbal exchange might lead to an action or decision of some kind.

You should begin by describing the setting—the time, the place, and what is happening there—in which the dialog takes place. Also, you should briefly describe the characters involved and the relationship between them. Enclose characters' exact words within quotation marks; enclose descriptions or other comments within parentheses. Use the example that follows as a guide.

SETTING: Elena and Dan are walking away from the movie theater, discussing their reactions to the film they had just seen.

"Didn't you think the acting was great? I just think the whole cast did a great job," Elena said.

"The movie was short on plot, though. It really had no story at all," Dan said.

Before heading down the steps into the subway, Elena reached into her purse for her wallet.

"Oh no!" she cried. "My wallet's gone!"

"Now, take it easy. You're probably just not spotting it," Dan said soothingly. "Let's take a better look under the street light."

"No, it's gone," Elena said after searching. "It must have fallen out when I put my purse down at our seats. We have to hurry back!"

When Elena and Dan arrived back at the theater, only the staff remained. "I've lost my wallet," Elena told an usher. "Please let us into the auditorium. We need to look for it at our seats."

The usher agreed.

"I'm sorry about this, Dan," Elena said with some embarrassment as they searched.

"Hey, it could happen to anybody."

After searching without success, Elena said, "I've lost thirty dollars and all my I.D. cards. What's most depressing is that somebody took my wallet—not just the money, but everything else too."

(Continues on next page)

Just then the usher approached them. "Would you describe your wallet for me?" she asked Elena.

"It was denim," Elena answered. "Blue denim with tan trim."

"Then here you are," the usher said with a grin, handing Elena her wallet.

"That's it! Thank goodness!" said Elena, beaming.

"Someone turned it in right after the movie." Then the usher giggled. "I guess you're lucky the movie was *Act of Kindness*. That must have inspired the right emotion."

Many of us enjoy a good argument. A good argument is not an emotional experience in which people's feelings get out of control, leaving them ready to start throwing things. Instead, it is a rational discussion in which each person advances and supports a point of view about some matter. We might argue with a friend, for example, about where to eat or what movie to go to. We might argue about whether a boss or a parent or an instructor is acting in a fair or unfair manner. We might argue about whether certain performers or sports stars deserve to get paid as much as they do. In an argument (such as the one going on in the above cartoon), the two parties each present supporting evidence. The goal is to determine who has the more solid evidence to support his or her point of view.

Argumentation is, then, a part of our everyday dealings with other people. It is also an important part of much of what we read. Authors often try to convince us of their opinions and interpretations. Very often the most important things we must do as critical readers are

1 Recognize the **point** the author is making.

2 Decide if the author's support is **relevant**.

3 Decide if the author's support is **adequate**.

This chapter will give you practice in doing the above, first in everyday arguments and then in textbook material.

The Basics of Argument: Point and Support

A good **argument** is one in which you make a point and then provide persuasive and logical evidence to support it. Here is a point:

Point: Even though the apartment is nice, I don't think you should move there.

This statement hardly discourages us from moving into the apartment. "Why do you say that?" we might legitimately ask. "Give your reasons." Support is needed so we can decide for ourselves whether a valid argument has been made. Suppose the point is followed by these three reasons:

1. The closest washer and dryer are in a laundromat three miles away.

2. Next door to the apartment building is an all-night bar.

3. Several bugs scurried into dark holes when the kitchen sink cabinet door was opened.

Clearly, the details provide solid support for the point. They give us a basis for understanding and agreeing with the point. In light of these details, we may consider looking for another apartment to rent.

We see here a small example of what clear thinking in an argument is about: making a point and then providing support that truly backs up that point. A **valid argument** may also be described as a conclusion supported by logical reasons, facts, examples, and other evidence.

Let's look at another example:

Point: The corner convenience store is run poorly.

We don't yet know if we would agree that the store is run poorly. We might trust the person who made the statement, but we can't judge for ourselves until we learn the supporting details. Here are those details:

1. Milk is routinely kept on the shelves several days after the suggested date of sale.

2. The "fresh" fruits and vegetables are often spotted and wrinkled.

3. At busy times of the day, there's not enough help in the store, so the lines are very long.

Again, the solid support convinces us that a logical point has been made.

Argument in Reading

Point and Support in an Argument

In everyday life, of course, people don't simply say, "Here is my point" and "Here is my support." Nor do writers state their basic ideas so directly. Even so, the basic structure of point and support is still at work beneath the surface, and to evaluate an argument, you need to recognize the writer's point and support.

You have already practiced point and support in the main ideas chapter (pages 15–40). The following practice exercise will deepen your understanding of point and support—the basic principles of argument.

PRACTICE 1

In each group, one statement is the point, and the other statements are support for the point. Identify each point with a **P** and each statement of support with an **S**.

> *Hint:* If it sounds right to insert the word *because* in front of a sentence, you probably have a statement of support. For example, we could say, *"Because* the closest washer and dryer are three miles away, *because* the apartment building is close to an all-night bar, and *because* several bugs were visible below the kitchen sink, I've come to the conclusion that I should not move into that apartment."

1. _____ A. Affordable daycare facilities often lack professionally trained staff and fail to follow adequate child-safety procedures.

   _____ B. It's hard for working parents to find reliable, affordable daycare.

   _____ C. Excellent daycare can cost $15,000–$20,000 a year per child.

   _____ D. For many working parents, the oldest form of daycare—adult relatives who live nearby—is unavailable.

2. _____ A. According to some medieval philosophers, laughing dishonored humans because it made them look like monkeys.

_____ B. Some medieval theologians believed that all laughing mocked God's creation and therefore endangered the human soul.

_____ C. Many people objected to comedy, believing that laughing encouraged drunkenness and improper behavior.

_____ D. In the Middle Ages, many people considered laughing harmful.

3. _____ A. A bone marrow transplant can increase the chances of survival for thousands of people who are diagnosed with leukemia and other blood-related diseases each year.

_____ B. More people should agree to donate bone marrow if their marrow matches the type of a patient in need.

_____ C. Only about 30 percent of patients can find a match among their own family members.

_____ D. People can donate marrow easily and safely: it can be collected in about forty-five minutes and is naturally replaced by the body within two to three weeks.

Relevant Support in an Argument

Once you identify the point and support of an argument, you need to decide if each piece of evidence is **relevant**—in other words, if it really applies to the point.

The critical reader must ask, "Is this reason relevant support for the argument?" In their enthusiasm for making an argument, people often bring up irrelevant support. For example, the fan of potato chips in the cartoon shown does not offer relevant support for his point that potato chips are diet food. Or as another example: In trying to get your cousin to take you to dinner, you might say, "You just got your paycheck." The fact that she just got her paycheck is beside the point; the question is whether she wants (or is able) to spend any of it on you.

An excellent way to develop your skill in recognizing relevant support is to work on simple point-support outlines of arguments. By isolating the reasons of an argument, such outlines help you think about whether each reason is truly relevant. Paying close attention to the relevance of support will help you not only in your reading, but also in making and supporting points in your own writing.

✓ Check Your Understanding

Consider the following outline. The point is followed by six facts, only three of which are relevant support for the point. See if you can check (✓) the **three** relevant statements of support.

Point: Pigs make good pets.

____ 1. When a pig weighs over 180 pounds, it is called a hog.

____ 2. Pigs are friendly and intelligent.

____ 3. In 1965, a pig named "Old Faithful" gave birth to thirty-six piglets in one litter.

____ 4. Pigs are easily housebroken.

____ 5. Pigs, like people, can get sunburn.

____ 6. Pigs can be taught to walk on a leash.

Now read the following comments on the six items to see which numbers you should have checked and why.

Explanation

1. What an animal is called has no bearing on how good a pet it will make. And for many people, the fact that pigs can weigh over 180 pounds is a reason they are *not* good pets. So you should not have checked number 1.

2. People tend to like pets who like them back and with whom they can interact. You should have checked number 2.

3. Admittedly, Old Faithful's accomplishment is nothing to oink at, but how many pet owners want thirty-six more pets than they started out with? You should not have checked number 3.

4. Given modern standards of cleanliness, being easily housebroken is even more attractive to many pet owners than friendliness or a genius IQ. You should have checked number 4.

5. Most people would prefer a pet for whom they wouldn't have to buy a lifetime supply of sunscreen. Therefore, you should not have checked number 5.

6. Since humans enjoy taking walks with their pets, the ability to keep an animal under control outdoors is important. Number 6 is the third number you should have checked.

PRACTICE 2

Each point is followed by three statements that provide relevant support and three that do not. In the spaces, write the letters of the **three** relevant statements of support.

Hint: To help you decide if a sentence is relevant or not, ask yourself, "Does this provide logical support for the point being argued?"

1. **Point: Married people have fewer health problems than unmarried people.**
   A. Married people suffer fewer incidents of back pain and headache than single people.
   B. The Centers for Disease Control keeps statistics on health issues affecting various segments of the population.
   C. Married people are more likely to be overweight than single people.
   D. Serious psychological disorders are more common among unmarried people than married people.
   E. High blood pressure afflicts more single people than married people.
   F. On the average, people marry at a later age now than they did a generation ago.

   Items that logically support the point: _____   _____   _____

2. **Point: "Dress-down" Friday in offices has positive effects.**
   A. No one knows exactly how the custom of dressing casually on Fridays started.
   B. Whatever its origins, dressing casually on Fridays has become very widespread.
   C. Dressing casually on Fridays provides a break in the routine, which energizes workers.
   D. Casual dress seems to reduce stress by creating a more relaxed atmosphere.

   E. Informality also seems to lead to more friendliness and cooperation between employees.

   F. Some employers complain that workers abuse the custom by wearing outfits that belong on the beach—or in the bedroom.

   Items that logically support the point: _____   _____   _____

3. **Point: People should consider alternatives to traditional burial practices.**

   A. A sympathetic, well-trained funeral director can be very helpful during a difficult time.

   B. A biodegradable coffin buried in a plot marked by shrubbery is easier on the environment than a traditional coffin and headstone.

   C. People may feel that giving their loved ones anything other than an expensive, conventional burial is somehow disrespectful.

   D. Families can avoid the expense of maintaining a cemetery plot by cremating, instead of burying, the dead.

   E. Many states permit burial on home property, which can be a more convenient burial location than a cemetery.

   F. Burial grounds provide valuable information to genealogists, sociologists, and other people interested in the past.

   Items that logically support the point: _____   _____   _____

Adequate Support in an Argument

A valid argument must include not only relevant support but also an **adequate** amount of support—enough to prove the point. For example, it would not be valid to argue "A government tax cut is a bad idea" if one's only support was "My taxes will still be too high." Such an important issue would require more support than one person's tax situation. Arguing a point that doesn't have adequate support is called "jumping to a conclusion."

✓ *Check Your Understanding*

In the argument below, three supporting reasons are given, followed by four possible conclusions. The evidence (that is, the supporting reasons) adequately supports only one of the points; it is insufficient to support the other three. Choose the **one** point that you think is adequately supported, and put a check mark (✓) beside it.

Support

● Lately Valerie has looked thinner and paler than usual.

● She used to go to all the parties, but now she stays home in the evenings.

● At work, she has been seen crying in the ladies' room.

Which **point** is adequately supported by all the evidence above?

____ A. Valerie is seriously ill.

____ B. Something is troubling Valerie.

____ C. Valerie has broken up with her boyfriend.

____ D. Valerie owes a great deal of money.

Explanation

The correct answer is B. From her behavior, we can safely conclude that something is troubling Valerie, but we have very little evidence about what is troubling her. Answer A is not well supported. The fact that Valerie hasn't been looking well makes us wonder if she's seriously ill, but we have no other evidence for that conclusion. Answer C is also poorly supported. The fact that Valerie hasn't been going to parties does make us wonder whether or not she's broken up with her boyfriend, but we have absolutely no other evidence to support that conclusion. Finally, except for the evidence showing that Valerie is troubled in some way, answer D has no evidence at all to support it, so it too is a poorly supported conclusion. We simply have insufficient information to decide anything more than this: something is troubling Valerie.

PRACTICE 3

For each group, read the three items of support (the evidence). Then check (✓) the **one** point that is adequately supported by that evidence.

Group 1

Support

- In one study, fifteen of the thirty women who listened to music during childbirth labor had no need for anesthesia.
- Studies indicate that the body produces pain-reducing hormones when a person listens to enjoyable music.
- Patients who had suffered a stroke gained lasting benefits after listening for three weeks to recorded music.

Point: Which of the following conclusions is best supported by all the evidence above?

____ A. Music can have a role in curing diseases of all types.

____ B. Music can be a helpful tool in dealing with some physical problems.

____ C. Music should be a resource in every medical office.

____ D. Music can also have negative effects on our physical well-being.

Group 2

Support

- "Living out of a suitcase"—being away from home and our familiar routine—and coping with planes, trains, buses, and rental cars can be exhausting.
- While on vacation, we often eat too much, drink too much, get too little sleep, work too hard at sightseeing, and in general overextend ourselves.
- Also, we tend to expect a vacation to be a "dream come true," and so we feel frustrated, angry, and let down if anything is less than perfect.

Point: Which of the following conclusions is best supported by all the evidence above?

____ A. A vacation trip with young children can be very difficult.

____ B. A vacation trip isn't always restful.

____ C. The expense of a vacation trip is a big worry for most people.

____ D. The best vacation is one spent dieting and exercising.

Group 3

Support

- Athletes often privately credit their victories to their own ability and their losses to bad breaks, lousy officiating, or the other team's exceptional performance.

- After receiving poor exam grades, most students in a half dozen studies criticized the exam, not themselves; generally, students interpret good grades to be the result of their own efforts.

- On insurance forms, drivers have explained accidents in such words as these: "An invisible car came out of nowhere, struck my car, and vanished"; "As I reached an intersection, a hedge sprang up obscuring my vision, and I did not see the other car"; "A pedestrian hit me and went under my car."

Which **point** is adequately supported by the evidence above?

____ A. Most people lack the skills they need to perform well at work and school.

____ B. People accept more responsibility for good deeds than for bad ones.

____ C. People tend to perform at a rather high level most of the time.

____ D. People accept more responsibility for successes than for failures.

Group 4

Support

- An increased amount, or volume, of blood in the circulatory system can elevate blood pressure.

- If the heart is pumping with too much force, that increases blood pressure by straining the circulation.

- The condition of the artery wall is also important: when the wall thickens, the artery becomes narrower, and the pressure of the blood flowing through it rises.

Which **point** is adequately supported by the evidence above?

____ A. High blood pressure is a mysterious, silent killer.

____ B. Factors in high blood pressure include stress, a fatty diet, and lack of exercise.

____ C. Factors in high blood pressure include the blood, the heart, and the arteries.

____ D. High blood pressure can be controlled by medications and lifestyle changes.

Group 5

Support

● A happily married man or woman might attribute a spouse's distracted manner to stress at work.

● An unhappily married man or woman might attribute a distracted manner to a decline in affection.

● A happily married man or woman might attribute a spouse's unexpected gift to a desire to show love.

● An unhappily married man or woman might consider an unexpected gift as evidence of guilt about something.

Which **point** is adequately supported by the evidence above?

____ A. Men or women who surprise their partners with gifts have probably been cheating on them.

____ B. Happily and unhappily married spouses tend to interpret their partners' behaviors differently.

____ C. People who are happily married are often deluding themselves about reality.

____ D. Spouses should give each other gifts more often.

Support in an Argumentative Essay

Following is an essay on a highly debatable point—whether or not to end the death penalty. Read it and decide whether the support for the point is both relevant and adequate. Then read the explanation that follows.

Second Thoughts of a "Hanging Judge"
Donald A. McCartin

1 In 1978, the first time Jerry Brown was governor of California, he appointed me to a judgeship in the Superior Court of Orange County. It was a gutsy move on his part, a liberal Democrat naming a right-wing Republican to the bench. I served there until 1993, after which I sat on assignment on death cases throughout California.

2 During that time, I presided over 10 murder cases in which I sentenced the convicted men to die. As a result, I became known as "the hanging judge of Orange County," an appellation that, I will confess, I accepted with some pride.

3 The 10 were deemed guilty of horrifying crimes by their peers, and in the jurors' view as well as mine they deserved to die at the hands of the state.

4 However, as of today, not one of them has been executed (though one died in prison of natural causes).

5 I am deeply angered by the fact that our system of laws has become so complex and convoluted that it makes mockery of decisions I once believed promised resolution for the family members of victims.

6 That said, I have followed the development of legal thinking and understand why our nation's Supreme Court, in holding that "death is different," has required that special care be taken to safeguard the rights of those sentenced to death. Such wisdom protects our society from returning to the barbarism of the past. And though I find it discomfiting and to a significant degree embarrassing that appellate courts have found fault with some of my statements, acts or decisions, I can live with the fact that their findings arise out of an attempt to ensure that the process has been scrupulously fair before such a sentence is carried out.

7 I can live with it and, apparently, so can the men I condemned. The first one, Rodney James Alcala, whom I sentenced to die more than 30 years ago for kidnapping and killing 12-year-old Robin Samsoe, was, just last year, again sentenced to death for killing Samsoe and four other young women who, it has subsequently been determined, were his victims around the same time.

8 I need not go into the permutations of Alcala's legal journey. Behind bars since 1979, he has not harmed, nor can he harm, any other young women. But harm has been done, and that's what infuriates me. Robin Samsoe's mother has been revictimized time and time again as the state of California spent millions upon millions of dollars in unsuccessful attempts to finally resolve the case against her daughter's murderer.

9   Had I known then what I know now, I would have given Alcala and the others the alternative sentence of life in prison without the possibility of parole. Had I done that, Robin's mother, Marianne, would have been spared the pain of 30 appeals and writs and retrial. She could have dealt then and there with the fact that her daughter's killer would be shut away, never again to see a day of freedom, and gone on to put her life together. And the people of California would have not have had to pay many millions of tax dollars in this meaningless and ultimately fruitless pursuit of death.

10   It makes me angry to have been made a player in a system so inefficient, so ineffective, so expensive and so emotionally costly.

11   I watch today as Gov. Brown wrestles with the massive debt that is suffocating our state and hear him say he doesn't want to "play games." But I cringe when I learn that not playing games amounts to cuts to kindergarten, cuts to universities, cuts to people with special needs—and I hear no mention of the simple cut that would save hundreds of millions of dollars, countless man-hours, unimaginable court time and years of emotional torture for victims' family members waiting for that magical sense of "closure" they've been falsely promised with death sentences that will never be carried out.

12   There is actually, I've come to realize, no such thing as "closure" when a loved one is taken. What family members must find is reconciliation with the reality of their loss, and that can begin the minute the perpetrator is sent to a prison he will never leave. But to ask them to endure the years of being dragged through the courts in pursuit of the ultimate punishment is a cruel lie.

13   It's time to stop playing the killing game. Let's use the hundreds of millions of dollars we'll save to protect some of those essential services now threatened with death. Let's stop asking people like me to lie to those victims' family members.

14   The governor doesn't have the power to end the death penalty by himself, but he can point the way. He could have a huge financial impact on California by following the lead of Illinois and commuting the sentences of the more than 700 men and women on California's death row to life without parole.

Donald A. McCartin (1925–2012) was a California Superior Court judge.

Questions about the Selection

1. What is the author's point? _____

2. What is his support for his point? _____

   _____

   _____

3. Is his support relevant? _____ (Note that the credentials of the author are often part of deciding whether support is relevant.)

4. Is his support adequate? _____

Explanation

The author's point is that the death penalty should be abolished. His support is that our legal system makes it almost impossible to execute a murderer, costing the state millions of dollars and leaving the victim's family in continuing pain and anguish over the lack of resolution. Since the author was a retired Superior Court judge who had a lifetime of experience in considering the death penalty and who in fact once favored the death penalty, his support can be seen as relevant and—for some people, if not all—adequate.

Argument in Writing

Most of the papers you are asked to write in this book involve a certain amount of persuasion—to make a point and then effectively support that point. But in an argument paper, where a debatable issue is involved, you need to think more critically, making certain that your support is relevant and adequate to the point you are arguing.

Many issues in everyday life are the subject of argument. Is single life preferable to married life? Should abortions be banned? Should gay marriages be legalized in every state? Should students be given vouchers to go to the school of their choice? Should the death penalty exist? Should people be allowed to end their own lives? Should the United States be involved in overseas wars? Should assault rifles be banned? Should contraceptives be distributed in schools?

For these and many other complex issues, there are no easy answers, and arguments about them are bound to persist. Typically, even when one of these issues goes in some form before the U.S. Supreme Court, where all the support is examined in enormous detail, the judges are often unable to reach a unanimous opinion. Faced with a complex issue, we must try our best to think as clearly as we can about it. We must decide what we individually think after close consideration of all the evidence available.

A Note on Kinds of Evidence

Evidence comes in a number of forms: examples, facts and/or statistics, expert opinions, personal experience, and common-sense reasoning.

PRACTICE 4

The following exercise will sharpen your sense of how each of these common forms of evidence can be used to support a point. Label each set of supporting details with one of the following:

> **A. Examples**   **B. Facts and/or statistics**   **C. Expert opinion**
> **D. Personal experience**   **E. Common-sense reasoning**

Point: Hitting children is not a good way to discipline them.

___ 1. Child psychologist Dr. Phil McGraw has said: "I believe spanking genuinely confuses children. I believe they think to themselves something like, 'OK, let me get this right. You are supposed to love me, nurture me and protect me from harm, and now you are standing there, five times my size, and hitting me and inflicting physical pain? Hmmm . . . I don't get it.'"

___ 2. According to a recent Canadian study, almost 20 percent of those who remembered being physically punished had suffered depression, and 43 percent had abused alcohol at some point in their life. By comparison, only 16 percent of people who were not hit or slapped complained of having suffered depression, and only 30 percent abused alcohol.

___ 3. I got spanked once by my mother in front of others and am still mad about it. It was so sudden and unexpected that she made me cry. I was embarrassed that I stood there crying, and for a long time I hated my mother for putting me in that position. I don't want to run the risk of having my child have a similar reaction.

___ 4. Why is it okay for an adult to hit a child when it isn't even acceptable for an adult to pick on someone his own size? There are times we disagree with our colleagues, but that doesn't give us the right to haul off and hit them. The only reason children might deserve a "swat" is that we're big and they're small—and that is a morally and ethically indefensible reason.

___ 5. Many parents find that making a child serve a "time-out" alone in his or her room gets a more desirable response than spanking. Also, children who have privileges taken away will often respond more favorably than children who are disciplined by spanking.

PRACTICE 5: Writing an Argument Paragraph

Write an argument paragraph that supports one of the following points:

- Marijuana should (*or* should not) be legalized in every state.
- Abortion should (*or* should not) be legal.
- Smartphones should (*or* should not) be allowed in schools.
- Sugar-rich drinks should (*or* should not) be banned from stores.
- Online classes are (*or* are not) preferable to in-person classes.

A Model Paragraph

Here are two student models of argument paragraphs. The assignment was to advance an argument about single-sex schools. One student argued in favor of such schools; the other student argued against them.

> Students clearly benefit from single-sex schools, which should be available to all. For one thing, it has been proven that students do better academically when they attend single-sex schools. A study in Australia followed 270,000 students over a period of 20 years. Of those students, the boys and girls who attended single-sex schools scored from 15 percent to 22 percent higher on standardized tests than the students attending co-ed schools. Also, single-sex schools do a better job of serving the different educational needs of boys **and** girls. Social scientists David and Myra Sadker have demonstrated how boys' and girls' brains develop differently and at different rates. Girls tend to develop language abilities at an earlier age, while boys' spatial abilities often develop sooner. The result is that in co-ed schools, girls are viewed as "better" at reading and writing, while boys are thought to be "better" at math and science. But in single-sex schools, where teachers can deal with only one gender, boys and girls can develop excellent language and spatial skills at their own natural pace. A final reason single-sex schools benefit students is that they take away much of the social stress that gets in the way of students' learning. Especially during the high-school years, boys and girls are distracted by their growing attraction to potential boyfriends and girlfriends. The result is that they can't concentrate fully on their studies. Students who attend single-sex schools can have a social life outside of school, but still concentrate on their schoolwork during the day.

Single-sex schools may have some good points, but in general, they are a poor idea. First, they discriminate against whichever sex is excluded. Remember when there were schools for blacks and schools for whites? The Supreme Court decided there was no such thing as "separate but equal," and they were right. Schools for blacks were poorly equipped and had much less funding. The same principle applies here. If the sexes are educated separately, depending on who is running things, one is going to get a better deal than the other. In addition, single-sex schools will contribute to an unhealthy feeling of superiority for one's own sex. Boys and girls will both come out of such schools thinking that the other sex couldn't hack it in their schools. They'll believe that the other sex is intellectually inferior. Last, and most importantly, single-sex schools prevent boys and girls from learning to interact with the other sex. The world is made up of men and women, and for the rest of their lives, students are going to have to live with and work with and probably marry people of the opposite sex. High school is the natural time to learn to understand people of the other sex and how to get along with them. Without that essential time together, boys and girls are going to go out into the real world seriously handicapped in their social skills. They'll never get that opportunity back to spend their days working and studying and playing alongside people of the other sex.

● For each paragraph, underline the topic sentence—the sentence that expresses the main idea.

● For each paragraph, circle the addition words that move the reader from one supporting point to the next.

● Both paragraphs present evidence partly in the form of common-sense reasoning. Which paragraph also uses facts and/or statistics and expert opinion? _____

Writing Your Own Paragraph or Essay

1. Explore the topic you may want to write about (marijuana, abortion, smartphones, sugar-rich drinks, or online classes) by freewriting about it, or asking questions such as *what, when, where, how,* and *why* about it, or making a list of all the details you can think of about it. Prewriting will help you determine the topic for which you can provide the best supporting details.

2. You may also want to quickly research the topic by going online and Googling "marijuana pro and con" or "abortion pro and con" or "smartphones in schools pro and con" or "sugary drinks pro and con" or "online classes pro and con." You will find millions of articles on these topics! As you read through several of them, chances are you will clarify your point of view about a given topic and whether you would like to argue for or against it.

3. Prepare a scratch outline of your paragraph or essay. Decide upon the separate and distinct supporting points that back up your point. Remember that there are five kinds of evidence you can cite: examples; facts and/ or statistics; expert opinion; personal experience; and common-sense reasoning.

4. Then go on to write the first and later drafts of your paper. Chances are that as you write, you will think even more clearly about your point of view. Revise as need be.

5. When you feel you have the final draft of your paper, read it aloud to make sure that every sentence reads smoothly and clearly. Use a grammar handbook, if necessary, to see what corrections are needed. Make the required corrections to remove the trouble spots.

Writing a Longer Argument Paper with Sources

Turn to pages 452–457 for an extended argument essay in which a student uses a standard academic format for her paper as well as a standard method for documenting sources.

ARGUMENT IN READING AND WRITING: Mastery Test 1 (Reading)

In each group, one statement is the point of an argument, and the other statements are support for that point. In the space provided, write the letter of the point of each group.

_____ 1. A. Horror movies give us a chance to feel smarter than the characters, who often do incredibly stupid things such as investigating the moaning sounds in the dark basement of a haunted house.

B. Horror movies also provide a great bonding experience between friends by allowing us to share screams and grab each other for comfort.

C. Horror movies give us a chance to explore our deepest fears ("There's a crazed killer in the basement! There's something horrible lurking in the woods!") while knowing we are safe.

D. Horror movies deserve the popularity they have in American culture.

_____ 2. A. The Internal Revenue Service is the only government agency with the power to take people's property and salaries without a hearing or court order.

B. Legal loopholes allow wealthy, well-connected Americans to avoid paying their fair share of income tax.

C. The U.S. income tax system needs to be reformed.

D. The current tax on interest earned in bank accounts punishes people for saving their money.

_____ 3. A. Requirements should be ended for teacher certification since studies show that whether teachers are certified is irrelevant to their effectiveness.

B. Tenure should be made more difficult to obtain so that weak teachers can be weeded out after two or three years on the job.

C. Bold steps should be taken to improve the U.S. education system and to reduce the gap between the good schools in suburbs and the poor schools in inner cities.

D. Substantial bonuses of $15,000 or more should be awarded annually to good teachers for as long as they teach in schools in low-income areas.

(Continues on next page)

_____ 4. A. A defendant charged with assault and battery would be foolish to show up in the courtroom wearing a black leather jacket, jeans, and boots.

      B. The woman who dresses in sweatpants for a job interview with a major retail company isn't likely to be hired.

      C. Someone who shows up at a wedding wearing jeans and tennis shoes is likely to be considered rude.

      D. People make judgments about us based on the way we dress.

_____ 5. A. Our schools must spend time dealing with such social problems as substance abuse and teenage pregnancy, which Japanese schools are not expected to do.

      B. U.S. schools are not entirely to blame for the lower achievement of their students compared with the skills of Japanese students.

      C. Many U.S. teenagers cut back on their study time by taking a part-time job, which is virtually unheard of in Japan.

      D. Many U.S. parents work full-time and leave homework decisions to their children, whereas Japanese mothers make sure their children study several hours each night.

ARGUMENT IN READING AND WRITING: Mastery Test 2 (Reading)

A. Each point is followed by three statements that provide relevant support and three that do not. In the spaces, write the letters of the **three** relevant statements of support.

1–3. **Point: We should use more solar energy.**

    A. Unlike oil and coal, energy from the sun is unlimited.

    B. The sun nourishes plants and animals.

    C. Solar energy is nonpolluting.

    D. Wind and water power have been used for centuries.

    E. Solar energy is less effective in cloudy climates.

    F. Solar energy is extremely cost-effective.

Items that logically support the point: _____   _____   _____

4–6. **Point: High-heeled shoes are a health risk.**

    A. It is difficult to walk fast in high-heeled shoes.

    B. Although males have worn high-heeled shoes in some cultures and historical periods, they do not wear high-heeled shoes in our society.

    C. Long-term wearing of high-heeled shoes increases the likelihood of developing back and foot disorders.

    D. Many women wear high-heeled shoes to work.

    E. High-heeled shoes increase the risk of falling on a slippery surface.

    F. High, narrow heels easily catch in sidewalk cracks and gratings, resulting in falls.

Items that logically support the point: _____   _____   _____

7–9. **Point: Cats and dogs benefit from being neutered.**

    A. Cats and dogs should be taken to a veterinarian at least once a year for a checkup and vaccinations.

    B. Neutering reduces the likelihood that a cat or dog will develop certain common forms of cancer.

    C. If you adopt an animal from a local shelter, the shelter may neuter your new pet.

    D. Neutered cats and dogs tend to be more content to stay at home, where they're safest.

    E. On average, neutered cats and dogs live longer than unneutered ones.

    F. Purebred cats and dogs are more likely than mixed breeds to suffer from inherited disorders.

Items that logically support the point: _____   _____   _____

(Continues on next page)

B. (10.) In the following group, one statement is the point of an argument, and the other statements are support for that point. In the space provided, write the letter of the point.

_____ A. Some nutritionists believe that dividing food intake into "three square meals a day" is a poor way to fuel metabolism.

B. Many healthcare professionals now consider traditional American eating and activity patterns unhealthy.

C. Heart specialists say today's jobs involve insufficient physical activity.

D. According to healthcare professionals, fast food eaten "on the run" contributes to dangerously high levels of fat and cholesterol and forces the digestive system to work too hard and too fast.

ARGUMENT IN READING AND WRITING: Mastery Test 3 (Reading)

A. Each point below is followed by three statements that provide relevant support and three that do not. In the spaces, write the letters of the **three** relevant statements of support.

1–3. **Point:** Not all stereotypes are negative views of groups.

    A. Asians are often stereotyped as a "model minority," presumably smarter and harder-working than others.

    B. Redheaded women are supposed to be sultry, sexy, and gorgeous.

    C. On the other hand, redheads are also supposed to be hot-tempered—a negative stereotype.

    D. Women in general are stereotyped as having a "maternal instinct" and nurturing: in other words, as good mothers and good caregivers.

    E. Other stereotypes of women depict them as being illogical and weak.

    F. Most stereotypes are oversimplified at best and outright false at worst.

Items that logically support the point: _____ _____ _____

4–6. **Point:** Arranged marriage, as it is still often practiced in India, has its advantages.

    A. The extended family of an arranged couple may be overbearing and meddling.

    B. The partners in an arranged marriage are generally compatible in their backgrounds, upbringing, beliefs and values.

    C. Strong social pressure may force an arranged couple to stay together, even if one or both are very unhappy.

    D. Over the course of their marriage, arranged couples often learn to love each other deeply.

    E. If love is absent in the arranged marriage, one or both of the couple may seek it in an affair.

    F. Arranged couples generally have plenty of physical and emotional support from their extended families.

Items that logically support the point: _____ _____ _____

(Continues on next page)

B. In the group below, read the three items of support (the evidence). Then, in the space provided, write the letter of the point that is adequately supported by that evidence.

Support

- In the early 1900s, classrooms were crowded, stuffy, poorly lit, and conducive to the spread of disease.
- Classroom "learning" consisted mainly of memorizing questionable facts.
- Physical punishment was considered the best way to teach good behavior.

_____ 7. Which **point** is adequately supported by all the evidence above?
    A. A century ago, most education was a very negative experience.
    B. Teachers in the early 1900s were poorly trained.
    C. Parents a century ago objected to physical punishment of their children.
    D. A century ago, few students completed high school.

C. Read the paragraphs below and then answer the questions that follow.

¹The lack of childcare places women at a disadvantage in the workplace. ²First of all, women are sometimes prevented from taking paid positions when good childcare is unavailable. ³Participation in many social activities is also difficult for these same women. ⁴In addition, childcare problems force women to stay in part-time jobs with lower pay, little career mobility, and no fringe benefits. ⁵Finally, the childcare dilemma discourages women from putting in the time necessary to seek and accept job promotions. ⁶Women with childcare responsibilities thus often have no choice but to remain in jobs for which they are overqualified.

_____ 8. Which sentence is the point of the argument?

_____ 9. Which sentence is **not** relevant support for the author's argument?
    A. Sentence 2   C. Sentence 4
    B. Sentence 3   D. Sentence 5

¹Animals can be useful in promoting mental stability and health. ²By forming close relationships with animals, we can demonstrate the kinship of all living things. ³Experiments in prisons have shown that convicts who are allowed pets become less violent. ⁴Also, patients in nursing homes show greater responsiveness and a more positive attitude when they have an opportunity to share affection with dogs and cats. ⁵When some autistic children were given the opportunity to interact with dolphins, they made great strides, including speaking for the first time in their lives.

_____ 10. Which sentence is **not** relevant support for the author's argument?
    A. Sentence 2   C. Sentence 4
    B. Sentence 3   D. Sentence 5

ARGUMENT IN READING AND WRITING: Mastery Test 4 (Writing)

Write a paragraph or an essay arguing and supporting a point. Choose one of the following ideas that you have not written about before:

- Marijuana should (*or* should not) be legalized in every state.

- Abortion should (*or* should not) be legal.

- Smartphones should (*or* should not) be banned in schools.

- Sugar-rich drinks should (*or* should not) be banned from stores.

- Online classes are (*or* are not) preferable to in-person classes.

Writing Your Own Paragraph or Essay

1. Explore the topic you may want to write about (marijuana, abortion, smartphones, sugar-rich drinks, or online classes) by freewriting about it, or asking questions such as *what, when, where, how*, and *why* about it, or making a list of all the details you can think of about it. Prewriting will help you determine the topic for which you can provide the best supporting details.

2. You may also want to quickly research the topic by going online and Googling "marijuana pro and con" or "abortion pro and con" or "smartphones in schools pro and con" or "sugary drinks pro and con" or "online classes pro and con." You will find millions of articles on the topics! For example, here are just some of the pros and cons found by Googling that would help you think about one of the topics:

   - Online classes make going to college easier for students. They can "go to class" at their own convenience. They can also work at their own pace, rather than having to keep up with other students.

   - Online classes require students to have a great deal of self-discipline. In addition, since students aren't right there in the classroom with the instructor, they may have more trouble motivating themselves to study and learn the subject.

   As you read through a series of pros and cons about a given topic, chances are you will clarify your point of view about that topic and whether you would like to argue for or against it. Do not hesitate to explore the pros and cons for the other topics as well. Your goal is to find a topic that you feel very strongly about and that you think you can support with solid evidence.

(Continues on next page)

3. Prepare a scratch outline of your paragraph or essay. Decide upon the separate and distinct supporting points that back up your point. Remember that there are five kinds of evidence you can cite: examples; facts and/or statistics; expert opinion; personal experience; and common-sense reasoning.

4. Then go on to write the first and later drafts of your paper. Chances are that as you write, you will think even more clearly about your point of view. Revise as need be.

5. When you feel you have the final draft of your paper, read it aloud to make sure that every sentence reads smoothly and clearly. Use a grammar handbook, if necessary, to see what corrections are needed. Make the required corrections to remove the trouble spots.

ARGUMENT IN READING AND WRITING: Mastery Test 5 (Writing)

Write an essay arguing the following point.

- Contraceptives should (*or* should not) be available in schools.

Writing Your Essay

1. Here are some pro and con statements to help you think about this topic:

   - Distributing contraceptives in high school amounts to condoning teen sexual activity. High-school students should be encouraged to postpone sexual activity until they are older, not given the message that it's okay to be sexually active.

   - Most people who would use a contraception-distribution program are sexually active already. The program would help prevent unwanted pregnancies that might happen otherwise.

2. Explore the topic further by freewriting about it, or asking questions such as *what, when, where, how*, and *why* about it, or making a list of all the details you can think of about it. Prewriting will help you determine the topic for which you can provide the best supporting details.

3. Now research the topic further by going online and Googling "contraceptives in schools pros and cons." You will find over a million articles on the issue. As you read through some of them, chances are you will clarify your point of view about the topic and whether you would like to argue for or against it.

4. Prepare a scratch outline of your paragraph or essay. Decide upon the separate and distinct supporting points that back up your point. Remember that there are five kinds of evidence you can cite: examples; facts and/ or statistics; expert opinion; personal experience; and common-sense reasoning.

5. Then go on to write the first and later drafts of your paper. Chances are that as you write, you will think even more clearly about your point of view. Revise as need be.

6. When you feel you have the final draft of your paper, read it aloud to make sure that every sentence reads smoothly and clearly. Use a grammar handbook, if necessary, to see what corrections are needed. Make the required corrections to remove the trouble spots.

(Continues on next page)

Alternate Essay Assignment

Alternatively, write an essay arguing one of the following points that you have not written about before:

- Year-round schools would benefit both parents and children.
- All alcohol advertising should be banned.
- Cigarettes should be classified as a dangerous drug.
- Religion is not about going to church but about the way one lives one's life.
- Schools should offer students cash bonuses for high test scores.
- The government should cover the cost of every child going to a good preschool.
- Many celebrities today fail to act as appropriate role models for young people.
- To reduce the divorce rate, all couples should be required to live together for a year before marriage.

ARGUMENT IN READING AND WRITING: Mastery Test 6 (Writing)

Write an essay arguing the following point.

- Physicians should be allowed to assist in suicide.

Writing Your Essay

1. Here are some pro and con statements to help you think about this topic:

   - Physician-assisted suicide allows patients to opt out of suffering through a long, painful death. Enduring such a death is as agonizing for their loved ones as it is painful for the patients themselves.

   - If physician-assisted suicide is legal, then sick, elderly people will be pressured to make use of it. Instead of honoring and caring for our sick elders, we will become a society that wants to hurry them into death when they become unable to take care of themselves.

2. Explore the topic further by freewriting about it, or asking questions such as *what, when, where, how*, and *why* about it, or making a list of all the details you can think of about it. Prewriting will help you determine the topic for which you can provide the best supporting details.

3. Now research the topic further by first reading the essay by Steve Lopez on pages 349–351. Then go online and Google "physician-assisted death pros and cons." You will find many thousands of articles on the issue. As you read through some of them, chances are you will clarify your point of view about the topic and whether you would like to argue for or against it.

4. Prepare a scratch outline of your paragraph or essay. Decide upon the separate and distinct supporting points that back up your point. Remember that there are five kinds of evidence you can cite: examples; facts and/ or statistics; expert opinion; personal experience; and common-sense reasoning.

5. Then go on to write the first and later drafts of your paper. Chances are that as you write, you will think even more clearly about your point of view. Revise as need be.

6. When you feel you have the final draft of your paper, read it aloud to make sure that every sentence reads smoothly and clearly. Use a grammar handbook, if necessary, to see what corrections are needed. Make the required corrections to remove the trouble spots.

(Continues on next page)

Alternate Essay Assignment

Alternatively, write an essay arguing one of the following points that you have not written about before:

- Year-round schools would benefit both parents and children.
- All alcohol advertising should be banned.
- Cigarettes should be classified as a dangerous drug.
- Religion is not about going to church but about the way one lives one's life.
- Schools should offer students cash bonuses for high test scores.
- The government should cover the cost of every child going to a good preschool.
- Many celebrities today fail to act as appropriate role models for young people.
- To reduce the divorce rate, all couples should be required to live together for a year before marriage.

Part Two

Fifteen Selections
for Readers and Writers

Introduction to the Reading Selections

Part Two of the book is made up of fifteen high-interest essays that will provide extensive practice in reading and writing. This introduction will describe the format of the fifteen essays. It will briefly review the concept of point and support that is the key to becoming a better reader and writer. Finally, it will offer strategies for reading and writing about the essays.

Format of the Readings

Each of the fifteen essays contains the following:

- A *Preview* that presents helpful background information and arouses your interest in the selection.

- A *Words to Watch* section that gives the definitions of some of the words in the selection.

- An activity called *First Impressions* that asks you to write for ten minutes about the selection you have just finished reading.

- A *Vocabulary Check* that helps you learn words in a research-proven way: by seeing how they are actually used in the selection.

- A *Reading Check* that helps you practice and develop important reading skills: recognizing main ideas and the central point; identifying key supporting details; making inferences; and being aware of the writer's craft.

- *Discussion Questions* to help you deepen your understanding of a reading.

- *Two Paragraph Assignments* and *two Essay Assignments*—giving you a choice of topics for writing practice. As a general rule, you will be given both a paragraph and an essay assignment that involve a first-person "I" point of view, in which you are asked to provide evidence from your own personal experience. You will also be given a paragraph and an essay assignment that involve an objective point of view, in which you will be asked to provide evidence from research or your own general reasoning.

Point and Support

The most important principle in this book is that effective reading and writing share two basic parts: (1) a *point* and (2) *support* for that point. By keeping this principle in mind, you can become a better reader and writer. When you read, remember that an author's purpose is to make a point and support it with reasons, examples, and details. When you write, remember that to communicate effectively, you should follow the same basic plan: make a point and support it.

Reading Strategies

To become a better reader, get actively involved in each stage of the reading process. Here are ways to do so.

1 **Preview the selection.** In other words, look over what you will read—quickly but alertly—before you start to read it. Follow these steps:

● *Turn the title into a question.* For example, before reading the selection "College Athletes Should Be Paid," you might ask the question, "Why should college athletes be paid?" or "How much pay should college athletes receive?" Searching for the answer to your question will give you a reason for reading.

● *Read through the first several paragraphs and the last several paragraphs.* They will give you a quick general sense of what the selection is about.

2 Read the selection straight through to enjoy whatever it has to say about life and human nature. Don't get bogged down; instead, just try to understand as much as you can the first time through.

3 Now reread the selection, marking key information with a pen or pencil. Marking material will keep your mind alert and show you what to come back to later. Here are some suggestions on how and what to mark:

- Underline ideas that seem important.

- Write *Ex* in the margin to set off helpful examples.

- Put question marks beside any material you don't understand.

- Number any major series of items or ideas.

   Following each selection is a set of questions that help you apply important reading skills, almost all of which you have already practiced in this book. As you strengthen these skills enough to make them habits, your reading ability is sure to improve. Here are the skills:

- Understanding vocabulary in context

- Recognizing main ideas and the central point

- Identifying key supporting details

- Making inferences

- Being aware of the writer's craft

4 Note techniques that the author uses to communicate ideas. In this book, questions on these techniques appear under the head "The Writer's Craft." Being aware of these strategies will increase your understanding of what you read as well as improve your own writing. Questions on the writer's craft include the following:

- *Introductions and Conclusions.* What does an author do at the start of an essay to interest you in reading what he or she has written? And what kind of "caboose," or conclusion, does the author use at the end of an essay?

- *Types of Support.* How has the author supported his or her central point? As you've already learned, common methods of support include reasons, examples, details, and personal experiences.

- *Patterns of Organization.* How have the supporting details been arranged? As you have seen, authors often use a **time order**—telling the parts of a story in the order that they happened. Common word signals (also called *transitions*) that mark time order are *first, then, before, as, after, next,* and *finally.* (See also pages 154–156.)

An equally popular pattern of organization is a **listing order**—providing a series of reasons, examples, or details. Common word signals or transitions that mark listing order are *first of all, another, in addition, also,* and *finally. (*See also pages 151–153.)

Another pattern of organization is **illustration**—supporting an idea with one or more examples, and using transitions such as *for instance, for example,* and *such as*. (See also pages 197–199.)

A fourth pattern is **comparison or contrast**—showing how things are alike or (more often) different. Typical transitions for this pattern are (for comparison) *like, just as, similarly* and (for contrast) *but, however, in contrast,* and *on the other hand.* (See also pages 200–203.)

A fifth pattern worth noting is **cause-effect**—explaining the reasons why something happened or the results of something. Typical transitions for this pattern are *because, therefore, effect, consequently,* and *as a result.* (See also pages 203–204.)

- *Tone.* Just as a speaker's tone of voice reveals how he or she feels, a writer's tone communicates feelings. You can get a sense of how an author feels about his or her subject by looking at the wording of the selection. It will often indicate whether a selection's tone is humorous or serious, angry or friendly, formal or informal, sentimental or sarcastic, hopeful or discouraging, or simply objective (detached and factual).

- *Purpose.* Decide what type of writing you are reading. Is it intended to **inform** (give people information), to **entertain** (give people pleasure), or to **persuade** (change people's minds about an issue)? Or does it have a combination of these purposes?

- *Audience.* Decide for what kind of reader the selection was probably written. Was it meant for the general reader (anyone)? Or was the author writing for a smaller audience, such as researchers, parents, or students?

- *Titles.* Most authors choose their titles very carefully. Many times, a title clearly describes the topic of the essay, and sometimes it is the shortest possible summary of the central point of an essay. Look closely at titles for excellent clues about authors' ideas and their attitudes toward their topics.

Writing Strategies

You have already practiced in Part One the steps you should take to write effectively. In a nutshell, you should:

1   Use the prewriting strategies of freewriting, asking questions, and list making to begin to write about your topic. Remember that the heart of the matter is to advance an idea or point of some kind and to provide solid support for that idea.

2   Make a scratch outline.

3   Write several drafts, aiming all the while to make a clear point, to provide strong support for that point, and to organize your support. A pattern of organization and transitions will help you organize your support.

4   When you have revised and edited and think you are almost finished, read your paper out loud. It should read smoothly and clearly. Look closely for grammar and punctuation problems at any rough spots. Use a grammar and punctuation handbook to help identify and correct mistakes that you may be making.

Here are some other tips that will help you with your writing.

1   Learn from your instructor whether you should be writing a paragraph or an essay in response to a given selection.

2   When you have a choice, write about what you know. You will note that for many of the writing topics in Part Two, you are given the opportunity to draw upon your personal experiences and use an "I" or "my" point of view.

But you may also be expected to write papers on objective topics, for which you will not draw upon personal experience but, instead, on your own reasoned opinions. You may be asked, for example, to take a position on abortion or handguns or marijuana or teenage parents or alcohol advertising on TV or texting while driving or bullying—or any other topic.

3   If you don't know much about your topic, you should do some quick research and read about your topic. The easiest way to do this is to simply go onto the Internet, using the search engine Google (**www.google.com**) to get more information. For example, if you Googled "bullying," you would immediately have access to over forty million articles on that topic!

Using Google will help you get more information quickly about a given topic; it will also suggest ways you can narrow down your potential topic. For example, you might decide, after looking through a number of articles about bullying, that you will write an essay on the steps that schools should take to prevent bullying.

Keep in mind two notes of caution about use of the Internet:

● Never for a moment believe that "If it's on the Internet, it must be true." Technology today allows anyone to publish anything at any time. For a given article, an author or information provider should be clearly identified. That author or information provider should be a knowledgeable, qualified, impartial, and reliable authority on the data presented.

● Do not use someone else's words in writing your paper. That would be *plagiarizing*—in a word, stealing. Use other people's ideas only as a springboard for developing your own thoughts about a given topic.

① Growing Less Dumb

Eileen Brenoff

Preview

Even corny sayings often have a germ of truth in them. A plaque in a tourist shop got the author thinking about the benefits of growing older—and possibly wiser.

Words to Watch

Below are some words in the reading that do not have strong context support. Each word is followed by the number of the paragraph in which it appears and its meaning there. These words are indicated in the article by a small circle (°).

plaques (1): signs
obsess (7): think constantly [about something]
perspective (10): viewpoint
spontaneous (11): unplanned
infuriates (16): makes extremely angry

1   In the area of Indiana where I grew up, shops cater to the tourists who come to see the local Amish people, with their 19th century lifestyle and horse-drawn buggies. One popular local souvenir sold in those shops is kitchen plaques° printed with what are supposedly Amish sayings—folksy things like "Kissing don't last; cooking do," or "Throw the horse over the fence some hay."

2   I was never tempted to buy one of those corny plaques. But I'll admit, one of the sayings on them has come into my mind recently. It's not about cooking or kissing or farm life. It's this: "We grow too soon old and too late smart."

3   I think whoever came up with that line was on to something. At 54, I don't consider myself old (no wisecracks from you 18-year-olds in the back row, please), and there are plenty of times I could be smarter. But if I'm not always smart, at least I believe I'm becoming a little less dumb as the years go on.

4   What am I less dumb about today than when I was younger? I think of a number of things. For starters, I believe that I am less dumb about worrying; I am less dumb about decisions; I am less dumb about other people's opinions, and in general I am less dumb when judging other people.

5   First of all, let's talk about worrying. What were you worried about a week ago? How about two weeks ago? Can you remember? No? Well, neither can

I, and that's my point. When I was younger, I worried a lot. I was really good at it. I could take one minor worry—say, a tickle at the back of my throat—and spin it into a long, complicated worry that could ruin an entire day. "My throat feels scratchy. Maybe I'm getting a cold. In fact, maybe it's not just a cold. Maybe it's strep. Strep is really nasty. And oh, shoot, I'm supposed to go to the movies with Keith on Saturday. That's only three days away. Lemme see . . . if it is strep, and I get antibiotics tomorrow, will I still be contagious on Saturday? But I still won't feel good and the date will be a disaster and Keith will never ask me out again and you KNOW who he'll ask out next, that cute Suzanne from biology class, and . . . " By the time I had worked that worry over thoroughly, my imagination had Keith and Suzanne married and living in a half-million dollar house at the shore with their 2.5 adorable children, while I was friendless and miserable and living in a cold rented room with a goldfish as my only companion.

6   Let me just point out that this was a dumb way for me to spend my time.

7   The fact is, I've slowly come to realize, that the things I worry about hardly ever happen. A few days after I've worked myself into a lather over some issue, the problem has generally either disappeared or been resolved in some perfectly satisfactory way. All my worrying had absolutely no impact, except to make me anxious and depressed. So one way that I am now less dumb is this: When I find myself starting to obsess° about a possible problem—when those "What ifs?" start running through my head—I have learned to say a firm "STOP THAT!" to myself. I remind myself that the things I was worried about last week or last month have, in general, not actually happened; and if they *did* happen, well, then I dealt with them.

8   The second thing I am less dumb about now is making decisions. When I was younger, decisions scared me, so I wanted the people around me to do the deciding. I am talking about things as minor as choosing what to order in a restaurant ("Are you going to have the clam chowder? I'll get the clam chowder if you do") to as major as deciding where to go to college ("A girl in my home room's brother goes to State U and he likes it, so maybe I'll go there.") Never mind that I really wanted the taco salad; never mind that I didn't know a thing about State U or the girl's brother. I felt safer having someone else take the responsibility for my decision. The outcome? I ended up doing everything from eating food I didn't enjoy to attending a college that was ill suited to my needs.

9   Really, really dumb.

10   Slowly I've learned that making my own decisions is not only smarter, but it's very empowering. In order to make good decisions, I've had to start giving *myself* the same consideration that I used to reserve for other people. I've learned to respect *my* preferences and opinions and instincts, instead of hoping that someone else might magically know what's best for me. Sure, when I have an important decision to make, I still consult the people close to me; but it's to get their perspective° on my own thinking, not to ask them to tell me what to do. For better or worse, the decision is mine—I own it. And that's a lot more satisfying than my dumb old way.

11   In addition, I am less dumb about this: I worry MUCH less than I used to about what other people think. When I reflect upon my younger self, especially when I was in my teens and twenties, I imagine myself moving through life in a rigid shell of self-consciousness. I was petrified that I might draw attention to myself by doing something weird. And to me, "something weird" meant something fun, creative, joyous, outrageous, spontaneous . . . you get the idea. If it was outside the tight little mold of what "normal" people were doing, I didn't have the courage to do it anyway. I was too afraid of what people would think. Would they stare? Would they laugh?

12   But you know something funny? When I think back to the people I knew during those years, I have only the dimmest memories of the ones I thought of as "normal." They all blend together in my mind—the girls with the stylish outfits and perfect hair; the boys with the varsity letters and pricey cars. For the most part, I can't even remember their names. The people who I do remember are the ones like Mike, who threw himself into every school play with passion and great good humor; Caroline, who dyed her hair pink long before it was fashionable; Serena, who would sing at the top of her lungs in the hallways, and Carl, who sat in the courtyard at lunchtime playing his bongo drums. I liked those people; I admired them; I wish I'd had the courage to be more like them.

13   I'm glad to say I'm not that dumb anymore. I can't remember the last time I hesitated to do or say something because I was worried, "What will people think?" I have taken to heart the wise words of former first lady Eleanor Roosevelt, who said, "You wouldn't worry so much about what others think of you if you realized how seldom they do." Now, I sing in public; I speak up in meetings; I ask for extra napkins in restaurants; I change my hair color on a whim. I talk to strangers, I play patty-cake with other people's babies, and I pet strangers' dogs. In short, I have a blast. I wish I'd had as much fun when I was 15.

14   Finally, I am less dumb in my judgments of other people. When I was younger, I tended to think in very black and white terms. People were good or they were bad; an action was either right or it was wrong. To take an extreme example, if I heard of a person accused of abusing children, my response would

be, "Just kill him—don't even bother with a trial. Get rid of him like you would a mad dog." And the thought of anyone hurting a child still makes me sick deep in my soul. But as the years have gone by, I have learned some sad truths. One of them is that people who hurt children were often themselves harmed in the same awful way. They were not born monsters; at one point, they were the innocent victims. So my attitude now is different. I think, "Keep him away from children, forever. But look at him as another human being. If he was terribly wounded in life, try to help him."

15   For another example, my earlier black-and-white thinking made me assume that our political leaders in Washington were doing what they should do, and that I didn't really need to pay very much attention to their actions. They knew more than I did about what needed to be done, right?

16   I think I'm less dumb about that now, too. I pay a lot closer attention to what our elected officials are doing. Now my attitude is, "Hey, I want my representatives to stand up for everyday folks, for people who are just trying to stay above water in today's hard times." I've come to harshly judge the politicians who seem concerned mainly about tax breaks for the wealthy and the best interests of banks and big corporations. I want to call them out when they disregard the poor and the middle class and everyday people in this country. It infuriates° me when I see them ignore the economic realities most of us live with and hear them say, "If you're not doing well in life, it's because you're lazy and don't want to work." I want to say to them, "Hey, you probably started on third base, and you want to condemn people who never had a chance to get to first?" I want to ask them, "How in your endless pursuit of wealth did you let your heart grow so hard?" I don't wish them ill, but I definitely judge them as people who have lost their humanity.

17   Yes, I've changed with the years, and in general I'm happy about those changes. I'm more tolerant in some ways, less in others, and a lot more ready to speak my mind and live my life without apology. Let me just conclude by saying that, all in all, I am not the dumb kid I was once upon a time. But, you know what they say, at least in Indiana: We grow too soon old and too late smart. Maybe you can grow smart at a younger age than I did.

First Impressions

Freewrite for ten minutes on one of the following.

1. Did you enjoy reading this selection? Why or why not?

2. Brenoff describes herself as a lot more ready to speak her mind than she used to be. Would you describe yourself as generally willing to speak your mind? Or do you generally tend to keep quiet? Explain.

3. Brenoff describes ways in which she has grown "less dumb" over the years. Are there ways in which you feel you've grown "less dumb"? Explain.

Vocabulary Check

_____ 1. In the excerpt below, the term *cater to* means
   A. annoy.
   B. explain.
   C. serve.
   D. defend.

   "In the area of Indiana where I grew up, shops cater to the tourists who come to see the local Amish people, with their 19th-century lifestyle and horse-drawn buggies. One popular local souvenir sold in those shops is kitchen plaques...." (Paragraph 1)

_____ 2. In the excerpt below, the word *petrified* means
   A. extremely fearful.
   B. confident.
   C. hopeful.
   D. excited.

   "I imagine myself moving though life in a rigid shell of self-consciousness. I was petrified that I might draw attention to myself by doing something weird." (Paragraph 11)

_____ 3. In the sentence below, the word *whim* means a
   A. carefully thought out action.
   B. sudden impulse.
   C. suggestion by someone else.
   D. formal agreement.

   "Now, I sing in public; I speak up in meetings; I ask for extra napkins in restaurants; I change my hair color on a whim." (Paragraph 13)

Reading Check

Central Point and Main Ideas

_____ 1. Which sentence best expresses the central point of the selection?
  A. Brenoff believes that she, like most people, has spent too much time worrying.
  B. As she's grown older, Brenoff has become more tolerant in some ways, less tolerant in others, and a lot more ready to speak her mind.
  C. Although Brenoff was never tempted to buy a corny Amish plaque, she believes that the Amish were right about what's important in life.
  D. Brenoff has become less dumb in several important ways and hopes that her readers will become less dumb, too.

_____ 2. The main idea of paragraphs 5–6 is that
  A. most people can't remember what they worried about two weeks ago.
  B. Brenoff now realizes that it was dumb of her to spend so much time worrying.
  C. Brenoff used to worry that she would become friendless and miserable because of a disastrous date.
  D. Brenoff now realizes that she was dumb to worry about so much about whether a cold would develop into strep.

Supporting Details

_____ 3. When Brenoff was young, she often worried about
  A. being thought of as "corny."
  B. doing something "weird."
  C. not having enough money to fit in with the "normal" people.
  D. not going to the right college.

_____ 4. One mistake that Brenoff made as a result of failing to take responsibility for her decisions was
  A. going to the prom with someone she didn't really like.
  B. attending a college that didn't meet her needs.
  C. marrying the brother of one of her friends.
  D. voting for a politician who supported the death penalty for child abusers.

_____ 5. An example Brenoff gives of how she has become more tolerant is that she
  A. no longer wishes ill of people who endlessly pursue wealth.
  B. now tolerates public officials with whom she disagrees.
  C. now thinks of child abusers as human beings, not monsters.
  D. no longer condemns people who never had a chance to get to first.

Inferences

_____ 6. In paragraph 12, Brenoff suggests that
   A. it takes courage to stand out from the crowd.
   B. Brenoff was unwilling to stand out from the crowd in school.
   C. "normal" people can be boring.
   D. all of the above.

_____ 7. We can conclude from the selection that
   A. today's young people are smarter than when Brenoff was young.
   B. Brenoff feels that as people grow older, they have fewer worries.
   C. Brenoff enjoys life more today than she did when she was a teenager.
   D. all of the above.

Argument

_____ 8. Which evidence from the selection supports Brenoff's statement that she has more fun now than when she was 15?
   A. For the most part, she can't remember the names of the "normal" people she knew in school.
   B. She pays more attention to what our elected officials are doing.
   C. She sings in public, speaks out at meetings, and asks for extra napkins at restaurants.
   D. She harshly judges politicians who seem concerned mainly about tax breaks for the wealthy and the best interests of banks and big corporations.

The Writer's Craft

_____ 9. Brenoff begins her story by telling of the Amish plaques she used to see in Indiana shops because
   A. she knows that most people are very curious about the Amish way of life.
   B. she admires the Amish, with their 19th-century lifestyle and horse-drawn buggies.
   C. she uses a saying on an Amish plaque to introduce the theme of her essay.
   D. she wishes she were still living in rural Indiana.

_____10. Which of the following statements best describes Brenoff's purpose in writing this selection?
   A. To inform young people of the inevitable consequences of aging.
   B. To entertain readers with amusing stories of her youth in Indiana.
   C. To inform readers how much American life has changed since she was a girl.
   D. To gently persuade young people to worry less, be more independent in making decisions, and become wiser in passing judgment on others.

Discussion Questions

1. Brenoff ends her essay by saying that she hopes her readers grow smart at a younger age than she did. In what ways have you, like Brenoff, become "less dumb" than when you were younger? Do you think it's possible to become "smart" at a young age? Why or why not?

2. Brenoff says she now realizes that "the things I worry about hardly ever happen." Her worrying solved nothing; it only made her anxious and depressed. Do you agree with Brenoff that worrying is a "dumb" way to spend one's time? Or is worrying sometimes justified? Explain.

3. In Brenoff's opinion, people who condemn others for not doing well in life have "lost their humanity." Do you agree? Do you think that people don't do well in life because they're lazy and don't want to work? Or are there other reasons that some people don't succeed?

4. Brenoff thinks that whoever came up with the slogan "We grow too soon old and too late smart" had realized something important. Are there any slogans or sayings that you think are particularly meaningful—maybe even meaningful enough to live by? If so, explain what they are and why they hold special meaning for you.

Paragraph Assignments

1. In the selection, Brenoff states that she's come to the realization that the things she worries about hardly ever happen. Write about a time in your life when you "worried yourself into a lather" about something, only to have the problem disappear or get resolved. In writing your paper, be sure to describe what the situation was that you found yourself worrying about as well as how it got resolved.

   Alternatively, write a paragraph describing something you worried about that actually *did* happen, and how you dealt with it.

2. Many people have trouble making decisions, and tend to let other people make choices for them. Why do you think decision-making is difficult for people? Write a paragraph in which you explain reasons why making decisions can be difficult.

Essay Assignments

1. Write an essay in which you discuss three specific ways that a relative or friend of yours could become happier and less stressed by being "less dumb" and behaving more sensibly.

Here is one student's response to this assignment:

> My next-door-neighbor, Sally, seems to be running in twenty different directions every waking second of her life. She lives in a constant state of worry and stress, and though she complains of being the queen of multitasking, she never seems to actually accomplish anything. Her standard excuse is, "I don't have enough time!" But I believe time is not the problem. There are at least a few things Sally could change that might help de-stress her life.
>
> First of all, Sally needs to do some serious housecleaning. I won't go as far as saying that my neighbor is a hoarder, but she's not far from it. Boxes of old newspapers line the walls, laundry is crammed into closets, and the kitchen looks like a tornado blew through it. At least once a week, Sally is in a panic because she's lost something amid all the clutter. More often than not, she's late to appointments because she can't find her car keys. One time, she even lost her cat for six hours! Surely, a little home organization could help with the confusion in Sally's life.
>
> And those four glasses of wine every night that Sally says help her relax are probably actually adding to her stress. Sally often complains of tension headaches and lack of energy. I'm not saying that her drinking is solely to blame, but it sure can't help. And weight gain is something Sally worries about nonstop, though it doesn't seem to occur to her that the 600–800 calories of wine every evening is packing on the pounds. Plus, the cost of all that wine must make a big dent in the tight budget that Sally is always biting her nails over. What she spends on nearly two cases of wine a month could pay off one of her credit cards in a year.
>
> Finally, my neighbor might want to consider backing off of the caffeine. Sure, there's nothing wrong with a

couple cups of coffee to get going in the morning, but Sally is constantly downing coffee, energy drinks, and even those questionable 5-hour energy supplements. She jokes about how her hands are always shaking, but the stress that all that caffeine causes is no joke. I've seen Sally so jittery from caffeine that even the slightest stressor just about sends her over the edge. Only yesterday, she burst into tears over hitting three red lights on the way to work. Now that's over-caffeinated.

Honestly, Sally's life is not much more complicated than any of my friends' lives, but there are certain things in her life that make her more stressed—things she could change. Sure, cleaning the house and drinking less wine and caffeine is not suddenly going to make Sally's life perfect. But it should bring her a newfound sense of calm. And with that calm, I'll bet she gets more done and feels like she has more time.

2. In "Growing Less Dumb," Brenoff describes four different ways of thinking when she was younger that, now as an older adult, she believes were pretty dumb. She worried too much, she feared making her own decisions, she was overly concerned about what other people thought of her, and she judged people too quickly. Write an essay in which you describe three things you thought or did when you were younger that you think are pretty dumb now. Be sure to use vivid examples of these past three "dumb" behaviors and, as Brenoff does, mention how you think or act differently today.

Check Your Performance		**GROWING LESS DUMB**	
Activity	*Number Right*	*Points*	*Score*
Vocabulary Check (3 items)	_____	x 10 =	_____
Reading Check			
Central Point and Main Ideas (2 items)	_____	x 7 =	_____
Supporting Details (3 items)	_____	x 7 =	_____
Inferences (2 items)	_____	x 7 =	_____
Argument (1 item)	_____	x 7 =	_____
The Writer's Craft (2 items)	_____	x 7 =	_____
		TOTAL SCORE =	_____%

Enter your total score into the **Performance Chart: Fifteen Reading Selections** on the inside back cover.

2 College Athletes Should Be Paid

Ann Kaufmann

Preview

College athletics are hugely profitable—for the schools and the coaches. Is it right that the student-athletes remain unpaid? In this essay, Ann Kaufmann looks at the history of the college sports system, the justification for and against paying players, and some proposals for sharing the profits with the athletes who generate them.

Words to Watch

replicas (8): copies
compensation (9): money given to pay for loss, damage, or work done
contention (10): claim
royalties (15): percentages of income from the sale of something

1   Every fall hundreds of thousands of college football fans jam into stadiums throughout the United States, while millions more watch on TV. And every March, nearly 80 million people tune in to "March Madness," the National Collegiate Athletic Association's (NCAA's) men's college basketball championship tournament. Together, college football and men's basketball generate more than $6 billion in annual revenue—mostly through the sale of TV rights. Of this sum, the NCAA takes in nearly $800 million a year.

2   Because college football and men's basketball are so amazingly profitable, head football coaches at public universities earn on average more than $2 million a year. And top college basketball coaches routinely earn $4 million a year. Salaries for *assistant* coaches now commonly exceed $200,000, with some earning as much as $700,000.

3   Given these handsome salaries, how much do the players themselves earn? Well, if you follow college sports, you probably already know that these athletes aren't paid anything. In fact, they can be suspended for accepting so much as a free lunch from a fan. To do so would violate their status as amateurs, which the NCAA views as lying at the heart of college sports. According

to NCAA officials, the NCAA exists to protect college athletes from "excess commercialism."

4   However, in the past few years, critics have begun arguing that the NCAA doesn't protect college players. Rather, it cheats them out of the profits they help generate. The NCAA responds to this argument by pointing out that student athletes get something very valuable—athletic scholarships. But critics wonder just how much of a "gift" athletic scholarships actually are. Recent studies estimate that these scholarships fall on average about $3,500 short of the full cost of attending college annually. In addition, until very recently athletic scholarships had to be renewed every year. If an athlete "underperformed," was seriously injured, or even if he didn't fit into the offensive/defensive strategy of a new coach, there was a good chance his scholarship would be terminated. In October 2011, the NCAA began permitting colleges and universities to offer multiyear scholarships, but does not require them to do so. Some powerhouse schools, such as LSU, Alabama, and Texas, were opposed to this measure. Without the benefit of a four-year scholarship, college players can be "cut," just as if they were professional players.

5   Those opposed to the current system also challenge the notion that "student athletes" are getting a quality education. They point out that college football and basketball players often spend upwards of 50 hours a week during the season at their sport. Such an intense schedule makes it almost impossible for them to take any but the easiest courses.

6   Of course, the "carrot" held out to these athletes is the dream of making it to the NFL or NBA. But for the vast majority of college athletes, the dream of a pro career is just a dream. Today, the NBA drafts only one percent of men's college basketball players, while two percent of football players make it to the NFL. And by the time most college athletes figure out that they're not going to make the pros, they're hopelessly behind academically. Rather than a "win/win" situation, what they face is a "lose/lose" situation: if they quit football or basketball to spend more time on their studies, they lose their athletic scholarships.

7   Desmond Howard, who won the 1991 Heisman Trophy while playing for the Michigan Wolverines, questions the current system. "You see everybody getting richer and richer," he says. "And you walk around and you can't put gas in your car? You can't even fly home to see your parents?"

8   Not surprisingly, college players are sometimes tempted to take money "under the table." At the start of the 2010 football season, A. J. Green, a wide receiver at Georgia, confessed that he'd sold his own team jersey from a bowl game the year before, to raise cash for a spring-break vacation. While Green served a four-game suspension for violating his amateur status, the Georgia Bulldogs store profited by selling replicas° of his jersey for $39.95 and up. The NCAA banned the University of Southern California (USC) from taking

part in bowl games in 2010 and 2011 because star running back Reggie Bush had accepted gifts from agents several years earlier. And in 2011, a University of Miami booster was found to have provided dozens of University of Miami football players with money, cars, and even prostitutes. Every year brings similar scandals.

9   Although the NCAA punishes players for accepting cash and gifts, civil rights historian Taylor Branch views the NCAA itself as the true villain of college sports. According to Branch, "The tragedy at the heart of college sports is not that some college athletes are getting paid, but that more of them are not." In fact, Branch challenges the whole concept of "student athletes." He sees this term as a thinly disguised way to keep athletes from being able to sue for workers' compensation° if they are injured playing for their college or university. Because they are "student athletes," they are denied the basic rights of other university employees.

10   Joe Nocera, a columnist for the *New York Times*, also makes a strong case for why men's college football and basketball players should be paid. As he puts it, "The NCAA's . . . contention° that it is protecting the players from 'excessive commercialism' is ludicrous; the only thing it's protecting is everyone else's revenue stream." To Nocera it's a simple matter of justice that college athletes should share in the wealth. To accomplish that goal, he lays out a plan for paying them a fair portion of the enormous profits they help generate.

11   Nocera's plan consists of five elements. The first element would require college coaches to offer athletes real contracts, just as professional teams do. One college or university might think a star halfback is worth $40,000 a year; another might think he's worth $60,000. When a player chooses a school, he and his recruiters would automatically discuss money.

12   The second element in the plan is a salary cap for every team, along with a minimum annual salary for every scholarship athlete. A salary cap would equalize the amount every team could pay its players. Thus, it would prevent super-rich athletic departments, such as those at the University of Texas and Oklahoma State, from recruiting all the top players. Nocera proposes a $3 million salary cap for the football team and $650,000 for the basketball team. The minimum salary would be $25,000 per athlete. Critics of Nocera's plan point out that smaller schools may not be able to pay their athletes these sums. That's probably true. According to Nocera, schools that truly couldn't afford to pay their players would be forced to

cut back on their football and men's basketball programs. Who knows? They might even return to their basic mission of educating students.

13   The third element would be that every player who stays in school for four years would also get an additional two-year scholarship. He could use this scholarship to either complete his bachelor's degree or get a master's degree. A six-year scholarship would allow players to take fewer courses during their years of athletic eligibility. As a result, they would stand a better chance of succeeding at the courses they do take. It would also enable those players who do graduate within four years to pursue a graduate degree. This focus on academics would better prepare athletes for a future without football or basketball. The days of *having* to major in physical education just because it's easy would be gone.

14   The fourth element of the plan is that each player would have lifetime health insurance. As things now stand, if a college football player or basketball player is injured while playing sports, the college has no legal responsibility to pay his medical bills. And many former college football players suffer chronic pain by the time they are in their thirties—due to the punishment their bodies took while playing college ball.

15   The fifth element is that an organization would be created to represent both current and former college athletes. This organization might take the form of a players' union, which would manage the health insurance, bargain with the NCAA to set the salary

caps and salary minimums, pay out royalties°, and serve as an all-around counterweight to the NCAA.

16   Will Nocera's plan ever become a reality? Some doubt it. However, a lawsuit called the O'Bannon case now threatens the NCAA's longstanding refusal to pay its players. The case is named after the lead plaintiff, Ed O'Bannon, who led UCLA to a national basketball title in 1995. The other plaintiffs include basketball greats Oscar Robertson and Bill Russell. Together they are suing the NCAA for licensing their images without compensating them. If the NCAA loses, the decision could lead to a "restructuring" of the relationship between college athletes and the NCAA. Who knows? It might eventually lead to paying the players.

17   Some protest that doing away with amateurism would ruin the college "brand." But amateurism isn't the reason fans love college sports. What they love is cheering on the teams that represent their schools. That would be just as true if the athletes were being paid. It's a similar situation to what happened with the Olympics. Years ago, only amateur athletes could take part in the Olympics. And what happened when pro athletes finally could take part? The Olympics only got better.

18   Others argue that if colleges began to pay football and men's basketball players, then they would have to pay athletes who play other sports, such as wrestling, lacrosse, and tennis. But college football and men's basketball aren't like other college sports. Because of the huge profits they generate, college

football and men's basketball players should be considered employees as well as students. As James Duderstadt, the former president of the University of Michigan, put it, "Most sports can be justified as part of what a university does. But big-time football and men's basketball are clearly commercial entertainment and have been pulled away from the fundamental purpose of a university."

Paying college football and men's 19 basketball players would cause the vast majority of the "under the table" payment scandals to go away. Rather than being the only ones *not* to profit from the enormous revenues they generate, these athletes would at long last receive a slice of the pie. Let's do the right thing and give it to them.

First Impressions

Freewrite for ten minutes on one of the following.

1. Did you enjoy reading this selection? Why or why not?

2. In your opinion, *should* college athletes be paid? Why or why not?

3. Do you think college athletes, in general, get a good education? Or are they passed along and encouraged to take easy classes so they can continue playing?

Vocabulary Check

_____ 1. In the excerpt below, the word *violate* means
   A. support.
   B. go against.
   C. increase.
   D. determine.

   "In fact, they can be suspended for accepting so much as a free lunch from a fan. To do so would violate their status as amateurs, which the NCAA views as lying at the heart of college sports." (Paragraph 3)

_____ 2. In the excerpt below, the word *ludicrous* means
   A. sensible.
   B. ridiculous.
   C. common.
   D. worthy of thoughtful discussion.

   "As he puts it, 'The NCAA's . . . contention that it is protecting the players from "excessive commercialism" is ludicrous; the only thing it's protecting is everyone else's revenue stream.'" (Paragraph 10)

_____ 3. In the excerpt below, the word *chronic* means
   A. required.
   B. timely.
   C. little.
   D. long-lasting.

   "As things now stand, if a college football player or basketball player is injured while playing sports, the college has no legal responsibility to pay his medical bills. And many former college football players suffer chronic pain by the time they are in their thirties—due to the punishment their bodies took while playing college ball." (Paragraph 14)

Reading Check

Central Point and Main Ideas

_____ 1. Which sentence best expresses the central point of the selection?
   A. Just as the Olympics improved when its athletes were paid, college football and men's basketball would improve if its athletes were paid.
   B. Because college football and men's basketball are so demanding and so profitable, the athletes who play them should be paid.
   C. It's wrong that college football and men's basketball coaches get paid huge salaries while their players receive only scholarships that don't even cover the full cost of attending college.
   D. *New York Times* columnist Joe Nocera has offered a plan for making college football and men's basketball more fair to the players.

_____ 2. Which sentence best expresses the main idea of paragraph 4?
   A. Colleges and universities have recently started to offer athletes multiyear scholarships.
   B. The NCAA harms college athletes more than it helps them.
   C. Athletic scholarships aren't as great a gift as the NCAA claims they are.
   D. Without the benefit of a four-year scholarship, college players can be "cut," just as if they were professional players.

_____ 3. Which sentence best expresses the main idea of paragraphs 5–6?
   A. It's wrong to hold out to college athletes the dream of making it to the NFL or NBA.
   B. The great majority of college football and men's basketball players never make it to the professional level and also don't get a quality education.
   C. Because college football and basketball players practice so much, they don't have time to take any but the easiest courses.
   D. By the time college athletes figure out they're not going to make the pros, they're far behind academically.

Supporting Details

_____ 4. One part of Joe Nocera's plan is to
   A. provide money to small schools that otherwise couldn't afford to pay their athletes.
   B. make it easier for super-rich athletic departments to pay athletes more money than other schools.
   C. require colleges to pay small salaries to wrestling, lacrosse, and tennis players as well as larger salaries to football and basketball players.
   D. offer six-year scholarships to athletes who stay in school for four years.

_____ 5. The plaintiffs in the O'Bannon case are suing the NCAA for
   A. not providing workmen's compensation to them when they were injured.
   B. refusing to pay their health insurance.
   C. licensing their images without paying them.
   D. selling replicas of their college uniforms without paying them royalties.

Inferences

_____ 6. Paragraphs 1–3 suggest that
   A. college football and basketball coaches are overpaid.
   B. excess commercialism is harming college sports.
   C. college football and men's basketball are already extremely commercial.
   D. college football and men's basketball have not always been as profitable as they are today.

_____ 7. We can conclude from paragraphs 7–8 that
   A. most college football players have enough spending money.
   B. most college football players take money "under the table."
   C. the NCAA tends to "look the other way" rather than punish players for accepting cash and gifts.
   D. because they aren't paid, some college athletes feel there is nothing wrong with taking "under the table" payments.

Argument

_____ 8. Write the letter of the statement that is the point of the following argument. The other statements are support for that point.
   A. The NCAA does not really care about the well-being of college football and men's basketball players.
   B. Although the NCAA takes in nearly $800 million a year, it suspends college athletes who accept "under the table" payments.
   C. Because they are termed "student athletes," college football and basketball players cannot sue their colleges and universities for worker's compensation.
   D. The NCAA routinely licenses images of college athletes without compensating them.

The Writer's Craft

_____ 9. The author's primary purpose in this selection is to
   A. inform readers that college football and men's basketball players are being unfairly treated.
   B. inform readers of the potential dangers involved in participating in college sports.
   C. persuade readers to support a plan to pay college football and men's basketball players.
   D. entertain readers with stories about the difficulties facing student athletes.

_____ 10. In paragraphs 11–15, Kaufmann
   A. lists the major points in a plan to pay college football and men's basketball players.
   B. compares and contrasts how college football and basketball players will be paid at large schools with how they will be paid at small schools.
   C. gives reasons why college football and basketball players should be paid.
   D. provides step-by-step directions for setting up a system for paying college athletes.

Discussion Questions

1. Do you know of anyone who received a scholarship to play college football or men's basketball? If so, was this person's college career successful? Why or why not?

2. Historian Taylor Branch states that it is tragic that college football and men's basketball players are not paid. Do you agree or disagree? Explain.

3. According to Joe Nocera, schools that truly couldn't afford to pay their players would be forced to cut back on their football and men's basketball programs. Do you agree or disagree that some colleges should de-emphasize college football and men's basketball? Who might benefit if they did so? Who might lose out?

4. As the selection indicates, college football and men's basketball are enormously popular—and profitable. Overall, do you think our country's "love affair" with these sports is a good thing, a bad thing, or maybe a little of both? Explain.

Paragraph Assignments

1. Many college football and basketball players are encouraged to dream of eventually moving on to the NFL and NBA. However, as Kaufmann explains, this is a dream that will most likely lead to a rude awakening, since the reality is that only 1 to 2 percent of these players will succeed in becoming professional athletes. Have you ever had a dream that was shattered when you learned the truth about how things really work? Write a paragraph describing your experience. Your "shattered illusion" experience can be anything from learning the truth about Santa Claus to learning the truth about an extremely competitive or difficult career path.

   Here is one student's response to the assignment:

   > When I was a little kid, I was certain that I was going to be a star football player, but I remember the day that dream was shattered. My brother, Mike, was nine years older than I was, so I usually got his old toys to play with—everything from blocks to bikes. But my favorite things were his old football helmets and pads. I used to put them on, and even though they were way too big, I thought I was pretty cool. I practiced running patterns Mike taught me, and I even got pretty good at catching passes by the time I was in second grade. I couldn't

> *wait to play on a Pee Wee football team like Mike had done. He played for his high school team now, and I just knew I was going to follow in Mike's footsteps. However, the morning I asked my dad about sign-ups for the Pee Wee league, he just looked at me and grinned. He told me that I couldn't play. I was stunned. "But why not?" I asked. Then my dad explained that girls didn't get to play on football teams. It had never occurred to my seven-year-old brain that I would not be allowed to play a sport I loved just because I was a girl.*

2. Kaufmann writes, "Not surprisingly, college players are sometimes tempted to take money 'under the table.'" Do you sympathize with players who accept cash or gifts? Or do you think such players should be seriously punished? Write a paragraph in which you explain and defend your point of view.

Essay Assignments

1. Write an essay in which you discuss in detail your three main reasons for believing that college athletes should (*or* should not) be paid.

2. As Kaufmann points out, both athletes and non-athletes have criticized the NCAA rules prohibiting college athletes from receiving money and gifts. Some athletes are now accepting these gifts, evidently believing that certain rules deserve to be broken. Although the statement "rules are made to be broken" is not always the best advice, we've all broken rules. Write an essay in which you discuss a time when you broke a rule that you thought was either unfair or unnecessary. In the body of your essay, first present the rule and explain why you thought it was wrong. In the next paragraph, discuss breaking the rule—how you broke it and how that made you feel. In the third paragraph, discuss what happened. Did you get caught, or did you get away with it? Did your behavior help make a change in the rules?

Check Your Performance

COLLEGE ATHLETES SHOULD BE PAID

Activity	Number Right		Points		Score
Vocabulary Check (3 items)	_____	x	10	=	_____
Reading Check					
Central Point and Main Ideas (3 items)	_____	x	7	=	_____
Supporting Details (2 items)	_____	x	7	=	_____
Inferences (2 items)	_____	x	7	=	_____
Argument (1 item)	_____	x	7	=	_____
The Writer's Craft (2 items)	_____	x	7	=	_____
		TOTAL SCORE		=	_____%

Enter your total score into the **Performance Chart: Fifteen Reading Selections** on the inside back cover.

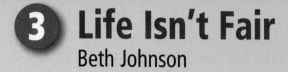

3 Life Isn't Fair

Beth Johnson

Preview

A memorable scene in a favorite book inspires the author to write about a well-intentioned, but destructive, lie we tell our children. Most lies, says the author, are harmless. But she adds that the lie with the most destructive potential is that people can expect a fair shake out of life.

Words to Watch

obliged (12): required
palatable (12): acceptable
reverence (14): respect and admiration
cosmic (16): huge
palatial (16): large and impressive, like a palace
menial (20): low-paying
sullen (23): bad-tempered
karmic (23): fated

1   There's a terrific book called *The Princess Bride* by William Goldman. It's full of laughs and breathtaking action, but what makes the book really memorable is a quiet scene that occurs two-thirds of the way into the book. In it, Goldman recalls a conversation he had with a friend's mother when he was a teenager. The friend, Ed Neisser, had just beaten him at badminton. According to Goldman, here's what happened next:

2   "[Ed] said, 'Don't worry, it'll all work out, you'll get me the next time,' and I nodded, and then Ed said, 'And if you don't, you'll beat me at something else.'

3   "I went to the porch and sipped iced tea and Edith was reading this book and she didn't put it down when she said, 'That's not necessarily true, you know.'

4   "I said, 'How do you mean?'

5   "And that's when she put her book down. And looked at me. And said it: 'Life isn't fair, Bill. We tell our children that it is, but it's a terrible thing to do. It's not only a lie, it's a cruel lie. Life is not fair, and it never has been, and it's never going to be.'"

6   That's it. That's what I remember best about *The Princess Bride*. And I've run into a number of people whose memories work the same way. When the subject of the book comes up, they

shake their heads in the way we do when we admire something too much for words and say something like, "What a great book. Remember the 'life isn't fair' part?" Or maybe they skip ahead a few paragraphs and quote another line of Goldman's: *"Some of the wrong people die."*

7   Why do I and my fellow *TPB*-lovers quote Goldman's words with such admiration and recall them so vividly?

8   We remember them, I think, because we see in Mrs. Neisser an adult who did an unusual and courageous thing. She had the kindness to pass on an important truth to a youngster whose welfare she cared about.

9   Kindness? you may be saying. It's kind to tell a kid that life will never be fair? What kind of kindness is that? Shouldn't a child be brought up to believe in justice? Shouldn't he be taught that evil never prospers, that good will be rewarded, that even when we lose at a game like badminton, things will somehow balance out along the way?

10   In considering those questions, observe Goldman's reaction upon hearing Mrs. Neisser's statement: *"'It isn't!' I said, so loud I really startled her. 'You're right. It's not fair.' I was so happy if I'd known how to dance, I'd have started dancing. . . . it meant so much to me to have it said and out and free and flying."*

11   What is going on here? Why did Goldman respond to Mrs. Neisser's words with such enthusiasm, even joy?

12   The word, I think, is relief. Relief because she has confirmed for him something he had always known was

true, but felt obliged° to pretend was not. His reaction teaches us something important about what children need, but rarely receive, from the adults in their lives. And that is honesty, even when dishonesty is a lot more palatable°.

13   I'm not addressing these words to parents who make a practice of lying to their kids for the parents' own selfish reasons. There are, unfortunately, plenty of lousy parents in the world. But the majority of us are heartbreakingly well-meaning. We love our kids and want them to have the best shot possible at happy lives. We would hurl ourselves under speeding trains to spare them pain. Part of what evokes the bottomless devotion we feel for them, I think, is their early, baby innocence. We melt, awestruck, as we watch our toddlers enfold any nearby child in the golden mantle of their universal acceptance. "I love him; he's my new best friend," they'll offhandedly remark of a kid whose name they haven't quite learned, a child whose color or creed or socio-economic class hasn't the slightest impact on them. At such moments we want to kneel at our children's feet and say, "Teach us."

14   Our reverence° for our children's innocence leads us into all sorts of irrational acts. We sneak quarters under their pillows long after they've stopped believing in the Tooth Fairy; we remind them to leave milk and cookies for Santa Claus years after they've figured out the odds of a fat guy in a red suit sneaking into their living room without setting off the burglar alarm (and probably without benefit of a chimney). But with quarters

and Christmas presents at stake, they are generally willing to play along with our need to view them, at least for one more year, as the trusting babes they once were. We know in the back of our minds that some wise guy on the playground will set them straight soon enough, and what's the harm in maintaining a pleasant fiction at home?

15   Which is all well and good; it's never hurt a kid to believe in Santa Claus and, more to the point, I've never known one who went off to college still believing. But the same can't be said, I think, for a larger and more pervasive fiction that we well-intentioned parents often impose on our children: that life is fair, that it's *supposed* to be fair, and that they have the right to expect it to act accordingly.

16   Most of us don't openly embrace the notion that the universe functions as a cosmic° vending machine: that you put in good behavior and get back worldly success. But in a hundred more subtle ways, we do suggest to our children that life plays by sportsmanlike rules, even as it's glaringly obvious that this isn't so. "Be nice to Jimmy, and he'll be nice to you," we say, despite plentiful evidence that Jimmy is a hellion completely uninterested in being nice to anyone. "Lots of boys care more about what's inside a person than what she looks like on the outside," we tell daughters as they're being ignored by male classmates who are busy lusting after the homecoming-queen candidates. "Geraldo's parents have more money than we do, but money can't buy important things like friendship," we say, while weekend after weekend kids flock to parties at Geraldo's palatial° house and sneer at our kids because they've never been to the Caribbean.

17   And, of course, life's unfairness is not confined to the growing-up years. Injustices large and small, tragic and commonplace, pop up everywhere. Studies show that tall, good-looking people are hired more readily and at higher starting salaries than short people of average looks. People who are fortunate enough to inherit money can live off their investments, while the children of the non-rich can expect to work hard all their lives. Babies are born drug-addicted and brain-damaged because of their parents' substance abuse. Adults who give priority to their families are viewed as less than team players and passed over for promotions.

Least fair of all, to quote our friend Goldman, "Some of the wrong people die." Children. Blameless drivers annihilated by drunks. Working-class couples on their first vacation in fifteen years. Newlyweds. High-school students meeting for prayer.

18   We parents know all these things. We not only know them; our own lives have been shaped, to differing degrees, by the universe's cool indifference to human standards of fairness. And yet most of us keep telling our children that for them it will be different; that they can and should expect a fair shake out of life.

19   It's not hard to understand why. That near-adoration with which we view our toddlers may give way to something more realistic as they grow older, but still, we can hardly bring ourselves to believe that their goodness and enormous lovableness will not be as appreciated by the world as it is by us. Furthermore, who wants to be the bearer of bad tidings? And isn't it a good thing if our children go into the world full of optimism?

20   That question reminds me of something a wise friend once said to me. We were discussing a woman we both know. Suzanne is bright and attractive, with a pleasant singing voice that occasionally lands her a role in the local musical theater. As she enters her 40s, however, Suzanne's life is anything but attractive. Divorced, with a child she loves but who spends most of his time with his father due to Suzanne's chaotic life, she lives in a tiny, trash-strewn apartment and bounces from job to

menial° job. Romantic relationships flare up regularly, but fizzle out within weeks. She's worked as a high-school teacher and was well liked by her students, but was too disorganized to keep the job. Now she tells people that she's doing temporary clerical work only until she gets her big break as a singer. Once in a while she takes the bus into the nearby city to audition for a nightclub job or two. Then it's back home for another few weeks of dodging bill collectors and loftily telling increasingly testy employers that she may be called to "the Coast" at any moment.

21   "You know where Suzanne's problems began?" my friend asked. "With parents whose message to her was, 'You're so beautiful and talented. You're sure to be a famous star.' I guess it's nice that her parents believed in her so much, but wouldn't it have been better for her if they'd said something realistic like, '*If* you work like crazy, *if* you put all your heart and soul and self-discipline into being better than anyone else, you *might, possibly,* someday get a lucky break? And by the way, you'd better figure out a way to pay the bills in the meantime'?"

22   I think my friend is right. I know that even today, when it's painfully clear Suzanne isn't going anywhere, her mother introduces her as "my Broadway-bound daughter." Suzanne has become so convinced that life is going to do the right thing and hand her what she wants that she can't see all she's wasted: the potential for mature, loving relationships with friends or a partner or her son; a rewarding career;

or a pleasant home. Instead, she's still waiting for that golden prize to drop out of the sky.

23   Suzanne's story is an extreme one; the implication that life is fair doesn't lead most children into a lifetime of fantasizing about a Broadway break. But the more common result, I think, is that many of us go through the precious, irreplaceable days of our lives with a kind of sullen° indignation that we haven't been treated better. Our jobs don't measure up to our early dreams. Our marriages are not endless sources of companionship and passion. Our children disappoint us. Our friends let us down. And we resent it; oh, do we resent it. My friend Michael had an older brother who was generally thought of as "the smart one" in the family. Although both boys went to college, Michael felt his parents expected him to fail and his brother to succeed. Sure enough, in the middle of his sophomore year, Michael announced that he was dropping out of school. "And they didn't do a *thing*!" Michael remembers, still outraged. "They just let me go off and get a job! If it'd been Joseph that said he was dropping out, they would have moved heaven and earth to change his mind, but they obviously thought, 'Oh, well; it's only Michael.'" To this day—and he's well into middle age—Michael blames his parents for his loss of a college education. He clings doggedly to the idea that he was treated unfairly—and maybe he was. But his insistence that life did him wrong has blinded him, most obviously to the fact that he could have finished college any

number of times without his parents' encouragement. Like Michael, many of us sink into a stew of self-pity as we contemplate how life *should* have been versus its reality. And the idea that life *should* have been sunshine and roses, blissful marriages, ever-rewarding work, thin thighs, perfect children, ideal health, and plenty of money is firmly rooted in the notion that it is fair. It's not. By human standards of justice, it's wildly unfair. The playing field is not level and it never will be. By and large, the rich get richer, the poor suffer, the same doors that swing open for the beautiful must be pried open by the plain. Whether the rich and the beautiful find inner peace through their good fortune is a question we must leave to them, but don't bother telling the poor and unattractive that they actually have the better karmic° deal.

So what's a parent to do? I think take   24 a lesson from Mrs. Neisser. Be straight with children. There will be plenty of chances. There's not a parent alive who hasn't heard an outraged child, in the context of discussing anything from bedtimes to allowance to appropriate movie fare to curfews, point out, "But that's not *fair*!" The follow-up comment is usually something like, "*You* get to stay up until 11. *Jennifer* got to watch *The Hunger Games. Everyone* is going to stay out all night after the prom. *Nobody* has to do chores to earn an allowance anymore." In response, look them in the eye and gently, lovingly, set them straight: "It may not be 'fair.' But few things are. I believe it's the best decision for this situation, and it's what we're going to do." And encourage them to be grateful when the sun shines, when days go smoothly, and above all, when love comes. It's all a gift, not a given. You never know which way the dice will roll next.

25   William Goldman doesn't let his readers forget that. Rather than wrapping up *The Princess Bride* tidily, he ends it on a most ambiguous note. We finish the last page not at all certain if our heroes escape from the villains; whether they live happily ever after (or even live at all) is very much in question. Is it fair to string readers along for 283 pages and then deny them the satisfaction of a neat ending? Maybe not. But what of it? The ending isn't fair; life isn't fair; the ultimate injustice is that none of us gets out of here alive. In that fact, finally, we're all treated impartially. It's what we do with the finite amount of time we're given—how we make our way through this maddening, beautiful universe, with its supreme disregard of our notions of fairness, that counts.

26   Life isn't fair. That's not a curse; it's a liberating reality. We can deny it and simmer in false hopes and resentment, or accept it and celebrate the breaks we get. In acceptance, we're choosing life itself.

First Impressions

Freewrite for ten minutes on one of the following.

1. Did you enjoy reading this selection? Why or why not?

2. Do you agree or disagree with Johnson's assertion that life isn't fair? Explain.

3. If you plan to have children, or already have them, will you tell them that life isn't fair? Why or why not?

Vocabulary Check

_____ 1. In the excerpt below, the word *evokes* means
   A. prevents.
   B. describes.
   C. contains.
   D. brings forth.

   "We love our kids and want them to have the best shot possible at happy lives. . . . Part of what evokes the bottomless devotion we feel for them, I think, is their early, baby innocence." (Paragraph 13)

_____ 2. In the sentence below, the word *pervasive* means
   A. widespread.
   B. depressing.
   C. rewarding.
   D. limited to one area.

> "But the same can't be said, I think, for a larger and more pervasive fiction that we well-intentioned parents often impose on our children: that life is fair, that it's supposed to be fair, and that they have the right to expect it to act accordingly." (Paragraph 15)

_____ 3. In the excerpt below, the word *ambiguous* means
   A. definite.
   B. unclear.
   C. fulfilling.
   D. humorous.

> "Rather than wrapping up *The Princess Bride* tidily, he ends it on a most ambiguous note. We finish the last page not at all certain if our heroes escape from the villains ..." (Paragraph 25)

Reading Check

Central Point and Main Ideas

_____ 1. Which sentence best expresses the central point of the selection?
   A. Mrs. Neisser was one of the few parents honest enough to tell children the truth about life.
   B. Many parents let their children believe that life is fair because they want them to approach the world full of optimism.
   C. Most parents are so in love with their children that it's hard for them to tell them the truth about life.
   D. Life isn't fair, and it's about time we stopped telling our children that it is.

_____ 2. The main idea of paragraph 16 is expressed in its
   A. first sentence.
   B. second sentence.
   C. third sentence.
   D. last sentence.

Supporting Details

_____ 3. In paragraph 23, Michael doesn't realize that
    A. his parents expected him to fail and his brother to succeed.
    B. he could have finished college without his parents' encouragement.
    C. he was actually smarter than his older brother.
    D. his parents didn't object when he dropped out of college.

_____ 4. Johnson states that if a child complains that a decision a parent makes isn't fair, the parent should tell the child that
    A. things will even out in the end.
    B. he or she received special treatment in the past.
    C. he or she should stop complaining because children in poor countries have it worse.
    D. the decision may not be fair, but few things are, and it's the best decision for this situation.

_____ 5. According to Johnson, Suzanne
    A. will eventually achieve her dream of becoming a Broadway star.
    B. has enormous talent but is too disorganized to become a star.
    C. would be better off if her parents had not encouraged her to believe she would become a star.
    D. has finally learned to accept the fact that a golden prize isn't going to drop out of the sky.

Inferences

_____ 6. Paragraph 16 suggests that
    A. parents deliberately try to mislead their children.
    B. good behavior generally leads to worldly success.
    C. despite what parents tell their children, money and good looks are important.
    D. Johnson wants her kids to become rich, like Geraldo's parents.

_____ 7. On the basis of paragraphs 19–21, we can conclude that Johnson believes
    A. it's good to be optimistic about life.
    B. being overly optimistic can lead people to hold out false hopes about life.
    C. young people should be taught that their dreams of success probably won't come true.
    D. Suzanne's parents deliberately misled her about her chances of becoming a Broadway star.

_____ 8. With which of the following statements would Johnson probably agree?
   A. In the United States, everyone has an equal opportunity to succeed.
   B. Plain-looking people tend to be appreciated just as much as people who are physically attractive.
   C. If a person works hard enough, he or she will definitely succeed.
   D. It's important to appreciate the good things you have because you never know what the future will bring.

The Writer's Craft

_____ 9. Johnson begins her essay with an excerpt from *The Princess Bride* because
   A. it was one of the most exciting books she had ever read.
   B. she approves of what Mrs. Neisser told William Goldman about life.
   C. she knows most Americans are interested in sports such as badminton.
   D. she knows that most of her readers have read the book.

_____10. In paragraph 25, Johnson describes the ambiguous ending of *The Princess Bride* in order to
   A. remind people that William Goldman is a very clever writer.
   B. encourage more people to read *The Princess Bride*.
   C. make the point that Goldman should have come up with a better ending.
   D. sum up her point about life's unfairness.

Discussion Questions

1. Do you agree with Johnson's basic premise that "life isn't fair"? What evidence do you have to support your answer?

2. Should parents ever tell their children "little white lies"—things that aren't exactly true? Under what circumstances do you think such untruths are acceptable?

3. The author mentions her friend Michael, who still resents his parents for allowing him to quit college. Do you know anyone who, like Michael, tends to blame other people for his or her own decisions? Explain. Why might people decide to blame others when they make the wrong decisions?

4. Johnson doesn't believe in shielding young people from life's harsh realities. Might there be any negative consequences to telling children about life's injustices? If so, what might they be?

Paragraph Assignments

1. Johnson writes that "Injustices large and small, tragic and commonplace, pop up everywhere." In fact, most of us have felt that we've been treated unfairly at one time or another. Write a paragraph about a time in your life when you felt you were treated unfairly. Describe the situation in detail. How did you react to this perceived injustice? Did you challenge it, or go along with it? If you had it to do all over again, would you react the same way—or differently?

2. In "Life Isn't Fair," Johnson describes Suzanne, a person whose overly optimistic view of the chances of her own success is harming her. But the opposite can be true as well. Being overly pessimistic can also have a negative effect on a person's life. Write a paragraph that supports the following point:

   Point: There are several reasons why being overly pessimistic can be just as harmful as being overly optimistic.

Essay Assignments

1. This essay centers on the idea that parents should teach their children that life isn't fair, even if the idea might be upsetting. What are other important things you think parents should teach their children? Write an essay about three such things.

2. Write an essay in which you develop three specific examples of how life has been unfair for three people you know. You may also want to include details on how well they have, or have not, coped with their situations. Devote a separate paragraph to each person, stating who he or she is and why life has been unfair. You could begin each of the supporting paragraphs of your essay with a topic sentence similar to the following:

   ● One person I know whose life has been unfair is _____.

   ● _____ is another person who could say "Life isn't fair."

   ● Finally, _____ is a strong example of "Life isn't fair."

   Be sure to include an introductory and a concluding paragraph for the essay.

Here is one student's response to this assignment:

We all experience times in our lives when things don't seem to be very fair. Perhaps we get passed over for a promotion we deserved. Maybe a friend lies to us, or it pours rain the entire time we're on vacation. Typically, we take the good with the bad and move on, realizing that sometimes life just isn't fair. However, some unfortunate people experience years or even a lifetime of unfairness. I know three people who have certainly had more than their fair share of unfair times.

One person I know whose life has been unfair is my Great Aunt Rachel. First of all, both Rachel's parents died when she was young, and she had to live in an orphanage for four years. At barely 18, she married a much older man. Aunt Rachel thought she had made a good choice marrying Uncle Mark, but she was wrong. After a few years of marriage, he began cheating on Aunt Rachel and even abusing her. I know some people think Aunt Rachel should have left her husband, but it wasn't that simple, particularly 50 years ago. She worked hard to raise her children and endured many years of unhappiness and sacrifice. Then when Rachel was in her early sixties, Mark abruptly left her for a younger woman. Today, Aunt Rachel has to work two low-paying jobs just to make ends meet. I've never heard her complain, and I always enjoy visiting Aunt Rachel, but I feel sad for how unfair her life has been.

Our neighbor down the street, Will, is another person who has experienced some serious unfairness in his life. Will was a star football player at the local high school, and he received a full scholarship to Notre Dame. He was full of big plans and dreams for his future until, in a split second, everything was taken away from him. Driving home from the gym one evening, Will was hit by a drunk driver. Will's injuries were so bad that he was in a coma for a week, and now he'll be in a wheelchair for the rest of his life. But Will's a real survivor. I don't think he spent very long feeling sorry for himself, even though he had every right to do so. Just this afternoon, I saw Will flying by the house in his "race wheelchair." He's training to qualify to be a wheelchair racer at the Boston Marathon next year, and I'll bet he makes it.

Finally, my friend, Candice, is definitely an example of someone who can claim that life isn't fair. I'm not sure I've ever known anyone with such random bad luck. Several years ago, Candice's house was completely destroyed by a tornado that barely touched the house right across the street from her. She picked herself up and moved to a part of the country where there are no tornadoes—and lost her home to a forest fire! Candice tried to have a sense of humor about it, but she was pretty upset. While trying to rebuild her life, Candice moved in with her elderly parents. Within a year, her dad was diagnosed with cancer, and her mom slipped and fell on some ice and broke her hip. When we talked last week, Candice said, "Sometimes I feel like I bring terrible luck to wherever I move." I assured her that she didn't, but I'm not sure I'd want her living in my house right now!

Aunt Rachel, Will, and Candice are three people I know personally who could say that life is not fair and really mean it. When I look at their lives, I don't get so dramatic or upset when some little thing strikes me as being unfair in my life. And all three share a common trait: they don't complain in spite of their circumstances. So as much as I feel sorry for all three people, I probably admire them even more. Life may have been terribly unfair to them, but they move forward anyway.

Check Your Performance   LIFE ISN'T FAIR

Activity	Number Right	Points			Score
Vocabulary Check (3 items)	_____	x	10	=	_____
Reading Check					
Central Point and Main Ideas (2 items)	_____	x	7	=	_____
Supporting Details (3 items)	_____	x	7	=	_____
Inferences (3 items)	_____	x	7	=	_____
The Writer's Craft (2 items)	_____	x	7	=	_____
		TOTAL SCORE		=	_____ %

Enter your total score into the **Performance Chart: Fifteen Reading Selections** on the inside back cover.

4 Managing Conflicts In Relationships

Rudolph F. Verderber

Preview

How do you handle the conflicts in your life? Do you withdraw or give in? Do you become aggressive or try to persuade? Or do you discuss and problem-solve? Whatever your methods, you will probably recognize them in the following excerpt from the widely used textbook *Communicate!* by Rudolph F. Verderber.

Words to Watch

disengagement (9): becoming free of a situation
contention (14): argument
entails (15): involves
coercion (15): force
obscured (16): hidden
degenerate (18): worsen
implement (20): carry out

1   Conflicts include clashes over facts and definitions ("Charley was the first one to talk." "No, it was Mark." or "Your mother is a battle-ax." "What do you mean, a 'battle-ax'?"); over values ("Bringing home pencils and pens from work is not stealing." "Of course it is." or "The idea that you have to be married to have sex is completely outdated." "No, it isn't."); and, perhaps the most difficult to deal with, over ego involvement ("Listen, I've been a football fan for thirty years; I ought to know what good defense is." "Well, you may be a fan, but that doesn't make you an expert.").

2   Although many people view conflict as bad (and, to be sure, conflict situations are likely to make us anxious and uneasy), it is inevitable in any significant relationship. Moreover, conflict is sometimes useful in that it forces us to make choices; to resolve honest differences; and to test the relative merits of our attitudes,

behaviors, needs, and goals. Now let's consider methods of dealing with conflict.

METHODS OF DEALING WITH CONFLICT

3 Left to their own devices, people engage in many behaviors, both negative and positive, to cope with or manage their conflicts. The various methods of dealing with conflict can be grouped into five major patterns: withdrawal, surrender, aggression, persuasion, and problem-solving discussion. Let's consider each of these methods in turn.

4 **Withdrawal.** One of the most common, and certainly one of the easiest, ways to deal with conflict is to withdraw. When people *withdraw*, they physically or psychologically remove themselves from the situation.

5 Physical withdrawal is, of course, easiest to identify. Suppose Eduardo and Justina get into a conversation about Eduardo's smoking. Justina says, "Eduardo, I thought you told me that whether you stopped smoking completely or not, you weren't going to smoke around the house. Now here you are lighting up!" Eduardo may withdraw physically by saying "I don't want to talk about it" and going to the basement to finish a project he was working on.

6 Psychological withdrawal may be less noticeable but is every bit as common. Using the same example, when Justina begins to talk about Eduardo's smoking in the house, Eduardo may sit quietly in his chair looking at Justina, but all the time she speaks, he is thinking about the poker game he will be going to the next evening.

7 Besides being quite common, both kinds of withdrawal are basically negative. Why? Because they neither eliminate nor attempt to manage the conflict. As researchers Roloff and Cloven note, "Relational partners who avoid conflicts have more difficulty resolving disputes." In the case of the physical withdrawal, Justina may follow Eduardo to the basement, where the conflict will be resumed; if not, the conflict will undoubtedly resurface later—and will probably be intensified—when Justina and Eduardo try to resolve another, unrelated issue. In the case of the psychological withdrawal, Justina may force Eduardo to address the smoking issue, or she may go along with Eduardo's ignoring it but harbor a resentment that may negatively affect their relationship.

8 Another reason why withdrawal is negative is that it results in what Cloven and Roloff call "mulling behavior." By *mulling* they mean thinking about or stewing over an actual or perceived problem until the participants perceive the conflict as more severe and begin engaging in blaming behavior. Thus, in many cases, not confronting the problem when it occurs only makes it more difficult to deal with in the long run.

9 Nevertheless, conflicts do occasionally go away if left alone. There appear to be two sets of circumstances in which withdrawal may work. First, when the withdrawal represents temporary disengagement° for the

purpose of letting the heat of the conflict subside, it can be an effective technique for managing conflict. Consider this example: Bill and Margaret begin to argue over inviting Bill's mother for Thanksgiving dinner. During the conversation, Margaret begins to get angry about what her mother-in-law said to her recently about the way she and Bill are raising their daughter. Margaret says, "Hold it a minute; let me make a pot of coffee. We can both relax a bit, and then we'll talk about this some more." A few minutes later, having calmed down, she returns, ready to approach the conflict more objectively. Margaret's action is not true withdrawal; it's not meant as a means of avoiding confrontation. Rather, it provides a cooling-off period that will probably benefit them both.

10   The second set of circumstances in which withdrawal may work is when a conflict occurs between people who communicate infrequently. Consider Josh and Mario, who work in the same office. At two office gatherings, they have gotten into arguments about whether the company really cares about its employees. At the next office gathering, Mario avoids sitting near Josh. Again, this form of withdrawal serves as a means of avoiding conflict rather than contributing to it. In this case, Mario judges that it simply isn't that important to resolve the disagreement. It is fair to say that not every conflict needs to be resolved. Withdrawal is a negative pattern only when it is a person's major way of managing conflict.

Surrender. A second method of managing conflict is to surrender. As you might suspect, *surrender* means giving in immediately to avoid conflict. Although altering a personal position in order to accommodate another can be positive when it's done in the spirit of cooperation, using surrender as a primary coping strategy is unhealthy. 11

Some people are so upset by the prospect of conflict that they will do anything to avoid it. For instance, Juan and Mariana are discussing their vacation plans. Juan would like just the two of them to go, but Mariana has talked with two of their friends who will be vacationing the same week about going together. After Juan mentions that he'd like the two of them to go alone, Mariana says, "But I think it would be fun to go with another couple, don't you?" Juan replies, "OK, whatever you want." Even though Juan really wants 12 the two of them to go alone, rather than describe his feelings or give reasons for his position, he gives in to avoid conflict.

13   Habitual surrender is a negative way of dealing with conflict for at least two reasons. First, decisions should be made on their merits, not to avoid conflict. If one person gives in, there is no testing of the decision—no one knows what would really be best. Second, surrender can be infuriating to the other person. When Mariana tells Juan what she thinks, she probably wants Juan to see her way as the best. But if Juan simply surrenders, Mariana might believe that Juan still dislikes her plan but is playing the martyr. And his unwillingness to present his reasons could lead to even more conflict.

14   The contention° that surrender is a negative way of dealing with conflict should be qualified to the extent that it reflects a Western cultural perspective. In some cultures, surrendering is a perfectly legitimate way of dealing with conflict. In Japanese culture, for instance, it is thought to be more humble and face-saving to surrender than to risk losing respect through conflict.

15   **Aggression.** A third method of dealing with conflict is through aggression. *Aggression* entails° the use of physical or psychological coercion° to get one's way. Through aggression, people attempt to force others to accept their ideas or wishes, thereby emerging as "victors" in conflicts.

16   Aggression seldom improves a relationship, however. Rather, aggression is an emotional reaction to conflict. Thought is short-circuited, and the person lashes out physically or verbally. People who use aggression are not concerned with the merits of an issue but only with who is bigger, who can talk louder, who can act nastier, or who can force the other to give in. With either physical or verbal aggression, conflict is escalated or obscured° but not managed.

Persuasion. A fourth method of 17 managing conflict is by persuasion. *Persuasion* is the attempt to change either the attitude or the behavior of another person in order to seek accommodation. At times during the discussion of an issue, one party may try to persuade the other that a particular action is the right one. Suppose that at one point in their discussion about buying a car, Sheila says, "Don't we need a lot of room?" Kevin might reply, "Enough to get us into the car together, but I don't see why we need more than that." Sheila and Kevin are now approaching a conflict situation. At this point, Sheila might say, "Kevin, we are constantly complaining about the lack of room in our present car. Remember last month when you were upset because we couldn't even get our two suitcases into the trunk and we had to put one of them in the back seat? And how many times have we been embarrassed when we couldn't drive our cars with friends because the back seat is too small for even two normal-sized people?" Statements like these represent an attempt at resolving the conflict through persuasion.

18   When persuasion is open and reasonable, it can be a positive means of resolving conflict. However, persuasion can also degenerate° into manipulation, as when a person says, "You know, if you back me on this, I could see to it that you get a few more of the good accounts, and if you don't, well . . ." Although persuasive efforts may fuel a conflict, if that persuasion has a solid logical base, it is at least possible that the persuasion will resolve the conflict.

19   **Discussion.** Λ fifth method of dealing with conflict is *problem-solving discussion*—the verbal weighing and considering of the pros and cons of the issues in conflict. Discussion is the most desirable means of dealing with conflict in a relationship because it provides for open consideration of issues and because it preserves equality. Resolving conflict through discussion is often difficult to accomplish, however, because it requires all parties involved to cooperate: the participants must be objective in their presentation of issues,

honest in stating their feelings and beliefs, and open to the solution that proves to be most satisfactory and in the best interests of those involved.

20   Problem-solving discussion includes defining and analyzing the problem, suggesting possible solutions, selecting the solution that best fits the analysis, and working to implement° the decision. In everyday situations, all five steps are not always considered completely, nor are they necessarily considered in the order given. But when two people perceive a conflict emerging, they need to be willing to step back from the conflict and proceed systematically toward a solution.

21   Does this process sound too idealized? Or impracticable? Discussion is difficult, but when two people commit themselves to trying, chances are that they will discover that through discussion they arrive at solutions that meet both their needs and do so in a way that maintains their relationship.

First Impressions

Freewrite for ten minutes on one of the following.

1. Did you enjoy reading this selection? Why or why not?

2. What conflict situations have you been involved in recently? How did you resolve them?

3. Which of Verderber's methods of managing conflicts might you try the next time you find yourself in a conflict situation? Why?

Vocabulary Check

_____ 1. In the sentence below, the word *harbor* means
   A. hold onto.
   B. avoid.
   C. give up.
   D. pretend.

   "Justina may force Eduardo to address the smoking issue, or she may go along with Eduardo's ignoring it but harbor a resentment that may negatively affect their relationship." (Paragraph 7)

_____ 2. In the excerpt below, the word *subside* means
   A. spread.
   B. rise.
   C. quiet down.
   D. remain.

   "There appear to be two sets of circumstances in which withdrawal may work. First, when the withdrawal represents temporary disengagement for the purpose of letting the heat of the conflict subside, it can be an effective technique for managing conflict." (Paragraph 9)

_____ 3. In the sentence below, the words *emerging as* mean
   A. losing to.
   B. realizing they are.
   C. pretending to be.
   D. becoming.

   "Through aggression, people attempt to force others to accept their ideas or wishes, thereby emerging as 'victors' in conflicts." (Paragraph 15)

Reading Check

Central Point and Main Ideas

_____ 1. Which sentence best expresses the central point of the selection?
   A. Many people have a negative view of conflict.
   B. There are five main ways, both positive and negative, with which people deal with conflict.
   C. Conflicts can force people to make choices and to test their attitudes, actions, needs, and aims.
   D. It is better not to intensify or hide conflict.

_____ 2. The main idea of paragraphs 9 and 10 can be found in the
  A. second sentence of paragraph 9.
  B. third sentence of paragraph 9.
  C. first sentence of paragraph 10.
  D. second sentence of paragraph 10.

Supporting Details

_____ 3. Verderber states that withdrawal
  A. never works.
  B. is the best way to deal with repeated conflicts.
  C. might work if a cooling-off period is needed or if the two people rarely see each other.
  D. is more effective in workplace or classroom situations than at home.

_____ 4. According to the selection, persuasion
  A. never works.
  B. tries to resolve conflict by changing another person's attitude or behavior.
  C. works only when the persuader has a higher status or more power than the other person.
  D. works because it appeals to a person's emotions.

_____ 5. TRUE OR FALSE? According to the author, discussion is the easiest way of dealing with conflict in a relationship.

Inferences

_____ 6. We can infer that the author of this selection
  A. believes that conflict should be avoided at all costs.
  B. feels that conflict is the best way to strengthen a relationship.
  C. feels that conflict can be positive if handled appropriately.
  D. believes that withdrawal is never an appropriate method of dealing with conflict.

_____ 7. Paragraph 14 suggests that Japanese people
  A. rarely, if ever, experience conflict.
  B. would rather lose an argument than lose respect.
  C. avoid all types of conflict situations.
  D. are more skilled at resolving conflicts than people in the United States are.

Argument

_____ 8. Three of the items below are supporting details for an argument. Write the letter of the statement that represents the point of these supporting details.
  A. People who use aggression are not concerned with the merits of an issue but only with who can force the other person to give in.
  B. Aggression usually harms a relationship.
  C. In aggression, thought is short-circuited and the person lashes out physically or verbally.
  D. With either physical or verbal aggression, conflict is escalated or obscured but not managed.

The Writer's Craft

_____ 9. Verderber supports his central point by providing
  A. examples of ways to manage conflicts.
  B. reasons why conflicts should be avoided.
  C. personal experiences he has had with conflict situations in his own family.
  D. statistics proving which method of conflict management is the best.

_____ 10. For what kind of audience did Verderber probably write this selection?
  A. A general audience of all ages
  B. College students taking a course in communication skills
  C. Couples experiencing relationship problems
  D. Graduate students preparing to become therapists

Discussion Questions

1. Which of Verderber's five methods of dealing with conflict do you or people you know typically use? Give examples.

2. Why do you think Verderber regards discussion as "the most desirable means of dealing with conflict in a relationship"? And why might he feel that discussion "is often difficult to accomplish"?

3. Assume someone you know is having a problem at home or in school. Suggest ways that this person could be encouraged to deal effectively with his or her specific conflict.

4. Verderber writes that conflict is sometimes useful because it forces us to make choices and test attitudes. When in your life has conflict been a *good* thing? What did you learn from it?

Paragraph Assignments

1. What is your typical approach when dealing with conflict? Decide if you're usually a withdrawer, surrenderer, aggressor, persuader, or problem-solver. Then write a paragraph supporting your choice by giving an example or two of your behavior in past conflict situations.

2. What advice would you give to Eduardo and Justina, the couple in the reading who are in conflict about Eduardo's smoking? What do you think Eduardo should do? What should Justina do? Write a paragraph advising the couple on how to handle their problem.

Essay Assignments

1. Write an essay in which you describe three people you know, defining each as one of the following: a withdrawer, a surrenderer, an aggressor, a persuader, or a problem-solver. Write a paragraph about each person and his or her approach to dealing with conflict.

Here is one student's response to this assignment:

> Every one of us deals with confrontation and conflict in our own way. Conflict, particularly among friends or family, is always nerve-racking, so we usually deal with it in ways that feel most comfortable and natural to us. And what feels most natural is usually a reflection of our personalities. In my family, there are some very different personalities. As a result, my brother, mother, and father all deal with conflict in vastly different ways.
>
> My brother, Mike, is an aggressor. He is not interested in resolving situations—he's more concerned about proving he's right and getting his way. He's reluctant to ever just drop an argument, even when he's wrong. When Mike lost money on a football bet with a friend, he argued that he shouldn't have to pay it because the quarterback got injured on the first play. The more his friend disagreed with Mike (as he should have!), the more vicious Mike became. When Mike finally accused his friend of being a con man and a jerk, the friend just told Mike to forget the bet. Even then, Mike demanded that his friend agree that he was right.
>
> On the opposite end of the conflict spectrum is my dad, who instantly surrenders when conflict arises. It's hard to imagine where my brother gets his aggression from, because

Dad simply backs down when faced with an argument. I recall a confrontation with our neighbor after Dad had been trimming a tree that belonged to the neighbor but hung over onto our property and made a mess. I know Dad always thought he was actually doing the neighbor a favor. However, when the neighbor took issue with it and said Dad was destroying his property, Dad just shrugged and said, "I'm sorry. You're right." Years later, Dad still fumes about that tree, but he won't discuss it with our neighbor.

Splitting the difference between Dad and Mike is my mom, the persuader. She listens calmly to the opposing side of an argument and then, just as calmly, makes a really good case for her viewpoint. She rarely gets huffy or seems offended in the midst of conflict. Just last week, Mom was shortchanged by accident at the grocery store. The checker rolled her eyes and angrily told my mom that it was impossible, since the computer figured out how much cash to give back. Mom nodded and didn't get upset. She simply said, "But you hand me the cash, not the computer. I'm sure it was just a mistake." In the end, Mom got a big apology from both the checker and the store manager!

When it comes to my family, everyone has very different styles of handling conflict. It's definitely something to see when our entire family gets in an argument. It usually ends up with Dad walking away, Mike yelling, and my mom trying to calm everyone down. As for me, I just try staying out of conflict in the first place!

2. At the beginning of his essay, Verderber lists the three causes for most conflicts: facts and definitions, values, and ego involvement. Reread the examples he gives for each cause, and you'll probably recall a conflict you've been in based on each one of these causes. Write an essay with this thesis statement: "I have been involved in conflicts that stemmed from facts/definitions, values, and ego involvement." Then proceed to describe and detail those conflicts in the body of your essay, using one paragraph for each cause.

   Alternatively, choose one of the three causes, and write an essay in which you describe and detail three separate conflicts you've been involved in based on that particular cause.

Check Your Performance

MANAGING CONFLICTS IN RELATIONSHIPS

Activity	Number Right		Points		Score
Vocabulary Check (3 items)	_____	x	10	=	_____
Reading Check					
Central Point and Main Ideas (2 items)	_____	x	7	=	_____
Supporting Details (3 items)	_____	x	7	=	_____
Inferences (2 items)	_____	x	7	=	_____
Argument (1 item)	_____	x	7	=	_____
The Writer's Craft (2 items)	_____	x	7	=	_____

TOTAL SCORE   =   _____%

Enter your total score into the **Performance Chart: Fifteen Reading Selections** on the inside back cover.

5 Controlling Your Destiny

Guadalupe Quintanilla

Preview

Guadalupe Quintanilla made history as the first Hispanic woman to become an administrator at the University of Houston in Texas. She was nominated to be a U.S. assistant attorney general, has served as a representative to the United Nations, and has spoken at countless conferences, both in the United States and abroad. But the most remarkable thing about Quintanilla is not where she is now, but how far she has traveled to get there.

Words to Watch

bewildered (4): confused
architect (22): creator
flip side (24): disadvantages (as opposed to advantages)
perspective (27): point of view
assertive (27): forceful and confident

1   I dropped out of first grade when I was thirteen years old. Yes, you read that correctly; I was a thirteen-year-old first-grader, and I quit school.

2   I was born in 1937 in Nogales, Mexico, just a few miles south of the Arizona border. When my parents separated, I went to live with my grandparents in a rural town deep in southern Mexico. There were no schools there—there weren't even any paved roads. Still, I learned a great deal. My grandparents ran a little store inside our house, and I helped out there. As a five-year-old, I would stand on a carton to use the telephone and call in orders. Sometimes when the suppliers heard a child's voice, they would hang up, but some of the other suppliers became accustomed to talking with me. I learned to read and write, and to work with numbers.

3   Then my grandfather began to lose his sight. We moved to Brownsville, Texas, in hopes that the doctors there could help him; but sadly, they could not, and he became completely blind.

4   In Brownsville, I was enrolled in school, and then the trouble began. Although I could read and write well, I could do those things only in Spanish. Unfortunately, the IQ test I was given was in English, and I didn't understand any of the questions. I scored 64 points,

which classified me as seriously mentally retarded. Although I was 12, I was put into first grade—in a class of six-year-olds. No one even tried to teach me. The teacher had me cut out pictures and take little kids to the bathroom. Because everyone was speaking a language I didn't understand, I was bewildered° by what was going on around me, and the other children teased me for being so stupid.

5   After four months, things came to a head. I was alone at recess, as usual, and a man cutting the grass greeted me, saying "*Buenas tardes.*" I was so excited to hear someone speak to me in Spanish, *la lengua de mi alma, la lengua de mi abuelita!* ("The language of my soul, the language of my grandmother!") Eagerly I answered him. Like a flash, a teacher swooped down, grabbed me by the arm, and marched me to the principal's office, where she and the principal both shouted strange English words at me. To this day, I do not know why they were so angry—was it something about this particular man, or was it simply that I was not supposed to speak Spanish at all?

6   What I do know is that I was humiliated more than I could bear. There was no force on earth that could make me go back to that place. I went home and told my family I was quitting school . . . and that is how I became a thirteen-year-old first-grade dropout.

7   Actually, I was very happy to be at home. I thought school was not essential for a girl, and nobody—least of all me—thought I should prepare to support myself. My grandparents, who were very loving and kind to me, were also very traditional; they raised me to be a good Hispanic wife and mother. My grandmother taught me to cook and clean and sew. I read novels and poetry and newspapers to my grandfather for hours. Everyone assumed that my life's job would be caring for a home and children.

8   Because my grandfather was getting older, he wanted to know that I would be protected after he was gone. In our world, "protected" meant "married," and so, at age 16, I married, and my grandparents came to live with my husband and me. Within five years I had my three children—Victor, Mario, and Martha. My life was simple and happy. I took care of everyone: my husband, my children, and my grandparents, and I could not have been more traditional—I would even put my husband's shoes on his feet and tie the laces for him.

9   But my traditional upbringing had not prepared me for everything, and soon after my children started school, I saw something bad happening. Victor, Mario, and Martha were as bright as they

could be; they knew so many stories and songs and rhymes and prayers; they were quick-witted and funny. And yet, when they began bringing home report cards, their grades were poor. They were put in a group called "Yellow Birds," which I soon realized was the label for "slow learners."

10   All my memories of my own school days came flooding back. I had been labeled "retarded"; I had accepted the idea that school was not for me. But I could not accept that idea for my beautiful, bright children. I *knew* they were not "slow learners"!

11   I visited their school and talked to their teachers and principal, something which was very difficult for me. People think that Hispanic parents do not care about education, because they are not likely to do things like call the teachers or join the PTA. In fact, the opposite is true: Most Hispanic parents have such great respect for education that they would never interfere with their child's schooling. They think, "She's *la maestra*; she must be right!" But I went to the school, and the principal told me the truth. He said, "Your children are confused. They speak only Spanish at home. They don't know how to learn in English."

12   I realized the principal was right. Yes, in our Spanish-speaking home, it was clear that my children were very bright, but in an English-speaking school, they were lost—just as I had been lost in that first-grade classroom.

13   I knew what I had to do. In order to help my children succeed, I was going to have to learn English, and learn it well.

14   That was the beginning of a long, difficult journey for me. At that time in Brownsville, there were no English language programs for adults, so I would have to find another way to learn. I went to the local high school to ask if I could sit in on some classes. But when the school administrators looked at my records, they saw the word "retarded" and told me, "You'd just be taking space in the classroom away from someone who could learn." I asked an administrator at the local hospital, where I served as a volunteer, if I could sit in on their nursing classes. No, I was told—not without a high-school diploma. I got the same answer at Texas Southmost College and at the telephone company, where operators were being trained.

15   I was so discouraged. I walked home from the telephone company in the rain, crying, feeling like a complete failure. But somehow the next day, I woke up with fresh courage. I went back to the college, found a Spanish-speaking student, and asked him, "*Quién decide quién asiste a la escuela aquí?*" ("Who decides who goes to school here?") He told me it was the registrar. I looked through the faculty parking lot until I found the spot marked RESERVED FOR REGISTRAR and waited by that car for hours until a man came to get into it. Fortunately, he spoke Spanish. I told him that I *had* to attend classes in order to become educated and help my children. I don't think he had much hope for me. "You've never gone to school at all," he said. "How can you handle college classes?"

16   "Just let me try," I said.

17   Finally he agreed, and I tried. And it was terribly, terribly difficult. I got up at 4:00 a.m. to study. I had a long bus ride to school. At noon I hurried home to fix my husband's lunch. I'd rush back to class, then go home again to be there when my children returned from school. There were times I went to the ladies' room during break and cried. I would look at myself in the mirror and say, "What are you doing? Why don't you go home and watch *I Love Lucy* on TV?"

18   But I did it. Even today, I can hardly understand how. I believe it was the love for my children that motivated me. I made the dean's list that first semester. I began to think that I could do more than just learn English; I began to think that I, the first-grade dropout, the "retarded" girl, could earn a college degree.

19   I will not take the time to tell you the whole long story here. But I *did* earn my college degree, and then I earned a master's degree, and then a doctoral degree in education. I joined the faculty of the University of Houston, where I still teach today. And my children, the "slow learners"? The oldest, Victor, is an attorney in San Antonio, Texas, specializing in estate planning. The second, Mario, is an emergency-room physician in Houston. And my youngest, Martha, is an attorney, who has just retired as chief of the Family Violence Division of the Dallas district attorney's office.

20   Now I would like to tell you not just about me, but about some of the things I have learned on my journey. Let me start with a few lines by the great Mexican poet Amado Nervo. He wrote:

21   *"Porque veo al final de mi rudo camino que yo fui el arquitecto de mi propio destino."*

22   (**"When I got to the end of my long journey in life, I realized that I was the architect° of my own destiny."**)

23   I insist that every student in every class I teach—whether it's Hispanic Women in Literature, Public Speaking in Spanish, or Latin Folklore of the Southwest—memorize those lines. They contain, in my opinion, the most important lesson a person can learn: that your future lies in your own hands. You—and only you—are the architect of your own destiny.

24   I think that lesson is especially important, and in some ways especially difficult, for Hispanic women. Our world is changing rapidly, but for many of us, cultural expectations still carry a lot of weight. The traditional ways can be very comfortable; the closeness and support of the Latino family can be a very wonderful thing. But the flip side° is that many of our young people find it hard to separate from the family and to learn to make independent decisions. Again and again, I see promising Latino students—both male and female—grow so homesick at the university that they drop out. I've heard "Our culture gives us strong roots, but we need to strengthen our wings." I think that is true.

25   In my own case, I met with a lot of resistance when I returned to school. My grandfather actually stopped speaking to me because to him, it was demeaning to the family to have a woman "on the street"—meaning in the world

outside of the home. He believed that by going "out there," I was neglecting my family. That was painful for me—to feel the disapproval of someone I loved and respected so much—but I had to stand firm for what I believed was right for me and my children. For women especially, trying to achieve that kind of independence is difficult. As we try to blossom in the Anglo world, we must respect the traditions of our parents; but at the same time, we must recognize—and help *them* recognize—that sometimes those traditions can hold us back.

26   We may not even realize how our culture makes us out of sync with the larger society. Once when Mario and Victor were teenagers, they and another Latino boy were invited to a concert by an Anglo friend. They said they'd be home at 5:00 p.m. At 5:15, when they weren't back, the other Hispanic mom called me and asked if I'd heard anything. At 5:30 I called the Anglo boy's mom to ask if she knew why they were late. She was *so* angry with me! She said, "I have company! The boys know what they're doing!" and actually hung up on me. I was astonished! Why was she angry? I realized she thought I was ridiculously overprotective. And by her standards, I guess I was. But to me and the other Hispanic mom, it was perfectly normal.

27   From one perspective°, that kind of protectiveness is simply loving. But we need to be aware of the downside. A fascinating study was done here in Houston about why many Latino children, in general, do not do as well in school as Anglo children. One thing that the study found is that most Latino children are less likely to ask questions. When they need help, they don't say so. I see that even at the university level. And I think part of the reason is that, in general, Latino children are accustomed to living in a supportive, protective family environment where they don't *have* to ask for much. Someone is always saying, "Do you need this? Would you like that? Can I help you?" As a result, these children, according to research, don't learn to speak up and ask for themselves. It's interesting, isn't it, that there is no word for "assertive°" in Spanish? The closest is *agresivo*, and the meaning of that is quite different. To be assertive means to be clear about what you want. It means going after what you want. It does not mean being aggressive, or angry, or rude, or somehow unwomanly.

28   But assertiveness is not a value that our culture promotes. And that is our loss, because if you develop the ability to be assertive, there's no telling what you might accomplish. Let me tell you a story that illustrates what I mean. Some years back I was driving through a pretty neighborhood here in Houston. I thought, "When I retire, I'd like to live here." Later I saw a house in that neighborhood come up for sale and called the real estate agent to ask about it. But he told me no, the house was not actually for sale. I said, "But there's a sign in the yard." He insisted no, there'd been some mistake, and it wasn't for sale.

29   Well, I thought about that for a while. I knew the house was for sale; why would the agent tell me it wasn't?

Hmm—could it be my Spanish accent? So I had Mario call. He has a Spanish name, of course, but he doesn't have an accent. And he was *Dr.* Quintanilla, the emergency room physician. Well, he got a different answer. The agent told Mario the house *was* for sale, but for a very high price. Then we had a friend of Mario's call. He is an Anglo, a police officer named Robert Jones. The agent told Robert Jones the house was for sale—and for *one-third the price* he had told Mario.

30   When Robert told me that, I said, "Buy the house, but have the contract made out to 'Robert Jones or his assignees'"—meaning that Robert could turn the house over to whomever he wanted. Of course, I was actually the buyer. When Mario and I went with Robert to the closing and the real estate agent realized who had really bought the house, he was so furious he would not even speak to us.

31   And you know what? Since that time, we have bought six more houses in that neighborhood. When we own them all, we'll rename the street "Quintanilla Drive."

32   That's what being assertive can do for you. I say, "Don't get mad. Get ahead."

33   Other specific advice for young women? I can think of three things:

34   **Get your degree before you marry.**

35   **Remember that no one can build *your* future better than you can.**

36   **Realize the great importance of having choices in your life.**

37   Why wait to marry? As I stress to young women again and again, it's tremendously important to have the *freedom of choice in your life*. And I see how terribly difficult it is for my students to pursue their dreams when they are trying to juggle a marriage and children. In addition, when you are very young, it is unlikely that you have the maturity to look into the future and know what you're going to want in a year, or five years, or ten. I have never regretted my husband or children, but certainly it would have been wiser for me to have waited until I was older to marry.

38   And the other points are all tied together with the first. Once you earn a degree, you have the ability to support yourself; you have a choice. If you choose to stay home to care for your children, that's fine. But if you feel cooped up in the house because you have no ability to support yourself and have no belief in yourself—no, that is not fine; you are worthy of more.

39   I have shown you this line of poetry before. But I will leave it with you again as a message from a first-grade dropout, a "retarded" student, a young mother of three children who were being told they could not succeed:

40   **"When I got to the end of my long journey in life, I realized that I was the architect of my own destiny."**

41   Please, believe these words. They are true. Your own life, like mine, can be the proof.

First Impressions

Freewrite for ten minutes on one of the following.

1. Did you enjoy reading this selection? Why or why not?

2. Which part of Quintanilla's story impressed you the most? Why?

3. Why does Quintanilla say, "Don't get mad. Get ahead"?

Vocabulary Check

_____ 1. In the excerpt below, the word *humiliated* means
   A. disappointed.
   B. deeply embarrassed.
   C. refreshed.
   D. revealed.

> "Like a flash, a teacher swooped down, grabbed me by the arm, and marched me to the principal's office, where she and the principal both shouted strange English words at me. To this day, I do not know why they were so angry. . . . What I do know is that I was humiliated more than I could bear. There was no force on earth that could make me go back to that place." (Paragraphs 5–6)

_____ 2. In the excerpt below, the word *demeaning* means
   A. very important.
   B. disgraceful.
   C. remarkable.
   D. helpful.

> "In my own case, I met with a lot of resistance when I returned to school. My grandfather actually stopped speaking to me because to him, it was demeaning to the family to have a woman 'on the street'—meaning in the world outside of the home. He believed that by going 'out there,' I was neglecting my family." (Paragraph 25)

_____ 3. In the excerpt below, the term *out of sync with* means
   A. in conflict with.
   B. appreciated by.
   C. in harmony with.
   D. related to.

> "We may not even realize how our culture makes us out of sync with the larger society. . . . I realized [the Anglo boy's mom] thought I was ridiculously overprotective. And by her standards, I guess I was. But to me and the other Hispanic mom, it was perfectly normal." (Paragraph 26)

Reading Check

Central Point and Main Ideas

_____ 1. Which sentence best expresses the central point of the selection?
   A. The author wants young Hispanics to respect their parents' traditions but also recognize that sometimes those traditions can hold them back.
   B. Quintanilla was determined to learn English after she learned that her children had been labeled "slow learners" in school.
   C. Even though Quintanilla's three children had been labeled "slow learners" in school, two have become attorneys and one has become a physician.
   D. Quintanilla wants young Hispanics to take a more active role in shaping their destiny, and uses her own success as an example.

_____ 2. The implied main idea of paragraph 14 is that
   A. when Quintanilla was a young mother, there were no English language programs for adults in Brownsville.
   B. Quintanilla had a very difficult time finding a way to learn English.
   C. the high school administrators didn't think Quintanilla could learn because she had once been labeled "retarded."
   D. a local high school, hospital, and telephone company all refused to help Quintanilla learn English.

_____ 3. The main idea of paragraph 27 is expressed in its
   A. first sentence.
   B. second sentence.
   C. third sentence.
   D. last sentence.

Supporting Details

_____ 4. Quintanilla dropped out of school because
   A. she had to care for her grandfather, who was going blind.
   B. she had been humiliated for speaking to a man in Spanish.
   C. her grandfather didn't want her to get an education.
   D. she wanted to get married and have children.

_____ 5. Quintanilla finally learned English
   A. by serving as a volunteer at a local hospital.
   B. by sitting in on a high-school English class.
   C. by convincing the registrar at a college to let her enroll there.
   D. by going through a training program for operators at the telephone company.

_____ 6. Quintanilla got a good price on a house in a nice Houston neighborhood by
   A. having her son, the doctor, buy it for her.
   B. threatening to sue the real estate agent who told her it wasn't for sale.
   C. getting an Anglo friend to buy it for her.
   D. informing the real estate agent that she was a well-respected professor at the University of Houston.

Inferences

_____ 7. We can infer from the following excerpt that
   A. Quintanilla realized that teachers and principals aren't always right.
   B. most Hispanic parents want their children to get a good education.
   C. the principal Quintanilla spoke with knew that Quintanilla's children weren't slow learners.
   D. all of the above.

> "I visited their school and talked to their teachers and principal, something which was very difficult for me. People think that Hispanic parents do not care about education, because they are not likely to do things like call the teachers or join the PTA. In fact, the opposite is true: Most Hispanic parents have such great respect for education that they would never interfere with their child's schooling. They think, 'She's *la maestra*; she must be right!' But I went to the school, and the principal told me the truth. He said, 'Your children are confused. They speak only Spanish at home. They don't know how to learn in English.'" (Paragraph 11)

Argument

_____ 8. Which of the following points is supported by the details in the excerpt below?
   A. Latino parents shouldn't care so much about their children.
   B. In order to succeed academically, Latino students need to break away from their families.
   C. Academic standards should be relaxed for Hispanic students.
   D. Hispanic females do better in college than Hispanic males.

> "I think that lesson is especially important, and in some ways especially difficult, for Hispanic women. Our world is changing rapidly, but for many of us, cultural expectations still carry a lot of weight. The traditional ways can be very comfortable. The closeness and support of the Latino family can be a very wonderful thing. But the flip side is that many of our young people find it hard to separate from the family and to learn to make independent decisions. Again and again, I see promising Latino students—both male and female—grow so homesick at the university that they drop out. I've heard 'Our culture gives us strong roots, but we need to strengthen our wings.' I think that is true." (Paragraph 24)

The Writer's Craft

_____ 9. Quintanilla begins her story by describing herself as a thirteen-year-old first-grade dropout because
  A. doing so helps her to illustrate how far she has come in life and that others can do the same.
  B. she wants to prove that anyone can go from being a dropout to a university professor.
  C. she wants to make the point that schools in the U.S. don't help the children of immigrants.
  D. she wants to point out that American schools have changed greatly since she was a girl.

_____ 10. In paragraphs 28–31, the story Quintanilla relates illustrates her point that
  A. most Anglos are racists.
  B. there is no word for *assertive* in Spanish.
  C. it's important to be assertive.
  D. it's important to be aggressive.

Discussion Questions

1. Why do you suppose the people at the Brownsville school were so quick to characterize Quintanilla as "retarded"? Do you think the same thing could happen today? Why or why not? What could her school have done to give her a better chance to succeed?

2. Quintanilla says that Hispanic parents are less likely than Anglo parents to question teachers because Hispanics are highly respectful of educators. Have you observed different ethnic groups seeming to have different attitudes towards teachers? What do you think might explain those differences?

3. One reason that Quintanilla quit school was that she and her family did not believe education was necessary for girls. In your experience, does this attitude still exist? Why would people think boys need education more than girls?

4. Quintanilla agrees with the saying, "Our culture gives us strong roots, but we need to strengthen our wings." What does this statement mean? Do you agree that the statement is generally true about Hispanic culture—or other cultures you're familiar with? Why or why not?

Paragraph Assignments

1. When the college registrar asks Quintanilla how on earth she thinks she's going to get through college classes when she has no education at all, she simply replies, "Just let me try." We have all had things we would like to at least *try* doing, but we run into all kinds of roadblocks: not enough education, a lack of required experience, not enough money, or even our own fear. Write a paragraph describing several obstacles that you feel often prevent people from trying to go in new directions.

2. Quintanilla describes the conflict between traditional Latino culture, with its emphasis on family ties, and the larger society, which rewards assertiveness. This opposition brought her into conflict with her grandfather, who opposed her going back to school.

   Think about a time in your life when you've disagreed with a person of a different generation. The person could be a parent, a grandparent, another adult, or even a child. Then write a paragraph that supports the following point:

   My feelings about _____ brought me into conflict with _____.

   In writing your paper, discuss the conflict in detail and then explain how (or if) it was resolved.

Essay Assignments

1. Although Quintanilla appreciates many aspects of Hispanic culture, she does not shy away from criticizing certain aspects of it. Think about American culture. If you could, what would you change about it? Then write an essay that supports the following thesis statement:

   Thesis: If I could change three things about American culture, I would change American attitudes toward _____, _____, and _____.

   In the body of your essay, explain why you would change each aspect of American culture. What positive results might these changes have?

2. Write an essay in which you detail three ways that you have made yourself—or intend to make yourself—an "architect of your own destiny," in the words of the Mexican poet quoted by Lupe Quintanilla.

Here is one student's response to this assignment:

When I decided to totally change my life at 51, most of my friends thought I was crazy. I had worked for most of my adult life as a clerk at an insurance office. There's nothing wrong with that, but I wanted more. "You're too old!" some friends said. "But your job is secure!" coworkers pointed out. Still, I wanted some adventure, more education, and a new career. Some people thought I had lost my mind, but before I was 55, I achieved those goals and created my own life "makeover."

First of all, I quit my job and spent four months hiking the Appalachian Trail alone. I'm divorced, and my children are grown, so I no longer thought this would be selfish or irresponsible. I had studied hiking the trail for years, and even practiced a handful of overnight hikes. I knew I had enough money saved to do this, and I could think of no greater challenging adventure. It was difficult, often lonely, and even frightening at times (bears!). But when I stood high atop the Georgia mountains near the end of the trail, it was the best feeling imaginable.

Next, I returned to school at our local community college. I'd always wanted to go to college, but life got in the way like it does for a lot of people. I continued working part time at a restaurant while studying culinary arts. It wasn't always easy making ends meet, but the restaurant work combined with my classes was leading me toward a long-held dream—to be a chef. I was much older than most of the people in my classes, but everyone supported me. I'd had a lot more years of cooking practice, so before I knew it, younger students were asking my advice. Two years later, I graduated near the top of my class.

And today I'm happily employed as the head chef at Romano's, a fancy Italian restaurant right down the street from my old job! It's really exciting to be in charge of a menu. I've even created some new dishes that have been favorably reviewed in our local newspaper. I have to say, this job is a great deal more satisfying to me than organizing files at an insurance office was. And I'll admit it—it's fun to see the surprised faces of old coworkers when they come in for lunch sometimes. The same ones who said, "You're crazy!" when I quit are now saying, "Wow. You actually did it!"

It might be a bit of a cliché to say that you're the master of your own destiny, but it's true. I think a lot of people become so used to their lives that it doesn't occur to them that they can change them if they really want to. All it takes is careful planning, some faith and confidence, and a vision for your new future. Before you know it, that vision will become a reality.

Check Your Performance

CONTROLLING YOUR DESTINY

Activity	Number Right	Points		Score
Vocabulary Check (3 items)	_____	x 10	=	_____
Reading Check				
Central Point and Main Ideas (3 items)	_____	x 7	=	_____
Supporting Details (3 items)	_____	x 7	=	_____
Inferences (1 item)	_____	x 7	=	_____
Argument (1 item)	_____	x 7	=	_____
The Writer's Craft (2 items)	_____	x 7	=	_____
		TOTAL SCORE	=	_____%

Enter your total score into the **Performance Chart: Fifteen Reading Selections** on the inside back cover.

6 Forget What You Know about Good Study Habits

Benedict Carey

Preview

Remember what your teachers used to tell you about how to study? You probably were told to sit in one place, probably at a desk with a good light over your left shoulder, and focus on only one subject at a time. But, as Benedict Carey explains, these ideas might be just the opposite of what you *should* be doing when you need to learn new material.

Words to Watch

cognitive (4): having to do with reasoning or mental processes
retention (6): the ability to remember
auditory (8): relating to the process of hearing
Falstaff (9): a funny, talkative character in several of Shakespeare's plays
neural scaffolding (11): supports that help the brain retain information
aesthetic (17): artistic
intuitive (17): instinctive
immersion (18): deep involvement
subsequently (24): later
connotation (28): implied meaning

1   Every September, millions of parents try a kind of psychological witchcraft to transform their summer-glazed campers into fall students, their video-bugs into bookworms. Advice is cheap and all too familiar: Clear a quiet work space. Stick to a homework schedule. Set goals. Set boundaries. Do not bribe (except in emergencies).

2   And check out the classroom. Does Junior's learning style match the new teacher's approach? Or the school's philosophy? Maybe the child isn't "a good fit" for the school.

3   Such theories have developed in part because of sketchy education research that doesn't offer clear guidance. Student traits and teaching styles surely interact; so do personalities and at-home rules. The trouble is, no one can predict how.

4   Yet there are effective approaches

to learning, at least for those who are motivated. In recent years, cognitive° scientists have shown that a few simple techniques can reliably improve what matters most: how much a student learns from studying.

5   The findings can help anyone, from a fourth grader doing long division to a retiree taking on a new language. But they directly contradict much of the common wisdom about good study habits, and they have not caught on.

6   For instance, instead of sticking to one study location, simply alternating the room where a person studies improves retention°. So does studying distinct but related skills or concepts in one sitting, rather than focusing intensely on a single thing.

7   "We have known these principles for some time, and it's intriguing that schools don't pick them up, or that people don't learn them by trial and error," said Robert A. Bjork, a psychologist at the University of California, Los Angeles. "Instead, we walk around with all sorts of unexamined beliefs about what works that are mistaken."

8   Take the notion that children have specific learning styles, that some are "visual learners" and others are auditory°; some are "left-brain" students, others "right-brain." In a recent review of the relevant research, published in the journal *Psychological Science in the Public Interest*, a team of psychologists found almost zero support for such ideas. "The contrast between the enormous popularity of the learning-styles approach within education and the lack of credible evidence for its

utility is, in our opinion, striking and disturbing," the researchers concluded.

9   Ditto for teaching styles, researchers say. Some excellent instructors caper in front of the blackboard like summer-theater Falstaffs°; others are reserved to the point of shyness. "We have yet to identify the common threads between teachers who create a constructive learning atmosphere," said Daniel T. Willingham, a psychologist at the University of Virginia and author of the book *Why Don't Students Like School*?

10   But individual learning is another matter, and psychologists have discovered that some of the most hallowed advice on study habits is flat wrong. For instance, many study skills courses insist that students find a specific place, a study room or a quiet corner of the library, to take their work. The research finds just the opposite. In one classic 1978 experiment, psychologists found that college students who studied a list of 40 vocabulary words in two different rooms—one windowless and cluttered, the other modern, with a view of a courtyard—did far better on a test than students who studied the words twice, in the same room. Later studies have confirmed the finding, for a variety of topics.

11   The brain makes subtle associations between what it is studying and the background sensations it has at the time, the authors say, regardless of whether those perceptions are conscious. It colors the terms of the Versailles Treaty with the wasted fluorescent glow of the dorm study room, say; or the elements of the Marshall Plan with the

jade-curtain shade of the willow tree in the backyard. Forcing the brain to make multiple associations with the same material may, in effect, give that information more neural scaffolding°.

12   "What we think is happening here is that, when the outside context is varied, the information is enriched, and this slows down forgetting," said Dr. Bjork, the senior author of the two-room experiment.

13   Varying the type of material studied in a single sitting—alternating, for example, among vocabulary, reading, and speaking in a new language— seems to leave a deeper impression on the brain than does concentrating on just one skill at a time. Musicians have known this for years, and their practice sessions often include a mix of scales, musical pieces, and rhythmic work. Many athletes, too, routinely mix their workouts with strength, speed, and skill drills.

14   The advantages of this approach to studying can be striking, in some topic areas. In a study recently posted online by the journal *Applied Cognitive Psychology*, Doug Rohrer and Kelli Taylor of the University of South Florida taught a group of fourth graders four equations, each to calculate a different dimension of a prism. Half of the children learned by studying repeated examples of one equation, say, calculating the number of prism faces when given the number of sides at the base, then moving on to the next type of calculation, studying repeated examples of that. The other half studied mixed problem sets, which included examples of all four types of

calculations grouped together. Both groups solved sample problems along the way, as they studied.

15   A day later, the researchers gave all of the students a test on the material, presenting new problems of the same type. The children who had studied mixed sets did twice as well as the others, outscoring them 77 percent to 38 percent. The researchers have found the same in experiments involving adults and younger children.

16   "When students see a list of problems, all of the same kind, they know the strategy to use before they even read the problem," said Dr. Rohrer. "That's like riding a bike with training wheels." With mixed practice, he added, "each problem is different from the last one, which means kids must learn how to choose the appropriate procedure— just like they had to do on the test."

17   These findings extend well beyond math, even to aesthetic° intuitive° learning. In an experiment published last month in the journal *Psychology and Aging*, researchers found that college students and adults of retirement age were better able to distinguish the painting styles of 12 unfamiliar artists after viewing mixed collections (assortments, including works from all 12) than after viewing a dozen works from one artist, all together, then moving on to the next painter.

18   The finding undermines the common assumption that intensive immersion° is the best way to really master a particular genre, or type of creative work, said Nate Kornell, a psychologist at Williams College and the lead author of the study. "What seems to be happening in this case is that the brain is picking up deeper patterns when seeing assortments of paintings; it's picking up what's similar and what's different about them," often subconsciously.

19   Cognitive scientists do not deny that honest-to-goodness cramming can lead to a better grade on a given exam. But hurriedly jam-packing a brain is akin to speed-packing a cheap suitcase, as most students quickly learn—it holds its new load for a while, then most everything falls out.

20   "With many students, it's not like they can't remember the material" when they move to a more advanced class, said Henry L. Roediger III, a psychologist at Washington University in St. Louis. "It's like they've never seen it before."

21   When the neural suitcase is packed carefully and gradually, it holds its contents for far, far longer. An hour of study tonight, an hour on the weekend, another session a week from now: such so-called spacing improves later recall, without requiring students to put in more overall study effort or pay more attention, dozens of studies have found.

22   No one knows for sure why. It may be that the brain, when it revisits material at a later time, has to relearn some of what it has absorbed before adding new stuff—and that that process is itself self-reinforcing.

23   "The idea is that forgetting is the friend of learning," said Dr. Kornell. "When you forget something, it allows you to relearn, and do so effectively, the next time you see it."

24   That's one reason cognitive scientists see testing itself—or practice tests and quizzes—as a powerful tool of learning, rather than merely assessment. The process of retrieving an idea is not like pulling a book from a shelf; it seems to fundamentally alter the way the information is subsequently° stored, making it far more accessible in the future.

25   Dr. Roediger uses the analogy of the Heisenberg uncertainty principle in physics, which holds that the act of measuring a property of a particle (position, for example) reduces the accuracy with which you can know another property (momentum, for example): "Testing not only measures knowledge but changes it," he says—and, happily, in the direction of more certainty, not less.

26   In one of his own experiments, Dr. Roediger and Jeffrey Karpicke, also of Washington University, had college students study science passages from a reading comprehension test, in short study periods. When students studied the same material twice, in back-to-back sessions, they did very well on a test given immediately afterward, then began to forget the material.

27   But if they studied the passage just once and did a practice test in the second session, they did very well on one test two days later, and another given a week later.

28   "Testing has such bad connotation°; people think of standardized testing or teaching to the test," Dr. Roediger said. "Maybe we need to call it something else, but this is one of the most powerful learning tools we have."

29   Of course, one reason the thought of testing tightens people's stomachs is that tests are so often hard. Paradoxically, it is just this difficulty that makes them such effective study tools, research suggests. The harder it is to remember something, the harder it is to later forget. This effect, which researchers call "desirable difficulty," is evident in daily life. The name of the actor who played Linc in *The Mod Squad*? Francie's brother in *A Tree Grows in Brooklyn*? The name of the co-discoverer, with Newton, of calculus?

30   The more mental sweat it takes to dig it out, the more securely it will be subsequently anchored.

31   None of which is to suggest that these techniques—alternating study environments, mixing content, spacing study sessions, self-testing, or all the above—will turn a grade-A slacker into a grade-A student. Motivation matters. So do impressing friends, making the hockey team, and finding the nerve to text the cute student in social studies.

32   "In lab experiments, you're able to control for all factors except the one you're studying," said Dr. Willingham. "Not true in the classroom, in real life. All of these things are interacting at the same time."

33   But at the very least, the cognitive techniques give parents and students, young and old, something many did not have before: a study plan based on evidence, not schoolyard folk wisdom or empty theorizing.

First Impressions

Freewrite for ten minutes on one of the following.

1. Did you enjoy reading this selection? Why or why not?

2. Were you surprised by any of the information in this selection? If so, what information?

3. What are some studying methods you use that work particularly well for you? What are some you have tried that were *not* helpful?

Vocabulary Check

_____ 1. In the sentence below, the word *sketchy* means
    A. vivid.
    B. written.
    C. vague.
    D. detailed.

    "Such theories have developed in part because of sketchy education research that doesn't offer clear guidance." (Paragraph 3)

_____ 2. In the sentence below, the word *hallowed* means
    A. unusual.
    B. inventive.
    C. highly respected.
    D. based on research.

    "But individual learning is another matter, and psychologists have discovered that some of the most hallowed advice on study habits is flat wrong." (Paragraph 10)

_____ 3. In the excerpt below, the word *paradoxically* means
    A. understandably.
    B. unexpectedly.
    C. unfortunately.
    D. reliably.

    "Of course, one reason the thought of testing tightens people's stomachs is that tests are so often hard. Paradoxically, it is just this difficulty that makes them such effective study tools, research suggests." (Paragraph 29)

Reading Check

Central Point and Main Idea

_____ 1. Which sentence best expresses the central point of the entire selection?
  A. A few simple techniques can improve students' ability to learn new material.
  B. Research has shown that people should study in different places, study mixed problem sets, and not cram for tests.
  C. People should be aware of and practice study techniques that are based on solid evidence, not folk wisdom or unproved theories.
  D. Despite the enormous popularity of the learning-styles approach in education, there is little evidence that it is useful.

_____ 2. The implied main idea of paragraphs 10–12 is that
  A. it's not necessary for students to find a specific place, a study room or a quiet corner of the library in which to study.
  B. although experts have long advised students to find one specific place to study, research shows that students retain information better when they vary the places in which they study.
  C. scientists have learned that the brain makes subtle associations between what it is studying and the background sensations it has at the time.
  D. students who studied a list of 40 vocabulary words in two rooms did better on a test than students who studied the words twice in the same room.

Supporting Details

_____ 3. TRUE OR FALSE? The author believes that some students are "visual learners," while others are "auditory" learners.

_____ 4. The author compares varying the type of material studied in a single setting to
  A. riding a bike with training wheels.
  B. giving the brain more neural scaffolding.
  C. the way musicians mix scales, musical pieces and rhythmic work in a practice session.
  D. speed-packing a cheap suitcase.

_____ 5. When studying for a test, the author recommends
    A. cramming.
    B. studying the same material twice in the same quiet room.
    C. requiring students to put in more overall study effort.
    D. spacing out periods of study over a week or so.

Inferences

_____ 6. The selection suggests that
    A. most educators closely follow the latest news in psychological research.
    B. the principles of effective studying are by now widely known.
    C. many teachers and students still hold mistaken beliefs about studying.
    D. researchers now have a clear idea how student traits and teaching styles interact.

_____ 7. The author suggests that
    A. intensive immersion is the best way to study for tests.
    B. one goal of education should be for students to retain information long after they are tested on it.
    C. teaching effective study techniques will turn failing students into A students.
    D. only elementary school students can benefit from studying mixed problem sets.

Argument

_____ 8. Which of the statements below does **not** support the point of the argument?

Point: Varying the type of material studied in a single setting seems to leave a deeper impression on the brain than does concentrating on just one skill.

    A. Children who studied mixed problem sets did twice as well as children who did not.
    B. When students studied the same material twice, in back-to-back sessions, they did very well on a test given immediately afterward, then began to forget the material.
    C. College students and retired adults were better able to distinguish the painting styles of 12 unfamiliar artists after viewing mixed collections.
    D. Musicians routinely practice a mix of scales, musical pieces, and rhythmic work during one session.

The Writer's Craft

_____ 9. Which of the following statements best describes the writer's purpose?
   A. To inform readers that most of what they know about good study habits is wrong.
   B. To warn the American public that we will fall behind other countries if we don't do a better job of educating our young people.
   C. To persuade American educators to require more standardized testing, not less.
   D. To persuade readers to adopt study techniques that have been scientifically proven to be effective.

_____ 10. What kind of conclusion does Carey use at the end of his essay (paragraphs 31–33)?
   A. He summarizes his main points.
   B. He provides a closing thought.
   C. He provides a recommendation.
   D. All of the above.

Discussion Questions

1. After reading this selection, do you plan to change the way you study? If so, which piece of Carey's advice would you be most likely to follow? Explain.

2. Carey admits that the study techniques he presents, which contradict common wisdom about good study habits, have not caught on. Why do you think this is the case?

3. The author notes that there are excellent instructors who are very outgoing, and others who are very reserved. A psychologist is quoted as saying, "We have yet to identify the common threads between teachers who create a constructive learning atmosphere." From your experience, can you identify any "common threads" between excellent instructors you have known?

4. Although Carey concedes that "the thought of testing tightens people's stomachs," he calls testing one of the most powerful learning tools we have. Do you agree or disagree? Explain.

Paragraph Assignments

1. Of the study techniques suggested in this article, which one or ones are you most likely to try yourself? Write a paragraph explaining what they would be and how you would put that technique or techniques into practice.

    Here is one student's response to this assignment:

    > I am actually excited about trying the study technique of mixing up content. I've been involved in soccer all my life, and I know from that experience how valuable it is to mix up conditioning drills. For instance, a good practice session might involve going from a difficult practice to an easy one and back again, or quickly moving from a drill that stresses passing to one that emphasizes dribbling. That variety keeps me focused and challenged in a way that working on just one skill does not. I'm going to apply that technique to my study of Spanish. Instead of spending an hour on vocabulary, for instance, I'm going to try breaking that hour into shorter periods in which I do some vocabulary, some speaking, some listening, and some reading. All those skills use different parts of the brain, just like passing and dribbling in soccer do. It makes sense to me that getting the whole brain involved will have good results.

2. Carey's article details how "some of the most hallowed advice on study habits is flat wrong." As it turns out, studying in the same place every time is not the best idea. And spacing out studying is far more likely to help you actually *learn* something than spending an entire night cramming for an exam. Based on what you've learned in the article, write a one-paragraph summary of study tips for students today.

Essay Assignments

1. As the essay points out, excellent teachers are far from all alike. Write an essay about three teachers whom you considered to be excellent. (Alternatively, write about two teachers you thought were very good and one you thought was *not* good.) Explain how their particular approaches to teaching helped (or did not help) you learn effectively.

2. If you were to become a teacher, what three steps would you take to insure your students really learn the subject you would be teaching? In particular, what directions and safeguards would you use so that students would be fully engaged and truly benefit from the class?

Check Your Performance

FORGET WHAT YOU KNOW ABOUT GOOD STUDY HABITS

Activity	Number Right	Points	Score
Vocabulary Check (3 items)	_____	x 10 =	_____
Reading Check			
Central Point and Main Ideas (2 items)	_____	x 7 =	_____
Supporting Details (3 items)	_____	x 7 =	_____
Inferences (2 items)	_____	x 7 =	_____
Argument (1 item)	_____	x 7 =	_____
The Writer's Craft (2 items)	_____	x 7 =	_____
		TOTAL SCORE =	_____ %

Enter your total score into the **Performance Chart: Fifteen Reading Selections** on the inside back cover.

7 To Tony Lopez, with Love

Steve Lopez

Preview

In the following selection, Steve Lopez, long-time columnist for the *Los Angeles Times*, writes about one of the most painful topics imaginable: his father's death. Not only does Lopez pay tribute to his father; he also offers a challenge to the medical profession—and to all of us—to be more realistic about death and dying.

Words to Watch

jalopies (2): noisy old cars
brood (4): children
flophouses and hovels (4): cheap and run-down places to stay
sensibilities (8): emotional responses
abundant (11): plentiful
anguish (12): intense suffering
palliative (13): soothing; easing pain
hospice (13): a place in which the dying are made as comfortable as possible
beatification (16): in the Roman Catholic Church, the first step toward making someone a saint

1   My dad never called a tow truck. That would have cost too much.

2   It didn't matter where he broke down in his second-hand jalopies°. Tony Lopez was a Depression-era guy who watched his wallet and dropped daily pocket change into a cigar box to pay for annual family vacations in Santa Cruz or Tahoe. When his car conked out, my dad called my Uncle Mike, who was cut from the same cloth. Mike would drive for miles and use a chain to tow my dad to safety, and they'd check junkyards for used parts and make the needed repairs themselves.

3   Remember the days of towing by chain, with sparks flying when the drooping links hit the pavement? That was my dad. It's a miracle he didn't go up in a ball of flames.

4   Tony Lopez didn't hire plumbers or landscapers. He did it himself or called friends, and he returned the favor when they needed help. He was frugal, for sure, but there wasn't much cushion in a bread truck driver's paycheck. Before checking into a motel, he was known to find out whether the bed could be taken apart so some of his brood° could sleep on the box spring to save the

cost of a bigger room. On a trip to Europe, my father, brother and I stayed in flophouses and hovels° near railroad stations, once sleeping in the bedroom of a house where the owner had just plucked a chicken and left feathers everywhere.

5   "That's where they get you!" he'd declare if soup and salad were not included in the price of a meal.

6   And yet for a guy who would drive 50 miles for a nickel discount on a gallon of gas, especially if they gave you juice glasses with every fill-up, my dad was always ticked off if I reached for the check at a restaurant. When I bought my first house, he insisted on helping with the down payment to lower my monthly burden. With his three kids and four grandchildren, he was as generous with his love as his money, sticking with us even when we screwed up.

7   Tony Lopez died the other day at the age of 83 after a long illness that he fought like a mule, literally hanging on to the rails of his bed to keep from being dragged into history. He used to bump into the undertaker around town, hold up his hand and say, "Not yet," as if he were waiting for a sale on funerals. But his time was finally up, and he went quietly Sunday morning, dying in his own home with my mother and sister at his side.

8   I want to thank him for the love and support, the memories, the sensibilities°, the laughs.

9   Tony Lopez, a scrappy little four-sport high school athlete known as a fierce competitor, raised a daughter who inherited his fight. If you went by statistics, my sister Debbie would have been gone a couple of years ago, done in by ovarian cancer that spread to her brain. But she's still battling.

10   Tony Lopez, never too shy to clown around in a crazy wig or wacky hat, raised a son who became a comedian, inheriting my dad's ability to connect with everyone, including strangers. My dad got tears in his eyes laughing about the time my brother Johnny edited my Aunt Milly's bumper sticker from "Say No To Drugs, Yes to Burritos—New Mecca Cafe," so that it said "Say Yes to Drugs." Milly drove around like that for months, wondering why she got so many peculiar looks.

11   Tony Lopez didn't go to college and never moved out of the little town he grew up in, but he sent his first son to college on that once-abundant° and adequately funded California dream of giving your kids greater opportunities

than you'd ever had. The son went to San Jose State to become a journalist who shares his dad's suspicion of authority, and the journalist would like to thank his dad for this last gift—a story that has lent support to others, and perhaps some insights, on the hard choices around death and dying.

12   Those who have followed the tale of my dad's months-long decline, or have been through this themselves, know the anguish° of decisions about life-extending medical procedures and where final days should be spent. I'd see but a shadow of my dad, curled up in half surrender, and want for him to slip away. Then he'd surprise me with a glance or a whispered "hello," and I didn't want to let go.

13   I came to appreciate the merits of palliative° and hospice° care, which help both patient and family prepare for the inevitable. But death is in charge and comes when it's ready, and after the hearse pulls away, an instant of relief gives way to a chill that creeps into your bones.

14   I believe more strongly than ever that everyone ought to have the option of doctor-assisted aid in dying. I can't tell you how many people have asked me why we keep loved ones alive with cruel limitations, but humanely end the suffering of animals.

15   Let Tony Lopez's passing stand as a call for doctors to be more up front in laying out the hard realities of medical limitations. And let it stand as a call for families to share their own attitudes with each other as to how much compromise is acceptable. Too many people are hanging on against their own wishes, only because they didn't make their feelings known in advance healthcare directives and other forms (which anyone can get from the Coalition for Compassionate Care of California, **www.coalitionccc.org**).

16   In his final days, my father was treated with grace and dignity by nurses and aides who grew up in Nigeria and Tonga, among other places, and they served our family and a noble profession well. And if my mother and sister were nuns, they would surely pass beatification° and go directly to sainthood for the way they loved and cared for my father.

17   My heartfelt thanks, as well, to readers who have checked in by the hundreds with their own stories and words of support.

18   Peace, Dad.

19   You had a heck of a good run.

First Impressions

Freewrite for ten minutes on one of the following.

1. Did you enjoy reading this selection? Why or why not?

2. Have you ever had to cope with the death of a loved one? Describe the experience.

3. Steve Lopez is grateful to his dad "for the love and support, the memories, the sensibilities, the laughs." Which of your family members do you feel most grateful to? Why?

Vocabulary Check

_____ 1. In the excerpt below, the word *frugal* means
   A. careful about money.
   B. hard-working.
   C. overly cautious.
   D. impatient.

   "He was frugal, for sure, but there wasn't much cushion in a bread truck driver's paycheck. Before checking into a motel, he was known to find out whether the bed could be taken apart so some of his brood could sleep on the box spring to save the cost of a bigger room." (Paragraph 4)

_____ 2. In the excerpt below, the word *inevitable* means
   A. further suffering.
   B. death.
   C. basics.
   D. events that can be controlled.

   "I came to appreciate the merits of palliative and hospice care, which help both patient and family prepare for the inevitable. But death is in charge and comes when it's ready.... (Paragraph 13)

_____ 3. In the sentence below, the word *directives* means
   A. changes.
   B. payments.
   C. laws.
   D. instructions.

   "Too many people are hanging on against their own wishes, only because they didn't make their feelings known in advance healthcare directives and other forms ..." (Paragraph 15)

Reading Check

Central Point and Main Ideas

_____ 1. Which sentence best expresses the central point of the selection?
   A. Witnessing his father's death has made journalist Steve Lopez realize just how generous his father was.
   B. Steve Lopez uses the occasion of his father's death to express love and appreciation for his dad and to discuss the hard choices concerning death and dying.
   C. Through observing his dad's months-long decline, Steve Lopez has come to appreciate the advantages of certain types of end-of-life care.
   D. After witnessing his father's lingering death, Steve Lopez has come to realize that doctors should be more honest with families about what can realistically be done for dying patients.

_____ 2. The implied main idea of paragraphs 1–5 is that
   A. Tony Lopez didn't believe in paying people to do jobs that he could do himself.
   B. the Depression shaped Tony Lopez's attitude toward money.
   C. Because he had grown up during the Depression and never made much money at his job, Tony Lopez tried to save money whenever possible.
   D. Tony Lopez was a poor man who could barely support his family.

_____ 3. The implied main idea of paragraph 15 is that Steve Lopez
   A. believes that doctors need to be more willing to discuss what can and cannot be done for dying patients.
   B. wants to use his father's death to encourage others to deal with end-of-life issues.
   C. believes that too many people are clinging to life without really wanting to.
   D. wants families to share with each other their own attitudes about death and dying.

Supporting Details

_____ 4. Steve Lopez believes it's a miracle that his dad
   A. helped him pay for the down payment on his house.
   B. let him attend college and become a journalist.
   C. didn't get badly burned while towing his car with chains.
   D. outlived the town undertaker.

_____ 5. Steve Lopez believes that people should
   A. receive all the life-extending medical procedures available.
   B. put elderly loved ones in nursing homes rather than have them cared for at home.
   C. hire American-born nurses to care for their terminally ill loved ones.
   D. fill out advance healthcare directives and similar forms while they still can.

Inferences

_____ 6. The selection suggests that Tony Lopez
   A. sacrificed so that his children could have more than he had.
   B. believed in the value of education.
   C. had a great sense of humor.
   D. all of the above.

_____ 7. In paragraph 12, Steve Lopez suggests that
   A. his dad's last illness was quick and painless.
   B. he was torn between wanting his dad to die and wanting him to keep living.
   C. very few people have to make the kind of decisions about life-extending medical procedures that he had to make.
   D. all of the above.

Argument

_____ 8. Which of the following statements does **not** support the point of the argument?

   Point: There are various choices to be considered with regard to death and dying.

   A. Some people deserve to be made saints for the way they love and care for others.
   B. People can make their feelings known in advance healthcare directives.
   C. People need to decide whether they wish to receive at-home hospice care or die in a nursing home or hospital.
   D. Some people believe in the option of doctor-assisted aid in dying.

The Writer's Craft

_____ 9. In paragraphs 16 and 17, Lopez's tone is
      A. politely respectful.
      B. sentimental.
      C. deeply appreciative.
      D. sorrowful.

_____ 10. Steve Lopez organizes his essay by
      A. telling the story of his dad's life in time order.
      B. contrasting his dad's life with his own.
      C. illustrating his dad's memorable qualities and drawing lessons from his death.
      D. listing things that families should discuss before any of them become terminally ill.

Discussion Questions

1. Why do you think Steve Lopez opens this essay with stories about his father never calling a tow truck, doing his own plumbing repairs, and saving money on hotel rooms? How do these stories support Lopez's central point?

2. These days it's possible for people to be kept alive with the aid of machines, even when they have no awareness of their surroundings and when there is no possibility of recovery. Would you want to be kept alive in such a way? Why or why not?

3. In the essay, Steve Lopez calls for families to share their own attitudes with each other about end-of-life issues. Why might it be difficult for some families to discuss these matters? Do you think your family would be willing to discuss these issues? Explain.

4. Lopez writes, "I believe more strongly than ever that everyone ought to have the option of doctor-assisted aid in dying." In your opinion, should doctors be allowed to help patients end their lives? Why or why not?

Paragraph Assignments

1. Choose an adjective that you think Steve Lopez would use to describe his father. Then write a paragraph supporting your choice of that adjective. Your topic sentence might be something like this: "I believe Steve Lopez would describe his father as 'tough' _or_ 'loving'" (or name some other quality).

2. Write a paragraph that describes the obituary you would like to be written about your life.

Here is one student's response to the assignment:

> The main point I hope my obituary conveys is that although I was a man who may never have been the very best at one thing, I was decent at a lot of things. It may sound strange to want to be remembered as someone who was great at nothing, but all of the things I could do in an average way tell the story of my life. The obituary should mention that I loved bass fishing. I never caught a monster fish, but the early mornings on the lake with my son were cherished hours. I also spent a lot of time playing guitar. No one ever asked for my autograph or offered me a record deal, but my wife asked me to play "Moon River" about a thousand times over the years. And the obituary should point out that I liked trying my hand at writing. I wasn't exactly Shakespeare, and not one of my pieces was ever published. Even so, I filled notebook after notebook with the best words I could think of to describe the wonderful world around me. So I hope, when my life on this world ends, these things about me will be remembered.

Essay Assignments

1. Lopez uses a number of brief anecdotes—stories—to help the reader understand what his father was like. Choose a person that you know very well. Write an essay in which you tell three stories about that person. Use each story to illuminate some aspect of your subject's personality.

2. Lopez writes, "I believe more strongly than ever that everyone ought to have the option of doctor-assisted aid in dying. I can't tell you how many people have asked me why we keep loved ones alive with cruel limitations, but humanely end the suffering of animals." Should we have the option to end the lives, and therefore the suffering, of family members who are terminally ill? Write an essay that argues either for or against this option. Present three clear and strong arguments for your side of this debate. You might want to research this topic by Googling phrases such as "euthanasia debate" or "doctor-assisted death."

Check Your Performance   TO TONY LOPEZ, WITH LOVE

Activity	Number Right		Points		Score
Vocabulary Check (3 items)	_____	x	10	=	_____
Reading Check					
Central Point and Main Ideas (3 items)	_____	x	7	=	_____
Supporting Details (2 items)	_____	x	7	=	_____
Inferences (2 items)	_____	x	7	=	_____
Argument (1 item)	_____	x	7	=	_____
The Writer's Craft (2 items)	_____	x	7	=	_____
		TOTAL SCORE		=	_____%

Enter your total score into the **Performance Chart: Fifteen Reading Selections** on the inside back cover.

8 A Path to Marriage

Jean Sutton

Preview

Jean Sutton grew up in West Oak Lane, a mostly African American community in northwest Philadelphia, and attended Franklin & Marshall College in rural Lancaster, Pennsylvania. There, she met her future husband. Jean's essay offers valuable suggestions about preparing for adult life, choosing a mate, and building a strong marriage.

Words to Watch

vulnerable (5): not protected
mentor (9): someone older and more experienced who provides advice and support
savvy (10): well-informed
potential (11): the possibility of becoming something in the future
acknowledged (12): accepted
monks (14): priests
despair (27): a feeling of hopelessness

1   "If I died, you'd have nothing. I have nothing to leave you."

2   Those are harsh words to hear when you're only 11, but I knew my mother was only telling me the truth.

3   "Don't make the same mistake I did," she said. "Educate yourself. Don't grow up expecting that a man will always provide for you. Anything can happen."

4   She knew what she was talking about. She had learned that lesson the hard way. With only an eighth-grade education, she had few job opportunities available to her. She provided childcare out of our home, a row house in a working-class neighborhood of Philadelphia. My father was a high-school graduate who had joined the military, and had then gone to work in a steel plant.

5   Then my father died suddenly. My mother and I were forced onto the emotional roller coaster that follows the

death of a loved one. Our sorrow was compounded by the financial impact of my father's loss. My mother struggled to make ends meet. We had to give up our car, and we very nearly lost our house. At a very early age, I realized how vulnerable° an uneducated woman is.

6   I think that was my first lesson in selecting a mate and in preparing myself for adulthood. I learned that I wanted to be a financial equal in a marriage. I didn't want to have to marry in order to survive. I didn't want to be unable to support myself if my man was no longer around. I set about the task of becoming self-sufficient. I completed my formal education and am now an assistant vice president at an insurance company. I am happily married, but I have also prepared myself for life's unexpected events.

7   From my elementary years on, I was a good student. I enjoyed school, but beyond that, I never forgot that education would provide me with the opportunities my mother hadn't had. When it was time for college, Franklin & Marshall College in Lancaster, Pennsylvania, offered me a scholarship. F&M is a very good school with a small minority enrollment. When I attended, there were 1,500 students, of whom about 50 were African American. I had gone to a Catholic high school with white students, so being with white people was not that big a deal. For me, the adjustment was more about class than about race. In high school, we'd all worn uniforms, so it wasn't so obvious who had money and who didn't.

8   But at F&M I really saw the difference. Now that I was living around people who

had always had money, I felt poor in a way I never had before. My classmates were surprised that I took my work-study job in the cafeteria so seriously. If they had jobs, it was just to earn pocket money. But I needed my job so that I could buy a winter coat. In the summers I worked full-time in order to buy textbooks for the next year. Although I tried hard to find affordable used books, one year I ran out of money before the second semester began. That term I developed a new schedule. I would sleep in the evening while my dorm mates studied. Then I would borrow the books I needed and study through the night. I took special satisfaction in making the dean's list that term!

Because F&M didn't have a large 9 enrollment of Black students, the Black Student Union made special efforts to help us get to know each other. The BSU assigned each of us incoming students a mentor°, and early in my freshman year they hosted a dance. My mentor noticed me sitting on the sidelines and asked one of the older students to invite me to dance. That student was Rod Sutton, the man I would later marry. I told Rod that I didn't feel like dancing. He said, "Okay, but then I'm going to sit and talk with you."

10   What I first noticed about Rod was the same thing most people notice— that he's *big*: a big, tall man with a big voice. And being from inner-city Newark, New Jersey, he's very street savvy°. As we sat and talked, however, I sensed that this big, loud guy was also kind and gentle. I felt a bond with him, as we had both grown up in the city without much money.

11   For a full year after that first meeting, Rod and I were just friends. Yes, for real, *friends*. And since I was just his friend, he wasn't trying to impress me. He was just being himself. During that year, we had long talks about how we wanted our lives to turn out. He talked about his plan to teach and to attend graduate school. He told me that he wanted to complete his education before he got married. He talked about the girls he'd known in his old neighborhood who had become teenage mothers, and how sad he was that those smart, talented girls would be unlikely to ever realize their full potential°. He said he didn't want to bring a child into this world before he was ready to be a devoted, responsible parent.

12   Wow, I thought. Even as he was criticizing teenage pregnancy, he did it in a way that didn't trash the girls involved. He acknowledged° that they were smart and talented. He respected them. That impressed me.

13   Other things impressed me as well. During our friendship, I had the chance to hang out with Rod and his friends. Many of those friends were good-looking guys, attractive and smart. But some were disrespectful of their own girlfriends or were involved in relationships built on guilt or control. Once I heard one of these guys call his girlfriend the "b" word right to her face. She shrugged it off as if it were nothing. Can you believe that the next day she was walking across the campus with him, arm in arm? When Rod heard such things, he always spoke up to the guy. He would criticize the disrespectful attitude toward "the young lady," as he always carefully referred to the girl.

14   As Rod and I exchanged our life stories, I came to respect him even more. I learned that this gentle, kind man had been an angry, troubled kid who had been repeatedly kicked out of school for fighting. He'd finally been sent to a kind of last-chance school, one run by monks°. There, gradually, he had turned around. As I heard him talk about how his attitude had changed and as I watched him in his daily life, I could see he was for real. He was consistent in his actions as well as his words. He wasn't saying things because he thought they were what I wanted to hear. He didn't just talk the talk—he walked the walk.

15   We began to date, and my good opinion of Rod kept growing. After we graduated from F&M, he got a job teaching elementary school. He lived in Philly but commuted to Camden, New Jersey, every day. That first winter, the temperature fell to zero after a storm that dropped seven inches of snow.

The schools in Philly and Camden were closed, but Rod left for work so early in the morning that he missed the announcement and drove all the way to Camden anyway. Here was a single guy, no wife or children to support, and yet he had such a strong work ethic he always showed up at work, often earlier than anyone else.

16   Watching him, I thought, He's hard-working, considerate, respectful, and a communicator. What more could a girl ask for?

17   Then I saw him interact with an elderly woman. When we were in a department store, Rod noticed her carrying a heavy shopping bag and struggling to open the door. "Let me help you with that, ma'am," he said. He took her bag and opened the door for her. "Thank you!" she said with a smile. He stood and watched her go until he was sure she was okay.

18   That sealed the deal for me. On top of everything else, he cared about our elderly! To this day, he respects the senior women in our church. He visits the sick and shut-ins. He goes beyond simply opening the door or helping with a bag. He engages them in a way that makes each one feel like the most important person in the world. I tease him about how he flatters the seniors, but I admire the care and respect that he shows. Given all the wonderful things I'd observed in Rod over the years, there was no question in my mind about what to say when he asked me to marry him.

19   My appreciation for his good qualities has only continued to grow since our wedding many years ago.

Before my mother passed away, she was seriously ill for many months, and I was her sole caregiver. When I came down with the flu, Rod stepped in without hesitation. He visited her every single day, making sure she had a good meal and fresh water by her bedside. Some days he sat with her for hours, just to keep her company.

20   In parenthood, as well as elsewhere in our lives, Rod and I are true partners. We agreed that we wanted to wait to start our family until we felt really ready. I know that during the years before we had a child, Rod took some criticism from men he knew. They'd pressure him, saying things like "Don't you know how to make a baby?" They'd say it in a joking way, but you know a lot of guys would have been bothered by that. They were implying he wasn't a "real man" until he had fathered a child. But Rod never let such things get to him. He made it clear that *we* were going to make that decision; that we were a team, and that no outside pressure was going to influence us. I am so grateful that Rod felt the same way I did—that bringing a new human being into the world is a very serious decision, and not something to be done lightly.

21   We did make that decision in our own time, and our family now includes Paige, who is 13; Justin, 11; and Abu, an 8-year-old we're in the process of adopting. Abu has gone through a lot in his short life, and we are all excited about his move from the foster-care system to his forever home. In Rod's career as a teacher and now as an assistant principal, he has seen so many angry,

scared, neglected children. He's worked very hard to help them, but as a teacher you can do only so much. We feel we've been very blessed in our own lives, and we've always wanted to share our good fortune with another child.

22   So by now you know that I'm a big fan of my husband and an advocate of marriage. But rest assured that marriage is not easy. It takes a lot of negotiating° and hard work. That's why it is so important to have patience in selecting and getting to know your mate. You cannot get to know someone in a day, a week, or even a month. It takes time. A good rule of thumb is to know your mate through at least four seasons before you get married. Don't rush!

23   And don't just listen to what a guy *says*. Words are easy. Observe his *actions*. Observe how he treats his family and close friends. That will be a good indication of how he'll treat you.

24   I see so many of the girls I grew up with settle for, in my opinion, far less than they deserve. We African American women face some special challenges. To begin with, we simply outnumber our marriageable men. So many of our men are in prison. And there is a widespread belief that high-achieving Black men don't marry Black women, that they go outside the race. I don't know how true that is, but many women believe it.

25   So I think a lot of women end up saying, "Well, this guy is halfway decent and not in prison," and they settle. And the result is so much divorce and so many children growing up without fathers. I understand why it happens. When your friends are getting married and having babies, it's easy to get swept up in the excitement of that. You don't want to be left behind. But marriage and parenthood are too important to go into for less than the right reasons.

26   I am convinced that good men, loving men, dependable men who hold themselves to high standards, are out there. Hold out! Give it time. Look in the right places—places like school, church, and work. I'll tell you where *not* to look—in bars and clubs. Sure, a good guy could be at a club. But in general, guys hanging out in clubs are looking for someone for a while, not for a lifetime.

27   Ladies, love yourself enough to, first, be the best person that you can be. Then love yourself enough to demand of your partner all that is rightfully yours. Take the time to be certain that the love you have is a love that will always be there. I'm not talking about the sexy love of your youth. I'm talking about a love that will be there at the end of your life, holding your hand when you take your last breath—a love that lasts not only through joy and fun, but also through sickness and despair° and whatever life may bring. Do not settle for less. Love yourself enough to hold out for all that you deserve.

First Impressions

Freewrite for ten minutes on one of the following.

1. Did you enjoy reading this selection? Why or why not?

2. Which part of Sutton's story impressed you the most? Why?

3. Sutton says that "marriage is not easy." Are you inclined to agree? Why or why not?

Vocabulary Check

_____ 1. In the excerpt below, the word *compounded* means
   A. hidden.
   B. weakened.
   C. increased.
   D. explained.

> "Then my father died suddenly. My mother and I were forced onto the emotional roller coaster that follows the death of a loved one. Our sorrow was compounded by the financial impact of my father's loss." (Paragraph 5)

_____ 2. In the excerpt below, the words *self-sufficient* mean
   A. attractive.
   B. important.
   C. interesting.
   D. independent.

> "I didn't want to have to marry in order to survive. I didn't want to be unable to support myself if my man was no longer around. I set about the task of becoming self-sufficient." (Paragraph 6)

_____ 3. In the excerpt below, the words *advocate of* mean
   A. supporter of.
   B. opponent of.
   C. newcomer to.
   D. substitute for.

> "Given all the wonderful things I'd observed in Rod over the years, there was no question in my mind about what to say when he asked me to marry him. My appreciation for his good qualities has only continued to grow since our wedding many years ago. . . . So by now you know that I'm a big fan of my husband and an advocate of marriage." (Paragraphs 18–19 and 22)

Reading Check

Central Point and Main Ideas

_____ 1. Which of the following sentences best expresses the central point of the selection?

    A. Sutton's father died when she was still a girl, leaving herself and her mother without much money.

    B. Sutton met her future husband when both were students at Franklin & Marshall College.

    C. Sutton believes that young Black women should not rush into marriage, but should first become self-sufficient and wait for a respectful, considerate partner.

    D. Sutton noticed that Rod Sutton was a hard worker, respectful of women, and kind to elderly people.

_____ 2. Which sentence best expresses the main idea of paragraph 8?

    A. Despite not having as much money as her classmates at F&M, Sutton succeeded academically.

    B. Sutton needed her work-study job so that she could buy a winter coat.

    C. One year, Sutton ran out of money before the second semester began.

    D. Sutton took special satisfaction in making the dean's list at F&M.

Supporting Details

_____ 3. The sudden death of Sutton's father made Sutton realize that

    A. we need to tell people we love them before it's too late.

    B. her parents' marriage was not a happy one.

    C. an uneducated woman is powerless to support herself.

    D. all of the above.

_____ 4. What "sealed the deal" for Jean about marrying Rod Sutton was that he

    A. spoke up to guys who called their girlfriends the "b" word.

    B. traveled through a snowstorm to get to his teaching job in Camden, New Jersey.

    C. helped an elderly woman carrying a shopping bag.

    D. helped to care for Jean's elderly mother when she became seriously ill.

_____ 5. Sutton states that it's important, when choosing a partner, to

    A. look for someone who has high standards.

    B. see how he (or she) treats close friends and family members.

    C. be patient.

    D. all of the above.

Inferences

_____ 6. From paragraph 13, we can infer that
   A. Jean liked some of Rod's friends more than she liked him.
   B. Rod sometimes called Jean the "b" word.
   C. Jean would never tolerate a boyfriend calling her the "b" word.
   D. Jean forced Rod to speak to his friends about the way they treated women.

_____ 7. Paragraph 15 suggests that
   A. Jean Sutton thought Rod was crazy for going to work in seven inches of snow.
   B. Jean Sutton admires people who have a strong work ethic.
   C. Jean Sutton had never met a hard-working man before she met Rod.
   D. Rod Sutton nearly had an accident on his way to work.

_____ 8. On the basis of "A Path to Marriage," we can infer that
   A. Rod Sutton's respectful attitude toward women earned Jean's love and admiration.
   B. Rod Sutton hadn't always had a respectful attitude toward women.
   C. finding a good, dependable man to love is impossible for most African American women.
   D. physical attraction is the most important factor in selecting a mate.

The Writer's Craft

_____ 9. Sutton's primary purpose in writing this essay is to
   A. inform readers of the difficulties faced by African American women trying to find the right man to marry.
   B. persuade readers, especially African American women, to achieve their full potential and then look for a partner that is truly their equal.
   C. predict that in the future, more and more marriages will end in divorce because women looking for husbands end up settling for far less than they deserve.
   D. entertain readers with a heartwarming story of how two young people got together.

_____10. In paragraphs 20–21, the story Sutton relates illustrates her point that
   A. children add a great deal to a marriage, and no marriage should be without them.
   B. too many couples yield to peer pressure and have children too soon.
   C. married couples need to be equal partners who make decisions together.
   D. teachers can do only so much to heal the wounds that parents have inflicted on children.

Discussion Questions

1. After reading what Jean Sutton has to say about relationships, do you think she believes in "love at first sight?" Why or why not?

2. Sutton says several times that it's more important to pay attention to what a romantic partner *does* than what he *says*. Do you think her advice is worthwhile? Why or why not?

3. Sutton mentions that her husband, Rod, was teased by some male friends for not having a child sooner. Why do you think men would put pressure on each other that way? What did you think of Rod's response?

4. Jean Sutton describes her husband Rod as a true partner. Based on her description, what qualities must a mate have to be considered a true partner? Are those qualities ones that are important to you? Are there others you would add?

Paragraph Assignments

1. It is apparent that Jean and Rod Sutton have a good marriage. Among the couples you know, who do you think has the best marriage? Write about that couple and their relationship. Include details about their words and actions that reveal why you admire their marriage.

   Here is one student's response to the assignment:

   > Although I haven't known my neighbors, Bert and Marion, that long, I can tell that they have an exceptionally good marriage. The first time I met the two of them, Bert was down on his hands and knees in their front yard planting petunias, while Marion sat near a slightly-opened window, offering him quiet gardening tips. Bert explained that Marion had a bad cold and didn't feel like planting

the flowers in the chilly spring wind, so he was doing the best he could. "If her flowers aren't in the ground by April 15th, all hell breaks loose," Bert said with a playful wink toward Marion, who waved happily through the window. Since that day, I've witnessed a strong bond of respect, friendship, and affection between these two elderly people. Once, when I dropped by for coffee, Marion pulled out several photo albums and both cried and laughed as she showed me nearly 50 years' worth of pictures of their life together. "Bert was such a good father," Marion said as she gazed at a photo, taken decades ago, of Bert with their two sons. "He changed diapers and cooked dinner and sang lullabies back when most men didn't do those sorts of things. It was wonderful." At that moment, Bert walked in and sat down at the table and just put his hand on Marion's without saying anything for a while as he turned the pages of a photo album. Finally, he looked up with a twinkle in his eyes and said, "Let's face it, dear. My lullaby singing was not what any sane person would call 'wonderful.'" As Marion burst out laughing, I found myself silently hoping that one day I'd have a marriage as strong as theirs.

2. Early in her essay, Jean Sutton writes, "I didn't want to have to marry in order to survive." She then goes on to list the steps she took to make herself self-supporting. What steps are *you* taking to make *yourself* self-supporting? Write a paragraph in which you describe these steps, providing specific examples.

Essay Assignments

1. As she grew to know Rod Sutton, Jean noticed some very specific characteristics she admired in him—for instance, his work ethic, his ability to communicate, and his respectful attitude towards older people. What are two or three characteristics that *you* would like to see in a potential mate? Write about those characteristics and why they are important to you. As Sutton does, give examples of how those characteristics can be expressed.

2. While the Suttons obviously have a good marriage, not every American couple fits this description. Sadly, in the United States, nearly 50 percent of first marriages end in divorce, and the rates are even higher for second and third marriages. How, then, can committed couples ensure that their relationship will survive? Pretend you are a counselor, and suggest, in

an essay, three strategies that couples should adopt to preserve their relationship. For each strategy, write a separate paragraph that gives it a name and includes specific examples of behaviors that should be either avoided or adopted.

Check Your Performance   **A PATH TO MARRIAGE**

Activity	Number Right	Points	Score
Vocabulary Check (3 items)	_____	x 10 =	_____
Reading Check			
Central Point and Main Ideas (2 items)	_____	x 7 =	_____
Supporting Details (3 items)	_____	x 7 =	_____
Inferences (3 items)	_____	x 7 =	_____
The Writer's Craft (2 items)	_____	x 7 =	_____
		TOTAL SCORE =	_____%

Enter your total score into the **Performance Chart: Fifteen Reading Selections** on the inside back cover.

⑨ Consequences of Social Class

James M. Henslin

Preview

We've all heard that America is the land of opportunity. And we've been told that no matter who our parents are or what they do for a living, we can become anything we want. However, as James M. Henslin tells us below, the social class we were born into has more to do with our future success than we might like to think.

Words to Watch

subculture (4): separate social group
blighted (5): decaying
outstanding (8): still unpaid
commodity (12): product
docile (21): easy to manage
prestigious (28): high-status

1   *The man was a C student throughout school. As a businessman, he ran an oil company (Arbusto) into the ground. A self-confessed alcoholic until age forty, he was arrested for drunk driving. With this background, how did he become president of the United States?*

2   *Accompanying these personal factors was the power of social class. George W. Bush was born the grandson of a wealthy senator and the son of a businessman who himself became president of the United States after serving as a member of the House of Representatives, director of the CIA, and head of the Republican Party. For high school, he went to an elite private prep school, Andover; to Yale for his bachelor's degree; and for his MBA to Harvard. He was given $1 million to start his own business. When that business (Arbusto) failed, Bush fell softly, landing on the boards of several corporations. Taken care of even further, he was made the managing director of the Texas Rangers baseball team and allowed to buy a share of the team for $600,000, which he sold for $15 million.*

3   *When it was time for him to get into politics, Bush's connections financed his run for governor of Texas and then for the presidency.*

4   Does social class matter? And how! Think of each social class as a broad subculture° with distinct approaches to life, so significant that it affects almost every aspect of our lives—our health, family life, education, religion, politics, and even our experiences with crime and the criminal justice system. Let's look at how social class affects our lives.

Physical Health

5   *If you want to get a sense of how social class affects health, take a ride on Washington's Metro system. Start in the blighted° Southeast section of downtown D.C. For every mile you travel to where the wealthy live in Montgomery County in Maryland, life expectancy rises about a year and a half. By the time you get off, you will find a twenty-year gap between the poor blacks where you started your trip and the rich whites where you ended it.*

6   The principle is simple: As you go up the social-class ladder, health increases. As you go down the ladder, health decreases. Age makes no difference. Infants born to the poor are more likely to die before their first birthday, and a larger percentage of poor people in their old age—whether 75 or 95—die each year than do the elderly who are wealthy.

7   How can social class have such dramatic effects? While there are many reasons, here are three basic ones. First, social class opens and closes doors to medical care. Consider this:

8   *Terry Takewell (his real name), a 21-year-old diabetic, lived in a trailer park in Somerville, Tennessee. When Zettie*

Mae Hill, Takewell's neighbor, found the unemployed carpenter drenched with sweat from a fever, she called an ambulance. Takewell was rushed to Methodist Hospital, where he had an outstanding° bill of $9,400.

9   *When the hospital administrator learned of the admission, he went to Takewell's room, got him out of bed, and escorted him to the parking lot. There, neighbors found him under a tree and took him home.*

10   *Takewell died about twelve hours later.*

11   *Zettie Mae Hill said, "I didn't think a hospital would just let a person die like that for lack of money."*

12   Why was Terry Takewell denied medical treatment and his life cut short? The fundamental reason is that health care in the United States is not a citizens' right but a commodity° for sale. Unlike the middle and upper classes, few poor people have a personal physician, and they often spend hours waiting in crowded public health clinics. When the poor are hospitalized, they are likely to find themselves in understaffed and underfunded public hospitals, treated by rotating interns who do not know them and cannot follow up on their progress. . . .

13   A second reason is lifestyles, which are shaped by social class. People in the lower classes are more likely to smoke, eat a lot of fats, be overweight, abuse drugs and alcohol, get little exercise, and practice unsafe sex. This, to understate the matter, does not improve people's health.

14　　There is a third reason, too. Life is hard on the poor. The persistent stresses they face cause their bodies to wear out faster. The rich find life better. They have fewer problems and more resources to deal with the ones they have. This gives them a sense of control over their lives, a source of both physical and mental health.

Mental Health

15　Sociological studies from as far back as the 1930s have found that the mental health of the lower classes is worse than that of the higher classes. Greater mental problems are part of the higher stress that accompanies poverty. Compared with middle- and upper-class Americans, the poor have less job security and lower wages. They are more likely to divorce, to be the victims of crime, and to have more physical illnesses. Couple these conditions with bill collectors and the threat of eviction, and you can see how they can deal severe blows to people's emotional well-being.

16　　People higher up the social class ladder experience stress in daily life, of course, but their stress is generally less, and their coping resources are greater. Not only can they afford vacations, psychiatrists, and counselors, but *their class position also gives them greater control over their lives, a key to good mental health.*

17　　As is starkly evident from the following Thinking Critically section, social class is also important when it comes to the medical care people receive for their mental problems.

Thinking Critically

Mental Illness and Inequality in Medical Care

18　Standing among the police, I watched as the elderly naked man, looking confused, struggled to put on his clothing. The man had ripped the wires out of the homeless shelter's main electrical box and then led police on a merry chase as he ran from room to room.

19　I asked the officers where they were going to take the man, and they replied, "To Malcolm Bliss" (the state hospital). When I commented, "I guess he'll be in there for quite a while," they said, "Probably just a day or two. We picked him up last week—he was crawling under cars at a traffic light—and they let him out in two days."

20　The police explained that the man must be a danger to himself or to others to be admitted as a long-term patient. Visualizing this old man crawling under cars in traffic and thinking about the possibility of electrocution as he ripped out electrical wires with his bare hands, I marveled at the definition of "danger" that the hospital psychiatrists must be using.

21　Stripped of its veil, the two-tier system of medical care is readily visible. The poor—such as this confused naked man—find it difficult to get into mental hospitals. If they are admitted, they are sent to the dreaded state hospitals. In contrast, private hospitals serve the wealthy and those who have good insurance. The rich are likely to be treated with "talk therapy" (forms of psychotherapy), the poor with "drug therapy" (tranquilizers to make them docile,° sometimes called "medicinal straitjackets").

For Your Consideration

22 How can we improve the treatment of the mentally ill poor? Take into consideration that the country is in debt and the public does not want higher taxes. What about the more fundamental issue—that of inequality in health care? Should medical care be a commodity that is sold to those who can afford it? Or do all citizens possess a fundamental right to high-quality health care?

Family Life

23 Social class also makes a significant difference in family life, in our choice of spouse, our chances of getting divorced, and how we rear our children.

24 **Choice of Husband or Wife** Members of the capitalist class place strong emphasis on family tradition. They stress the family's history, even a sense of purpose or destiny in life. Children of this class learn that their choice of

husband or wife affects not just them, but the entire family, that it will have an impact on the "family line." These background expectations shrink the field of "eligible" marriage partners, making it narrower than it is for the children of any other social class. As a result, parents in this class play a strong role in their children's mate selection.

25 **Divorce** The more difficult life of the lower social classes, especially the many tensions that come from insecure jobs and inadequate incomes, leads to higher marital friction and a greater likelihood of divorce. Consequently, children of the poor are more likely to grow up in broken homes.

26 **Child Rearing** Lower-class parents focus more on getting their children to follow rules and obey authority, while middle-class parents focus more on developing their children's creative and leadership skills. Sociologists have traced this difference to the parents' occupation. Lower-class parents are closely supervised at work, and they anticipate that their children will have similar jobs. Consequently, they try to teach their children to defer to authority. Middle-class parents, in contrast, enjoy greater independence at work. Anticipating similar jobs for their children, they encourage them to be more creative. Out of these contrasting orientations arise different ways of disciplining children; lower-class parents are more likely to use physical punishment, while the middle classes rely more on verbal persuasion.

27　　Working-class and middle-class parents also have different ideas about how children develop. Working-class parents think that children develop naturally—they sort of unfold from within. If parents provide comfort, food, shelter, and other basic support, the child's development will take care of itself. Middle-class parents, in contrast, think that children need a lot of guidance to develop correctly. Among the consequences of these contrasting orientations is that middle-class parents read to their children more, make more efforts to prepare them for school, and encourage play and extracurricular activities that they think will help develop their children's mental and social skills.

Education

28　　Education increases as one goes up the social class ladder. It is not just the amount of education that changes, but also the type of education. Children of the capitalist class bypass public schools. They attend exclusive private schools where they are trained to take a commanding role in society. Prep schools such as Andover, Groton, and Phillips Exeter Academy teach upper-class values and prepare their students for prestigious° universities.

29　　Keenly aware that private schools can be a key to upward social mobility, some upper-middle-class parents do their best to get their children into the prestigious preschools that feed into these exclusive prep schools. Although some preschools cost $23,000 a year, they have a waiting list. Parents even solicit letters of recommendation for their 2- and 3-year-olds. Such parental involvement and resources are major reasons why children from the more privileged classes are more likely to go to college—and to graduate.

Religion

30　　One area of social life that we might think would not be affected by social class is religion. ("People are just religious, or they are not. What does social class have to do with it?") The classes tend to cluster in different denominations. Episcopalians, for example, are more likely to attract the middle and upper classes, while Baptists draw heavily from the lower classes. Patterns of worship also follow class lines: The lower classes are attracted to more expressive worship services and louder music, while the middle and upper classes prefer more "subdued" worship.

Politics

31　　As I have stressed throughout this text, people perceive events from their own corner in life. Political views are no exception to this symbolic interactionist principle, and the rich and the poor walk different political paths. The higher that people are on the social class ladder, the more likely they are to vote for Republicans. In contrast, most members of the working class believe that the government should intervene in the economy to provide jobs and to make citizens financially secure. They are more likely to vote for Democrats. Although the working class is more liberal on *economic* issues (policies that increase government spending), it is more conservative on *social* issues (such as opposing abortion and the Equal Rights Amendment). People toward the bottom of the class structure are also less likely to be politically active—to campaign for candidates or even to vote.

Crime and Criminal Justice

32   If justice is supposed to be blind, it certainly is not when it comes to one's chances of being arrested. The white-collar crimes of the more privileged classes are more likely to be dealt with outside the criminal justice system, while the police and courts deal with the street crimes of the lower classes. One consequence of this class standard is that members of the lower classes are more likely to be in prison, on probation, or on parole. In addition, since those who commit street crimes tend to do so in or near their own neighborhoods, the lower classes are more likely to be robbed, burglarized, or murdered.

First Impressions

Freewrite for ten minutes on one of the following.

1. Did you enjoy reading this selection? Why or why not?

2. What images come to your mind when you hear the term "social class"? What characteristics do you associate with lower, middle, and upper class?

3. Henslin discusses the different standards of medical care available to wealthy and poor people. Most industrialized nations, including Canada, provide universal health care for their citizens. Would you support such a system in the United States? Why or why not?

Vocabulary Check

_____ 1. In the excerpt below, the phrase *couple with* means
   A. live together.
   B. add to.
   C. compare to.
   D. contrast with.

> "Compared with middle- and upper-class Americans, the poor have less job security and lower wages. They are more likely to divorce, to be the victims of crime, and to have more physical illnesses. Couple these conditions with bill collectors and the threat of eviction, and you can see how they can deal severe blows to people's emotional well-being." (Paragraph 15)

_____ 2. In the excerpt below, the word *orientations* means
   A. privileges.
   B. laws.
   C. outlooks.
   D. rewards.

> "Working-class parents think that children develop naturally—they sort of unfold from within. If parents provide comfort, food, shelter, and other basic support, the child's development will take care of itself. Middle-class parents, in contrast, think that children need a lot of guidance to develop correctly. Among the consequences of these contrasting orientations is that middle-class parents read to their children more ..." (Paragraph 27)

_____ 3. In the sentence below, the word *subdued* means
   A. realistic.
   B. energetic and emotional.
   C. long-lasting.
   D. quiet and restrained.

> "Patterns of worship also follow class lines: The lower classes are attracted to more expressive worship services and louder music, while the middle and upper classes prefer more 'subdued' worship." (Paragraph 30)

Reading Check

Central Point and Main Ideas

_____ 1. Which sentence best expresses the central point of the selection?
   A. Poorer mental and physical health is the most striking difference between the poor and the middle class.
   B. In the United States, it's almost impossible for someone to rise above the social class he or she was born into.
   C. Compared to the poor, the rich have fewer problems and more resources to deal with the ones they have.
   D. Social class affects almost every aspect of our lives.

_____ 2. The main idea of paragraph 31 is expressed in its
   A. first sentence.
   B. second sentence.
   C. third sentence.
   D. last sentence.

Supporting Details

_____ 3. According to the selection, poor people who are seriously mentally ill
  A. often become long-term mental patients.
  B. usually receive "talk therapy" instead of drugs.
  C. are often ignored.
  D. are often given tranquilizers to make them docile.

_____ 4. Henslin states that members of the capitalist class
  A. tend to believe that children sort of unfold from within.
  B. tend to stress the family's sense of destiny or purpose in life.
  C. are generally not as religious as working-class people.
  D. tend to be liberal on economic issues and conservative on social issues.

_____ 5. According to the selection, which of the following is *not* characteristic of the lower social classes?
  A. They are more likely to believe that the government should intervene in the economy.
  B. They are more likely to try to teach their children to defer to authority.
  C. They are more likely to smoke, eat a lot of fats, and be overweight.
  D. They are more likely to encourage their children to be creative.

Inferences

_____ 6. On the basis of paragraphs 1–4, we can infer that the author believes that
  A. attending Andover, Yale, and Harvard made George W. Bush well-qualified to be president.
  B. George W. Bush would probably never have become president if he had not been born rich.
  C. George W. Bush inherited his leadership ability from his grandfather and father.
  D. George W. Bush was an excellent businessman.

_____ 7. We can infer from paragraphs 8–11 that
  A. Terry Takewell died because he couldn't afford to pay his hospital bill.
  B. Terry Takewell died because his diabetes was left untreated.
  C. Terry Takewell's neighbors cared more about him than did the hospital administrator who escorted him to the parking lot.
  D. all of the above.

Argument

8. Label the point of the following argument with a **P** and the two statements of support with an **S**. Label with an **X** the statement that is neither the point nor the support of the argument.

____ A. Middle- and upper-class people usually have a personal physician, while poor people often spend hours waiting in crowded public health clinics.

____ B. When the poor are hospitalized, they are likely to find themselves in understaffed and underfunded public hospitals.

____ C. In the United States, there is a two-tier system of medical care.

____ D. The health care reform passed by Congress in 2010 was intended to reduce some of the inequality that has characterized medical care in the United States.

The Writer's Craft

_____ 9. In general, Henslin explains the effects social class has on people's lives and also
   A. contrasts the lives and beliefs of upper-class people with the lives and beliefs of lower-class people.
   B. lists factors that help explain why some people are wealthier than others.
   C. narrates a history of social class from early American times to the present.
   D. defines the term "social class" and provides examples of typical upper-class, middle-class, and lower-class people.

_____ 10. Henslin's main purpose in this selection is to
   A. entertain readers with colorful stories about the unbelievable situations that poor people get themselves into.
   B. inform readers of ways in which social class determines much about our lives.
   C. persuade readers that they should do everything in their power to overcome the limits of the social class they were born into.
   D. persuade readers that we should raise taxes on the rich in order to pay for better health care for the poor.

Discussion Questions

1. In paragraph 22, the author asks, "Should medical care be a commodity that is sold to those who can afford it? Or do all citizens possess a fundamental right to high-quality health care?" What do you think? Explain your position.

2. The selection compares child-rearing practices of lower-class parents with child-rearing practices of middle- and upper-class parents. Think about how you were raised. Which style of child-rearing did your parents follow? Explain. If you have or are planning to have children, which style of child-rearing would you use? Why?

3. When discussing social class in America, some argue that social classes are fluid in the United States—in other words, that anyone can rise in social class on the basis of his or her willingness to work hard. Do you agree with this argument? Why or why not?

4. Do you think that the author presents an accurate picture of the way social class affects family life, religion and politics? Why or why not? How would you describe your own views of family, religion, and politics? Do they fit what the selection describes as characteristic of your social class? Explain.

Paragraph Assignments

1. Have you ever felt out of place or uncomfortable because of your social class? Even children understand the embarrassment of being teased for something that might reflect their class, from the clothes they wear to what they bring to school for lunch. As we grow older, and the details of social class become more complex, we may feel out of place at a social function or simply in the company of certain people. Write a paragraph about a time that you felt this way. Be sure to include details about how felt and how you handled it.

2. Do you support the idea of universal health care for all Americans? Or do you prefer the current system, where health care is linked to employment and income? Write a paragraph stating and defending your answer. You may want to research this topic by Googling "universal health care pro and con."

Essay Assignments

1. Write an essay in which you observe ways, within your own family, or within the families of people you know, that social class has played a role.
   Here is one student's response to the assignment:

   > My dad and his brother, Uncle Will, grew up in a family that was pretty poor. Their dad owned a small butchering business that barely made ends meet. Although Dad and Uncle Will were fairly close when they were kids, their lives took very different turns. Dad worked three jobs and put himself through college. Today, he's a sales director for a large company. Uncle Will barely finished high school and has worked as a janitor, making a small salary, for 35 years. My uncle's lower social class has definitely influenced his life and ways of thinking.
   >
   > For one thing, Uncle Will still thinks that college is a waste of time and money. As a result, he never encourages his children to think about college. It doesn't matter that Uncle Will's own brother was able to better his life through a college degree. Most of my uncle's coworkers and friends believe that education makes no difference and that "real work" has more to do with working hard all your life than with some fancy title. Sometimes, Uncle Will makes sarcastic comments about how my dad's job is just pushing paper around.
   >
   > My uncle also believes that government is the enemy and that nothing he can do will ever make a difference. I've watched Uncle Will get up and leave the room when the news comes on, because it makes him so angry. He's never even registered to vote, because, in his words, "It won't make any difference." When I've tried to explain that every vote matters, he just laughs and shakes his head. Because he's never had much money, position, or status, I think Uncle Will feels powerless. His view is that "the suits" make all the rules and laws, and he has no say in the matter. He just works, goes home, and pretty much disregards the world around him.
   >
   > And, finally, Uncle Will has never paid much attention to his health. Like his father, Will has smoked since he was 16. And even though he must know that it's unhealthy, he's never tried to quit. Also, because of Uncle Will's income, much of the food he eats is cheap fast food, and as a result, he's pretty overweight. To Uncle Will, smoking, eating greasy food, and drinking too much beer are not necessarily bad habits—they're the same things nearly all of his friends do. If my dad ever

says anything about these habits, Uncle Will gets mad and claims that my dad thinks he's better. "It was good enough for Dad!" is his standard comeback.

My Uncle Will's lower social class certainly colors the way he lives and how he sees things. It's particularly interesting to me since he and my dad grew up together, but now they could not be more different. Because I love my uncle, I wish he had made some different choices when he was younger. Somehow, my dad saw that he didn't have to remain in the social class to which he was born. Uncle Will never realized that was possible.

2. According to the information in this selection, if parents born into the lower class wanted to give their children a chance of moving into the middle class, what are some steps they could take? Write an essay in which you describe three such actions and how they might affect the children.

Check Your Performance   **CONSEQUENCES OF SOCIAL CLASS**

Activity	Number Right	Points	Score
Vocabulary Check (3 items)	_____	x 10 =	_____
Reading Check			
Central Point and Main Ideas (2 items)	_____	x 7 =	_____
Supporting Details (3 items)	_____	x 7 =	_____
Inferences (2 items)	_____	x 7 =	_____
Argument (1 item)	_____	x 7 =	_____
The Writer's Craft (2 items)	_____	x 7 =	_____
		TOTAL SCORE =	_____ %

Enter your total score into the **Performance Chart: Fifteen Reading Selections** on the inside back cover.

10 The Ugly Truth about Beauty

Dave Barry

Preview

Why are women so very critical of the way they look? And why are men so very . . . not? Humorist Dave Barry explores this difference between the sexes in a way that ties together supermodels, lawn care, and a well-known plastic doll.

Words to Watch

regimen (5): process
mutation (8): an organism resulting from a DNA change
bolster (9): make stronger

1 If you're a man, at some point a woman will ask how she looks.

2 "How do I look?" she'll ask.

3 You must be careful how you answer this question. The best technique is to form an honest yet sensitive opinion, then collapse on the floor with some kind of fatal seizure. Trust me, this is the easiest way out. Because you will never come up with the right answer.

4 The problem is that women generally do not think of their looks in the same way that men do. Most men form an opinion of how they look in the seventh grade, and they stick to it for the rest of their lives. Some men form the opinion that they are irresistible stud muffins, and they do not change this opinion even when their faces sag and their noses bloat to the size of eggplants and their eyebrows grow together to form what appears to be a giant forehead-dwelling tropical caterpillar.

5 Most men, I believe, think of themselves as average-looking. Men will think this even if their faces cause heart failure in cattle at a range of 300 yards. Being average does not bother them; average is fine, for men. This is why men never ask anybody how they look. Their primary form of beauty care is to shave themselves, which is essentially the same form of beauty care that they give to their lawns. If, at the end of his four-minute daily beauty regimen°, a man has managed to wipe most of the shaving cream out of his hair and is not

bleeding too badly, he feels that he has done all he can, so he stops thinking about his appearance and devotes his mind to more critical issues, such as the Super Bowl.

6   Women do not look at themselves in this way. If I had to express, in three words, what I believe most women think about their appearance, those words would be: "not good enough." No matter how attractive a woman may appear to be to others, when she looks at herself in the mirror, she thinks: woof. She thinks that at any moment a municipal animal-control officer is going to throw a net over her and haul her off to the shelter.

7   Why do women have such low self-esteem? There are many complex psychological and societal reasons, by which I mean Barbie. Girls grow up playing with a doll proportioned such that, if it were human, it would be seven feet tall and weigh 81 pounds, of which 53 pounds would be bosoms. This is a difficult appearance standard to live up to, especially when you contrast it with the standard set for little boys by their dolls . . . excuse me, by their action figures. Most of the action figures that my son played with when he was little were hideous-looking. For example, he was very fond of an action figure (part of the He-Man series) called "Buzz-Off," who was part human, part flying insect. Buzz-Off was not a looker. But he was extremely self-confident. You could not imagine Buzz-Off saying to the other action figures: "Do you think these wings make my hips look big?"

8   But women grow up thinking they need to look like Barbie, which for most

women is impossible, although there is a multibillion-dollar beauty industry devoted to convincing women that they must try. I once saw an Oprah show wherein supermodel Cindy Crawford dispensed makeup tips to the studio audience. Cindy had all these middle-aged women applying beauty products to their faces; she stressed how important it was to apply them in a certain way, using the tips of their fingers. All the women dutifully did this, even though it was obvious to any sane observer that, no matter how carefully they applied these products, they would never look remotely like Cindy Crawford, who is some kind of genetic mutation°.

9   I'm not saying that men are superior. I'm just saying that you're not going to get a group of middle-aged men to sit

in a room and apply cosmetics to themselves under the instruction of Brad Pitt, in hopes of looking more like him. Men would realize that this task was pointless and demeaning. They would find some way to bolster° their self-esteem that did not require looking like Brad Pitt. They would say to Brad: "Oh *yeah*? Well, what do you know about *lawn care*, pretty boy?"

10   Of course many women will argue that the reason they become obsessed with trying to look like Cindy Crawford is that men, being as shallow as a drop of spit, *want* women to look that way. To which I have two responses:

11   1. Hey, just because *we're* idiots, that does not mean *you* have to be; and

12   2. Men don't even notice 97 percent of the beauty efforts you make anyway. Take fingernails. The average woman spends 5,000 hours per year worrying about her fingernails; I have never once, in more than 40 years of listening to men talk about women, heard a man say, "She has a nice set of fingernails!" Many men would not notice if a woman had upward of four hands.

13   Anyway, to get back to my original point: If you're a man, and a woman asks you how she looks, you're in big trouble. Obviously, you can't say she looks bad. But you also can't say that she looks great, because she'll think you're lying, because she has spent countless hours, with the help of the multi-billion-dollar beauty industry, obsessing about the differences between herself and Cindy Crawford. Also, she suspects that you're not qualified to judge anybody's appearance. This is because you have shaving cream in your hair.

First Impressions

Freewrite for ten minutes on one of the following.

1. Did you enjoy reading this selection? Why or why not?

2. Barry says that most women think their appearance is "not good enough." Aside from Barbie dolls, what factors might influence women to feel that way?

3. Do you agree that men are less critical of their own appearances than women are of theirs? Why do you think there is less pressure on men to look attractive?

Vocabulary Check

_____ 1. In the sentence below, the word *bloat* means
  A. bleed.
  B. run.
  C. sneeze.
  D. expand.

> "Some men form the opinion that they are irresistible stud muffins, and they do not change this opinion even when their faces sag and their noses bloat to the size of eggplants and their eyebrows grow together to form what appears to be a giant forehead-dwelling tropical caterpillar." (Paragraph 4)

_____ 2. In the excerpt below, the word *dutifully* means
  A. oddly.
  B. obediently.
  C. quickly.
  D. carelessly.

> "Cindy had all these middle-aged women applying beauty products to their faces; she stressed how important it was to apply them in a certain way, using the tips of their fingers. All the women dutifully did this, even though it was obvious to any sane observer that, no matter how carefully they applied these products, they would never look remotely like Cindy Crawford, who is some kind of genetic mutation." (Paragraph 8)

_____ 3. In the excerpt below, the word *demeaning* means
  A. insulting.
  B. difficult.
  C. strange.
  D. disgusting.

> "I'm just saying that you're not going to get a group of middle-aged men to sit in a room and apply cosmetics to themselves under the instruction of Brad Pitt, in hopes of looking more like him. Men would realize that this task was pointless and demeaning." (Paragraph 9)

Reading Check

Central Point and Main Ideas

_____ 1. Which sentence best expresses the implied central point of the selection?
   A. Women have been brought up to believe that they should look like real-life Barbie dolls, even though this is impossible.
   B. In our society, women tend to have lower self-esteem than men.
   C. Because of the way they have been brought up, most women spend far more time worrying about their appearance than men do.
   D. It is impossible for men to tell women the truth about how they look because women will not believe them.

_____ 2. The implied main idea of paragraphs 8 and 9 is that
   A. middle-aged women who try to look like Cindy Crawford are foolish.
   B. men have more important things to do than to compare themselves to Brad Pitt.
   C. the beauty industry convinces many women that they should try to look like Cindy Crawford, an impossible task.
   D. in contrast to women, men have not been led to believe that their looks are the most important thing about them.

Supporting Details

_____ 3. The author's son played with an action figure that was
   A. attractive and self-confident.
   B. hideous-looking but self-confident.
   C. neither attractive nor self-confident.
   D. worried about the size of his hips.

_____ 4. One thing the author has never heard a man say is
   A. "I'm shallow as a drop of spit."
   B. "Honey, you look bad."
   C. "Honey, you look great."
   D. "She has a nice set of fingernails."

Inferences

_____ 5. We can infer from paragraph 5 that the author believes that
   A. most men are ugly, not average-looking.
   B. most men are afraid to ask people how they really look.
   C. most men don't spend much time grooming themselves or thinking about the way they look.
   D. the Super Bowl is a critical issue.

_____ 6. On the basis of paragraph 6, we can infer that the author believes that
    A. most women have an unrealistically negative view of their own appearance.
    B. most women waste time in front of mirrors because they're spoiled and lazy.
    C. many women become uncontrollably angry when they see themselves in a mirror.
    D. it is impossible for a woman to ever be pleased with her appearance.

_____ 7. We can conclude from the last two paragraphs that many women
    A. overestimate the amount of attention men pay to women's appearances.
    B. dislike men because they care so little about their own appearance.
    C. are annoyed that the beauty industry forces them to spend countless hours worrying about their appearance.
    D. believe that men with shaving cream in their hair are big trouble.

Argument

_____ 8. Write the letter of the statement that is the point of the following argument. The other statements are support for that point.
    A. Dave Barry states that despite how attractive a woman is, she thinks she looks like a dog when she sees herself in the mirror.
    B. Dave Barry uses exaggeration throughout his essay in order to poke fun at women's obsession with looking beautiful.
    C. According to Dave Barry, women are wasting their time trying to look like supermodel Cindy Crawford, who is "some kind of genetic mutation."
    D. According to Dave Barry, women spend 5,000 hours per year worrying about their fingernails.

The Writer's Craft

_____ 9. Barry probably titled his essay "The Ugly Truth About Beauty"
    A. to attract the reader's attention with the surprising suggestion that there's something ugly about beauty.
    B. to suggest the "ugly truth" that men don't even notice most of the efforts women make to look beautiful.
    C. to make the point that being overly concerned about one's physical appearance is not a good way to live.
    D. for all the above reasons.

_____10. What type of conclusion does Barry use in the final paragraph of his essay?

    A. A summary of his thesis.

    B. A summary of his thesis and main supporting details.

    C. A summary and a closing thought.

    D. A summary, a closing thought, and a recommendation for further action.

Discussion Questions

1. Although Barry's essay is written for laughs, he obviously has something serious to say about women and men and their feelings about their appearances. In non-humorous language, how would you rephrase his main points?

2. Think about the women you know. How much time would you say that they devote to clothing, hairstyles, and makeup? On the basis of your answer, do you agree with the author's view that women spend far too much time worrying about how they look? Why or why not?

3. Do you agree or disagree with the author's negative view of the role Barbie dolls play in shaping American girls' image of themselves? Once the girls have grown up, to what extent would you say that external forces, such as the media and the fashion industry, influence their feelings about their own appearances? Explain your reasoning.

4. Do you agree with Barry that men are generally satisfied with their own appearance? Why might their standards be so different from those of women?

Paragraph Assignments

1. Do you think Barbie dolls really influence girls—and, later, women—to have unrealistic expectations about their looks? Why or why not? Write a paragraph defending your answer.

    Here is one student's response to the assignment:

> Some people argue that the super-perfect looks of Barbie dolls negatively influence young girls, but I'm not buying it. Barbie is thin as a rail, ridiculously proportioned, and has eyes nearly as big as her hands. Do little girls really want to look like that? I doubt it. I believe the appeal of the Barbie doll is

> *similar to the appeal of a flashy cartoon character—something fun to play with but not something to turn into. It is only when a girl observes her mother or other women in her life trying in vain to attain a ridiculous level of physical perfection that Barbie becomes a bad influence. Then a simple toy becomes a constant reminder of what a young girl is expected to become. But if the girl's mother has a healthy and realistic concept of beauty, the girl's concept of her Barbie doll is also realistic. In that case, a Barbie remains nothing more than a harmless (though a bit odd-looking) doll.*

2. Most people would agree that there's nothing wrong with wanting to look good. But wanting to look good too often turns into insecurity and unhappiness with one's appearance. Write a paragraph in which you explain the difference between a healthy and an unhealthy concern for one's looks.

Essay Assignments

1. Whether we like it or not, beauty matters. Research has shown that better-looking people tend to be more popular, earn more money, and even get better seats at restaurants. Think about three people you know (you can include yourself, if you want) who vary in appearance from not all that attractive to pretty darned attractive. How does each person's appearance make a difference in his or her life and interactions with other people? Are there any differences in these people's confidence and self-image? Write an essay that presents each person and describe how each individual's beauty, or lack of it, affects his or her life.

2. This essay focuses on the different emphases that women and men put on their own physical appearance. But there are numerous other ways that men and women tend to think and act differently. Write an essay in which you spell out three ways in which, in your experience, men and women are different. Provide examples to support your claims.

Check Your Performance

THE UGLY TRUTH ABOUT BEAUTY

Activity	Number Right		Points		Score
Vocabulary Check (3 items)	_____	x	10	=	_____
Reading Check					
Central Point and Main Ideas (2 items)	_____	x	7	=	_____
Supporting Details (2 items)	_____	x	7	=	_____
Inferences (3 items)	_____	x	7	=	_____
Argument (1 item)	_____	x	7	=	_____
The Writer's Craft (2 items)	_____	x	7	=	_____
		TOTAL SCORE		=	_____ %

Enter your total score into the **Performance Chart: Fifteen Reading Selections** on the inside back cover.

11 Rethinking Sleep
David K. Randall

Preview

"You need eight hours of sleep a night!" That's one of those standard truths that "everybody" knows. And yes, we do need adequate sleep to function at our best, mentally and physically. But how and when we get those hours of sleep may have a greater impact than we realize.

Words to Watch

affliction (2): a disorder
amorous (6): related to love
off-kilter (7): unbalanced
insomniacs (7): people who have difficulty sleeping
cognitive (9): reasoning or thinking
hone (11): improve
sequential (12): uninterrupted

1   Sometime in the dark stretch of the night it happens. Perhaps it's the chime of an incoming text message. Or your iPhone screen lights up to alert you to a new e-mail. Or you find yourself staring at the ceiling, replaying the day in your head. Next thing you know, you're out of bed and engaged with the world, once again ignoring the often quoted fact that eight straight hours of sleep is essential.

2   Sound familiar? You're not alone. Thanks in part to technology and its constant pinging and chiming, roughly 41 million people in the United States—nearly a third of all working adults—get six hours or fewer of sleep a night, according to a recent report from the Centers for Disease Control and Prevention. And sleep deprivation is an affliction° that crosses economic lines. About 42 percent of workers in the mining industry are sleep-deprived, while about 27 percent of financial or insurance industry workers share the same complaint.

3   Typically, mention of our ever-increasing sleeplessness is followed by calls for earlier bedtimes and a longer night's sleep. But this directive may be part of the problem. Rather than helping us to get more rest, the tyranny of the

eight-hour block reinforces a narrow conception of sleep and how we should approach it. Some of the time we spend tossing and turning may even result from misconceptions about sleep and our bodily needs: in fact neither our bodies nor our brains are built for the roughly one-third of our lives that we spend in bed.

4   The idea that we should sleep in eight-hour chunks is relatively recent. The world's population sleeps in various and surprising ways. Millions of Chinese workers continue to put their heads on their desks for a nap of an hour or so after lunch, for example, and daytime napping is common from India to Spain.

5   One of the first signs that the emphasis on a straight eight-hour sleep had outlived its usefulness arose in the early 1990s, thanks to a history professor at Virginia Tech named A. Roger Ekirch, who spent hours investigating the history of the night and began to notice strange references to sleep. A character in *The Canterbury Tales*, for instance, decides to go back to bed after her "firste sleep." A doctor in England wrote that the time between the "first sleep" and the "second sleep" was the best time for study and reflection. And one 16th-century French physician concluded that laborers were able to conceive more children because they waited until after their "first sleep" to make love. Professor Ekirch soon learned that he wasn't the only one who was on to the historical existence of alternate sleep cycles. In a fluke of history, Thomas A. Wehr, a psychiatrist then working at the National Institute of Mental Health in Bethesda, Md., was conducting an experiment in which subjects were deprived of artificial light. Without the illumination and distraction from light bulbs, televisions or computers, the subjects slept through the night, at least at first. But, after a while, Dr. Wehr noticed that subjects began to wake up a little after midnight, lie awake for a couple of hours, and then drift back to sleep again, in the same pattern of segmented sleep that Professor Ekirch saw referenced in historical records and early works of literature.

6   It seemed that, given a chance to be free of modern life, the body would naturally settle into a split sleep schedule. Subjects grew to like experiencing nighttime in a new way. Once they broke their conception of what form sleep should come in, they looked forward to the time in the middle of the night as a chance for deep thinking of all kinds, whether in the form of self-reflection, getting a jump on the next day, or amorous° activity. Most of us, however, do not treat middle-of-the-night awakenings as a sign of a normal, functioning brain.

7   Doctors who peddle sleep aid products and call for more sleep may unintentionally reinforce the idea that there is something wrong or off-kilter° about interrupted sleep cycles. Sleep anxiety is a common result: we know we should be getting a good night's rest but imagine we are doing something wrong if we awaken in the middle of the night. Related worries turn many of us into insomniacs° and incite many to reach for sleeping pills

or sleep aids, which reinforces a cycle that the Harvard psychologist Daniel M. Wegner has called "the ironic processes of mental control."

8   As we lie in our beds thinking about the sleep we're not getting, we diminish the chances of enjoying a peaceful night's rest.

9   This, despite the fact that a number of recent studies suggest that any deep sleep—whether in an eight-hour block or a 30-minute nap—primes our brains to function at a higher level, letting us come up with better ideas, find solutions to puzzles more quickly, identify patterns faster and recall information more accurately. In a NASA-financed study, for example, a team of researchers led by David F. Dinges, a professor at the University of Pennsylvania, found that letting subjects nap for as little as 24 minutes improved their cognitive° performance.

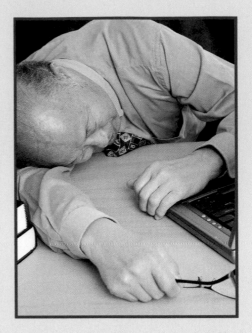

10   In another study conducted by Simon Durrant, a professor at the University of Lincoln, in England, the amount of time a subject spent in deep sleep during a nap predicted his or her later performance at recalling a short burst of melodic tones. And researchers at the City University of New York found that short naps helped subjects identify more literal and figurative connections between objects than those who simply stayed awake.

11   Robert Stickgold, a professor of psychiatry at Harvard Medical School, proposes that sleep—including short naps that include deep sleep—offers our brains the chance to decide what new information to keep and what

to toss. That could be one reason our dreams are laden with strange plots and characters, a result of the brain's trying to find connections between what it's recently learned and what is stored in our long-term memory. Rapid eye movement sleep—so named because researchers who discovered this sleep stage were astonished to see the fluttering eyelids of sleeping subjects— is the only phase of sleep during which the brain is as active as it is when we are fully conscious, and seems to offer our brains the best chance to come up with new ideas and hone° recently acquired skills. When we awaken, our minds are often better able to make connections that were hidden in the jumble of information.

12   Gradual acceptance of the notion that sequential° sleep hours are not essential for high-level job performance

has led to increased workplace tolerance for napping and other alternate daily schedules.

13   Employees at Google, for instance, are offered the chance to nap at work because the company believes it may increase productivity. Thomas Balkin, the head of the department of behavioral biology at the Walter Reed Army Institute of Research, imagines a near future in which military commanders can know how much total sleep an individual soldier has had over a 24-hour time frame thanks to wristwatch-size sleep monitors. After consulting computer models that predict how decision-making abilities decline with fatigue, a soldier could then be ordered to take a nap to prepare for an approaching mission. The cognitive benefit of a nap could last anywhere from one to three hours, depending on what stage of sleep a person reaches before awakening.

14   Most of us are not fortunate enough to work in office environments that permit, much less smile upon, on-the-job napping. But there are increasing suggestions that greater tolerance for altered sleep schedules might be in our collective interest. Researchers have observed, for example, that long-haul pilots who sleep during flights perform better when maneuvering aircraft through the critical stages of descent and landing.

15   Several Major League Baseball teams have adapted to the demands of a long season by changing their sleep patterns. Fernando Montes, the former strength and conditioning coach for the Texas Rangers, counseled his players to fall asleep with the curtains in their hotel rooms open so that they would naturally wake up at sunrise no matter what time zone they were in—even if it meant cutting into an eight-hour sleeping block. Once they arrived at the ballpark, Montes would set up a quiet area where they could sleep before the game. Players said that, thanks to this schedule, they felt great both physically and mentally over the long haul.

16   Strategic napping in the Rangers style could benefit us all. No one argues that sleep is not essential. But freeing ourselves from needlessly rigid and quite possibly outdated ideas about what constitutes a good night's sleep might help put many of us to rest, in a healthy and productive, if not eight-hour-long, block.

First Impressions

Freewrite for ten minutes or so on one of the following.

1. Did you enjoy reading this selection? Why or why not?

2. How much sleep do you typically get each night? Do you feel that amount is adequate? Why or why not?

3. Will reading this selection cause you to change your sleep habits? If so, in what ways will you change them?

Vocabulary Check

_____ 1. In the sentence below, the word *misconceptions* means
   A. pregnancies.
   B. research.
   C. clever insights.
   D. mistaken ideas.

   "Some of the time we spend tossing and turning may even result from misconceptions about sleep and our bodily needs: in fact neither our bodies nor our brains are built for the roughly one-third of our lives that we spend in bed." (Paragraph 3)

_____ 2. In the sentence below, the word *segmented* means
   A. divided into parts.
   B. put together.
   C. not disturbed.
   D. completely restful.

   "But, after a while, Dr. Wehr noticed that subjects began to wake up a little after midnight, lie awake for a couple of hours, and then drift back to sleep again, in the same pattern of segmented sleep that Professor Ekirch saw referenced in historical records and early works of literature." (Paragraph 5)

_____ 3. In the sentence below, the word *diminish* means
   A. improve.
   B. reflect on.
   C. reduce.
   D. ignore.

   "As we lie in our beds thinking about the sleep we're not getting, we diminish the chances of enjoying a peaceful night's rest." (Paragraph 8)

Reading Check

Central Point and Main Ideas

_____ 1. The central idea of the selection is that
   A. people who call for earlier bedtimes and a longer night's sleep to combat sleeplessness have a narrow view of sleep.
   B. the more we worry about not getting enough sleep, the less sleep we get.
   C. in contrast to people in the United States, people in countries such as China, India, and Spain sleep in various and surprising ways.
   D. freeing ourselves from the idea that we must sleep eight straight hours may help us find rest in a more healthy and productive manner.

_____ 2. The main idea of paragraph 15 is stated in the
   A. first sentence.
   B. second sentence.
   C. third sentence.
   D. last sentence.

Supporting Details

_____ 3. TRUE OR FALSE? People cannot fall into a deep sleep during a 30-minute nap.

_____ 4. Historical records and early works of literature have provided evidence that
   A. people got more sleep when there were no light bulbs, computers, cellphones, or computers to bother them.
   B. the Chinese have always gotten more sleep than people in other countries.
   C. many people used to sleep, wake up for a while, and then go back to sleep.
   D. those who did heavy physical labor usually slept straight throughout the night.

_____ 5. According to the selection, our dreams are filled with strange plots and characters because
   A. they reflect our anxiety about not getting enough sleep.
   B. we are too exhausted to dream in a logical, sequential pattern.
   C. our brains are trying to decide what information to keep and what to toss.
   D. we are over-stimulated by the pings and chimes of modern technology.

Inferences

_____ 6. We can infer from paragraphs 1 and 2 that
   A. technology is one of the factors depriving us of sleep.
   B. before the invention of computers and cellphones, no one was sleep-deprived.
   C. office workers tend to be more sleep deprived than other people.
   D. people today need less sleep than people a hundred years ago.

_____ 7. The author would probably agree with which of the following statements?
   A. Long-haul pilots who sleep during flights should be fired.
   B. The Texas Rangers had a winning season because players were encouraged to take naps.
   C. More companies should offer employees the chance to nap at work.
   D. Companies should encourage their employees to go to bed earlier and get a longer night's sleep.

Argument

_____ 8. Which of the statements does **not** support the point of the argument?

Point: Recent research shows that deep sleep, including naps, improves cognitive performance.

   A. A NASA-financed study found that letting subjects nap for as little as 24 minutes improved their performances.
   B. Researchers at the City University of New York found that short naps helped subjects identify more connections between objects than those who simply stayed awake.
   C. Millions of Chinese workers put their heads on their desks for a nap after lunch.
   D. The amount of time a subject spent in deep sleep during a nap predicted his or her later performance at recalling a short burst of melodic tones.

The Writer's Craft

_____ 9. The author concludes his essay with
   A. statistics about the value of taking naps.
   B. a series of examples that show that a straight eight-hour sleep has outlived its usefulness.
   C. a summary of his main ideas.
   D. an anecdote about his own sleep habits.

_____10. In general, this reading is organized according to which of the following patterns?
   A. Illustration: provides examples that show it's not natural or desirable to sleep eight straight hours.
   B. Time order: tells of changing attitudes toward sleep since the 1600s.
   C. Contrast: contrasts modern American attitudes toward sleep with the attitudes of people in different countries and at different times.
   D. Listing order: lists reasons why it is better to take naps during the day than to sleep eight hours at night.

Discussion Questions

1. About how many hours of sleep a night do you get? If you're sleep-deprived, what factors tend to reduce the amount of sleep you get? Is there anything you can do to get more sleep?

2. If you were entirely in charge of your schedule—if you were not bound by any work or personal commitments—when and how much do you think you would sleep? Would your sleep schedule be different than it is now?

3. As the author points out, daytime napping is common in many countries, from India to Spain, but it has not yet caught on in the United States. Do you think it ever will? Why or why not?

4. The essay mentions the way that electronic media—cell phones and computers, etc.—can interfere with our sleep. Do you find yourself losing sleep because of such devices? What could you do to minimize their effect on you?

Paragraph Assignments

1. Write a paragraph in which you describe changes you would have to make in your own daily routine in order to consistently get eight hours of sleep a night.

2. Imagine that you have been chosen by your coworkers to write a letter to your boss attempting to convince him or her to allow everyone to take naps on the job. Write the paragraph of the letter where you state your case. Use arguments of your own in addition to the evidence presented in Randall's essay. Your topic sentence could be, "I definitely feel that allowing workers to take one or two twenty-minute naps a day would be beneficial to our company."

Essay Assignments

1. Write an essay in which you detail three reasons why you at times (or often) do not get enough sleep, along with possible solutions that might help you get more sleep.

Here is one student's response to the assignment:

> Eight hours every night—according to doctors, that's how much sleep we're **supposed** to get in order to remain healthy. But I can't imagine how anyone actually gets that much rest a few times a week, much less every night! I'll admit it, though. There are quite a few things I do that I don't have to do that definitely interfere with getting enough sleep. And I can come up with solutions for the top three reasons why I'm not getting eight hours a night.
>
> One reason my sleep is less than perfect is that I go out with friends at least a few times a week. It's okay on the weekend when I can sleep in, but on weeknights I often don't get home until midnight, and I have to get up around 6:00 for work. I really don't want to give up hanging with friends completely, but I suppose I could probably get home an hour or two earlier. I guess I could live with just going out to get pizza and not continuing on to a movie or a club.
>
> However, if I'm not out with friends, I'm either watching TV or on the computer. Often, I'm doing both at the same time! I get so involved with what I'm doing that I lose track of time, and the next thing I know, it's midnight again. And sometimes I get so wound up in a scary movie or a conversation online that I can't get sleepy. Then I lie awake in bed for another hour or more. The solution? Turn off the screens, and, instead, read a book or listen to music. That sounds a lot more relaxing and sleep-inducing.
>
> Finally, I could actually sleep until 7:00 if I exercised after work, when I have more time, instead of waiting until the morning. I really like to get 30 or more minutes of running in three times during the week, but I always find some excuse for not running in the evening. Those excuses are usually pretty flimsy. For example, during the winter I've been known to say that it's too dark and cold after work. But it's even colder in the morning! Mostly, I've just gotten in the habit of thinking about food and fun right after work. I can change that habit. And I bet I'd sleep better after exercising before bed.

> *It's true that I rarely get a good night's sleep, but that's definitely something I can fix if I just make a handful of adjustments. It's funny, because sometimes I feel like I just don't have the energy to make changes in my life. Then I realize that if I were more rested, I'd have the energy to change!*

2. It is estimated that more than 20 percent of Americans suffer from insomnia and that more and more of these people are becoming dependent on some type of drug to help them sleep. In his essay, Randall refers to the "ironic process of mental control." Why is the process of taking certain drugs in order to control our minds ironic? When we take drugs to alter our minds, we *lose* the ability to control our thought processes.

   Imagine that you had a friend who asked you for advice to help him with his insomnia. Instead of drugs, suggest three natural ways to combat sleeplessness. Write an essay that presents these three ideas and explains how they work. If you need help coming up with ideas, a Google search of "beating insomnia naturally" or "how to sleep well without drugs" will bring up literally millions of results.

Check Your Performance   **RETHINKING SLEEP**

Activity	Number Right	Points	Score
Vocabulary Check (3 items)	_____	x 10 =	_____
Reading Check			
Central Point and Main Ideas (2 items)	_____	x 7 =	_____
Supporting Details (3 items)	_____	x 7 =	_____
Inferences (2 items)	_____	x 7 =	_____
Argument (1 item)	_____	x 7 =	_____
The Writer's Craft (2 items)	_____	x 7 =	_____
		TOTAL SCORE =	_____ %

Enter your total score into the **Performance Chart: Fifteen Reading Selections** on the inside back cover.

12 Marijuana Today

Mark Bowden

Preview

The laws against marijuana use have been ineffective, expensive, and unevenly enforced. There is a strong case to be made, says former *Philadelphia Inquirer* columnist Mark Bowden, for legalizing pot. (In fact, since this essay was written, the states of Washington and Colorado have legalized the possession of small amounts of marijuana.) Whether people should actually smoke pot, though, is another question entirely.

Words to Watch

disabuse (10): correct
contrition (10): regret
revelry (12): celebration
leverage (16): influence
clarity (18): clearness

1 I knew when I saw my father sitting at the kitchen table that I was in trouble.

2 I was a teenager, returning home late from a night out with my friends. I was high. As we did most nights, my friends and I had been smoking pot. Nearly everyone I knew my age smoked pot.

3 My father was usually asleep long before I got home. I took a quick inventory of my state of mind and concluded that so long as my conversation with him was casual and brief, there was a chance he wouldn't notice that I was cockeyed stoned. One of the virtues of pot, or so I thought then, was this ability to play it straight. Fear was especially useful. It could straighten out your thinking in a hurry.

4 As was his style, he confronted me head-on.

5 "Mark, do you smoke?" he asked.

6 I could not lie to my father. Even to this day, I'm not sure why exactly; I hope it was because I respected him and knew he did not lie to me.

7 "Yes," I told him, and then braced myself.

8 He was furious, but not about my marijuana use. He had not even considered the possibility of an illicit drug. He was worried that I was smoking

cigarettes! I nearly swooned with relief.

9   I was not a cigarette smoker. They gave me a headache and left a god-awful taste in my mouth. They were addictive and caused cancer. No way. My father had been a heavy smoker in his youth, and he had quit cold turkey when the first of the surgeon general's warnings had come out. So he could not comprehend why one of his own sons would even consider flirting with the habit.

10   I did not disabuse° him. While I might not have been able to look my father in the eye and lie, I was expert at withholding the complete truth. I bore the cigarette scolding manfully, expressed agreement and contrition°, and gave the old man my word I would never smoke another cigarette. I have kept that promise.

11   It took me a little longer to stop smoking dope. Having raised five children of my own and entered upon grandfatherhood, I can report two things: (1) I think we ought to repeal laws against marijuana possession; (2) I no longer think smoking pot is a good idea.

12   Tomorrow, April 20, or 4/20, has become an unofficial national holiday for lovers of weed. There are supposedly 420 chemical elements in cannabis, or something like that. The reasons for 4/20 becoming the toker's special day are suitably confused, about as certain as most trains of thought under the influence. The revelry° both celebrates the substance and protests its illegality. I'm with them on the latter issue, not so much on the former.

13   Marijuana smoking is, if anything, more commonplace today than when I was a wannabe hippie 40 years ago. My sons, now grown, tell me that it was easier for them to get pot in high school in Chester County than it was to get beer. Generations of Americans have grown up getting high, long enough for everyone to know that all the old horror stories about its use are ridiculously exaggerated. No one I knew who smoked dope as a kid—and, as I said, just about everyone I knew did—turned into a heroin or cocaine addict.

14   I do know some folks who became alcoholics, and a number of them are no longer around. I believed then and I believe today that alcohol is a far greater public health and safety threat than marijuana. Tobacco, also legal, is an even greater curse.

15   Yet the war on weed rages on. Thirty-seven years after a special commission formed by Congress and President Richard Nixon concluded that punitive marijuana laws cause more social harm than the drug itself, nearly half of the drug arrests in this country are for pot. The numbers grow annually. More people were arrested for pot possession in America last year than ever before in our history, more than 800,000. In Pennsylvania, possession is a misdemeanor, and the possible prison sentence goes from 30 days to a year, depending on whether the amount is more or less than 30 grams. Although there are horrific exceptions, most of these offenders, unless they were involved in serious drug trafficking or some other illegal activity when

arrested, do not go to jail for simple possession. Still, what a tremendous waste of money and manpower! One of the strongest arguments against such misdemeanor drug laws is that they are completely ineffective.

16   More than that, the prohibition of marijuana gives police an undue amount of leverage° over average citizens. When something as widespread as pot possession is illegal, police can use it as an excuse to harass whole classes of otherwise law-abiding citizens. It should come as no surprise that the majority of those possession busts were young black and Latino men, even though surveys show that most of the marijuana users in this country are white.

17   I stopped smoking dope many years ago. I have always urged my children not to use it, just as I have counseled them to avoid using other drugs and getting drunk. The effects of pot use are more subtle than drunkenness, which leads many to conclude that marijuana is a less dangerous intoxicant than alcohol, but its very subtlety poses a unique threat. Because you can go to class high, go to work high, drive high, and otherwise function with apparent normality, it is easier to abuse marijuana constantly than alcohol, and that "normality" you feel isn't the truth. Marijuana doesn't make you out of control. It just makes you stupid. And while I haven't surveyed the most recent medical reports, I suspect the health effects of inhaling pot smoke are likely to be at least as harmful as the substance that so concerned my dad.

For me, as with most users, getting high was a symptom of boredom and rebellion. Once I grew up and found work that I loved, competitive work that demanded real effort and mental clarity°, I realized that the effects of getting high, the confusion and silliness, were a disadvantage. When I had children, the responsibility I felt for them weighed on me in a nice way, but also in a way that ruled out getting high. Weed began to induce less joy than worry. What if, feeling temporarily silly and indifferent, I failed my family in some way, large or small?   18

I know I am not alone in this. These are the kinds of decisions adults in our society make every day about their health, their responsibilities, and their happiness. Lots of people don't agree with me, including some of my friends. That may make them misguided, in my view, but it certainly shouldn't make them criminal.   19

First Impressions

Freewrite for ten minutes on one of the following.

1. Did you enjoy reading this selection? Why or why not?

2. In your opinion, should marijuana be legalized? Why or why not?

3. If marijuana were legalized, do you think its usage would increase, decrease, or stay about the same? Explain.

Vocabulary Check

_____ 1. In the excerpt below, the word *illicit* means
   A. easily purchased.
   B. illegal.
   C. able to be smoked.
   D. expensive.

   "He was furious, but not about my marijuana use. He had not even considered the possibility of an illicit drug. He was worried that I was smoking cigarettes!" (Paragraph 8)

_____ 2. In the sentence below, the word *punitive* means
   A. unenforceable.
   B. effective.
   C. relatively weak.
   D. intended to punish.

   "Thirty-seven years after a special commission formed by Congress and President Richard Nixon concluded that punitive marijuana laws cause more social harm than the drug itself, nearly half of the drug arrests in this country are for pot." (Paragraph 15)

_____ 3. In the sentence below, the word *induce* means
   A. rule out.
   B. demonstrate.
   C. bring about.
   D. become an example of.

   "When I had children, the responsibility I felt for them weighed on me in a nice way, but also in a way that ruled out getting high. Weed began to induce less joy than worry." (Paragraph 18)

Reading Check

Central Point and Main Ideas

_____ 1. Which sentence best expresses the central point of the entire selection?

A. Although the author smoked marijuana regularly as a teenager, he has always urged his children not to use it.

B. The author believes that it is a waste of time and money to jail people for possessing marijuana.

C. The author has come to believe that smoking marijuana is probably less harmful than consuming alcohol.

D. Although the author no longer approves of smoking marijuana, he thinks laws against its possession ought to be repealed.

_____ 2. The implied main idea of paragraphs 13–14 is that

A. marijuana smoking is now more commonplace than when the author was young.

B. generations of Americans have grown up smoking pot, proving that the old horror stories against its use are exaggerated.

C. alcohol and tobacco are far greater health hazards than marijuana use, which is commonplace.

D. none of the people who the author smoked dope with as a kid turned into heroin or cocaine addicts.

_____ 3. The implied main idea of paragraph 15 is that

A. a special commission concluded that punitive marijuana laws cause more social harm than the drug itself.

B. arresting people for marijuana possession is a waste of money and manpower and does nothing to reduce use of the drug.

C. more Americans than ever are smoking pot, while the number of people arrested for pot possession continues to grow.

D. even though hundreds of thousands of people every year are arrested for marijuana possession, most do not go to jail.

Supporting Details

_____ 4. Which of the following statements was **not** true of the author's youth?

A. He gave up smoking pot before he gave up smoking cigarettes.

B. He often smoked pot with his friends.

C. He successfully hid his pot smoking from his father.

D. He agreed with his dad that smoking cigarettes was harmful.

_____ 5. During the administration of President Nixon, a special commission concluded that
   A. nearly half of the drug arrests in the United States were for pot.
   B. punitive marijuana laws are more harmful to society than the drug itself.
   C. only people involved in serious drug trafficking should go to jail for possessing marijuana.
   D. punitive marijuana laws have little effect on people's behavior.

Inferences

_____ 6. On the basis of paragraphs 1–10, we can infer that
   A. the author frequently lied to his father.
   B. the author's father would have been even more furious to learn that his son was smoking pot.
   C. the author's father considered smoking marijuana less harmful than smoking tobacco.
   D. the author did not believe the surgeon general's warnings about cigarettes.

_____ 7. In paragraphs 17–19, the author suggests that
   A. although people can still function while high, they don't function nearly as well.
   B. there are negative health consequences to smoking marijuana.
   C. some of the author's friends still smoke marijuana.
   D. all of the above.

Argument

_____ 8. Which of the following statements does **not** support the following point?

Point: We ought to repeal laws against marijuana possession.

   A. Police use pot possession as an excuse to harass blacks and Latinos.
   B. None of the people the author smoked pot with as a kid turned into heroin or cocaine addicts.
   C. Inhaling pot is at least as harmful as smoking cigarettes.
   D. A government study concluded that punitive marijuana laws cause more harm than the drug itself.

The Writer's Craft

_____ 9. The author begins his essay with
   A. shifting to the opposite.
   B. going from broad to narrow.
   C. a brief story.
   D. a series of questions.

_____10. The author's primary purpose in this selection is to
   A. inform readers that smoking marijuana is not nearly as dangerous as it is made out to be.
   B. persuade readers that we should decriminalize marijuana possession.
   C. persuade readers that we need to pay more attention to alcohol abuse and less attention to marijuana abuse.
   D. entertain readers with examples of the silly things that pot smokers say and do.

Discussion Questions

1. Before reading this essay, were you in favor of the legalization of marijuana, or were you opposed to it? Did the essay change your thinking in any way?

2. One of the criticisms of marijuana is that it is a "gateway drug"—in other words, its use leads to later experiments with harder, more harmful drugs. Do you agree with the statement that using marijuana leads to other forms of drug abuse? Why or why not?

3. Bowden writes, "I believe today that alcohol is a far greater public health and safety threat than marijuana. Tobacco, also legal, is an even greater curse." Given the dangers posed by alcohol and tobacco, should these substances be made illegal? Why or why not?

4. The author confesses that for him, "getting high was a symptom of boredom and rebellion." Do you think this is the main reason young people smoke pot, or might there be other reasons? What are some other behaviors in which bored, rebellious youngsters engage?

Paragraph Assignments

1. Bowden begins his essay with the story of an encounter between him and his father, on a night when he came home stoned. Most people know the feeling of coming home, as teens or young adults, and finding an

angry parent (or other family member) waiting to confront them about a problem. Write a paragraph about such an experience in your own life. Use dialog to make the encounter vividly alive.

Here is one student's response to the assignment:

> The angriest I've ever seen my dad was during my Christmas break this year when I came home from a party at four in the morning. When I was a senior in high school, I always had to be home by midnight. But since I'm now in college, I just figured that that rule no longer applies, even though I'm still living at home. I mean, I'm an adult, right? Wrong! My dad met me at the door with his hand out. "Give me your keys. You're grounded for the rest of the month," he said loudly. His eyes were bloodshot, and his voice shook with anger. "What!?" I sputtered. "You can't—" My dad cut me off mid-sentence. "Oh yes I can, and I will. Don't you **dare** tell me what I can or can't do in my house," he bellowed, inches from my face. My dad is usually pretty mild-mannered, so I knew I was in big trouble. In a lame attempt to defend myself, I just said, "I lost track of time. My watch is broken." My dad calmed down over the next few days. I don't think it was a coincidence, however, that I got a new watch for Christmas.

2. Bowden writes that "when something as widespread as pot possession is illegal, police can use it as an excuse to harass whole classes of otherwise law-abiding citizens." When police do something like this, it is considered an abuse of the power they have. Technically, they have the legal right to arrest anyone for possession of marijuana, but targeting blacks and Latinos is unfair. Have you ever witnessed someone in a position of power being unfair or rude? Write a paragraph describing what happened.

Essay Assignments

1. Like marijuana, there are many things that are illegal in the United States—or parts of the United States— that some people feel should be legalized. These range from the right to keep chickens in your backyard, to being able to drink at 18, to allowing same-sex marriage. Similarly, there are quite a few things that are legal that some people feel should be *illegal*. Some examples include assault weapons, the death penalty, talking on cell phones while driving, and even high caffeine energy drinks like Red Bull. Write an essay in which you argue that something

that is illegal should be legal or vice versa. Your thesis should be similar to one of the following:

- Even though _____ is illegal, I feel it should be legal for three reasons.

- Even though _____ is legal, I feel it should be illegal for three reasons.

The body of your essay, then, will present your three reasons.

2. Bowden clearly presents several ways he was concerned his life would be negatively affected if he continued to smoke pot: his job would suffer, his family might be in danger, and his health would deteriorate. Have you ever known, or do you know, someone who grew up but was never able to kick a habit of drugs or alcohol that started during his or her teen years? How is that person's addiction affecting his or her life? Write an essay about the person you know or have known. Present and detail three ways that addiction is hurting that individual's life. Consider such things as opportunities that may have been wasted, money spent on drugs/alcohol, relationships harmed, health affected, legal problems, and so on.

Check Your Performance   **MARIJUANA TODAY**

Activity	Number Right	Points	Score
Vocabulary Check (3 items)	_____	x 10 =	_____
Reading Check			
Central Point and Main Ideas (3 items)	_____	x 7 =	_____
Supporting Details (2 items)	_____	x 7 =	_____
Inferences (2 items)	_____	x 7 =	_____
Argument (1 item)	_____	x 7 =	_____
The Writer's Craft (2 items)	_____	x 7 =	_____
		TOTAL SCORE =	_____%

Enter your total score into the **Performance Chart: Fifteen Reading Selections** on the inside back cover.

13 The Bitter Truth about Sugar

Emily Carlin

Preview

The fact that America is getting fatter is beyond dispute. Since the early 1980s, we have been growing steadily heavier; more than 75 percent of adults and one-third of our children are now overweight if not obese. Many serious illnesses are linked to being overweight, and the rates of those diseases are skyrocketing. What in the world has happened to us in the last few decades? This article identifies a major culprit and explains how it has been quietly added to our food supply in shocking quantities.

Words to Watch

ostracism (3): exclusion

endocrinologist (12): a doctor who specializes in treating disorders of the endocrine system, such as diabetes. The endocrine system is a collection of glands that secrete hormones directly into the bloodstream.

triglycerides (18): a type of fat found in the blood

hankering (25): craving

diminished (25): gotten smaller

scoffed at (41): made fun of

subsidies (45): money paid by the government to support certain businesses

perimeter (49): border

abhorrent (50): distasteful

calibrated (50): adjusted

unprecedentedly (51): never before known or experienced

explicit (56): fully and clearly expressed

1   You hear it all the time. Americans are slobs. *Fat* slobs.

2   We have no self-control, no will power. We know if we ate less and exercised more, we could be lean and healthy, but it's just too hard to do that. We're eating ourselves into all kinds of awful diseases and early graves because we're undisciplined and lazy and we just don't care.

3   We know that being obese makes us targets of bullying and social ostracism° as children and costs us workplace promotions as adults. And still, we keep choosing to be fat.

4   We're puzzled, it's true, that our

ancestors didn't suffer from obesity and diabetes at anything close to the rate we do. It's odd that small children—even newborn babies—are fatter than ever. Even our pets are heavier than they were a generation ago. Still, everyone says that being fat and unhealthy is our personal responsibility. It's our fault alone that we've gotten to this point, and we should hang our heads in shame.

5   Right?

6   Most people—overweight ones included—would say "Yes." They'll tell you in a second that obese individuals are at fault because they eat too much and don't exercise enough. Through the poor choices they've made in diet and lifestyle, they've "chosen" to be this way.

7   They're wrong.

8   Personal choice is only part of a larger puzzle. We American consumers are unwitting participants in a huge and deadly experiment run by the corporate food industry. We are rats released in the clean, well-lighted laboratory of the modern-day supermarket, where we fill our shopping carts with a thousand varieties of attractively packaged, deceptively labeled poison. As the food processing industry grows ever richer, and our government passively looks on, we are testing how much sugar the human body can absorb before it is irreversibly damaged.

Let's Talk about Sugar

9   We've always known that too much sugar isn't good for us. Sweet desserts make us fat; sugary drinks rot our teeth.

10   But the truth about the sugar in our foods today is much more complicated—and deadlier—than a matter of a few extra pounds and some cavities.

11   To start, we need to define what we mean by "sugar." For the purposes of this discussion, we'll talk primarily about *fructose*, the super-sweet molecule that is part of all caloric sweeteners. Fructose aliases include cane sugar, beet sugar, organic turbinado sugar, high fructose corn syrup (HFCS), honey, maple syrup, agave syrup, molasses, or any of the other *forty-plus names for sugar* that show up on food labels.

12   Why focus on fructose? In the words of Robert Lustig, M.D., a pediatric endocrinologist° and author of the 2012 book *Fat Chance: Beating the Odds Against Sugar, Processed Food, Obesity, and Disease*, fructose is "the Voldemort of the dietary hit list," the nutritional equivalent of the lethal super-villain in the Harry Potter series.

13   Here's a simplified overview of some of the ways fructose affects our bodies:

14   Unlike other nutrients, which are broken down and used by various parts of the body (such as the pancreas, the digestive tract, the muscles, and the brain), fructose goes straight to the liver. When we consume a large amount of fructose, as we usually do, the liver is overwhelmed. Unable to gradually process all that fructose, it turns it into liver fat.

15   A fatty liver, in turn:

16   ● Is at risk for developing cirrhosis (a potentially fatal disease usually

associated with alcoholism), liver scarring, and even liver cancer.

17 • Causes *insulin resistance*. Insulin is the hormone that regulates the amount of sugar in the blood. When the cells in a person's body become insulin resistant, they stop responding normally to this important hormone. The result is Type 2 diabetes—the kind that used to be called "adult onset" diabetes, but which is now epidemic among children. People with Type 2 diabetes have abnormally high blood sugar. Their condition can lead to heart attacks, strokes, blindness, kidney failure, and poor circulation, resulting in amputation.

18 • Releases fats into the bloodstream as triglycerides°, which are associated with "bad cholesterol" and increased risk of heart disease.

19 And there's more. When we eat naturally occurring sugar—say, in the form of a banana—that sugar contains not only fructose, but also the less-sweet molecule of *glucose*. Once in our bodies, glucose has two important functions. First, it stimulates the production of insulin, the hormone that regulates our blood sugar and fat storage. Second, it triggers the production of another hormone called *leptin*. Leptin tells our brains that we're no longer hungry and should stop eating. In short, insulin and leptin are essential for normal fat storage and appetite control.

20 Fructose, on the other hand, does neither of these things. You already know that fructose contributes to insulin resistance. But it has another insidious effect: it actually *blocks* leptin from reaching the brain. Without leptin, the brain never gets the message, "Stop eating." We never feel satisfied. We just keep eating.

21 So the problem with fructose is not only that it provides what are commonly called "empty calories": it *actively damages our health*. It contributes to diabetes, obesity, and heart disease. It interferes with our brain's ability to know when we're full. It is no exaggeration to say that it is toxic.

Our Hard-Wired Sweet Tooth

22 Now, none of this would be a problem if we didn't love sugar so much. But we do. We're hard-wired for it.

23 Initially, our taste for sugar was a blessing, not a curse. Sweetness was nature's way of telling our ancestors that a food was safe to eat. In nature, there are no sweet foods that are poisonous.

24 In addition, we craved sugar because we needed the extra fat it quickly provided. Our ancestors had to work hard for every bite they consumed. Whether they were hunters or harvesters, they expended a lot of energy just staying alive. For a brief time every year when fruit was in season, they gorged themselves on it. Those sweet calories gave their bodies the extra fat needed to survive demanding life stages like puberty, pregnancy, and nursing.

25 Unfortunately for us, our hankering° for sweets hasn't diminished° since our ancestors' day—even though our

activity levels certainly have. And now, sugary foods are available 24/7, not only during a brief harvest season. In fact, to say that sugar-packed foods are "available" to us is a little like saying oxygen is "available." We're practically swimming in the stuff.

26   In the average supermarket, about 80 percent of the packaged foods available to consumers include added sugar. And the worst part is that so much of it is hidden.

27   The manufacturers of those foods get very indignant at the idea of "hidden sugars." "The labels are right there," they say. "All the shoppers have to do is read them."

The Tangled Web of Nutritional Labels

28   But reading nutritional labels is easier said than done. Let's look at one such label. This is from Kellogg's Honey Smacks cereal. (It used to be called "Sugar Smacks." Kellogg's P.R. people apparently decided that "honey" sounded healthier than "sugar.")

29   One of the first things you might notice about the Honey Smacks nutritional label is that while it lists the percentage provided of the recommended daily value (RDV) of fat, sodium, cholesterol, potassium, and carbohydrates, it does not list an RDV for sugar. That's because the Food and Drug Administration (FDA) has not set any such value. Despite all the evidence that excessive consumption of sugar significantly contributes to widespread, chronic disease among Americans, the FDA consistently submits to

pressure from food industry lobbyists and declines to set a recommended maximum daily level.

30   The American Heart Association (AHA), however, has been bolder. It recommends that adult women consume no more than 5 teaspoons of added sugar a day (about 20 grams); adult men 9 teaspoons (about 36 grams), and children 3 teaspoons (about 12 grams). In contrast, surveys have shown that the average American consumes 22.2 teaspoons (almost 90 grams) of added sugar a day. More than half that sugar is in the form of sodas and other beverages.

31   Secondly, you'll notice that while "sugar" is listed as the first ingredient in Honey Smacks—meaning that the cereal contains more sugar than any other ingredient—the ingredients also

include "dextrose" and "honey." Those two ingredients are sugar in slightly different forms.

32   Third, you will see that in every ¾-cup serving of Honey Smacks (and most kids consume much more than that amount in a sitting), there are 15 grams of sugar—that's more than 3½ teaspoons of sugar per serving. This already exceeds the AHA's maximum daily sugar allowance for children, and we haven't even left the breakfast table yet. (By comparison, a Krispy Kreme glazed donut contains less than that— 10 grams of sugar.)

33   Now, Honey Smacks is an easy target of criticism. It is consistently ranked as one of the unhealthiest cereals on the market. By weight, Honey Smacks is *more than 55 percent sugar*. But many other foods that are widely considered "good for you" are equally surprising, once you look beyond the attractive packaging.

34   Take yogurt, for instance. Yogurt is generally thought of as "health food." And before the processed-food industry got hold of it, it was. A six-ounce Greek yogurt with no added sweeteners contains 16 grams of sugar. That sugar is lactose, the sugar that occurs naturally in milk. Unless you're lactose-intolerant, lactose is no problem. But compare that serving of Greek yogurt to a six-ounce serving of Yoplait, a yogurt brand very popular with children. The Yoplait contains 27 grams of sugar—that's 11 grams, or 2.75 teaspoons, more than the Greek yogurt.

35   Nowhere on the Yoplait label does it explain that there is any difference between the 16 grams of naturally occurring sugar and 11 grams of added sugar. Food labels don't have to provide that information. When the FDA has requested such labeling, the food processors have responded that revealing the amount of "added sugar" would be the same thing as giving away their recipes, and their competitors could copy their formulas. Again, the FDA gave in to the food industry and backed off implementing requirements for sugar. So the only way you and I can figure out how much added sugar is in a processed food is to do the kind of supermarket detective work described above—hardly something most American consumers have the time or the know-how to accomplish.

36   And so, when a well-meaning dad gives a child a container of Yoplait, believing it to be a wholesome snack, he is giving her a serving of yogurt *plus as much sugar as is in eight ounces of Coca-Cola.*

The Sugar-Industrial Complex

37   In the face of all this—as the rates of obesity, diabetes, heart disease, hypertension, and other diet-related health problems reach devastating levels in the U.S. and beyond, and the evidence piles ever higher that the sugar in our diet is largely to blame— you might reasonably ask, "What are we going to do about this?"

38   And if you do, the processed-food industry will confidently answer, "Not a darn thing."

39   There *was* one remarkable attempt to tackle the question from the inside. In

the spring of 1999, a secret meeting was held in Minneapolis, at the headquarters of the Pillsbury Company. The attendees included top executives from industry giants Nestlé, Kraft, Nabisco, General Mills, Procter & Gamble, Coca-Cola, and Mars. The meeting and its aftermath are described in a 2013 Pulitzer Prize-winning book, *Salt Sugar Fat: How the Food Giants Hooked Us*, by journalist Michael Moss.

40   At the meeting, two top Pillsbury executives laid out the facts: how Americans were growing ever fatter and unhealthier; how advertising aimed at children encouraged exactly the opposite of good eating habits; and how the ever-growing availability of convenient, cheap, super-sized processed foods packed with sugar, salt, and fat were contributing to this state of affairs. The executives even compared their industry's role in damaging Americans' health with the role of the tobacco industry. These executives made it plain: We're harming children's health, they told the assembled giant food companies. We're doing it knowingly. We need to be more responsible. Let's talk about working together, as an industry, to make processed foods healthier.

41   They were shot down, instantly. The head of General Mills led the charge. He scoffed at° the idea that the industry shared any part of the blame for America's health crisis. We just give shoppers what they want, he said. It's up to them to choose whether or not to buy it.

42   And so business went on as usual. Only for the food industry, "business as usual" becomes more sophisticated with each passing year. It takes advantage of every technological breakthrough to better understand not only what consumers want, but also how to make them want *more* of it. Companies use brain scans that reveal that a hefty dose of sugar makes our brains light up exactly the way that cocaine does. They've discovered that the sweeter they make their breakfast cereals, the sweeter kids want their cereals to be. Like lab animals, children are easily trained to crave ever-higher amounts of sugar. In fact, there is a whole host of evidence that suggests that sugar is actually addictive, just like alcohol (which is derived from fermented sugar).

43   And knowing all this, the food industry is loading its products ever more heavily with sugar. It does this for the most understandable of reasons. It's making tons of money. And much of that profit is connected to its use of high fructose corn syrup (HFCS).

44   It does all this not only without interference from our government, but with its enthusiastic cooperation. It is estimated that members of Congress spend five hours of each day meeting with professional lobbyists (people whose job it is to persuade lawmakers to favor their cause). Many of the mostly successful and highly paid lobbyists are employed by the food industry. As a result of their work, our government permits   absurd,   health-damaging

actions such as allowing food stamps to be used to purchase sodas and classifying HFCS as "safe."

The Sweet Success of High Fructose Corn Syrup

45   In recent years, HFCS has become the sweetener of choice for the food industry. While sugar derived from sugar cane has become increasingly expensive, due in part to hurricanes in the Caribbean that damaged the cane crop, the cost of corn has plummeted, thanks to government subsidies° to farmers. As a result, the food industry has turned enthusiastically to cheap HFCS, which is now the most commonly used sweetener in the United State. And "most commonly used" hardly does it justice—it's *everywhere*.

46   HFCS is like a gift from heaven for the industry. It's 75 percent sweeter than cane sugar. Not only is it cheap, and not only does it sweeten food, but it causes baked goods to turn an appetizing color *and* increases the shelf life of processed foods. (In order to make foods last a long time, food processors not only add HFCS but also routinely strip their products of fiber, further increasing their health-damaging qualities. But that's an appalling subject for another day). The average American eats *42 pounds* of HFCS a year.

47   Because it is so cheap, and because the food processors understand so well consumers' insatiable hunger for (and possibly even addiction to) sweets, HFCS is turning up in the most unlikely places. You'd expect heavy doses of sweeteners in candies, cookies, and other dessert-like foods, but a quick label-reading supermarket tour reveals HFCS's presence in barbecue sauce, baby's crackers, ketchup, lemonade, dog food, stuffing mix, juice boxes, frozen entrées, salad dressings, hamburger buns, macaroni and cheese, frozen pizza . . . the list goes on and on. And the name? *High Fructose* Corn Syrup? That should give you a clue about its effects on our bodies. It is to diabetes and obesity what fertilizer is to a garden.

Where Do We Go From Here?

So here are a few final thoughts.   48

1. Yes, it would be beneficial for   49 people with obesity-related health problems to exercise more and eat less. Particularly, it would benefit them to concentrate their shopping on the perimeter° of the supermarket, where the roughly 20 percent of the supermarket's foods that are unprocessed (fresh fruits, vegetables, meats, fish) reside. In addition, it would benefit us all to learn to cook from-scratch meals that utilize whole grains and unprocessed fruits and vegetables.

2. The kind of changes needed to   50 bring about #1 will require time, effort, and education. We've been raised in a culture that values convenience above all things. Many of us don't know how to cook. The idea of giving up our Lunchables and Velveeta Shells & Cheese, our Coca-Cola and Froot Loops is abhorrent°. And why wouldn't it be? We've grown up watching nearly

5,000 food ads a year, each scientifically calibrated° to appeal to our youthful appetites.

51   But think about this. If a foreign enemy were sneaking a substance into our food that caused skyrocketing rates of diabetes, heart disease, obesity, and hypertension, creating an unprecedentedly° huge public health crisis that would tax our medical system to its utmost and had the potential to cripple our economy, would we expect our government to do something in response?

52   Why does the American food industry get a free pass when it is—quite openly—doing the same thing?

53   Government regulation of dangerous substances is not a new thing. Our government has played a role in regulating the distribution of two other toxic substances: alcohol and tobacco. It has acknowledged that depending upon "personal responsibility" is not an adequate response for substances that can inflict such serious social damage.

54   It is time for the government to step up to the plate in a similar way regarding sugar. It should take a variety of steps, including the following:

55   • Limit the amount of sugar added to processed foods.

56   • Require explicit°, easily understood labeling on processed foods, showing their natural *and* added sugar content.

57   • Impose sugar taxes to raise the costs of highly sweetened foods.

58   • Ban advertisements of sugary foods aimed at children.

59   • Ban the use of HFCS.

60   The idea that we've "chosen" to become a sick, obese society is a cynical lie, happily promoted by the processed-food industry. "Freedom of choice" and "personal responsibility" are meaningless concepts when our food environment has been dramatically manipulated—some might say *poisoned*—and the government has turned a blind eye. For the sake of generations to come, we must educate ourselves about the sugar-coated toxins in our foods and demand action.

First Impressions

Freewrite for ten minutes on one of the following.

1. Did you enjoy reading this selection? Why or why not?

2. Did any of the facts or statistics in this article surprise you? Which ones?

3. Will you make any changes in your own shopping and eating habits after reading this article? Why or why not?

Vocabulary Check

_____ 1. In the excerpt below, the word *insidious* means
   A. harmful.
   B. unreal.
   C. positive.
   D. calming.

   "You already know that fructose contributes to insulin resistance. But it has another insidious effect: it actually *blocks* leptin from reaching the brain. Without leptin, the brain never gets the message, 'Stop eating.'" (Paragraph 20)

_____ 2. In the excerpt below, the word *implementing* means
   A. preventing.
   B. putting into effect.
   C. advertising.
   D. explaining.

   "When the FDA has requested such labeling, the food processors have responded that . . . their competitors could copy their formulas. Again, the FDA gave in to the food industry and backed off implementing requirements for sugar." (Paragraph 35)

_____ 3. In the sentence below, the word *insatiable* means
   A. irregular.
   B. decreasing.
   C. easily satisfied.
   D. unable to be satisfied.

   "Because it is so cheap, and because the food processors understand so well consumers' insatiable hunger for (and possibly even addiction to) sweets, HFCS is turning up in the most unlikely places." (Paragraph 47)

Reading Check

Central Point and Main Ideas

_____ 1. Which sentence best expresses the central point of the selection?
   A. Many Americans are overweight because they eat too much and don't exercise enough, but these are not the only reasons.
   B. Although high fructose corn syrup is found in many foods, consuming large amounts of it is harmful to one's health.
   C. The food processing industry is harming our health by getting us addicted to foods that contain too much added sugar.
   D. Because of the influence of professional lobbyists, our government has done little to regulate the food processing industry.

_____ 2. The main idea of paragraph 45 is found in its
   A. first sentence.
   B. second sentence.
   C. third sentence.
   D. last sentence.

Supporting Details

_____ 3. Brain scans reveal that a large dose of sugar has the same effect on the brain as
   A. a glass of wine.
   B. smoking a cigarette.
   C. cocaine.
   D. a cup of coffee.

_____ 4. Which of the following is **not** a reason that the food industry adds HFCS to foods?
   A. It is both cheaper and sweeter than cane sugar.
   B. It is more easily digested than cane sugar.
   C. It makes baked goods look more appetizing.
   D. It increases the shelf life of processed foods.

Inferences

_____ 5. The implied main idea of paragraphs 22–27 is that
   A. our ancestors needed to consume sugary foods to survive demanding life stages like puberty, pregnancy, and nursing, but we don't.
   B. manufacturers of processed foods are taking advantage of our hard-wired craving for sugar by adding sugar to packaged foods.
   C. although our craving for sweets hasn't diminished, we don't need to consume them as much as we used to.
   D. most of the packaged foods available to consumers include added sugar.

_____ 6. The fact that there are forty-plus names for fructose that show up on food labels suggests that
   A. most American consumers have become very knowledgeable about different types of sugar.
   B. it can be difficult for American consumers to know just how much sugar they are consuming.
   C. the U.S. government strictly regulates the amount of each type of sugar that processed foods contain.
   D. all of the above.

_____ 7. The selection suggests that
   A. it's healthier to eat bananas and other naturally sweet fruits than processed foods containing high fructose corn syrup.
   B. everyone should gradually reduce their consumption of sugary foods to zero.
   C. people who consume high fructose corn syrup will definitely develop Type 2 diabetes.
   D. all of the above.

Argument

8. Label the point of the following argument with a **P** and the three statements of support with an **S**.

   ____ A. The processed-food industry puts HFCS in products that don't need to be sweetened in order to increase consumer demand for these products.

   ____ B. The processed-food industry adds sugar to already sweet products such as yogurt.

   ____ C. The processed-food industry has contributed to high levels of obesity and diabetes among the American public.

   ____ D. The processed-food industry has been training children to crave ever higher amounts of sugar.

The Writer's Craft

_____ 9. Which of the following best describes how the writer introduces this selection?

     A. She makes a broad statement that narrows down to a specific point.

     B. She introduces an idea that is the opposite of the point of the selection.

     C. She asks a series of challenging questions.

     D. She provides an anecdote that illustrates the point of the story.

_____ 10. Which of the following statements best describes the writer's purpose?

     A. To inform overweight people that being overweight is not entirely their fault.

     B. To entertain readers with outrageous examples of the many ways that food manufacturers sneak sugar into processed foods.

     C. To persuade readers to push the government to regulate how much added sugar goes into processed foods and to ban the use of HFCS.

     D. To criticize American consumers for not taking the time to learn just how much added sugar goes into processed foods.

Discussion Questions

1. Do you have any idea how much sugar you consume on an average day? Do you suspect the amount is higher than is good for you? What are some ways you would be willing to lower your sugar intake?

2. According to the head of General Mills, the processed-food industry bears no responsibility for damaging Americans' health because it is "simply giving shoppers what they want." Do you agree with his opinion? Why or why not? Cite evidence from the selection to support your response.

3. The author makes several suggestions to consumers—including encouraging them to shop the perimeter of supermarkets and to learn to cook from-scratch meals using natural ingredients. Do you think the people you know would be willing to change their shopping and eating habits in response to these recommendations? Would you? Why or why not?

4. Given the power of the food industry, do you think it's likely that the government will ever regulate sugar in the same way it regulates tobacco and alcohol? What steps would have to be taken to make such regulation occur? Would you be willing to take part in such an effort? Explain.

Paragraph Assignments

1. How did your family eat as you were growing up? Were there lots of fast food and processed foods? Were soda and fruit punch in the refrigerator? Or did you eat fresh vegetables, whole grains, and fresh fruit? Write a paragraph in which you describe your family's diet. Then add whether this is a diet you want to stick with in your own life, or if there are changes you'd like to make.

2. At the end of the essay, Carlin concludes that not only has our food environment been dangerously manipulated, but the government has refused to deal with this crisis. She also explains that many government officials are persuaded to ignore the problem by highly paid lobbyists who work for the food industry. Essentially, then, the government has put money and politics ahead of the best interests of American citizens.

   Can you think of another instance or issue where the government has refused to do the right thing? Write a paragraph about this situation. Your paragraph can focus on either something that the federal government has ignored or something disregarded by your local or state government.

Essay Assignments

1. Carlin writes, "We've been raised in a culture that values convenience above all things." Most Americans do seem to prefer doing everything as quickly and painlessly as possible. Some might argue that conveniences such as drive-through restaurants or microwave ovens or instant foods are beneficial because they free up time for more important things. On the other hand, others might argue that our reliance on convenience makes us lazy.

   Write an essay that supports one of the following thesis statements:

   ● Increasing our dependence on modern conveniences may be harmful at times.

   or

   ● Modern conveniences are good things that benefit us.

   In the body of your essay, present three examples of modern conveniences that help support your thesis. In each paragraph, describe how these conveniences are either beneficial or detrimental to society.

2. Today, the majority of Americans are overweight, and one in three is obese (weighing 20 percent more than normal body weight standards). Although hidden and unhealthy sugar in the foods we eat clearly adds to our nation's weight problem, it is obviously not entirely to blame. Carlin points out other factors that can lead to weight gain: too much

food, too little exercise, and unwillingness or inability to cook—things that "require time, effort, and education."

Think about your own health. Whether or not you're overweight, what are three things you could change or work on in your life to improve your health and/or weight? Then write an essay that presents your three ideas for improving your health/weight. Your thesis could be something similar to this: "My health would definitely be better if I paid more attention to three specific areas of my life."

Here is one student's response to the assignment:

I'll admit it—I'm not exactly the healthiest person I know. It's not like I stay up all night partying or hang out in freezing weather without a coat on, but I am guilty of ignoring most of the sensible advice out there for staying healthy. As a result, I get sick a few times a year, and I don't feel all that great a lot of the time. And though it's hard for me to admit, I'm beginning to look a little out of shape, too. It's probably time for me to stop being lazy about my physical well-being. There are at least three specific things I could do to improve my health.

It would require some focused effort on my part, but I know I should get at least a few hours of exercise a week. It shouldn't really be that hard, right? After all, we're talking about less than 30 minutes a day. My problem has always been that I associate exercise with pain and agony. But the fact is, I actually like walking my dog, Mr. Bones, around the neighborhood in the evening when I take the time to do it. And that's exercise! Typically I just let him out in the backyard to run around. But I think I can bear to miss one stupid reality TV show and walk around the block a couple times instead. I'm sure Mr. Bones would appreciate it, too.

And I might have to do a little learning and listening, but I'm sure I'd feel better if I had a better understanding of which foods are healthy and which ones are not. Of course, I'm aware of the fact that the half-gallon of peanut butter ice cream that I eat every week is really not a good idea. But I tend to think of "healthy" food as being something like rabbit food or birdseed—not filling and definitely not tasty. However, whenever my girlfriend makes dinner for us, it's always incredible even though she's a total health-food freak. When she talks about which foods are healthiest and how to prepare them, I usually tune her out with a yawn. But I think I'll start listening to her and try learning something. Like Mr. Bones, I'm sure she'd appreciate it too.

Finally, I really need to set aside some time every single day to just relax and clear my head. I'm not quite ready to commit to bubble baths, but just sitting still without any interference from my phone or the TV or computer or friends would be helpful. Sometimes, my head is still so busy and buzzing from the day that I can't turn it off at night and go to sleep. And when I don't sleep, I feel terrible the next day. I read recently that one of my favorite football players meditates every evening for 20 minutes in order to relax. I never thought of meditation as something an NFL offensive lineman would do! Maybe I should try it. Twenty minutes isn't too much time to sacrifice, and I'm sure my brain would appreciate it.

When it comes to looking after my health, there are definitely a few things I could do to make sure I'm looking after it a little more closely. Because I can be a bit lazy, I'm sometimes reluctant to put forth extra effort, learn something new, or give up any of my free time. However, as time goes by and I continue to refuse to make changes, I find myself getting a little fatter, a little more prone to illness, and a little more stressed out. That's no way to live. As they say, there's no time like the present. And I'm ready to move forward into healthier times.

Check Your Performance   THE BITTER TRUTH ABOUT SUGAR

Activity	Number Right	Points	Score
Vocabulary Check (3 items)	_____	x 10 =	_____
Reading Check			
Central Point and Main Ideas (2 items)	_____	x 7 =	_____
Supporting Details (2 items)	_____	x 7 =	_____
Inferences (3 items)	_____	x 7 =	_____
Argument (1 item)	_____	x 7 =	_____
The Writer's Craft (2 items)	_____	x 7 =	_____
		TOTAL SCORE =	_____%

Enter your total score into the **Performance Chart: Fifteen Reading Selections** on the inside back cover.

(14) Diamonds Aren't Forever

Ruth A. Rouff

Preview

"Mark and Lindsey are shopping for a ring!" It's a feature of nearly every American engagement—The Ring. And not just any ring, but a *diamond* ring. But why is a diamond ring so necessary? This essay reveals the not-so-romantic truth behind one of the most successful marketing campaigns in history.

Words to Watch

signify (5): symbolize; be a sign of
multi-faceted (6): on several levels; having many aspects
enlisted (6): requested the cooperation of
frugal (13): simple, plain, and costing little

1　It's no secret that we Americans are exposed to advertising virtually from the cradle to the grave. Aside from print advertising, the amount of time we spend watching TV commercials alone is staggering. One source estimated that by the time a person turns sixty, he or she will have "wasted" *three years* watching TV commercials.

2　Of course, advertisers and their clients don't think of their messages as a waste of time—far from it. They see them as serving the vital purpose of keeping us informed about important goods and services. But it's one thing to convince us to spend money on a particular brand of toothpaste or frozen dinner. It's quite another to manipulate us into feeling as if we must spend large sums of money on things we don't really *need* but have been told that we *should* want.

3　One surefire way advertisers get us to spend lots of money on nonessential items is to hit us where we are most vulnerable—not in the head, but in the heart. What they do is suggest that if we *truly* love a person, we will show it by how much we spend on him or her. And if that statement is true, then its opposite is also true. The less expensive the gift—well, you don't want those you love thinking you're *cheap*, do you?

4　The history of diamond engagement rings is a classic example of the way that advertisers play upon our emotions to stimulate demand for a particular product. As strange as it may now seem, giving diamond rings to symbolize engagement is a fairly recent custom. Oh, in the 1800s and earlier, European royalty exchanged diamond engagement rings, but Americans usually didn't. In fact, back in colonial times, the Puritans frowned upon jewelry and instead gave thimbles as a sign of commitment. The thimble was then used by the bride-to-be as she sewed her wedding clothes and linen. After the wedding, the thimble was cut to show that it was no longer needed. The rim of the thimble was then worn on the finger like a ring.

5   This charming custom gradually died out, along with Puritanism. By the middle of the 19th century, the practice of giving rings to signify° engagement became commonplace. These engagement rings were usually not diamonds—because diamonds were very rare. However, something happened in 1870 that would forever change the jewelry industry. Huge diamond mines were discovered in South Africa. Since diamonds were literally being scooped out of these mines by the ton, the price of the gems rapidly dropped. By the 1890s, inexpensive diamond engagement rings were well within the reach of many Americans. Mass-market retailers such as Sears and Roebuck began featuring modestly priced rings in their mail-order catalogs. In the late 1930s, the average price of a diamond engagement ring was only $80. This drop in price was not what the De Beers Company, which

had a monopoly on the South African diamond mines, wanted to see.

So in 1938, De Beers hired an 6 American advertising agency, N.W. Ayer, to boost diamond prices by changing American attitudes toward diamonds. They wanted to get the message across to young men that diamonds were a gift of love: the larger and finer the diamond, the greater the expression of love. Similarly, young women had to be encouraged to view diamonds as an essential part of romantic courtship. As if waging a great military campaign, N.W. Ayer used a multi-faceted° approach to promote the giving of costly diamond engagement rings:

- Movie stars were given diamonds to use as their symbols of undying love.

- Journalists were paid to write magazine stories that stressed the size of diamonds that celebrities presented to their loved ones. Glossy close-ups of ring-laden hands accompanied the stories.

- Speakers were sent around to high schools across the country to lecture students about diamond engagement rings.

- The British royal family was even enlisted° to wear diamonds rather than other jewels.

As Ayer explained in a 1948 company report, "We spread the word of diamonds worn by stars of screen and stage, by wives and daughters of political leaders, by any woman who can make the grocer's wife and the mechanic's sweetheart say 'I wish I had what she has.'"

7   But the masterstroke of the campaign was the slogan, "A Diamond Is Forever," which is now considered the most recognized advertising slogan of all time. The genius of the slogan was that since "diamonds are forever," they should never be resold. As a result, secondhand diamonds—which would have increased supply and lowered prices—never entered the market.

8   The ad campaign was amazingly successful. By 1941, the retail sale of diamonds had increased over 50%, and nearly everyone viewed a diamond ring as an essential part of an engagement.

9   These days, the price of diamond engagement rings continues to rise. In 2007, the average cost in the United States was $2,100. In 2011, the average cost of a jewelry-store diamond ring was between $3,500 and $4,000, with larger stones selling for even more. And, of course, the matching wedding band is extra.

10   Ironically, given the number of American marriages that end in divorce, a diamond may be forever, but marriages often aren't. The National Center for Health Statistics recently predicted that one-third of new marriages among younger people will end in divorce within 10 years and 43 percent within 15 years.

11   Despite such statistics, we will continue to think of Mother's Day, Valentine's Day, Christmas, anniversaries, and birthdays as days to reaffirm bonds of love. But in the cold, hard eyes of the jewelry industry, these days are golden marketing opportunities.

- "Every Kiss Begins with Kay," proclaims Kay Jewelers.
- "True love has a beginning but no ending," says a slogan on the Tiffany.com website.

The message is that if you *really* love your partner, you'll want to shower her (or him) with jewelry throughout her (or his) life.

12   But what if, after all that spending, true love *isn't* forever? Well, high-powered divorce lawyers now advertise in many of the same magazines that carry ads for jewelry.

13   If you're like most people, you're probably thinking, "But I still want a diamond engagement ring, just like the one my mother had." There's nothing wrong with that. After all, very few of us desire a totally frugal° lifestyle.

14   But keep in mind that advertisers are doing their best to pressure us into wanting what *they* think we should want. And remember, too: love can't be reduced to dollar signs.

15   If it could, the rich would never get divorced.

First Impressions

Freewrite for ten minutes on one of the following.

1. Did you enjoy reading this selection? Why or why not?

2. Do you think advertisers have done an effective job on selling the American public about the importance of diamonds?

3. The author points out that advertisers manipulate us into feeling that we should want certain things, even if we don't need them. What are some examples of non-essential products that are heavily advertised? How are we persuaded to want them?

Vocabulary Check

_____ 1. In the excerpt below, the word *virtually* means
   A. online.
   B. purely.
   C. unclearly.
   D. almost.

   "It's no secret that we Americans are exposed to advertising virtually from the cradle to the grave.... One source estimated that by the time a person turns sixty, he or she will have "wasted" *three years* watching TV commercials." (Paragraph 1)

_____ 2. In the excerpt below, the word *modestly* means
   A. moderately.
   B. well-behaved.
   C. highly.
   D. secretly.

   "By the 1890s, inexpensive diamond engagement rings were well within the reach of many Americans. Mass-market retailers such as Sears and Roebuck began featuring modestly priced rings in their mail-order catalogs." (Paragraph 5)

_____ 3. In the following excerpt, the word *masterstroke* means
   A. brilliant idea.
   B. major error.
   C. first step.
   D. ending.

> "But the masterstroke of the campaign was the slogan, 'A Diamond Is Forever,' which is now considered the most recognized advertising slogan of all time. The genius of the slogan was that since 'diamonds are forever,' they should never be resold." (Paragraph 7)

Reading Check

Central Point and Main Ideas

_____ 1. Which sentence best expresses the central point of the selection?
   A. Despite current beliefs, giving diamond rings to symbolize engagement is a fairly recent custom.
   B. In 1938, De Beers hired the N.W. Ayer advertising agency to change American attitudes toward diamonds.
   C. Given the number of American marriages that end in divorce, a diamond may be forever, but marriages often aren't.
   D. The history of diamond engagement rings is a classic example of the way that advertisers play upon our emotions to stimulate demand for a particular product.

_____ 2. Which sentence best expresses the main idea of paragraphs 5–6?
   A. After huge diamond mines were discovered in South Africa, the price of diamond engagement rings dropped.
   B. Because the price of diamonds dropped after diamond mines were discovered in South Africa, the De Beers Company hired an ad agency to promote the giving of costly diamonds.
   C. The American ad agency N.W. Ayer tried to convince young people to view diamonds as a gift of love.
   D. The De Beers Company, which had a monopoly on the South African diamond mines, was not happy to see the average price of a diamond engagement ring drop.

Supporting Details

_____ 3. Which of the following tactics was *not* employed as part of N.W. Ayer's campaign to promote the giving of costly diamond engagement rings?
A. Movie stars were photographed wearing diamonds.
B. Speakers lectured high-school students about diamond engagement rings.
C. The First Lady of the United States was photographed wearing an expensive diamond ring.
D. The slogan "A Diamond Is Forever" was created.

_____ 4. By 1941, the retail sale of diamonds had increased more than
A. 5%.
B. 15%.
C. 50%.
D. 100%.

Inferences

_____ 5. We can infer from paragraph 4 that the Puritans
A. preferred very large, expensive weddings.
B. placed more value on hard work and thrift that on displays of wealth.
C. had servants do much of their housework.
D. had small families.

_____ 6. We can conclude from this selection that
A. it is natural for most people to prefer diamonds to other precious stones.
B. diamonds are the rarest precious stones.
C. the demand for diamonds has been artificially stimulated.
D. people who purchase expensive diamond rings are less likely to divorce than those who do not.

_____ 7. We can infer from this selection that the author believes that
A. students of advertising should study the classic N.W. Ayer ad campaign for diamonds.
B. diamond engagement rings are no longer as popular as they once were.
C. jewelry companies have recently begun marketing jewelry as a sound investment, rather than as an expression of love.
D. divorce rates among the rich are lower than divorce rates for those who are not rich.

Argument

_____ 8. Three of the items below are supporting details for an argument. Write the letter of the statement that represents the point of this argument.
   A. By the 1890s, inexpensive diamond engagement rings were well within the reach of many Americans.
   B. Contrary to popular belief, diamonds have not always been costly.
   C. Retailers such as Sears and Roebuck began featuring modestly priced diamond engagement rings in their mail-order catalogs.
   D. In the late 1930s, the average price of a diamond engagement ring was only $80.

The Writer's Craft

_____ 9. The author's purpose in writing this selection is to
   A. criticize engaged couples for buying diamond rings.
   B. inform readers about the techniques used to promote the sale of diamond engagement rings.
   C. entertain readers with amusing stories about engagement customs.
   D. persuade jewelers to reduce the selling price of diamond engagement rings.

_____10. In paragraphs 8–9, the author
   A. lists specific facts and figures to show how successful the diamond engagement ring marketing campaign was.
   B. lists specific ways that the advertising agency promoted diamond engagement rings.
   C. explains the reasons why people like diamonds so much.
   D. contrasts the prices of diamond engagement rings and wedding bands.

Discussion Questions

1. As a result of reading this selection, has your attitude toward the giving of expensive jewelry changed, or stayed about the same? Explain.

2. The author describes advertisers who suggest that if we truly love a person, we will show it by spending lots of money on her or him. Do you agree that spending money on someone demonstrates love? Why or why not? Have you ever felt guilty or resentful about the amount of money you spent on a gift? Explain.

3. The author describes the Puritan practice of giving a thimble as a sign of commitment as a "charming custom." Do you agree with her? Why or

why not? Can you think of any religious groups today that frown upon jewelry? If so, what reasons do they give for doing so?

4. The author describes the N.W. Ayer campaign for De Beers as a classic example of the way advertisers play on our emotions to stimulate demand for a particular product. Can you think of some other examples of advertisements that manipulate our emotions? Do any of them use celebrities to convince us to buy their products? Explain.

Paragraph Assignments

1. Regardless of your gender or marital status, if you were to become engaged right now, would you want to give or receive a diamond engagement ring? Why or why not? Write a paragraph explaining your answer.

Here is one student's response to the assignment:

> I know that a big diamond engagement ring is supposed to be the ultimate sign of love and dedication, but there are at least a few reasons why I would not want one. To begin with, it seems like such an incredible waste of money. Today, the average price for a diamond ring is four thousand dollars! Are you kidding me? For that amount of money, my fiancé and I could spend two weeks in the Caribbean. Lifelong romantic memories trump a shiny stone on my hand any day. Secondly, the idea that a big gaudy ring means love is just a lot of marketing. My mom wears her grandmother's engagement ring on her right hand, and it's a simple silver band with a **very** small diamond. When I asked her why it was so plain, she told me that the whole "big diamond thing" began only about 60 years ago as a way for jewelers to sell more diamonds. So a big ring is not necessarily a sign of devotion—it's a sign that marketing works. Finally, I don't even really like diamonds! Who wants a clear colorless stone in a ring? If my fiancé insisted on buying me a ring, I'd ask for an amethyst. Then with the $3500 he'd save, we could start planning our romantic vacation right away.

2. Many holidays and special occasions have traditions connected with them—things that we're "supposed" to do, even if we don't really want to. Think of one such tradition you would like to see discontinued. Write a paragraph explaining your choice.

Essay Assignments

1. As the author notes, nearly half of all American marriages these days end in divorce. Write an essay in which you present three reasons in particular that you believe divorce is prevalent. To help you think knowledgeably about this subject, you may want to Google "reasons for divorce" and research some of the many opinions and theories expressed there. Be sure to include introductory and concluding paragraphs for your essay.

2. The diamond engagement ring is only one part of planning a wedding that many people accept as a necessity. Write an essay about three other customs that have become an expected part of an engagement or wedding. In your essay, discuss both the positive and the negative aspects of these customs. For example, you might want to write about some of the following:

   ● newspaper announcements
   ● "registering" for gifts the couple wants
   ● bridal showers
   ● bridesmaids' dresses
   ● elegant (but costly) white wedding gowns
   ● the bride's family paying for the wedding
   ● fancy invitations
   ● expensive entertainment
   ● seating arrangements at the reception

Check Your Performance   **DIAMONDS AREN'T FOREVER**

Activity	Number Right	Points	Score
Vocabulary Check (3 items)	_____	x 10 =	_____
Reading Check			
Central Point and Main Ideas (2 items)	_____	x 7 =	_____
Supporting Details (2 items)	_____	x 7 =	_____
Inferences (3 items)	_____	x 7 =	_____
Argument (1 item)	_____	x 7 =	_____
The Writer's Craft (2 items)	_____	x 7 =	_____
		TOTAL SCORE =	_____%

Enter your total score into the **Performance Chart: Fifteen Reading Selections** on the inside back cover.

Today's Jobs Crisis: What Students Need To Know

Donald Bertram

Preview

After years of hard work, you hope to have a certification or college degree. You may also have a sizable student loan waiting to be paid off. But you can also expect you'll have your pick of good jobs, right? Wrong. These days, finding a job in America is not an easy task, as Donald Bertram explains in the following selection.

Words to Watch

capital equipment (5): equipment that can be used to create wealth
Shangri-La (18): an imaginary paradise
bureaucracies (19): organizations that divide work into various departments
Spartan (19): basic; without frills
tenured (20): permanent
viable (28): practical
rhetoric (28): talk
credential (28): proof of ability
roiling (31): stirred up
commodities (32): things that are bought and sold
vying (32): competing

1　Finding a job in America may be more difficult than it has ever been before. What are the factors that make the job hunt so much more challenging today—and what must students do to increase their chances for employment? Above all, how can students avoid an all-too-common trap in today's economy: post-high-school study and significant debt, but no job to show for it?

Many Jobs Have Disappeared Forever

To begin with, students must 2 recognize a hard truth: Many jobs in America have disappeared forever. There is a well-known story about a meeting that President Barack Obama had with the late Steve Jobs of Apple Computer, America's most profitable corporation. Apple at one time boasted that its products were made in the United States. But now almost all of its millions of iPods, iPhones, iPads, and other products are manufactured overseas—benefiting *hundreds of thousands* of workers there. Why can't all that work making Apple products come home, Obama was said to have asked. Jobs's reply was unambiguous: "Those jobs aren't coming back," he said.

"I'm the only human that works here. The other 17,000 employees are computerized robots. Would you like to speak with C76-78X?"

3   The globalization of jobs is simply a reality of today. Many American companies, like Apple, have shipped their jobs overseas to places like China, India, and Latin America, where workers are willing to work for a fraction of the pay they would receive in the United States. Companies go overseas because they are increasingly owned by institutional investors who focus on the bottom line, rather than on what might be better, in the long run, for American workers. "American business is about maximizing shareholder value," says Allen Sinai, chief global economist at the research firm Decision Economics.

4   Once companies decided to set up manufacturing sites in other countries, with cheaper costs and higher profits, American manufacturing could not compete, and many blue-collar manufacturing jobs for the middle class disappeared. Thirty or forty years ago, the country had an abundance of low-skill, decent-paying manufacturing jobs in the automobile, steel, textile, furniture, apparel and electronics assembly industries, among others. Instead of going to college, a person could work in a factory and still enjoy a middle-class life with a house, a yearly vacation, and the chance to eat steak in a restaurant on a Saturday night. But those days are gone.

5   Relatedly, the manufacturing jobs that *do* remain in America have been reduced by automation, which has helped companies cut over 6 million jobs since 2000. As one executive said, "You basically don't want workers. You try to find capital equipment° to replace them." Today there are all kinds of factory robots that perform tasks that once gave people a living wage.

6   The rapid growth of computer-based technology has also eliminated many traditional jobs. Picture the 1960s advertising agency in the cable TV show *Mad Men*, and think about the abundance of people there who were hired to do jobs now handled electronically by small machines. Secretaries have been replaced by word processing, voice mail, e-mail and

scheduling software; accounting staff by Excel; people in the art department by desktop design programs. And today the need for workers of all kinds has been reduced by, for example, online banking, self-service checkouts at the supermarket, and the use of home computers or smartphones to do one-click ordering of food, clothing, shoes, health and beauty aids, books, music, movies, games, tools, and an endless range of sports, electronics, and automotive products.

7   Also cutting deeply into American jobs has been "outsourcing"— the transfer of many white-collar jobs to the much cheaper labor market overseas. Enabled by global computer networks, questions and problems that were once dealt with by workers in the U.S. are now answered by someone at a computer and phone station in India. The back-office operations of banks, investment houses, and insurance companies are increasingly handled by bright, talented people, hired at low wages, in countries halfway around the world. And many companies have or plan to set up white-collar operations in other countries. A case in point: Pharmaceutical giant Merck & Co. Inc., which operates a plant near Philadelphia, announced plans to invest $1.5 billion in research development in China—enough to build a facility large enough to house 600 employees, who will work on discovering new drugs, testing them, and getting regulatory approval. Global competition for jobs with people in other parts of the world is a reality that is likely to increase over time.

The Reduced Value of a College Degree

A second key factor in today's economy is that not only have many jobs disappeared, but a college degree no longer means what it once did. In the past, a student with a college diploma could walk out the college door, and companies would almost be waiting on the doorstep, ready to offer him or her an interesting white-collar job. Today, chances are that unless students have prepared themselves for jobs in marketable areas, there will be no one waiting on their doorstep except the lenders who have provided them with the loans needed to earn their degree. [8]

Here are a few all-too-typical stories; there are countless others just like them. [9]

1. Kelsey, 23, graduated from a university in Ohio with a degree in marketing and $120,000 in student debt. Unable to get a job in her major, she is now working two restaurant jobs and has given up her apartment to live with her parents. Her mother, who co-signed on the loans, took out a life insurance policy on her daughter. "If anything ever happened, God forbid, that is my debt also," said her mother. [10]

Kelsey didn't seem like a perfect financial fit for a school that costs nearly $50,000 a year. Her father and mother have modest incomes, and she has four sisters. But when she visited the school, she was won over by faculty and admissions staff members who urge students to pursue their dreams rather than obsess on the sticker price. "I was [11] an 18-year-old and they really sold me," Kelsey says. "But no one told me that when I would graduate, I'd owe like $900 a month."

12   **2.** Michael, 22, graduated in 2010 with a creative writing degree. Today he is making just above the minimum wage in his job as a barista, serving customers at a Seattle coffeehouse. In the beginning he sent three or four resumés a day, but employers questioned his lack of experience or the practical worth of his major, and he has lost his job-hunting momentum. He is fortunate in getting financial help from his parents to help pay off student loans.

13   **3.** Laura, 29, unemployed and with $100,000 in student debt, graduated with honors and two B.A.s, served in the Peace Corps, then graduated with a master's degree in public administration. Despite her accomplishments, she searches fruitlessly for work and lives on food stamps in South Philadelphia. At last count, she had applied for more than 250 jobs, from government service to boutique clerk to waitress. She talked about the blue-collar parents that have supported her along the way: "My parents' hopes are in me, and I feel I'm letting them down. My generation wants to succeed, and given the chance, we could shine. But so many things are holding us back."

14   **4.** Wanda makes $8.50 an hour working for an employment training center in Florida. She dropped out of a for-profit college after she ran out of money, even with the loans. She has stopped opening her student loan bills but thinks they now total over $90,000. She's a single mother who knows she cannot pay it. "She's worse off than when she started," an adviser says. "Debt with no degree."

15   **5.** "I always used to say that I couldn't wait to get out of here when I graduate and have a career instead of just a job," Reid, 24, says as he sweeps the grocery store aisles where he still works as what he calls a "glorified janitor." Reid graduated 18 months ago with a degree in corporate finance. He hasn't been able to find a job in investment banking or wealth management as he had hoped, and his student loans are over $50,000 and growing. After a year of fruitless job searching, Reid lowered his expectations. No one was hiring investment specialists, because far fewer people had money to invest. "So I changed my approach and expectations," Reid explains. Although he was overqualified, he began applying for low-paying positions at call centers. "But even with those," he says, "they were looking for older, more experienced, and even better qualified workers. That's how bad the job situation is."

16   **6.** Eric got a degree in history from the University of Pennsylvania, and he still owes $20,000 for his degree. He's applied for a least 100 jobs—"any job that looked like something I can do"— but nothing has developed. Now he's a chess tutor for elementary school kids. He believes he was misled: "The good schools project this image that

if you have our degree, it's a ticket to any job you want—which is obviously total B.S.," he says. "I don't think I was properly informed of the negative side to all this. And he adds: "If this is what it's like for people who go to the best colleges, how is it for everyone else?"

FIVE IMPORTANT "DON'TS"

17 **Given the loss of so many jobs in America, and the fact that a college degree no longer means what it once did, here are five guidelines that students should keep in mind:**

18 **1. Don't choose a college because you've fallen in love with it.** Parents and students often fall in love with pretty campuses. To compete for the parent dollar, education experts say, college officials have long believed that they must manufacture nothing short of Shangri-La° University: heaven on earth, with cable and Internet. Health facilities, major athletic complexes, libraries, speedy Internet service—an entire society is replicated. "On the college tour," says one student advisor, "they don't take you to the philosophy department. They show you the gym." The appealing extras cost money, and all too often schools pass along those costs to incoming students in the form of ever-increasing tuition.

19 Listen to the advice of Barmak Nassirian, associate executive director of the American Association of Collegiate Registrars and Admissions Officers in Washington. Too many students, he says, don't understand that when they go to college, they're entering places of business, not cathedrals on a hill: "A lot of schools have stopped being anything but self-sustaining bureaucracies°." His advice: **"Pick a more Spartan° school near home, and commute."**

20 **2. Don't assume a college will give you important advice about either career prospects or student debt.** Some schools are responsible in educating students about today's job challenges. But as one expert has said, "Many colleges are just trying to fill seats. Warm bodies in classrooms help pay for the comfortable salaries of tenured° faculty and administrative personnel. They present school as an opportunity, but it reaches a point where they're just taking people's money. As a result, students leave school with serious debt and without a marketable degree."

21 Carl Van Horn, direction of the John J. Heldrich Center for Workforce Development at Rutgers University, is one of an increasing number of voices saying that colleges need to do better to prepare their students for today's changed labor market. Van Horn says, "Colleges have a moral responsibility to educate students about job prospects, but few offer anything other than advice to start a job search six weeks before graduation."

22 Today's reality is that a college degree itself is no ticket to success. About 50 percent of college graduates are working in jobs that don't require a bachelor's degree, according to economist Paul Harrington of Drexel University. Students in four-year

colleges, he says, don't give sufficient thought to how their majors connect to jobs in the real world.

23   As for student debt, the Obama administration has tried to make college pricing easier to understand. Colleges and universities are now required to post calculators on their Web sites that explain the net tuition price after grants and loans, but critics say the calculators can be confusing, misleading or hard to find. And the administration has proposed that colleges be required to offer a "shopping sheet" to make it easier for families to measure the true costs and benefits. "We just have to get them much more information," said Education Secretary Arne Duncan. "If you're going to college, you need to know not what the first year costs. You need to know what it's going to cost for the long haul." One student advisor has said, "When a college suggests that students take out $5,000 in loans, I wish they'd put 5,000 one-dollar bills on a table in front of them and explain that debt will follow them for life. Then maybe they could see just what they're getting into." Nassirian adds that lenders have been only too happy to work with schools. "What's better than owning a piece of a student for life?"

24   **In light of the above, an important rule of thumb is to not get into major debt.** Regard any student loan for more than $2,500 a year as a danger to your future. Like mortgages lugged around for life, student loans can follow you to the grave and can't be discharged in bankruptcy. Lenders can legally collect on those loans by attaching money from your wages and even from your social security.

25   **3. Don't start college unless you're reasonably sure you can finish.** The one thing worse than student debt is student debt without a diploma. Only about 40 percent of all four-year college students who start school ever complete it, and among community college students, just 1 in 5 earns an associate's degree within three years. Students drop out due to family demands and the need to find some kind of work. As a result, the United States has the highest college dropout rate in the industrialized world. The danger of dropping out is especially high for children of low-income families.

26   **4. Don't go to a for-profit school.** (To see a list of such schools, Google "for-profit schools" or go to **http:// en.wikipedia.org/wiki/List_of_for-profit_universities_and_colleges**.) Students at for-profit schools often complain that they were misled about educational costs and that their job prospects were exaggerated. Many for-profit institutions have a track record of very high tuitions—sometimes twice that of nonprofit schools—and low graduation rates. Government reports and lawsuits have accused some for-profit colleges of outright fraud, including doctoring attendance records or peddling near-worthless degrees. Never go to a for-profit school without checking first to see if there is a comparable program offered at a nearby community college.

27   **5. Don't assume that you will need a college degree. Instead, you may want to get a certification or some other postsecondary training in a growing career field.** Former Labor Secretary Robert Reich says, "Too many families cling to the mythology that their child can be a success only if he or she has a college degree." Such an assumption poorly serves candidates who might be better off taking career-related courses, attending a vocational-training school, or learning about other ways to enter the work force.

28   A report called *Pathways to Prosperity* recently released by Harvard University states, in some of the strongest terms yet, that a "college for all" emphasis may actually harm many American students—keeping them from having a smooth transition from adolescence to adulthood and a viable° career. The Harvard report concludes: "The American system for preparing young people to lead productive and prosperous lives as adults is clearly badly broken." It is a system that doesn't do a good job showing students the link between their learning and the jobs to which they aspire. The college-for-all rhetoric° should be broadened to become "post-high-school credential° for all."

29   And writing recently in *The Atlantic*, Jordan Weissman adds: "When there were fewer graduates, a generic college degree used to be a valuable credential. Now that the market is flooded, diplomas count less, and specific skills count more. This means that, in many instances, associate's and technical degrees may be more financially valuable than a liberal-arts degree. After all, some of the fastest growing job categories are expected to be in so-called 'middle-skill' positions such as nursing, which do not require a full, four-year education. It's one more sign that, for people seeking to fix America's employment picture, 'college for all' is the wrong mantra. We need to be talking about 'skills for all' instead."

30   Other voices express a similar conclusion: One unemployed college graduate observed, "I was raised to think that what you needed was a college degree," he said. "That's not the game anymore. It's what you major in." And an employment adviser comments: "Our current college system doesn't work. You get a degree but wind up in a high-school labor market job you could have had before college. But now you're worse off because you have all the debt you incurred getting that college degree." And an education researcher concludes: "The mainstream American approach to education is obsolete. The solution to today's problems starts with education—specifically, work-linked education, the teaching of particular skills to do a particular job. We should not be emphasizing college but career training."

Two Important "Do's"

31   **1. Do pursue some kind of post-high-school skills development.** In today's economy, job applicants with only high-school diplomas are among the worst off; just three out of 10 can expect to make $35,000 a year or more

in their lifetimes, predicts Georgetown University economist Jeff Strohl. One education reporter has said that in today's world facing the future even with a postsecondary degree "is like being a lifeboat in a roiling° sea," but "facing the future with a high-school degree is like being in the water."

32   And writes Adam Davidson in the *New York Times*: "Though it's no guarantee, a B.A. or some kind of technical training is at least a prerequisite for a decent salary. It's hard to see any great future for high-school dropouts or high-school graduates with no technical skills. They most often get jobs that require little judgment and minimal training, like stocking shelves, cooking burgers, and cleaning offices. Employers generally see these unskilled workers as commodities°—one is as good as any other—and thus each worker has very little bargaining power, especially now that unions are weaker. There are about 40 million of these low-skilled people in our work force. They're vying° for jobs that are likely to earn near the minimum wage with few or no benefits, and they have a high chance of being laid off many times in a career. . . . The rest of us, meanwhile, should go to school, learn some skills and prepare for a rocky road."

33   It's worth noting that most community colleges remain a bargain—a way to make postsecondary education affordable. Average tuition is often about $3,000 a year, compared to a four-year school costing tens of thousands more. And a student can save thousands more by commuting to a community college close to home.

2. Do sail your own ship in looking for a job. The Harvard report *Pathways to Prosperity* notes that much so-called career counseling is inadequate and nonexistent, with counselors lacking the expertise needed for quality career guidance in today's world. For that reason, you need to take charge of the fact that *it's up to you* to research career and job possibilities. Some students lack street smarts, and they just drift passively and blindly with the tide, not looking or planning ahead for the challenges and dangers that await. Don't be a patsy; your life is in your hands—no one else's.

Here's what you should start to do: Educate yourself about what all the adults in your life do to make a living. Educate yourself about the kinds of jobs that are available in the region of the country where you live. Educate yourself about the strongest jobs possibilities by visiting the *Occupational Outlook Handbook* (**www.bls.gov/ooh/**)—the government website that lists the strongest job possibilities for today. (Right now the fastest growing occupations up to 2020 are projected to be personal care aides, home health aides, masonry, carpenter and plumber helpers, veterinary technicians, physical and occupational therapy assistants, meeting and event planners, interpreters and translators, medical secretaries, and family therapists.) Use the Internet to educate yourself as well about how to prepare a good resumé and a good cover letter when applying for jobs, as well as how to handle a job interview.

36 And, in general, keep in mind that the U.S. economy is one that has shifted from the production of vital goods to a service-based collection of jobs. Ask yourself, "What kind of service-providing job can I prepare for?" For example, one of the largest growth fields in the country today is health care. If your funds are severely limited, consider earning a certificate as a personal care aide or home health aide; chances are that certificate will quickly get you a job with a regular paycheck you can use to gradually take courses in a promising career direction.

Final Thoughts

Knowledge is power. To secure a 37 meaningful job, you must first understand the challenges in today's economy. The first challenge is that many jobs have disappeared, and the second is that a college degree no longer leads to a job in the way it once did. With these facts in mind, apply the "don'ts" and "do's" presented here. Then proceed one careful step at a time in exploring directions you feel will have the best chance of opening job doors. Remember it's up to you to make the search for a good job a primary and ongoing goal in your life. I wish you success.

First Impressions

Freewrite for ten minutes on one of the following:

1. Did you enjoy reading this selection? Why or why not?

2. Did any of the facts or statistics in this article surprise you? Which ones?

3. In the selection, the author gives a series of "don'ts" and "do's" for today's students. Which piece of advice would you be most likely to follow? Why?

Vocabulary Check

_____ 1. In the excerpt below, the word *unambiguous* means
A. promising.
B. clever.
C. straightforward.
D. indirect.

> "Why can't all that work making Apple products come home, Obama was said to have asked. Jobs's reply was unambiguous: 'Those jobs aren't coming back,' he said." (Paragraph 2)

_____ 2. In the excerpt below, the word *generic* means
A. general.
B. specific.
C. competitive.
D. technical.

> "When there were fewer graduates, a generic college degree used to be a valuable credential. Now that the market is flooded, diplomas count less, and specific skills count more." (Paragraph 29)

_____ 3. In the sentence below, the word *incurred* means
A. reduced.
B. benefited from.
C. brought on yourself.
D. recycled.

> "But now you're worse off because you have all the debt you incurred getting that college degree." (Paragraph 30)

Reading Check

Central Point and Main Ideas

_____ 1. Which sentence best expresses the central point of the entire selection?
A. Globalization, automation, and outsourcing are the reasons why it is now difficult for many Americans to get good-paying jobs.
B. Because many American jobs have disappeared, students need to pursue some kind of post-high-school education that will provide them with marketable skills.
C. There are ways that today's students can avoid falling into the trap of becoming unemployed or under-employed.
D. Because they have failed to prepare themselves for the current job market, about 50% of college graduates are working in jobs that don't require a college degree.

_____ 2. The implied main idea of paragraphs 8–16 is that
A. today it's common for young college graduates to be deeply in debt and unemployed or underemployed.
B. many young American college graduates are deeply in debt due to the high cost of their college education.
C. today a college degree is worthless.
D. many of today's recent college graduates are surprised that they have to work so hard to obtain even low-paying jobs.

Supporting Details

_____ 3. According to the selection, the reason so many American jobs are now performed overseas is that workers in China, India, and Latin America
A. tend to work harder than Americans.
B. are willing to work for lower wages than American workers.
C. are, on average, better educated than American workers.
D. all of the above.

_____ 4. According to Education Secretary Arne Duncan,
A. not all students need to acquire a post-high-school education.
B. students need to know what college will cost for the long haul.
C. it is only important for students to know what the first year of college will cost.
D. students should avoid taking out any loans to pay for their college education.

_____ 5. According to Bertram, students should **_not_**
A. expect that their college will prepare them for today's job market.
B. automatically think that they need a four-year college degree.
C. enroll at a for-profit school when a community college offers a comparable program.
D. all of the above.

Inferences

_____ 6. From paragraphs 2–7, we can infer that
A. Steve Jobs was afraid to tell President Obama the truth about who built Apple products.
B. American workers are not skilled enough to be able to produce iPods, iPhones, iPads, and other Apple products.
C. many American businesses have no loyalty to American workers.
D. forty years ago, most Americans who earned a decent salary were college graduates.

_____ 7. On the basis of paragraphs 18–19, we can infer that
   A. most colleges are not interested in educating students.
   B. like other businesses, colleges need to make money to survive.
   C. colleges with the most up-to-date facilities provide the best education.
   D. all of the above.

_____ 8. We can infer from paragraph 23 that
   A. $5,000 is a lot of money to most recent college graduates.
   B. lenders are only too happy to get students into debt.
   C. many young people have no idea how much their college degrees will cost them.
   D. all of the above.

The Writer's Craft

_____ 9. The section "Many Jobs Have Disappeared Forever" (paragraphs 2–7)
   A. compares American businesses with businesses in China, India, and Latin America.
   B. presents a series of steps in the process of closing manufacturing sites in the United States and opening them in other countries.
   C. contrasts American attitudes toward competition with foreign attitudes toward competition.
   D. lists reasons why there are fewer American jobs than there used to be, and why these jobs are not coming back.

_____ 10. The author's purpose in writing this selection is to
   A. persuade students that they are better off simply getting a high-school diploma rather than going into debt to get a post-secondary credential.
   B. inform students that it is no longer necessary for them to get a college diploma.
   C. persuade students that they need to acquire the kind of education that will provide them with skills that are in demand in today's globalized economy.
   D. entertain readers with stories about foolish young people who have majored in impractical subjects and gone deeply into debt.

Discussion Questions

1. Has reading this selection changed your thinking about your educational and/or career goals? If so, in what ways?

2. According to paragraph 3 of the selection, institutional investors focus on the "bottom line" rather than what might be better for American workers in the long run. Do you think American companies have a duty to keep jobs in the United States? Why or why not?

3. In paragraph 25, Bertram states that "the one thing worse than student debt is student debt without a diploma." Do you know of anyone who started college but failed to finish? If so, why did this person fail to finish? Does he or she plan to go back?

4. Do you know how much it will cost you to obtain a post-secondary education? Do you know how soon you will have to start paying back any loans you take out? How might you find out this information?

Paragraph Assignments

1. Bertram presents a series of "don'ts" and "do's" to today's students. Of all the guidelines he gives, which do you think is the most significant? Write a paragraph that explains your reason for choosing this guideline. Be sure to explain what impact following it might have on a student's future college and career plans.

2. In the selection, Bertram recommends educating yourself about what the adults in your life do to make a living. Take his advice and speak with one or more people you know regarding what they do for a living. Be sure to ask how and why they got into this field, and whether or not they are satisfied with what they are currently doing. After you have these conversations, write a paragraph summing up what you've learned by talking with these people.

Essay Assignments

1. Imagine that you have completed your post-secondary education and that you now have skills for which there is a steady demand. Write a cover letter for a job that you would like to have. In your cover letter, describe the personal qualities and educational background that would make you an ideal candidate for the job. Look at some sample cover letters on the Internet to get an idea of the proper format for such a letter.

Here is one student's response to the assignment (which, as you'll see, appropriately involves a series of short paragraphs):

Kathryn Deakin
11 Berry Drive
Marlton, NJ 08091
856.870.9385
kathy2013@gmail.com

October 30, 2013

David N. Frost, M.D.
Attn. Office Manager
181 W. White Horse Pike, Suite 100
Berlin, NJ 08009

To Whom It May Concern:

I am a certified Medical Assistant who is seeking a position in a doctor's office near my home in West Berlin, New Jersey.

I've accumulated some significant work and life experience in the years since I graduated from Eastern Regional High School. As my enclosed resume indicates, I worked in responsible positions for several years at McDonald's, Wawa, and Virtua Hospital.

Along the way, I realized that the food-service industry was not what I wanted to do—because I missed feeling that I was making a difference in my everyday work. Fortunately, during my time at Virtua, I got to know a number of medical assistants, and their experience inspired me to study for a certification in that area.

After enrollment in a full-time medical assistant program at Camden County College, I served an externship at Family Practice Associates in Washington Township. There I had the satisfaction of connecting with patients in meaningful ways as I performed a number of medical assistant duties. After completing the externship, I took and passed the certification exam as a medical assistant.

I could probably secure a job as a medical assistant at a hospital. But because my externship experience was so positive, my dream is to work in a doctor's office. I am confident I will bring competence, responsibility, a friendly manner, and a strong work ethic to the position I secure.

I'll plan to give you a call next week to see that you received my letter. I'm available for an interview, and I believe you would find me worthy of consideration.

Sincerely,

Kathryn Deakin

Kathryn Deakin

2. Bertram states that because so much career counseling is inadequate and nonexistent, it's up to you to research career and job possibilities. Take a few minutes and brainstorm a list of careers and/or jobs that you are interested in. Then pick three items from this list and research three of them on the Internet, using such resources as the *Occupational Outlook Handbook* (**www.bls.gov/ooh/**) and others. Afterward, write an essay that, in your own words, presents the results of your research. Your thesis statement might be similar to one of the following:

  ● According to my research, three strong job possibilities in my region of the country are _____, _____, and _____.

or

  ● According to my research, there is a strong demand for _____ and _____, but not for _____.

Following an introductory paragraph, the body of your essay should describe in detail what the occupational outlook is for each career, what the salary is for each career, and what a person would need to do to prepare for each career. You might conclude your essay by stating which career would be the best of the three choices, and why.

Check Your Performance

TODAY'S JOBS CRISIS: WHAT STUDENTS NEED TO KNOW

Activity	Number Right	Points	Score
Vocabulary Check (3 items)	_____	x 10 =	_____
Reading Check			
Central Point and Main Ideas (2 items)	_____	x 7 =	_____
Supporting Details (3 items)	_____	x 7 =	_____
Inferences (3 items)	_____	x 7 =	_____
The Writer's Craft (2 items)	_____	x 7 =	_____
		TOTAL SCORE =	_____%

Enter your total score into the **Performance Chart: Fifteen Reading Selections** on the inside back cover.

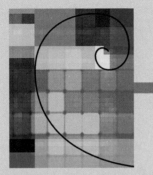

Part Three

Writing a Research Paper with Sources

Writing a Research Paper with Sources

For some papers that you write, you can develop your point simply by drawing upon your personal knowledge and experience. For other papers, you will want to support your point by using outside sources as well. Most often, those outside sources will be in the form of books and articles.

The best source for books will be a school or local library or an online book site such as Amazon or Barnes and Noble. (At both sites, you can often order an inexpensive used copy of a given book title.) The best source for articles, as pointed out on pages 279–280, is simply going online and using the research engine Google (**www.google.com**). For example, if you Googled the general topic of "hunger in America," you would find *more than 200 million articles*! Just looking at several of those articles could help you begin to think about how to narrow down and limit the topic. As you will see in the model paper that follows, one student decided to focus her paper on the reasons we should end hunger in America.

Two Cautions about Using Outside Sources

1 As mentioned on page 280, never for a moment believe that "If it's on the Internet, it must be true." Technology today allows anyone to publish anything at any time. For any given article that you find, you must clearly identify its author or source. Moreover, that author or source should be a *knowledgeable, qualified, and reliable authority* for the data presented. Look at the credentials cited and use your common sense to make sure you are getting legitimate examples, solid facts and/or statistics, and expert opinion.

2 When you are writing your paper, you must take care not *to plagiarize*—that is, to use another author's words and ideas as your own. If you cite another author's words, enclose those words in quotation marks and indicate the source. If you cite another author's ideas, indicate the source. The model paper that follows will show you how to document another person's or source's words or ideas. By using citations, you demonstrate that your work has been carefully researched. See the "Guide to Documentation" on pages 459–460.

A Model Research Paper with Sources

On first page: student's name, instructor's name, course and date submitted (written with date before month)

Double-space; leave 1″ margin on all four sides

Tilson 1

Last name and page number on every page, 1/2″ from top of page

Emily Tilson

Dr. Somers

English 112

31 March 2014

An Argument for Ending Hunger in America

Title (centered)

It is estimated that there are nearly 50 million people in our country who struggle with not having enough nutritious food to eat (Pringle 14). That's one out of every six people. Many Americans find it hard to believe that hunger could possibly exist on such a large scale in one of the richest countries on earth. However, while our hunger problem is often ignored or swept under the rug as something of a national embarrassment, it continues to grow. Not only is this unacceptable; it is also unnecessary. Hunger is a real and devastating problem in the United States, and there are compelling reasons for working toward putting an end to it.

In-text citation

To begin with, child hunger leads to serious health issues. In America, nearly 25 percent of children under the age of six live in households where there is some form of "food insecurity" (Pringle 25). The definition of *food insecurity* can range from a lack of healthy food to a complete absence of food, meaning a child might not eat for an entire day or longer. In early childhood, a child who is poorly fed is not only hungry—he or she will be sick more often, suffer from sadness and lethargy, and may develop problems such as speech and vision impairment. A school-aged child who is poorly fed misses up to 75 percent more school days due to illness than a healthy child and is far more likely to misbehave. Furthermore, a teen that is poorly fed is more likely to suffer depression, commit suicide, and become involved in violent crime than a healthily-fed teen (Berg 49). And it doesn't take an entire childhood of poor nutrition to cause these problems. A child that has gone hungry *only once* is two and a half times more likely to have health and

Tilson 2

emotional problems that could last a decade or longer (Park). Today, this means the physical and emotional well-being of nearly 17 million children in our country is at risk.

In addition, strange as it may sound, our country's obesity epidemic is directly linked to widespread food insecurity. When people do not have access to nutritious food, they can still be hungry and malnourished, even if they are very overweight. Poor people purchase cheaper food, and cheap food very often means unhealthy food high in fat, sodium, and empty calories. The situation isn't helped by the fact that since 1980, the price of fruits and vegetables has risen significantly while the price of desserts, snacks, and sodas has gone down. Poorer people do not necessarily make "poor food choices"—often, there is no other choice. Making matters worse, approximately 13 million people live in what are known as "food deserts," low-income areas that have no stores nearby that carry healthy food. In some of the poorest parts of Mississippi, for example, over 70 percent of people live 30 miles or more from a grocery store (Pringle 46). The majority of these people cannot afford or are unable to travel to stores that have healthy food. Instead, they eat what is available nearby—typically fast and fatty processed food. And the resulting obesity leads to numerous health problems such as high blood pressure, diabetes, and heart disease. Think this doesn't affect you? Think again. Obesity now costs our country up to $2,000 more a year per person in health care expenses (Mayo).

Another convincing reason for working toward ending hunger in America is less obvious than health concerns—we should end hunger because *we can*. How do we know we can? Because we've done it before. Between 1969 and 1979, thanks to the quick development of federal programs such as food stamps and free school meals, hunger all but disappeared in our country (Berg 75). However, that forward progress ended abruptly in the 1980s. During Ronald Reagan's presidency, federal funding for the poor was drastically slashed, and, thirty years later, hunger has returned with a vengeance. Today, the average federal nutrition assistance payment per person is $130 a month—barely $1.50 per meal (SNAP). No wonder so many people are suffering. It is estimated that if funding for federal nutrition assistance programs were increased by only 20 percent, it would cut national hunger in half. At 40 percent, hunger would be entirely eliminated (Berg 256). However, considering that the United States spent an astounding $660 billion on defense in 2012 and less than $18 billion on child nutrition programs, it is clear that focusing on tackling hunger is not a top priority (Final). Meanwhile, other countries have successfully tackled national hunger problems that were far worse than the current problems in the United States. In Ghana, West Africa, for example, the percentage of the population that was undernourished fell from *64 to 12 percent* in fewer than 20 years (Curtis). If Ghana, an exceedingly poor country, was able to tackle its hunger crisis, we should be able to do the same. That we continue to disregard hunger when it's a problem that can definitely be solved is both shameful and embarrassing.

Of course, the most obvious reason for why we should eliminate hunger in America is simply because it's the right thing to do. Many Americans support ending hunger for various reasons. Some approach it from a stance of fairness and equality. It just isn't right that so many millions of people should be sick and tormented because of malnutrition when America has more than enough healthy food available. In fact, worldwide, there is enough food on our planet for every person to have 4.3 pounds of healthy food every day (Lappe 8). Clearly, as the seventh richest country on Earth, America has plenty of resources. It is astoundingly unfair for so many millions of our citizens to suffer. Others look at hunger from a faith-based angle. Isaiah 58:10 says, "If you pour yourself out for the hungry and satisfy the desire of the afflicted, then shall your light rise in the darkness and your gloom be as the noonday." Shouldn't it be natural for caring human beings to want to "pour themselves out for the hungry"? Many people may assume that our government will take care of the hungry much in the same way it takes care of other national problems. But as former president Bill Clinton points out, "Hunger is not

Tilson 4

just a problem for politicians. We all have an ethical and moral obligation to help people who are suffering" (McGovern vii). Finally, some look at our growing hunger crisis and feel a sense of outrage and incredulousness. How can this even be happening here? How is it possible that we are *allowing* it to happen? "If another country was doing this to our kids, we would be at war," Academy Award winner and spokesperson for the *No Kid Hungry* campaign, Jeff Bridges, recently commented in the 2013 film *A Place at the Table*.

There are those, however, who do not support a movement to put an end to hunger in the United States. Some people do not believe there even is a hunger crisis. Many Americans associate hunger with horrific images of starving children in famine-stricken countries. They believe that if our children don't look like those children, they must not really be in danger. However, years of poor nutrition force millions of American children to "face a slow and steady starvation rather than sudden famine," according to a 2011 *ABC World News* report (Avila). Because this kind of starvation is not as visually dramatic, some people refuse to believe it is happening. Still others believe that those who claim to need help are simply lazy freeloaders who are intent on taking advantage of the welfare system. To begin with, the vast majority of people receiving food assistance receive no other form of government help, and many are reluctant or embarrassed to accept even that small amount of financial assistance. Furthermore, 41 percent of people on food stamps work one or more jobs, and more than 61 percent of those who receive help receive it for less than a year. Finally, over 80 percent of those receiving food stamps use the financial assistance to feed a child, an elderly person, or someone who is disabled (Berg 87). And there's not exactly a whole lot of freeloading going on when the average payment per person per meal is $1.50.

In summary, we need to recognize and address the ever-growing hunger problem in the United States. The health of millions of children is at serious risk. And obesity, affecting both children and adults, is directly linked to food insecurity. Furthermore, our country has the resources and ability to wipe out hunger, and it should go without question that it is our moral responsibility to help those in need. Many people feel that increasing funding for federal nutrition assistance would be too costly. However, consider this: The current generation of children is predicted to be the first ever in the history of United States to have a life expectancy shorter than its predecessor (Levine). Hunger is a significant factor in this prediction. Continuing to ignore hunger in America would be, without a doubt, far more costly.

Sources, listed in
alphabetical order
and double-spaced

Works Cited

Avila, Jim. "Hunger and Children in America: A Slow and Steady Starvation." *ABC World News Tonight*. American Broadcasting Company, 17 Aug. 2011. Web. 28 Mar. 2014.

Berg, Joel. *All You Can Eat: How Hungry Is America?* New York: Seven Stories Press, 2008. Print.

Curtis, Mark. "Country Successes in Reducing Hunger." *ActionAid: USA*. n.p. 11 Nov. 2011. Web. 28 Mar. 2014.

"Final Monthly Treasury Statement for Fiscal Year 2012." *Financial Management Service*. United States Department of Treasury, 30 Sep. 2012. Web. 28 Mar. 2014.

Lappe, Frances Moore, et al. *World Hunger: Twelve Myths*. New York: Grove Press, 1998. Print.

Levine, Susan, and Rob Stein. "Obesity Threatens a Generation." *The Washington Post*. The Washington Post Company, 17 May 2008. Web. 28 Mar. 2014.

"Mayo Clinic Study: Obesity Outweighs Smoking in Employer Health Cost." *Mayo Clinic Health System*. 1 May 2012. Web. 28 Mar. 2014.

McGovern, George, Bob Dole, and Donald Messer. *Ending Hunger Now*. Minneapolis: Fortress Press, 2005. Print.

Park, Alice. "Study: Effects of Childhood Hunger Last for Decades." *Time*. Time Incorporated, 2 Aug. 2010. Web. 28 Mar. 2014.

Pringle, Peter, ed. *A Place at the Table*. New York: Public Affairs, 2013. Print.

"SNAP (Food Stamps): Facts, Myths, and Realities." *Feeding America*, n.p. n.d. Web. 28 Mar. 2014.

Formatting and Documentation

If asked to do so by your instructor, you can use the Modern Language Association (MLA) formatting and documentation style. This is the style Emily used for her research paper.

General Formatting Guidelines

When you put together a formal research paper, there is a specific format that you should follow. Unless your instructor indicates that you should use alternative formatting, the following guidelines apply:

- To begin with, use good quality 8-1/2-inch × 11-inch paper when printing out your research paper.

- Make sure the margins on each page are set to 1 inch on all sides. The only exception to the 1-inch margin is the author's last name/page number in the upper right-hand corner of each page ("Tilson 1" on the student paper example). Your last name and the page number should be set 1/2 inch from the top of every page of your paper, including your Works Cited page.

- Double-space your entire paper, including the Works Cited page.

The first page of your paper will differ from the rest of your paper in these ways:

- In the upper left-hand corner, you will list your name, the name of your instructor, the name of your course, and the date you are turning your paper in. Note that the date is written like this: 31 March 2014. As before, double-space these lines.

- After the date, skip a line, and center the title of your paper on the page. Do not use all capital letters, italics, quotation marks, or boldface in your title. Also, do not underline the title or put a period at the end of it.

- Double-space again between your title and the first line of your paper. Remember to indent the first line of each paragraph.

In-text Citations

Whenever you quote someone or present information that is not widely known, like statistics, new ideas, and facts, you must credit the source of that information. An in-text citation is simply an easy way for the reader to refer to your Works Cited page to see the source you've used. Typically, you will present two types of in-text citations:

● When you have used information from ***printed material*** (a book or magazine, as opposed to a Web site), you will place the author or editor's last name and the page number where the information was found inside parentheses following the information.

    For example, the very first sentence of the student essay contains an in-text citation for a book. The author or editor's last name is Pringle, and the information was found on page 14. Now look at the Works Cited page. Peter Pringle is the editor of a book titled *A Place at the Table*.

● When you have used information from a ***Web site***, you will simply put the author's last name inside parentheses with no page number, since there are typically no numbered pages on Web sites. If the information you use is from an online source that shows no author, put the first word of the title of the article/story inside the parentheses instead.

    For example, look at the in-text citation for "Park" near the end of the second paragraph in Emily Tilson's paper. Referring to the Works Cited page, you can see that Alice Park is the author of an article about childhood hunger at the Web site for *Time*. Then, at the end of the third paragraph, you will see "Mayo" as an in-text citation. Here, no author's name is given on the Mayo Clinic's Web site, so the first word of the article is used instead.

Remember to put your in-text citations at the very end of the sentence that contains the cited material. Also, put the period outside the parentheses.

A Guide to Documentation

When to Cite a Source

When exactly should you cite a source? As previously mentioned, any time you present quoted material, or facts and statistics that are not well known, you should cite your source. However, sometimes the definition of what is "not well known" can get a little confusing. For example, think about the Civil War. It is widely known that many thousands of soldiers died. You would not need to back that fact up with a cited source. However, if you wrote, "It is estimated that 620,000 soldiers died in the Civil War," you would need to cite your source. Perhaps a Civil War buff might know that specific statistic, but in general, most people would not.

    But what about a fact like "General Robert E. Lee was initially reluctant to lead the Confederate Army"? That's a fairly well known fact, but there are certainly many people who might be surprised to read that. Should you cite your source or not?

    Your best bet is to use a citation whenever you present information that is new and/or surprising to *you*, or when you're unsure whether or not you should cite a source. You may risk having a few more citations than you need, but that's better than risking plagiarism. Still, you want to use common sense and not cite a source for everything in your paper. For example, you may have forgotten that the Civil War lasted from 1861 to 1865, but that is not a new or widely unknown fact. And remember that the whole point of using research in your paper is to back up *your* ideas and point of view. The last thing you want to do is just string together pages of statistics and other people's ideas.

The Works Cited Page

The Works Cited page is the final page of your paper, and it provides all the information needed to verify your sources. There are very specific guidelines when it comes to formatting your Works Cited list, and some students find the details a bit overwhelming and tedious. However, once you've worked through the first few entries, you'll get the general hang of it.

General Guidelines

- Center "Works Cited" at the top of a new page. Even if there is nearly a full page left at the end of your paper, do not begin the Works Cited list on that page.

- Determine whether you are citing a book or a Web site, and follow the specific guidelines (below) for each entry.

- Arrange your entries in alphabetical order. As discussed, you will use either the author's last name or, if there is no author listed, the first word of the title of the article/story you have cited.

  > *Note:* Use the first *main* word of the title. If the title begins with an article (*the, an, a*), do not list it by that word. For example, "The Problem of Childhood Hunger" would be alphabetically listed by the word "Problem." This is also the word you would use for your in-text citation.

- Double-space everything on the page. Do not add extra spaces between entries. If an entry takes more than one line, indent the second line one-half inch by spacing or by hitting the "tab" key on your keyboard.

Specific Entry Guidelines

Web site entries

For an example, look at the first entry on the Works Cited page of Emily's paper:

Avila, Jim. "Hunger and Children in America: A Slow and Steady Starvation."

ABC World News Tonight. American Broadcasting Company, 17 Aug. 2011.

Web. 28 Mar. 2014.

In this case, the source is a story from the Web site for *ABC World News Tonight*. The format for most Web site sources is as follows:

- Type the author's last name first, then a comma, and then the first name. Follow this with a period.

- Next, type the title of the article/story, followed by a period, and put quotation marks before the title and after the period.

- This will be followed by the name of the Web site. Type this in italics, followed by a period.

- Next, provide the name of the publisher. Often, you can find the publishing information near the bottom of the home page of a Web site. Type the publisher's name, and follow it with a comma.

- The date the story/article was written follows the comma. Place a period after the date. Remember that the date is written like this: 31 Mar. 2014. Note that in the Works Cited section, you will abbreviate the month.

- Next, indicate that this source is from the Internet by typing "Web" followed by a period.

- Finally, add the date that you accessed this story on the Web site. Because Web sites change and are updated so frequently, it's important to indicate when you visited the site.

Of course, sometimes not all of the information required is available. If no author is listed, simply begin with the title of the article/story. Sometimes there is no publishing information available, and other times no date is given for when the article was written. In these cases, you will put "n.p." for "no publisher" and "n.d." for "no date." In the final entry of Emily's Works Cited page, for example, there is no listed author. Additionally, there is neither a publisher nor a date:

"SNAP (Food Stamps): Facts, Myths, and Realities." *Feeding America,*

n.p. n.d. Web. 28 Mar. 2013.

Book Entries

Book entries tend to be a little less involved than Web site entries since books don't change. The second entry on the Works Cited page of Emily's paper is for a book:

> Berg, Joel. *All You Can Eat: How Hungry Is America?* New York: Seven Stories
> Press, 2008. Print.

The format for books is as follows:

● Type the author's last name, then a comma, then the first name. Follow this with a period.

● Next, type the title of the book in italics, followed by a period. (Note that if the title ends in punctuation, as in the above book, there is no need for a period.)

● Provide the name of the city where the book was published, followed by a colon.

● Next, give the name of the publisher, followed by a comma, and then the copyright date, followed by a period. Typically, you can find all this information on the copyright page, a page at the very beginning of the book.

● Finally, simply add the word "Print" followed by a period. This is to clearly differentiate your source from a Web source.

If there is more than one author, list the authors in the order in which they are listed on the book. (Note that the names of the additional authors are typed exactly as they appear on the book, first name before last name.) For example:

> McGovern, George, Bob Dole, and Donald Messer. *Ending Hunger Now.*
> Minneapolis: Fortress Press, 2005. Print.

If there is an editor rather than an author, simply place a comma and "ed." after the editor's name. For example:

> Pringle, Peter, ed. *A Place at the Table.* New York: Public Affairs, 2013. Print.

As you might expect, there are different guidelines when writing a Works Cited entry for a periodical, an interview, or even a text message. If you need more help with your Works Cited page, there are various Web sites such as the *Purdue Online Writing Lab* that detail the format of nearly every kind of Works Cited entry imaginable.

Limited Answer Key

An important note: To strengthen your reading skills, you must do more than simply find out which of your answers are right and which are wrong. You also need to figure out (with the help of this book, the teacher, or other students) *why* you missed the questions you did. By using each of your wrong answers as a learning opportunity, you will strengthen your understanding of the skills. You will also prepare yourself for the mastery tests in Part One and the vocabulary and reading comprehension questions in Part Two, for which answers are not given here.

Answers to the Practices in Part One

1   Main Ideas in Reading

Practice 1

1.	S	6.	S
	G		G
	S		S
	S		S
2.	G	7.	S
	S		S
	S		S
	S		G
3.	S	8.	S
	S		S
	S		G
	G		S
4.	S	9.	S
	S		S
	S		G
	G		S
5.	S	10.	S
	G		S
	S		S
	S		G

Practice 2

Answers will vary. Here are some possibilities:

1. computers, fax machines, television sets, microwave ovens, cell phones
2. taking out garbage, cleaning up after a pet, cleaning the toilet, writing a letter, ironing, taking a test
3. clear plots, interesting characters, action scenes, elements of humor
4. he/she won't listen, is a slob, is a know-it-all, is bossy, has a terrible temper

Practice 3

1.	S	3.	S
	S		S
	P		P
	S		S
2.	S	4.	S
	S		S
	S		S
	P		P

Practice 4

1. S   3. P
   S   S
   P   S
   S   S

2. S   4. S
   P   P
   S   S
   S   S

Practice 5

1. S   3. S
   S   P
   S   S
   P   S

2. S   4. S
   S   S
   P   S
   S   P

Practice 6

Group 2

A. SD
B. SD
C. MI
D. T

Group 3

A. SD
B. T
C. SD
D. MI

Group 4

A. T
B. SD
C. SD
D. MI

Practice 7

Paragraph 1

1. *Topic:* Cannibalism
2. *Main idea:* Sentence 1

Paragraph 2

1. *Topic:* The Great Wall of China
2. *Main idea:* Sentence 1

Paragraph 3

1. *Topic:* Chaperones
2. *Main idea:* Sentence 1

Paragraph 4

1. *Topic:* Cardiovascular disease
2. *Main idea:* Sentence 2

Practice 8

1. 2
2. 3
3. 1
4. 4

Practice 9

A. 2
B. C

2   Supporting Details in Reading

Practice 1

(Wording of answers may vary.)

A. **Main idea:** Researchers have identified four kinds of intimacy.

1. One kind of intimacy is physical.
2. Intimacy can come from intellectual sharing.
3. Another kind is emotional.
4. Intimacy can come from shared activities.

B. **Main idea:** . . . four basic types of crowds.

1. Casual crowd—people with little in common except for participating in a common event
   Minor detail: People looking through a department-store window
2. Conventional crowd—people who have assembled for a specific purpose
   Minor detail: People attending a baseball game or concert
3. Expressive crowd—people who have gotten together for self-stimulation and personal satisfaction
   Minor detail: People attending a religious revival or rock concert
4. Acting crowd—an excited, explosive collection of people
   Minor detail: People engaged in rioting, looting, or other aggressive behavior

Practice 2 *(Wording of answers may vary)*

A. 1. Act as matchmaking institution
   2. Establish social networks
   3. Provide employment
   4. Stabilize employment

B. 1. *Minor detail:* Plow fields and pull carts
   2. *Major detail:* Benefit when die naturally
   3. *Minor detail:* Used as fertilizer and cooking fuel
   4. *Major detail:* Easy to raise

Practice 3

A. B
B. C

Practice 4 *(Examples may vary.)*

A. A Pyrrhic victory—a victory won at enormous cost.
   Example—The Greek general Pyrrhus defeated a Roman army, but his own army suffered terrible losses.

B. Suppression—a deliberate attempt to avoid stressful thoughts.
   Example—To not think about an argument with his girlfriend, Jeff spends a lot of time with his buddies.

3 Main Ideas and Supporting Details in Writing

Practice 1 *(Wording of answers may vary.)*

A. *Point:* The flu has some very specific symptoms that make it different from a cold.
   Supporting details:
   1. Comes on suddenly
   2. Has a cluster of symptoms including fever, headache, and muscle aches
   3. Makes people feel weak and exhausted

B. *Point:* There are certain times you should definitely not text.
   Supporting details:
   1. In class
   2. While driving
   3. While talking to someone
   4. At important ceremonies, such as weddings and funerals

C. *Point:* You will get a lot more out of your doctor visit if you make a few simple preparations for it.
   Supporting details:
   1. Make a list of medications you are currently taking.
   2. Take along a list of symptoms.
   3. Write down any questions you want to ask the doctor.

D. *Point:* Attending college can be more stressful than many incoming students realize.
   Supporting details:
   1. Choosing a major
   2. Holding a part- or full-time job while in school
   3. Balancing studies with social life
   4. Accumulating debt

Practice 2

Answers will vary.

Practice 3

1. B, C, E
2. A, C, D
3. A, C, D
4. A, C, F

Practice 4

1. B
2. B
3. A
4. A

4 Understanding the Writing Process

There are no correct answers to the practice exercises in this chapter.

5 Relationships in Reading

Practice 1

1. also   4. First
2. For one thing   5. Third
3. In addition

Practice 2 *(Answers may vary.)*

1. After   4. before
2. Then   5. while
3. during

Practice 3 *(Wording of answers may vary.)*

A. Main idea: For several reasons, pork was America's most popular meat a hundred years ago.
1. Pigs grew quickly.
2. Pigs required little attention.
3. Pigs could be preserved cheaply.

B. Main idea: . . . aging process.
1. Our bodies simply wear out.
3. Our body chemistry loses its delicate balance.
4. Our bodies, with age, reject some of their own tissues.

Practice 4 *(Wording of answers may vary.)*

Main idea: People pass through three stages in reacting to unemployment.
1. Shock, followed by relief
2. Strong effort to find a new job
3. Self-doubt and anxiety if no job is found

Practice 5 *(Wording of answers may vary.)*

Main idea: Taking certain steps will help you to remember your dreams.
2. Put a pen and notebook near your bed.
3. Turn off your alarm so you can wake up gradually.
4. Write down the dream immediately.

Practice 6

1. B   6. A
2. A   7. A
3. A   8. B
4. B   9. A
5. B   10. B

6 Relationships in Writing

There are no correct answers to the practice exercises in this chapter.

7 More Relationships in Reading

Practice 1 *(Answers may vary.)*

1. For instance
2. for example
3. such as
4. including
5. illustration

Practice 2

A. *Term being defined:* Shaping; *definition*—1; *example 1*—2; *example 2*—10
B. Irony—saying one thing but meaning another
   Example—To end the famine in Ireland, Swift suggests the Irish should raise babies to be eaten.

Practice 3 *(Answers may vary.)*

1. Similarly   4. as
2. Just like   5. Just as
3. in the same way

Practice 4

(Answers may vary.)

1. however   4. despite
2. Although   5. In contrast
3. but

Practice 5 *(Wording of answers may vary.)*

A. Contrast: Japanese employment practices and U.S. employment practices
B. Contrast: school and home
   2. Public discipline   Private scolding
      in school   at home
   3. Much competition   Minimal competition
      in school   at home

Practice 6 *(Answers may vary.)*

1. Because   4. Since
2. as a result   5. Therefore
3. so

Practice 7 *(Wording of answers may vary.)*

A. *Main idea (the cause):* Chronic stress
Effect 1: Painful muscle tension
Effect 2: Weakening of body's immune system
Effect 3: Psychological disorders

B. *Main idea (the effect):* There are a number of motivations for shoplifting.
Major supporting details (the causes):
1. Poverty
2. Stretch a budget
3. Sense of excitement
4. Desire for social acceptance

Practice 8

1. A   6. B
2. C   7. C
3. B   8. A
4. C   9. C
5. A   10. B

8 More Relationships in Writing

There are no correct answers to the practice exercises in this chapter.

9 Inferences in Reading and Writing

Practice 1

1. C
2. B
3. C
4. B

Practice 2

1. B
2. A
3. B
4. B

Practice 3

A. 3, 4, 6
B. 1, 4, 6
C. 1, 4, 6

Practice 4

1. C; metaphor
2. B; simile
3. A; simile
4. A; metaphor
5. C; metaphor

Practice 5

1. C
2. B
3. C
4. B
5. C

10 Argument in Reading and Writing

Practice 1

1. S   3. S
   P   P
   S   S
   S   S

2. S
   S
   S
   P

Practice 2

1. A, D, E
2. C, D, E
3. B, D, E

Practice 3

Group 1: B
Group 2: B
Group 3: D
Group 4: C
Group 5: B

Practice 4

1. C   4. E
2. B   5. A
3. D

Practice 5

There are no correct answers to this exercise.

Acknowledgments

Text Credits

Barry, Dave. "The Ugly Truth about Beauty." From the *Miami Herald*, February 1, 1998. Copyright © 1998 by Dave Barry. Reprinted by permission.

Bertram, Donald. "Today's Job Crisis: What Students Need to Know." Reprinted by permission.

Bowden, Mark. "Marijuana Today." Reprinted by permission of the author.

Brenoff, Eileen. "Growing Less Dumb." Reprinted by permission.

Carey, Benedict. "Forget What You Know about Good Study Habits." From *The New York Times*, September 7, 2010 © 2010 *The New York Times*. All rights reserved.

Carlin, Emily. "The Bitter Truth about Sugar." Reprinted by permission.

Henslin, James M., "Consequences of Social Class." From *Essentials of Sociology: A Down-to-Earth Approach*, 9th edition, © 2011. Reprinted by permission of Pearson Education, Inc., Upper Saddle River, NJ.

Johnson, Beth. "Life Isn't Fair." Reprinted by permission of the author.

Kaufmann, Ann. "College Athletes Should Be Paid." Reprinted by permission.

Lopez, Steve. "To Tony Lopez, with Love." From the *Los Angeles Times*, February 22, 2012. Copyright © 2012 *Los Angeles Times*. Reprinted by permission.

McCartin, Donald A. "Second Thoughts of a 'Hanging Judge.'" From the *Los Angeles Times*, March 25, 2011. Reprinted by permission of Karen McCartin.

Quintanilla, Guadalupe. "Controlling Your Destiny." Reprinted by permission of the author.

Randall, David K. "Rethinking Sleep." From *The New York Times*, September 23, 2012 © 2012 *The New York Times*. All rights reserved.

Rouff, Ruth A. "Diamonds Aren't Forever." Reprinted by permission of the author.

Sutton, Jean. "A Path to Marriage." Reprinted by permission of the author.

Verderber, Rudolph. "Managing Conflicts in Relationships." From Verderber, *Communicate!*, 8th ed. © 1996 Wadsworth, a part of Cengage Learning, Inc. Reproduced by permission. www.cengage.com/permissions

Photo Credits

Part Two

Chapter 1, p. 282 Private collection; Chapter 2, p. 293 © PCN Photography/Alamy; Chapter 3, p. 304 © BSIP SA/Alamy; Chapter 4, p. 316 © Martin Norris/Alamy; Chapter 5, p. 326 courtesy Guadalupe Quintanilla; Chapter 6, p. 340 © PhotoAlto/Superstock; Chapter 7, p. 350 © Steve Lopez; Chapter 8, p. 359 courtesy Jean Sutton; Chapter 10, p. 382 © Avril O'Reilly/Alamy; Chapter 11, p. 392 © StockbrokerXtra/Alamy; Chapter 12, p. 402 © Vince Bevan/Alamy; Chapter 13, p. 412 © FDA/Alamy; Chapter 14, p. 425 © Blend Images/SuperStock; Chapter 15, p. 434 © RGB Ventures LLC dba SuperStock/Alamy.

Index